CONTEMPORARY ECONOMIC THOUGHT
THE CONTRIBUTION OF NEO-INSTITUTIONAL ECONOMICS

Also by ALLAN G. GRUCHY
MODERN ECONOMIC THOUGHT:
THE AMERICAN CONTRIBUTION

CONTEMPORARY ECONOMIC THOUGHT

THE CONTRIBUTION OF NEO-INSTITUTIONAL ECONOMICS

ALLAN G. GRUCHY

AUGUSTUS M. KELLEY • PUBLISHERS
CLIFTON 1972

First Published 1972

© 1972 Allan G. Gruchy

Published by

AUGUSTUS M. KELLEY · PUBLISHERS

305 ALLWOOD ROAD

CLIFTON, NEW JERSEY 07012

ISBN 0 678 00898 1

LCN 79-184664

Printed in the United States by
SENTRY PRESS
New York, N. Y., 10013

TYPOGRAPHY BY CHELSEA TYPESETTERS, INC., NEW YORK

IN MEMORIAM
S.A.G.
D.W.G.

CONTENTS

PREFACE

In recent years, while conventional economics has gained greatly in technical proficiency, it has been subjected to a great deal of criticism on the ground that it is becoming increasingly irrelevant to an understanding of many of the major problems of the real economic world. While conventional economists have much to say about the economics of decision making in both the private and the public sectors, they have given much less attention to problems of greater concern to the public such as the technological and organizational revolutions and their impacts on the structure and functioning of the industrial system, the exercise of economic power by organized business and organized labor, the role of the large industrial corporations in the determination of national priorities, the declining independence of the consumer, environmental deterioration and other social costs of continuous economic growth, and the growing gap between rich and poor nations. When economics is taken to be a "science of choice" or a "science of efficiency," as it is by conventional economists, it is much too narrow in scope to deal with these pressing economic and social problems. An economics that is largely limited to a study of maximizing behavior, and which ignores the social or cultural setting in which this behavior is carried on, is hardly prepared to cope successfully with the major economic issues of the second half of this century.

It is not surprising that an economics that centers its attention upon the mechanics of economic decision making and the achievement of short-run economic stability, and has little to say about long-term economic trends and the shift from welfare capitalism to guided capitalism, should come under severe attack. In the years since the close of the Second World War economists such as John Kenneth Galbraith, Gunnar Myrdal, Gerhard Colm, and Clarence E. Ayres have strongly criticized what passes as conventional economics. This criticism of course is not entirely new. In the pre-1939 period Thorstein Veblen and other institutionalists roundly objected to the orthodox Marshallian economics that dominated academic circles from 1890 to 1929. The headway made by these critics of orthodox economics was not inconsiderable. By 1932 Lionel Robbins, a well-known exponent of orthodox economics, was led to state in *An Essay on the Nature and Significance of Economic Science* that "in recent years, if they [the institutionalists] have not secured the upper hand altogether, they have certainly had a wide area of power in America." With the restoration of peace in 1945 and the new approach to economics as the science of economic decision making, conventional economists arrived at the comforting view that institutional economics had had its day, and that whatever there was worthwhile in it had been absorbed by the main stream of orthodox economic thought. This assessment of the rise and decline of institutionalism proved to be only wishful thinking. It was not long after the end of World War II that a new generation of heterodox economists returned to the task of criticizing conventional economics.

The new generation of heterodox economists may be said to work in the institutionalist tradition, but their economic heterodoxy is sufficiently different from Veblen's "old" institutionalism to warrant describing the postwar heterodox economics as "neo-institutionalism." Most of the main figures in the neo-institutionalist movement such as Galbraith, Myrdal, and Colm had little or no contact with Veblen's work in their early formative periods. As could be expected, they differ from Veblen in a number of important ways. Conventional critics cannot claim, as they did against Veblen, that the neo-institutionalists dispense with the basic concepts of inherited economics, since these new heterodox economists openly declare their indebtedness to the long line of economists since the time of Adam Smith. The neo-institutionalists do not reproduce Veblen's oversimplified analysis of psychological drives or instincts, nor do they duplicate his overemphasis upon the way in which technology molds human behavior. Looking at the industrial system a half-century later than did Veblen, the neo-institutionalists do not accept Veblen's theory of capitalist development. Whereas Veblen looked forward to the demise of the private enterprise system, the neo-institutionalists think in terms of preserving this system.

For those who wonder why the rift between neo-institutional and conventional economists continues after three-quarters of a century, it should be pointed out that this rift is maintained because neo-institutional and conventional economics are in essence two very different ways of comprehending economic reality, the one evolutionary and the other static or cross-sectional. Behind these different ways of grasping economic reality lies a difference in intellectual orientation or philosophical outlook which, as Clarence Ayres explains in *The Industrial Economy*, is not a "mere matter of opinion," but involves instead "our basic conceptions of the nature of man and of society." The neo-institutionalists' way of comprehending economic reality leads them to adopt a cultural or social view of this reality, while the conventional economists' manner of grasping economic reality makes them prone to pattern economics after the physical sciences. Since the static or cross-sectional approach to understanding economic reality does throw some light on the nature of this reality, much of the work of conventional economists falls within the scope of economics as it is viewed by neo-institutionalists. The main disagreement between the conventional and neo-institutional economists is over what should be included within the scope of economics. The neo-institutionalists include much more within the scope of economics than do conventional economists, because they assert that social science data, unlike the data of physical science, deal with purposive individuals living in a changing social world. If they are to explain the behavior of individuals and groups in the advanced industrial society of today, the neo-institutionalists find it essential to develop a theory of the industrial system in which the market system is embedded. When the neo-institutionalists replace the conventional economists' "market economics" with their "systems economics," they include the basics of market economics but they also go well beyond these basics. It is the position of the neo-institutionalists that their version of economics, being much more relevant to the pressing economic problems of the second half of the twentieth century, provides a much more satisfactory way of grasping the nature of economic reality than does conventional economics.

In this study four chapters are devoted to the contributions of economists whose work I regard as good examples of what I have described as neo-institutional economics. It is clear from an analysis of the work of these heterodox economists that they share similar views with respect to the nature and significance of the science of economics, and so it is possible to refer to a school of neo-institutional economists. While all members of this school may not neatly fit the image of a neo-institutionalist, there is enough unity in the work of these economists to regard them as members of a school that can be distinguished from the school of conventional economists. None of these heterodox economists has referred to his work as "neo-institutional economics." Being concerned with analyses of major economic problems, most of these economists have not taken time out to place their work in the stream of economic thought. It has been the objective of this study to do precisely this.

It is now well established that the problems that economists work on and the kinds of economic theories that they develop reflect the times in which they live. Economists as a whole do not draw their inspiration from some remote and pristine fountainhead of scientific universalism in spite of what some orthodox members of the economics profession assert. We are quite clearly living in a transitional era just as did the classical economists of the late eighteenth and early nineteenth centuries. The economics that is being fashioned today in the western world is reflective of the new era of planned participatory democracies that is unfolding. Like everything else the science of economics needs to change, both to explain the economic basis of the new era and to provide guidance as this era develops. Conventional economics, being an "intellectual" institution, suffers from a cultural lag and has the same difficulty in making adjustments to the new era that all institutions have. The neo-institutionalists regard their economics as something that will aid conventional economics in making this adjustment more readily and more effectively, so that the standard economics of tomorrow may be more relevant to the kinds of economic problems that will doubtlessly arise in planned participatory democracies.

In recent years dissenters from orthodox economics have received support from what is described as the New Left which has had a special appeal for young economists at a number of well-known universities. The critique of established economics presented by the Union for Radical Political Economics in many ways duplicates the critique previously developed by the institutionalists and the neo-institutionalists. A survey of the critiques of the radical economists of the New Left shows that they criticize orthodox economics on the grounds that its scope is too narrow, that it fails to account for the artificial scarcity created by large industrial enterprises, and that it is overly concerned with the technique of marginal analysis which keeps economists from studying the long-run non-marginal changes in the evolving industrial system. In addition the radical economists criticize standard economics because it takes consumer wants as given and does not explain how many of these wants are created by producers with the aid of advertising. They also criticize standard economics for the reason that it does not make enough use of the contributions of the other social sciences.

Since the neo-institutionalists have been criticizing the established economics along substantially the same lines for over a quarter of a century, they find little that is new in the criticisms of the radical economists. Where the neo-institutionalists and the radical economists differ is in regard to how economics may be used to deal with the important economic problems of the last third of the current century. The neo-institutionalists look forward to reforming the advanced industrial economy without eliminating private business enterprise whereas the radical economists of the New Left would like to establish "a whole new order" along either anarchist or socialist lines. Even on this latter point the members of the Union for Radical Political Economics have little to offer that is new since socialist proposals have in recent decades emphasized the need to decentralize the planned socialist society. What is new in regard to the position of the radical economists of the New Left is that their anarchistic and counter-culture leanings have led them to join the somewhat amorphous radical youth movement that is currently challenging the Establishment, its values, and its elitist-centralist control of the affluent society. It is evident, however, that the radical economists like other members of the radical youth movement have no clear vision of what they would like to see replace the existing social system.

In developing my views with regard to the nature and significance of neo-institutionalism I have benefited greatly from many contacts with members of the Association for Evolutionary Economics. This Association originated at a meeting of a small group of economic dissenters which was held in Washington, D.C., in December 1958. Since economic dissenters are more in agreement about what they dissent from than about what they consider to be the nature and scope of economics, I do not assign to any member of this Association responsibility for the views that I may hold with regard to the nature and significance of neo-institutional economics. I am also greatly indebted to my wife for her very proficient editorial work in connection with this study.

ALLAN G. GRUCHY
University of Maryland

CHAPTER I

NEO-INSTITUTIONALISM AND THE TREND OF ECONOMICS

The quarter of a century since the close of the Second World War, although a period of general economic prosperity in Western Europe and the United States, has been an era in which orthodoxy in economic thought has come under severe attack. This has occurred in the opinion of the critics of conventional or standard economics because this type of economics has grown increasingly irrelevant to the major issues of the times. The improvement in the technical proficiency of conventional economists in recent decades has not been matched by an improvement in their ability to explain the forces which are at work transforming the advanced industrial society into a new post industrial society that would be better adjusted to the demands of the technological revolution of the second half of the twentieth century. Nor have conventional economists of the Marshallian-Keynesian type been able to come forth with economic policy measures that can cope successfully with many of the problems of our affluent society.

In the post World War II decades a number of unconventional economists have come forth as severe critics of the established standard economics. These heterodox critics include such economists as John K. Galbraith, Gunnar Myrdal, Clarence Ayres, Adolph Lowe, Gerhard Colm and François Perroux, to mention only a few of the more prominent members of the growing group of dissenters from conventional economics. These dissenters from economic orthodoxy are not without roots in the past. In the United States economic dissent was nourished prior to 1939 by the work of Thorstein Veblen and later institutionalists such as John R. Commons, Wesley C. Mitchell and John M. Clark. In the United Kingdom the economics of dissent prior to 1939 drew support from John A. Hobson, Richard Tawney, G. D. H. Cole and other Fabians. The current generation of economic dissenters, while owing much

1

to the pioneer work of the pre-1939 dissenters, is dealing with an essentially new economic phenomenon — the affluent society of the post 1945 period in Western Europe and the United States. It is no longer a case as it was prior to 1939 of examining and criticizing a society with a relatively small affluent establishment. It is no longer a case of making proposals to cope with the problems of an economic system racked by recurring severe depressions. The economic dissenters of today observe that we have now learned how to prevent serious depressions and mass unemployment. They also observe that, while there are still sizeable minority groups that are subject to the evils of poverty, inadequate employment and economic insecurity, a large section of the population in the advanced industrialized nations of the West has access to a comfortable standard of living while a considerable part of the population enjoys what has been described as affluence.

While it is true that the United States and the major West European nations are only a few rich nations in a world of mostly poor countries, it is in the rich industrialized countries that the technological explosion is occurring. The rich industrialized nations constitute the center from which emanates the technological change that is transforming the world. It is for this reason that the heterodox dissenting economists pay special attention to the world's affluent nations. In doing so they call attention to the inadequacies of conventional economics as an instrument for explaining the problems of the affluent nations and for providing solutions to these problems. Conventional or standard economics with its emphasis on the essentials of classical micro-economics and on Keynesian macro-economics was fashioned prior to the advent of the affluent society. While in the opinion of the dissenting heterodox economists conventional economics has much that is worth preserving, nevertheless it is felt by these critics of conventional economics that it is much too narrow in scope to explain satisfactorily the pressing problems of an affluent society in a new technological age.

Keynes and the Economics of Depression

Economic and political developments in recent decades have had profound effects on the course of economic thought. What appeared to be a great advance in the development of economic science in the 1930's — the so-called Keynesian Revolution — has not measured up to the demands of the explosive decades of the 1950's and the 1960's. While it proved to be significant with respect to the problems of the depressed 1930's, Keynesian economics and economic policy proposals have come to have diminishing acceptance as post World War II problems have come to the surface. Keynes fashioned his economics in the light of the problems of his time. These were primarily the problems of the depressed interwar period, 1919-1939, in the United Kingdom. It should not be surprising to see that Keynes wrote much about unemployment, low production and depressed demand, for these were the pressing problems in the era in which he did his most fruitful writing. Likewise, it should not be surprising to find that Keynes had little to say about the problems of a full employment affluent society. He was not especially concerned with the roles of the large industrial corporation or the individual consumer in an affluent society, with the problem of the hidden and unpaid social costs of continuous economic growth, or with the question of what direction an affluent society should take.

With regard to the question of what direction economic activities should take Keynes was very explicit. He tells us in *The General Theory of Employment Interest and Money* that "I see no reason to suppose that the existing system seriously misemploys the factors of production which are in use. . . . *It is in determining the volume, not the direction, of actual employment that the existing system has broken down.*"[1] According to Keynes, at the time that he was writing and for the indefinite future, what was being produced was considered to be satisfactory from the point of view of general welfare. It was for Keynes only a matter of getting more of the same goods and services. For Keynes there was no problem of too many private goods and too few public goods, there was no problem of the corporate management of consumer demand, there was no problem of the quality of economic life, and so in general there was no problem of going beyond the private market mechanism to the clear and effective establishment of national economic priorities. This was a view about the use of the nation's factors of production that was quite unacceptable to the institutionalists of the 1930's. It was their position that *both* the volume and the direction of investment and employment were unsatisfactory from the point of view of the general welfare in the depressed 1930's.

In the post 1945 period an even more important problem than that of increased production and employment — and one to which Keynes never addressed himself — made its appearance. This is the

---

[1] John Maynard Keynes, *The General Theory of Employment Interest and Money* (New York: Harcourt, Brace and Co., 1936) p. 379. Italics supplied.

problem of how to provide guidance or direction for a full employment affluent society. The main deficiency in Keynes's economics was that it had little to say about what a nation does after it achieves full employment. How does a nation preserve full employment and, assuming that it does achieve full employment on a lasting basis, in what direction should the nation's economy move? Are we to assume that in the area of private production the market system dominated by a small number of large business enterprises will produce what the consumers as free agents would want to buy, or will these dominating enterprises induce consumers to purchase what these enterprises decide to produce? Will a full employment affluent society develop an imbalance between the production of private and public goods? These are some of the major problems of the post 1945 decades as they have appeared in the affluent United States and in a Western Europe now in the mass consumption stage of economic development, and looking forward in the near future to the prospect of entering the post mass consumption or mass service stage of economic development.

Keynes's economics was not constructed to aid in diagnosing the problems of an economy enjoying a fairly well sustained full employment and a high standard of living. Nor have his followers been able to remedy these limitations of Keynes's economics. In Western Europe, particularly in the Scandinavian countries, the Netherlands, France and the United Kingdom (when the British Labor Party is in office), Keynesian interventionism has been replaced by various forms of indicative national economic planning. This does not mean that Keynes's theory of aggregate income determination has been dispensed with, or that various economic policy tools widely used by Keynesians, such as deficit financing and countercyclical tax adjustments, have been abandoned by the major West European countries in the post war period. Few would deny that in the limited area of pure theory Keynes made some significant contributions. His heterodox critics, however, assert that he was not equally constructive in the broader area of the theory of the evolving industrial system, which is cultivated by present day institutionalists.

The new direction in economic thought and economic policy making since 1945 has dispensed with the Keynesian economic approach and economic philosophy which find expression in the policy of "interventionism." Keynesian interventionism is also subject to considerable attack in the United States which is the only large industrialized country where this interventionism continues to be accepted as the official national economic policy. Even the British Conservative Government, after a decade of low economic growth and recurring international balance of payments crises, in 1962 called for the acceptance of some kind of indicative national economic planning along the French lines to replace the Keynesian interventionism of the years 1951-1961. The Conservative Government established the National Economic Development Council in 1962. This Council set the United Kingdom on the path towards indicative national economic planning with the publication of a four year national economic plan.[2]

Institutional Economics in the Depressed 1930's

During the depressed 1930's in the United States there was a large infusion of institutionalist economic thinking into government circles. Writing in 1932 Lionel Robbins, a severe critic of the institutionalists, observed that "now we have the Institutionalists . . . in recent years, if they have not secured the upper hand altogether, they have certainly had a wide area of power in America."[3] What Robbins had in mind was the influence in government circles of economists who held views similar to those of such well known American institutionalists as John R. Commons, Wesley C. Mitchell, John M. Clark and Walton H. Hamilton. These heterodox economists were well aware that there was a great need for short-run economic measures that were designed to provide immediate relief for defaulting businessmen, farmers and home owners, and also for the millions of unemployed workers. They agreed with John M. Clark who, when appearing in 1931 before a government committee which was considering a bill to establish a national economic council, described the problem of coping with depression as one of using "the productive powers we have got, bringing them together with demand at a point that represents something like the full use of our productive powers."[4] This full employment goal was to be achieved, according to Clark and other institutionalists, by cutting taxes, increasing government spending and stimulating both private investment and consumption. But, unlike Keynes, the institutionalists did

---

[2] National Economic Development Council, *Growth of the United Kingdom Economy, 1961-1966* (London: Her Majesty's Stationery Office, 1963) p. 32.

[3] Lionel Robbins, *An Essay on the Nature and Significance of Economic Science* (London: Macmillan and Co., Second Edition, 1935) p. 114.

[4] John M. Clark, "Statement of Dr. John Maurice Clark, Professor of Economics, Columbia University," *Hearings before a Subcommittee of the Committee on Manufactures*, U. S. Senate, Oct. 22-Dec. 19, 1931, p. 212.

not stop there. They had what Keynes and his followers did not have; namely, a long view of the operations of the economic system which would enable them to view the depression, not only as a short-run cyclical problem, but also as a problem arising in the process of the industrialization of the American economy. While Keynes was not unaware of long-run economic trends, his main concern in the 1930's was with short-run or cyclical matters. Whereas Keynes did express some interest in long-run economic developments, it remained for his followers to eliminate largely whatever was long run in Keynes's economic thought, and to concentrate on timeless or short-run models of the economy if these followers were pure theorists, or to concentrate on the next turn in business conditions if they were economic advisers or practitioners.

Unlike Keynes and the Keynesians the institutionalists of the 1930's went beyond immediate economic policy proposals to suggest that the occurrence of the Great Depression should be taken as an occasion for raising two important questions: (1) where is the nation's economy heading and (2) is the direction in which the economy is moving a direction of which the people in general approve? To put these matters differently, the questions to be answered are: does the private enterprise economy secure satisfactory guidance where this guidance comes mainly from large private economic power groups and not from the more numerous but individually weaker economic power groups? And who really decides what consumers will purchase, and what will be the content of the affluence made possible by full employment and a high and sustained economic growth rate?

Wesley C. Mitchell, John M. Clark and other institutionalists developed a theory of the modern industrial society in which, because of the presence of large economic power groups, the market system no longer functioned in such a manner as to provide full employment and high levels of production on a sustained basis. The large industrial corporations and the large trade unions had severely reduced the flexibility of the private market mechanism and the effective functioning of this mechanism's equilibrating tendencies. Technological change had so altered the structure and functioning of the maturing industrial economy that *laissez-faire* capitalism disappeared during the 1930's. In the new phase of capitalist development that was established after 1929 what Gardiner C. Means had described as the "corporate revolution" could be domesticated effectively only by turning to a program of national economic guidance that would supplement and guide the private enterprise system towards what John R. Commons had called "reasonable capitalism." Going beyond Keynesian countercyclical measures, Mitchell, Clark, Tugwell and Means advocated what is today known in Western Europe as indicative national planning.

What the institutionalists of the pre-World War II period did was to place the economic decision making processes of the private and public sectors of the nation's economy within the broad framework of the maturing industrial economy. As a consequence of this theoretical procedure the impact of the nation's economic decision making process on the total industrial system and the reverse impact of the whole industrial system on the subsidiary economic decision making process were made the prime topics of investigation and analysis. The impact of the private economic decision making process on the total evolving industrial economy was revealed in terms of how the large industrial corporations not only prevented the economy from reaching a full employment equilibrium on a sustained basis, but also directed the economy towards ends that many individuals and groups believed to be inimical to the general welfare of the nation. It was for this reason that Wesley C. Mitchell in 1932 complained that the nation's private enterprise system was not producing an adequate supply of "serviccable" or "most urgently needed" goods. John M. Clark likewise lamented that the market system all too frequently produced "market values" but not "service values"; that is to say, values that would serve the general as well as individual welfare.

The influence of the institutionalists on national economic policy making was strongest during the early years of the New Deal. A number of factors contributed to the decline in their influence after 1935. Not having available to them during these years the national income accounting and gross national product statistics which became available after 1939 during the Second World War, the institutionalists could not construct national economic budgets and use them as a basis for national economic policy making. Consequently they were unable to quantify the national economic priorities and the planning proposals which they recommended. More importantly, the United States like the major West European countries was not politically prepared in the late 1930's to embark on any national economic planning program. The enthusiasm of the Roosevelt Administration for the kind of national economic guidance proposed by Rexford G. Tugwell, Mordecai Ezekiel, John M. Clark

and other institutionalists declined after 1937 as the Roosevelt
Administration's interest turned increasingly from domestic to inter-
national issues in the face of the advance of fascism in Western
Europe.

Economics in the Post 1945 Era

Since 1945 Keynesian economics has continued to dominate academic circles in both Western Europe and the United States. In
the United States very soon after the close of the Second World
War standard economists rewrote their textbooks in order to combine the economics of Marshall and of Keynes. As Paul A. Samuelson
has recently explained, standard economics textbooks now "provide
us with a 'neo-classical synthesis' that combines the essentials of the
theory of aggregative income determination with the older classical
theories of relative prices and of micro-economics."[5] What is true
of Samuelson's conventional economics textbook is true of almost
all other economics textbooks. But neither Marshall nor Keynes
developed an economics that was concerned with the major economic problems of the kind that have appeared in the post 1945 era.
Neither Marshall nor Keynes — nor any of their followers — ever
dealt extensively with such problems as the exercise of power by
large economic interest groups, the conversion of the market mechanism into a consumer want-creating rather than a consumer want-
serving mechanism, the decline of the free market system, and the
emergence of the government as a factor mediating among economic
power groups or providing direction for the economy. Nor were
Marshall and Keynes or their followers interested in problems such
as the rise of the affluent society in which the heavy social costs of
aimless economic growth are frequently ignored and in which the
quality of life falls as affluence rises, the development of a society
in which the production of private goods is elevated above the production of public goods, and the development of an industrial-military complex which at times subordinates the national interest to
private profit making.

The Keynesian influence in the economic field in the post 1945
era has led to a continuation of the pre-1939 concern in academic,
business and government circles with short-run developments in the
state of business and with measures designed to assure high levels

---

[5] Paul A. Samuelson, *Economics, An Introductory Analysis*, Sixth Edition
(New York: McGraw Hill, 1964) p. 809.

of employment and production in the immediate future. No special concern has developed in the Keynesian camp with such long-run questions as for what national purposes are employment and production levels being raised; or how has the technological revolution altered the structure and functioning of the modern industrial economy; or who really directs this economy, and how may this direction be altered so that it will be in conformity with what a large section of the general population thinks it should be? These are the questions that are being raised by the new post 1945 generation of institutionalists such as Galbraith, Myrdal, Colm, Ayres and other critics of the conventional Marshallian-Keynesian economics synthesis.

Post 1945 Keynesian economics has found expression in the work of the Council of Economic Advisers which has directed its attention mainly to the short-run problems of achieving full employment and stable economic growth. The Council's primary concern with the short-run aspects of unemployment, recession, price and wage developments and balance of international payments difficulties has prevented the Council from giving adequate attention to the need to adopt a long-range view of the development and the problems of the post mass consumption economy. This long-range approach would open the door to a consideration of such problems, now ignored by conventional economists, as the impact of the technological explosion on the structure and functioning of the modern industrial economy, the determination of long-term national economic and social goals and the need to establish relative priorities among these goals. Keynesians such as Walter W. Heller, Gardner Ackley and Arthur M. Okun, all formerly chairmen of the Council of Economic Advisers, were in the years 1960-1968 proponents of "gap economics" and the "new economics." These Keynesian versions of economics dealt with the gap between the economy's actual and potential total national output, and with measures designed to eliminate the production gap and to prevent inflation from developing once the gap was filled. The Keynesians of the 1960's made no special effort to fill the production gap with high priority goods and services. No new machinery was developed for the better determination of national economic and social goals and of priorities among these goals. Economic program formulation at the federal level was largely an *ad hoc* response to specific needs and special demands rather than a coordinated response to well established national priorities. The general position of the Keynesians in the

There is no econometric model of the process of industrialization which incorporates historical time during which technological change alters both the structure and the functioning of the developing industrial economy. Nor could such a model incorporate non-quantifiable data such as the power of economic interest groups, the elements of affluence or disamenities such as the loss of personal privacy and the destruction of wilderness areas and historical landmarks.

What the critics of conventional macro-economists and micro-economists assert is that the limited view of the scope of economics held by these economists causes them to ignore many of the most pressing problems of the affluent western economies. These conventional economists have failed to take the long view that goes beyond the short-run performance of the nation's economy and of the individual private and public units operating within it. They have failed to develop an economics that throws light on the nature and the problems of the post industrial society that is now shaping up in the United States and towards which Western Europe is now moving. An economics that would do this would have to investigate the process of industrialization and how this process affects the current and future operations of the mature industrial economy.

The Post Industrial or Post Mass Consumption Economy

The post industrial or post mass consumption society of the United States is a product of the technological revolution that occurred after 1945. As a consequence of this revolution there has emerged an automated and computerized society which by the year 2000 could very well be a super affluent society.[7] The post industrial society of today is a service oriented society in which the public sector is becoming increasingly important, the private market system is losing its importance, interest in efficiency is declining as affluence spreads and the inherited Puritanical work oriented values are being eroded by the rapid improvement in the standard of living of the majority of the population. The post mass consumption economy is best described as a public-private enterprise economy in which public enterprise plays a more crucial role than does private enterprise. As the year 2000 approaches it can be anticipated that

---

[7] Herman Kahn and Anthony J. Wiener, *The Year 2000, A Framework for Speculation on the Next Thirty-Three Years* (New York: The Macmillan Co., 1967) p. 214.

the government as a factor in economic life will become increasingly more significant. In the mature industrial stage which preceded the current post mass consumption stage of economic development the key institution was the large industrial corporation. It was the message of Berle and Means's study of the large corporation, *The Modern Corporation and Private Property* (1933), that in the early 1930's the large industrial corporation was the dominant economic institution, and was the factor that was most influential in the determination of the course of the nation's economic activity. In the third of a century since the publication of Berle and Means's landmark study the large industrial corporation has given way before the rise of the government as a factor responsible for the guidance of the nation's economic life. In 1929 government purchases at all levels amounted to only 10 per cent of gross national product. By 1970 these public purchases had risen to 23 per cent of gross national product. But more important, the ability and willingness of the government at the federal, state and local levels to influence the course of economic activities had increased in a way that cannot be quantitatively measured.

In recent decades the role of the government has become a major consideration for a number of reasons. The post industrial society is a learning society in which the scarcest resource is human capital. The provision of an adequate supply of this capital is the primary concern not of private business enterprise but of the government. Nothing is more important among the functions of the government in a modern industrial society than the provision of education and the sponsoring of scientific research. So significant is the role of the government in providing the education, skills and scientific research required by the modern industrial society that it is now appropriate to describe the government as a fourth factor of production to be added to the conventionally viewed factors of land, labor and capital.

The technological revolution or explosion of the past few decades which has created the affluent society has led to the widespread demand for some kind of social and economic planning. The pace of technological change has become so rapid in recent years that the failure to plan for this change can only lead to many undesirable consequences for man and his natural and social environments. Scientific progress and technological change are not achieved without a cost to society. In the United States the affluence made possible by the technological revolution has been accompanied by the production of many disamenities or external diseconomies which have

contributed to the lowering of the quality of life.[8] Whether planned
or not, the technological revolution is in process of greatly altering
the structure and functioning of the modern industrial economy.
Many industrialized countries have already come around to the
position that the preservation of the general welfare requires some
kind of social and economic planning. National planning is now well
established in the Scandinavian countries, the Netherlands and
France. The United Kingdom, Italy and Belgium have in recent
years turned to national planning as a means of coping with the
economic and social problems of a technological society.

There is much evidence that a considerable sentiment in favor
of economic and social planning is developing in the United States
even though the private business system has traditionally been
opposed to this planning. What brought the issue of national planning to the fore in recent years was the national priority crisis of the
1960's. The spectacle of a nation placing a man on the moon while
at the same time millions of its citizens live in poverty and squalor,
while its cities are becoming blighted and while throughout the
country the natural and social environments are rapidly deteriorating has given rise to a new interest in economic and social planning. The conflicting demands of government programs for
investment in human resources, environmental improvement, outer
and inner space, and defense have stimulated interest in a number
of congressional proposals for the establishment of a permanent
Commission on National Goals, a federal Office of Program Analysis
and Evaluation and a Council of Social Advisers similar to the
Council of Economic Advisers.[9] The Bureau of the Budget expressed its concern for an improvement in national economic and
social guidance by creating a Resources Planning Staff, which
dealt with the problem of establishing relative priorities among
the many programs of the Federal Government's departments
and agencies. The proposed Social Report of the President issued
by a Council of Social Advisers would provide a comprehensive
view of the nation in the light of which there could be made a
balanced assessment of national priorities.[10] This concern with rela-

    [8] Ezra J. Mishan, *The Cost of Growth* (New York: Frederick A. Praeger,
1967) pp. 53-99.
    [9] Gerhard Colm and Luther H. Gulick, *Program Planning for National
Goals* (National Planning Association, Washington, D.C., Planning Pamphlet No. 125, November 1968) pp. 19-20.
    [10] U.S. Department of Health, Education, and Welfare, *Toward a Social
Report* (Washington, D.C., 1969) p. 101.

tive national priorities is a logical extension of the interest in the planning-programming-budgeting system which has in recent years been put into operation by a number of federal government departments. All these proposals and programs for improving social and economic guidance in the United States are an indication of the recognition of the growing need to domesticate the technological revolution along lines that will lead to an increase in general welfare at a minimum of social and economic cost.

Neo-Institutionalism in the Post Industrial Society

Ayres, Galbraith, Myrdal and other critics of conventional economics broaden the scope of economics to include not only the standard analysis of the economic decision making process in the private and public sectors, but also an analysis of the maturing industrial system within which private and public economic decision making is carried on. They do not deny that conventional economics has within its limited scope made important contributions to economic analysis. What they do deny, however, is that conventional economics provides the kind of economic analysis that is needed to interpret the functioning of the post industrial economy and to handle satisfactorily many of the economic problems that have arisen in the technological society of the second half of the twentieth century. These critics of conventional economics define economics to be the study of the evolving system of human relations that disposes of scarce resources for the satisfying of private and collective wants. In so doing they develop a theory of the mature industrial economy which takes account of the forces at work changing this economy, the activities of the various economic power groups operating within the economy and the roles of these conflicting power groups in determining the direction in which the economy moves. These critics add a long view of the evolving industrial economy to what Gunnar Myrdal has described as the "nearsightedness" of conventional economists.[11]

The critics of conventional economics state that it is very important to analyze the process of industrialization and the forces at work in the development of the post mass consumption economy, because it is only in this manner that one can get a full understanding of the nature and the problems of this economy. The current industrial economy is an evolving system that cannot be fully explained by

---

[11] Gunnar Myrdal, *Challenge to Affluence* (New York: Pantheon Books, 1962) p. 87.

confining it within the mold of some econometric model with its quantified halfway approach to economic reality. No matter how much of economic reality such a model reveals — and there is no denying that a considerable part of economic reality will be uncovered — what is revealed will necessarily be far removed from the full reality of the total evolving industrial system. Conventional economics in its most refined form can only be at best a first and very limited approximation to the full reality of the post mass consumption economy.

It is clear that the critics of conventional economics such as Galbraith, Myrdal, Ayres and others of a similar intellectual bent work within the institutionalist tradition that was established in the United States by Thorstein Veblen in the early decades of this century. None of these heterodox critics, however, with the exception of Ayres was influenced in his formative years by Veblen's work. The image presented by these present day institutionalists is so different from the image presented by Veblen, it is appropriate to refer to work of the current institutionalists as "neo-institutional economics" to distinguish it from the "old" institutional economics of Thorstein Veblen. As a result of his powerful attack on marginalist economics Veblen gave the impression to the orthodox economists of his time and to later readers of his writings that he would largely dispense with the inherited standard economics. He seemed to imply that neither consumer sovereignty nor the principles of economic decision making would have a place in his technocratic regime of workmanship of the future. The view that Veblen was an unsophisticated technocrat, who had little regard for the fundamentals of standard economic theory, persists to this very day. As recently as 1968 Raymond Aron asserted that "Veblen made the mistake of thinking that the industrial order — the order of production — was sufficient unto itself," and was not subject "to the requirements of economic calculation."[12] This criticism cannot be levelled against the neo-institutionalists who do not dispense with the building blocks of standard economic theory. They very clearly state that they have taken much from the work of standard economists of the past and the present. For example, Ayres explains in *The Industrial Society* that "This is not to say that all the inquiries of all the economists have been a complete waste of time. . . . The investigations of economists

---

[12] Raymond Aron, *Progress and Disillusion, The Dialectics of Modern Society* (New York: Frederick A. Praeger, 1968) p. 187.

have given us a wealth of knowledge of price relationships the effect of which is to show how the various economic activities affect each other. All this is of great value."[13] Galbraith explains in *The New Industrial State* when referring to the work of standard economists that "I have drawn on their work, quantitative and qualitative, at every stage; I could not have written without their prior efforts."[14] Likewise François Perroux informs us in his article on the domination effect of large industrial corporations that his excursions beyond conventional economics involve no disavowal of standard economic theory.[15] Rather than dispense with conventional economics the neo-institutionalists accept it for what it is worth, and then go beyond it to develop a broader economics which is concerned not only with decision making in the market place but also with the guidance of the larger evolving economic system.

The neo-institutionalists of the present differ from Veblen in other important ways. Veblen's emphasis on the discipline of the machine process as a factor determining human behavior opened him to the criticism that his economic analysis was adversely affected by the acceptance of an untenable technological determinism. While neo-institutionalists accept industrial technology as an important factor that can influence the course of economic evolution, they do not impute to technology the power to shape mental attitudes or to condition economic behavior that Veblen was prepared to accord to technology.

Veblen's institutionalism was fashioned in an era when government played a minor role in economic life and the master institution was the large industrial corporation, which according to Veblen's interpretation was held in bondage to the investment bankers, the captains of finance. In Veblen's analysis of the American economy the government was a tool of the vested interests which aided these interests in exploiting the underlying population. Veblen saw the possibility of an affluent society but such a society did not arrive during his lifetime. Only a small class of the vested interests enjoyed what little affluence there was in the early decades of this century. Veblen analyzed the American economy in terms of a progressively

---

[13] Clarence E. Ayres, *The Industrial Economy* (Boston: Houghton Mifflin, 1952) p. 36.

[14] John Kenneth Galbraith, *The New Industrial State* (Boston: Houghton Mifflin, 1967) p. 402.

[15] François Perroux, "The Domination Effect and Modern Economic Theory," *Social Research*, Vol. 17, No. 2, June 1950, p. 188.

declining real national income and the eventual demise of the capitalist system. The institutionalists who followed Veblen in the 1930's paid increasing attention to the role of the government in economic affairs, but the main problems of the times were not those of an affluent society. Commons, Mitchell, Clark, Tugwell and Means were primarily concerned with the problems of long-term economic stabilization and the provision of at least a health and decency standard of living for all citizens. They were not primarily interested in the problems of a widely affluent society. They wrote in terms of a welfare state in which all citizens would be protected from the hazards of unemployment, insecurity and poverty.

The institutionalism of Veblen and his immediate followers was essentially the economics of a maturing industrial economy. Neo-institutionalism is the economics of an industrial economy that has not only matured but has passed into the current era of the post mass consumption society. The difference between the old institutionalism of Thorstein Veblen and the neo-institutionalism of Galbraith, Myrdal, Ayres, Colm, Lowe and Perroux is in large part the difference between the 1920's and the 1960's. The analysis presented in the following chapters provides an explication of this difference between the "old" and the "new" institutionalism and of its significance for the development of the economics of dissent.

CHAPTER II

INSTITUTIONAL ECONOMICS PRIOR TO 1939

Institutional economics prior to World War II was primarily an American intellectual development. John A. Hobson, Richard Tawney, G. D. H. Cole and other Fabians in the United Kingdom and Werner Sombart in Germany had criticized orthodox economics, but never with the vigor and tenacity which Thorstein Veblen had applied to the same task. In addition institutionalist thought in Western Europe never secured the academic foothold that it did in the United States where the large number of universities, many of them public institutions, provided more academic opportunity for the dissemination of the economics of dissent than was the case in Western Europe.

The final quarter of the nineteenth century in the United States was a period of great social change, economic disturbance and political agitation. The movement of the frontier to the West Coast coincided with the rapid industrialization of the American economy. One of the consequences of these years of economic and social strife was the development of considerable dissent in academic circles from the orthodox economics which was largely based on the work of Adam Smith, David Ricardo and John Stuart Mill. Prominent among the economic dissenters after 1880 were Simon N. Patten (1852-1922), Richard T. Ely (1854-1943) and Thorstein Veblen (1857-1929). There was much in common in the work of these three heterodox economists, who drew heavily upon the German historical school for inspiration and guidance. It was only Veblen's work, however, which left much of an imprint on the fabric of American economic thought. None of the other late nineteenth century exponents of economic heterodoxy duplicated in his work the brilliance and incisiveness of Veblen's economic analysis. Whereas Patten and Ely were relatively minor figures in the development of the economics of dissent, Veblen went on to provide a firm foundation for the economics of dissent which has come to be known as "institutional economics."

The Institutionalism of Thorstein Veblen

An analysis of Veblen's economics may very well begin with the observation that he described his economics as "evolutionary" or "cultural" economics.[1] In order to explain the American economic system Veblen needed a theory of society or culture which would be applicable to the economic system, and which would provide a general framework for his interpretation of this system. Veblen's theory of culture moves along the following lines.[2] Man is a self-active creature who seeks to satisfy his instinctive drives by using his reason and following customary and habitual ways of behaving. These ways of behaving give rise to institutions which are the key elements in human culture. Institutions develop over time as aids by means of which men organize and control individual and social behavior in order to satisfy their wants. Veblen divides all institutions into two types; namely, serviceable and disserviceable institutions. Serviceable institutions reflect man's workmanship and parental instincts or drives which lead to action that contributes to race survival. The instinct of workmanship finds expression in the manipulation of raw materials and the making of useful goods, while the parental bent causes the individual to have a regard for the welfare of the family, tribe and community. Disserviceable institutions reflect man's predatory or acquisitive drive which, if uncontrolled by cultural arrangements, will elevate the individual over the community and undermine the life process. The psychological dichotomy or conflict in man between serviceable and disserviceable drives or urges is reproduced in a cultural dichotomy or conflict between serviceable and disserviceable institutions. This cultural dichotomy finds further expression in the conflict between the classes, such as the priestly, military and business classes, which have predatory goals, and the working class which has serviceable goals leading to race survival.

---

[1] This survey of Veblen's economics and the economics of other institutionalists who were prominent prior to 1939 is based largely upon this writer's *Modern Economic Thought, The American Contribution* (1947). See also Joseph Dorfman, *The Economic Mind in American Civilization*, Volume III, 1865-1918 (1949) and Volumes IV and V, 1918-1933 (1959).

[2] Myron W. Watkins, "Veblen's View of Cultural Evolution," *Thorstein Veblen: A Critical Reappraisal*, edited by Douglas F. Dowd (Ithaca, New York: Cornell University Press, 1958) pp. 249-264.

Veblen explains that institutions and the culture in which they are embedded change over time in response to changes in science and technology. These changes in science and technology result from the impact of man's idle curiosity on his environment. It is man's idle curiosity that makes him a self-active and restless creature who is always breaking the cake of custom and habit that encrusts human behavior. Since science and technology never stand still, culture and the institutional basis of society are always undergoing change of some kind. Since all institutions do not change at the same rate, social or cultural lags develop. Some individuals or groups are interested in preserving old institutional arrangements because they stand to gain from these arrangements. These are the individuals and groups who are dominated by acquisitive or predatory instincts. Those individuals or groups who are disadvantaged by the maintenance of old institutions seek to bring about institutional changes. These are the individuals and groups who are dominated by the parental and workmanship drives. The conflicting objectives of those who want to preserve existing institutions and of those who want to change these institutions give rise to individual and class conflict. The working population is interested in self-preservation or race survival, which is threatened by social conflict. According to Veblen's interpretation the underlying population seeks to change the institutional basis of society so that it will better meet human needs and enhance the life process. There is no assurance, however, that any tribe, community or nation will be successful in this endeavor. The course of history is strewn with the remains of dead civilizations. Veblen was at heart a pessimist. While he saw the possibility of man developing a culture or an institutional complex that would enable him to survive, he felt that there was a very wide gap between the possibility and the certainty that a particular culture such as West European culture would survive.

Veblen emphasized that society or culture is a process and not a static system. It develops an existence of its own which is independent of the individuals and groups functioning within the society or culture. The factor that causes the social or cultural process to be ever emergent is technological change. The cultural process is non-teleological for the reason that it does not move towards any predetermined end. Men may seek to steer the cultural process towards ends that they have established as worthwhile. But according to Veblen's interpretation of the history of human culture, mankind has not been very successful in providing guidance for the evolution of society. The course of cultural evolution in Veblen's opinion is very largely a matter of drift.

Veblen's Concept of the Economic System

We are now in a position to shift from Veblen's general theory of society or culture to his specific theory of the economic system. In Veblen's analysis the economic system is an evolving process that is a part of the larger total social system. The economic system is concerned with the material aspect of culture or that part of culture which deals with the provision of material goods for the satisfaction of human wants. The economic system which originated when cultural development gave rise to the Stone Age has since that time passed through many stages of development. Veblen's main interest was in the era of large-scale or monopoly capitalism during the years 1880-1929. His writings spanned the period from the first large-scale merger movement, which began in the closing decade of the nineteenth century, to the final years of *laissez-faire* capitalism in the late 1920's. What Veblen developed was a theory of mature *laissez-faire* capitalism with special reference to the American scene. This phase of capitalist development was in Veblen's opinion a temporary phase. Technological change would continue to push the economic system into new eras of development as it had done since the Stone Age.

In Veblen's analysis the economic system contains within itself a basic conflict which reflects the conflict within man himself. The psychological dichotomy based on the conflict between man's drive to acquire for himself and his drive to protect and improve the community welfare is reproduced in the conflict between the disserviceable and serviceable economic institutions and the conflict between the vested interests and the workers. The economic system is a complex of institutions which men use as aids in the effort to produce the goods and services that are needed to meet their wants. Veblen explained that in some historical eras such as the Stone Age and the handicraft era mankind's acquisitive urge was effectively kept in check. In these eras the institutional arrangements for the control of the production and distribution of goods favored the meeting of basic needs and the survival of the human race. In other eras such as antiquity, feudalism and modern large-scale capitalism institutional arrangements were more favorable to predation and the sacrifice of community welfare to individual aggrandizement. In the monopoly capitalism of the period 1880-1929 business had come to dominate industry, and goods making was sacrificed to money making.

Veblen analyzed the economic system in terms of two basic flows; namely, the real flow and the financial flow. The real flow is concerned with the production of material goods, while the financial flow deals with the accumulation of pecuniary values or assets such as bank deposits, corporate securities, mortgages and other monetary claims. The real flow of the economy is related to the process of goods making. Goods can be classed as "economic values" when they have "brute serviceability," which is a quality that enables them to contribute to the life process or human survival. Brute serviceability is a form of "social serviceability" or social utility, which is more fundamental than personal or private utility. Private utility may reflect only the whim or caprice of the individual, whereas social serviceability reflects what is fundamental to human survival. Social or brute serviceability is a matter of the "mechanical" and "chemical" qualities of goods that make them useful for enhancing "human life on the whole."[3] In other words social serviceability is a matter of science and technology and the ultimate criterion of value is not subjective personal utility but science and technology. Not all material goods are "economic values" or values that contribute to race survival. Goods that incorporate a large element of fashion or that express class prestige or status are not economic values, since they express personal whim and caprice and do not enhance the life process. Only those material goods are economic values that contribute to individual welfare by improving the conditions leading to race survival.

According to Veblen's interpretation, "pecuniary values" are based on the principle of getting something for nothing and are inimical to race survival. Pecuniary values are increased by restricting output, misleading consumers with the aid of advertising and high pressure salesmanship, creating surplus profits and indulging in financial manipulations that sacrifice efficiency in goods making to profitability in money making. Pecuniary values are increased by subordinating the real flow of the economy to its financial flow. Whereas social welfare and race survival are enhanced by subordinating the financial flow to the real flow of goods making, personal aggrandizement is favored by elevating the community's financial flow over its

---

[3] Thorstein Veblen, *The Theory of the Leisure Class* (New York: The Macmillan Company, 1912) p. 99.

real flow. As Veblen saw it, the evolution of capitalism favored the financial flow over the real flow and sacrificed the production of economic values to the enlargement of pecuniary values. The main economic problem was to reverse this development by creating an economy in which the creation of economic values would become the nation's main concern.

Veblen asserted that it is necessary to regard the economic system as a process because the current economic system can be fully understood only by inquiring into how it came to be what it is, and by investigating the forces that are shaping its future. He explained in *Absentee Ownership and Business Enterprise in Recent Times* (1923) that he was inquiring into the "sequence of economic growth and change" in order to explain the economic situation that had come to a head in the past two decades. He criticized the orthodox economists who had taken the current economic system as something to be explained without inquiring into how the economic system came into being, or into what was the probable course of its future development.

Veblen abandoned the view of a competitive world which was the central consideration of the orthodox economics of his time. In its place he put a view of the economic system in which the core or heartland was occupied by large industrial corporations which were representative of the "key" or "staple" industries — the steel, coal, power, heavy machinery, chemical and transportation industries. Surrounding the core of large-scale industries were the middle-size and small-scale industries of a competitive nature along with agriculture and retailing. The core of the economy functioned like a vortex, expanding and drawing into itself a growing part of the economy as technological change replaced small-scale production with large-scale production. The drift of business enterprise was from the periphery of the economy into the expanding heartland of large-scale business enterprise.

In Veblen's economic analysis the large-scale industrial corporation is the "master institution." Its ownership is in the hands of absentee owners and its management is the responsibility of representatives of the absentee owners. Investment bankers, the "captains of finance," have a crucial role to play because they control the financial destiny of the large industrial corporations. Since they underwrite the sale of corporate securities, the captains of finance are in a position to control the expansion and mergers of industrial corporations.

Veblen was very much concerned with the operations of the large-scale private business enterprise. The aim of this enterprise was to maximize profits or pecuniary values. This was achieved by forming coalitions to eliminate cutthroat competition and to restrict production. Prices were set at levels that would create large surplus profits which went to the absentee owners or corporate pensioners. Prior to 1929 there was no effective challenge to the economic power wielded by the large industrial corporations and their interlocking directorates, which included investment bankers. The government exercised no control over business enterprise, since it was put in office by the business interests. Labor offered no challenge to business enterprise since it was largely unorganized. Where it was organized, as in the case of the members of the American Federation of Labor, labor emulated the self-seeking monopolistic practices of business enterprise. Farmers and consumers, both largely unorganized, were without economic power, and could offer no effective resistance to the large corporations and their financial guardians, the investment bankers.

The Drift of Business Enterprise

According to Veblen's interpretation the policies of those in control of the large business enterprises operating in the heartland of the industrial economy necessarily led to economic disaster. In periods of prosperity corporate managers would seek to enlarge the pecuniary assets of the absentee owners by enlarging the capital structure of the corporations. Veblen explains in *The Theory of Business Enterprise* (1904) that the expanding profits of business enterprises in periods of prosperity would serve as the basis for additional issues of common stocks and bonds. When the boom came to an end, however, because the expanding output could not be sold profitably, many overcapitalized firms would be forced into bankruptcy because they would be unable to meet the fixed charges on their overextended bond issues. In the ensuing period of depression new firms capitalized at lower levels would take the place of the bankrupt overcapitalized firms, and the foundation would be laid for the next period of business expansion.

Veblen asserted that, in spite of technological progress, recurring business cycles would carry the nation along a downward path towards the eventual destruction of the private capitalistic system. The growing concentration of industry and the increasingly effective restriction of production by the large corporations and the large trade unions would in the long run adversely affect the nation's "aggregate output" or "total gross output." The industrial system would be operated at a "progressively diminishing return."[4] Veblen explained that the difference between the nation's total gross output and the cost of producing this output — the wages paid to workers, the cost of raw materials and the depreciation on industrial capital — is the net product of industry which is claimed by the absentee owners. As recurring depressions become more severe this net product of industry would decline and eventually turn into a deficit. With the decline in real national income wages would fall to a level that could be no longer tolerated by the working population. At this point an industrial stalemate would make its appearance and the underlying population guided by spontaneously created leaders would overturn the capitalist system.

Veblen was not certain what the outcome of the industrial stalemate would be. He was certain, however, that the system of private business enterprise would pass away in the course of time because technological change would undermine its foundations. In Veblen's opinion the demise of capitalism would be followed by the establishment of a military dictatorship or a socialist state.[5] If the absentee owners and their representatives appealed to the government for protection from the working population, the workers might be defeated but only at the price of the establishment of a militaristic fascism which would sacrifice the propertied classes to its own interests. If the workers succeeded in overturning the capitalist system, they would establish a regime of workmanship or a socialist state. This socialist regime would establish a planned economy in which the net product of industry, the difference between total gross output and the cost of producing this output, would no longer be taken up by the absentee owners but would be absorbed partly by the workers and partly by the social investment of the state for the purpose of enlarging the nation's aggregate output. Veblen did not provide a detailed plan for the reconstruction of the economic system. His regime of workmanship would have been some kind of "industrial democracy" possibly along the lines of the Guild Socialism which was advocated by G. D. H. Cole and other English socialists

[4] Thorstein Veblen, *Absentee Ownership and Business Enterprise in Recent Times* (New York: The Viking Press, 1938) p. 422.

[5] Charles B. Friday, "Veblen on the Future of American Capitalism," *Thorstein Veblen, The Carleton College Veblen Seminar Essays*, edited by Carlton C. Qualey (New York: Columbia University Press, 1968) pp. 45-46.

prior to the First World War.[6] The main objective of Veblen's industrial democracy would be to restore goods making to its proper place and to allocate the nation's resources to the production of "economic values" which would enhance "human life on the whole."

Veblen's Concept of the National State

The state plays an important role in Veblen's theory of capitalism. Like Marx, Veblen viewed the state as a device for advancing the welfare of the vested interests and for exploiting the working population. The national state advanced the pecuniary welfare of the vested interests at home and abroad. The imperialistic wars that were waged by the national states of the advanced industrialized world created colonial empires which provided investment outlets for the propertied classes and also sources of raw materials for the industries that they owned. The output of industry that could not be sold at home because of the inadequate purchasing power of the workers was taken up by the state through military preparations and the conduct of warfare. In this manner domestic prosperity was made to depend in part upon the successful military ventures of the state.

Besides sustaining prosperity by providing outlets for what the private domestic markets could not absorb, the national state aided the vested interests in another way. Preparations for war and the actual carrying on of warfare served the purpose of reducing industrial unrest by stimulating the patriotic fervor of the underlying population. Veblen explains that the spirit of patriotism had its roots in the dim past when clans, tribes and communities found that the warlike spirit contributed a great deal to human survival. The spirit of patriotism is very closely allied with the spirit of sportsmanship, and both are today cultivated by the leisure class. In modern times when survival depends upon peace and not war between advanced industrialized nations, the vested interests find it convenient to use the spirit of patriotism to preserve their property and their privileges. The educational system, organized religion and the media of communication are used, according to Veblen's interpretation, to make the working population emulate the patriotic fervor of the vested interests and be prepared to go to war to defend the property of the vested interests.

---

6 Thorstein Veblen, "A Policy of Reconstruction," *Essays in Our Changing Order*, edited by Leon Ardzrooni (New York: The Viking Press, 1934) pp. 391-398.

In Veblen's analysis of the industrial system there was no permanent place for the national state. Industrialism had no respect for
national boundaries. The large industrial corporation drew its raw
materials from many international sources, and sold its output in
the markets of many countries. In this situation the national state
was an anachronism. It was an outmoded institution which served
the welfare of only the vested interests, and was doomed to disappear
with the private business system. In Veblen's future regime of workmanship or socialist state there would be nationalities but no national
states. Various nationalities would preserve their cultural identities,
and they would find political expression through some form of world
government.

Veblen's Criticism of Neo-Classical Economics

The year before Veblen published his first essay on an economics
topic Alfred Marshall published his *Principles of Economics* (1890),
which was to be the most widely used economics textbook during
much of Veblen's career as an economist. Marshall's *Principles* was
typical of the conventional economics of the period 1890-1930,
which was the subject of severe criticism by Veblen. Marshall's
neo-classical economics can be best described as "market economics."
It was primarily concerned with the optimal allocation of scarce
resources in a competitive market. Marshall took the state of the
industrial arts and the institutional framework as given data. He
analyzed the operations of a small-scale "representative firm" in a
competitive economic system in which the factors of production
were highly mobile, and human behavior was assumed to be rational
and therefore free from the influence of habit and convention. The
economic system was viewed not as an evolving process but as a
static mechanism. The main feature of this economic mechanism
was its tendency to establish an equilibrium. All market forces were
of a self-correcting and not a self-reinforcing nature. Any deviation
from equilibrium quickly called into action self-correcting forces
that would eliminate the original deviation and restore equilibrium.

Veblen criticized what he took to be the excessively abstract and
unrealistic "marginal-utility economics" of Alfred Marshall on two
main grounds. These were Marshall's view or concept of the economic system and his theory of human nature. It was Veblen's position that Marshall's view of the economic system was inadequate
because it was based upon an unsatisfactory preconception as to the
nature of the real economic world. Veblen asserted that Marshall's

preconception of normality led him to assume that there was a normal world of economic equilibrium lying behind the actual world of economic fluctuations, irregularities and conflicts. Veblen explained that economists would come closer to the real economic world if their economic analysis was based upon a preconception of process. Such a preconception would cause them to view the economic system as an evolving process in which change,. development and conflict were permanent rather than transitory features of economic activity.

Veblen also found Marshall's theory of human nature quite inadequate as an explanation of how people behaved in the real economic world. From Marshall's point of view, man was largely a rational creature, unhampered by habitual and conventional pressures, who was dominated by the desire to maximize gain or utility. Like other conventional economists, Marshall divorced the individual from his social environment so that he was essentially a non-social product, who was free to respond to the pecuniary stimuli of the competitive market place. Veblen substituted a social psychology for Marshall's individualistic and hedonistic psychology. He did not deny that men were at times capable of rational behavior. But, in Veblen's opinion, more important than reason in the guidance of human behavior were customs, habits and institutions behind which were operating powerful instinctive drives or propensities. Men used reason but only within a framework of historical circumstances, personal habituation and social convention.

The consequences of Veblen's criticism of Marshall's economics were as follows: Veblen did not deny the usefulness of "market economics." This type of equilibrium economics did throw some light on how scarce resources are allocated in a competitive economy. What Veblen strenuously objected to was what went along with the orthodox view of economics as primarily a study of the allocation of scarce resources in a competitive equilibrium. In other words, he objected to the orthodox economists' excessively rationalistic idea of the nature of human behavior, their view of technology and the institutional framework of society as given data, and their assumption that there were forces at work driving the economic system towards an equilibrium position. Veblen objected to the short-run view of the orthodox economists that led them to limit the scope of economics and to ignore the contributions of the related social sciences. The short-run approach of the orthodox economists caused them to pay little attention to the disruptive behavior of the large industrial corporations, the conflicts among economic classes, the impact of technological change on the structure and functioning of the economic system, the exercise of economic power by large economic interest groups, the decline of consumer sovereignty and many other important problems that emerge when a long-range view of the economic system is taken.

Veblen's Contributions to Economic Science

Veblen did not ignore the areas of micro-economics and macro-economics.[7] In the field of micro-economics he went beyond the competitive firm of Alfred Marshall's economics, and focused attention on the price and production policies of the "partial monopolies," or what are today known as the oligopolistic enterprises. In the area of macro-economics Veblen developed an elementary form of what is now known as national income economics. He analyzed the nation's total gross output and its component parts, and also the various claims on this national output. Veblen's major contributions, however, were not in micro-economics and macro-economics. His major contribution was to take a long view of the economic system which went far beyond the equilibrium analysis of the orthodox economists' market economics.

Veblen's long-range view led him to take the economic system to be an evolving process in which there is no tendency towards the establishment of an equilibrium position. The essence of the economic process is change, development and conflict. Regarding the economic system as an economic process enabled Veblen to take a view of economic reality that was different from the static, short-run view of the orthodox economists. It also enabled him to broaden the scope of economics to include matters for investigation that had been excluded by the orthodox economists. Veblen, unlike the orthodox economists, did not take technology and the institutional framework of society as given data. He emphasized the importance of explaining the impact of technological change on the structure and functioning of the economic system. The long view also enabled Veblen to distinguish between institutions that made for race survival and those that did not. Furthermore, by broadening the scope of inquiry Veblen could show the importance of having economists become aware of the contributions of related social sciences.

When Veblen applied his concept of the economic process to the

---

[7] Allan G. Gruchy, "The Influence of Veblen on Mid-Century Institutionalism," *The American Economic Review*, Vol. XLVIII, No. 2, May 1958, pp. 11-14.

American scene he developed a concept of the logic of the process of industrialization. This concept enabled Veblen to explain the course of industrialization as the economic system moved from competitive small-scale capitalism to monopolistic large-scale capitalism. If his economic analysis was to be significant, Veblen had to get beyond mere historical description. He succeeded in doing so by showing how technological change imposed a pattern or shape on the course of industrialization. Industrialization, he saw, is not just a haphazard random development. When he applied his logic of development to Germany in *Imperial Germany and the Industrial Revolution* (1915), Veblen was able to predict the probable course of German economic development and its political consequences. He did the same thing for Japan in his essay on "The Opportunity of Japan" (1915).[8] Veblen could explain Imperial Germany as a "disturber of the world's peace" by pointing to the cultural lag from which Germany suffered. After 1870 Germany had advanced industrially but had remained politically feudal in outlook. The feudal outlook being associated with a warlike spirit Germany felt constrained to use its new industrial strength for the purpose of conducting military ventures which were a constant threat in the early years of the twentieth century to world peace.

Veblen's genetic approach also led him to ask, where is the economy moving and why? Such questions were never raised by the orthodox economists because an economic system in equilibrium or moving towards an equilibrium position is not evolving or developing. It was obvious to Veblen that the American economic system was evolving, and would continue to do so because technological change was unceasing. For Veblen, if not for the orthodox economists, economic reality was a changing reality. The industrialization process thus opened the door to institutional change and the reconstruction of the economic system. Any economist who takes the economic system to be a process must necessarily deal with the question of social control. No particular form of social control is specified by the emergent nature of the economic process. All that is specified is that the economic system of today will not be the economic system of tomorrow. Veblen was not optimistic about mankind's ability to rise to the occasion and to control the evolution of the industrial system so that it would move in the direction of race survival.[9] It was

---

[8] Thorstein Veblen, *Essays in Our Changing Order*, pp. 248-266.
[9] Allan G. Gruchy, "Veblen's Theory of Economic Growth," *Thorstein Veblen: A Critical Reappraisal*, pp. 162-163.

Veblen's position, however, that man had to try his hand at social control because technological change would present him with the problem of dealing with an inevitably changing economic system.

The Limitations of Veblen's Evolutionary Economics

Much of the criticism of Veblen's economics stems from the fact that he was not interested in presenting his views with textbook clarity nor was he much interested in defending himself from his critics. When Veblen criticized orthodox economics, the vigor and harshness of his criticism was rather easily interpreted by his opponents as a move towards dispensing with all inherited economic theory. Had he written a general treatise on economics or been more of a theoretical system-builder, Veblen would have been forced to indicate what part of the received economics he was prepared to accept and with what part he would dispense.[10] With regard to Veblen's contributions to economic theory it is quite clear that he had theoretical insights that he failed to develop. He could have pushed his work in micro-economics and macro-economics much further than he did. Undoubtedly his lack of interest in mathematical economics would account for some of his failures to move further in these areas of economic analysis.

Veblen also failed to make much of value theory. He repudiated both the Marxian labor theory of value and the overly subjectivistic Austrian utility theory of value. What Veblen did was to go behind the price values in the market place to uncover a more basic value than price or market value. This more fundamental value he described as "economic value" which was grounded in "social serviceability." Social serviceability was the quality of an economic value that enabled it to contribute to human or race survival. Since Veblen analyzed social serviceability in terms of the mechanical, chemical and psychological aspects of utility, his criterion of value was scientific and technological. In other words the ultimate determinant of value was science and technology and not labor content or personal feeling. What Veblen was doing was to move towards an instrumental or technological concept of value, such as was developed later by Clarence E. Ayres. Veblen's treatment of the value problem remains scattered among his writings. He made no effort to present a detailed critique of orthodox value theory. Nor did he attempt to

---

[10] Joseph Dorfman, "The Source and Impact of Veblen's Thought," *Thorstein Veblen: A Critical Reappraisal*, pp. 11-12.

present his own value theory in any well developed manner. As was so frequently the case, Veblen had a fresh insight into a major economic problem but failed to make the most of this new insight.

With regard to his theory of the developing economic process, Veblen could have improved his position by emphasizing the point that he was not seeking to uncover any laws of economic development. He should have emphasized the point that the laws of pure economic theory have no counterpart in the theory of economic development. It would have strengthened Veblen's theoretical position if he had more clearly indicated what he meant by the logic of capitalist development. What he was really doing was developing a theory of industrialization and uncovering the logic inherent in the process of industrialization. Veblen did not take the time to explain fully what he meant by this logic, nor did he devote much time to explaining the role of technology as a cultural imperative operating within the process of industrialization. One of the unfortunate consequences of his failure to devote more time to these matters was that he opened himself to the criticism that his technological interpretation of economic evolution was excessively deterministic.[11]

Veblen's analysis of the future state of the economy was deficient in a number of ways. He laid himself open to the criticism that he was an unsophisticated technocrat who would construct an industrial system in which there was no concern for the requirements of economic calculation. Production would be carried on without concern for efficiency and marginal adjustments. If Veblen's regime of workmanship was viewed by him as a utopia of economic abundance, there would be no need for any economics of calculation. If, however, he regarded his future economic society as the next step after capitalism in the transition to socialism, his immediate objective was far from being utopian, and would still be very much concerned with the reduction of waste, the improvement of efficiency, the meeting of consumer preferences and other aspects of economic calculation that are normally found in a market system. Since Veblen's analysis remains unclear with regard to these matters, he continues to be criticized as an exponent of a crude kind of technocracy.[12]

A major deficiency on Veblen's part was his failure to look at the process of industrialization critically. He criticized the private business system very severely but he was not equally critical of the

---

[11] David Riesman, *Thorstein Veblen, A Critical Interpretation* (New York: Charles Scribner's Sons, 1953) pp. 84-87.

[12] *Ibid.*, pp. 92-98.

industrial system.[13] He did not draw attention to the possible evils of an industrial society. He did not call attention to the possible conflicts in an industrial society between the "managers" and the "managed," to the possible reappearance of power struggles and new class alignments in a socialist society, and to the possibility that those in charge of the management of the industrial system might endeavor to impose their values on the general population. Veblen did not investigate the impact of an industrial society on the quality of human life. Observations in recent decades of the functioning of the industrial state in the Soviet Union and other communist countries indicate that there are many obstacles to the securing of a life of high quality in an industrial society. John K. Galbraith's study of *The New Industrial State* (1967) suggests that the evils of an industrial society are not limited to experiments with industrialism being carried on in the socialist or communist countries.

The limitations of Veblen's "evolutionary" or "cultural" economics can be attributed in large part to the size of the task that he set for himself in the closing decade of the last century. The reconstruction of economics in any major way would tax the abilities of even the most gifted of economists. A major reconstruction of the science of economics by such a gifted thinker could at best only indicate the directions in which the reconstruction should take place. In the final analysis this was Veblen's major contribution. He broadly indicated the lines along which he thought the reconstruction of the inherited economics should move, and he left to others the task of working out the full implications of the questions with regard to the nature and scope of economic science that he had raised.

The Collective Economics of John R. Commons

John R. Commons (1862-1945), born only five years after Veblen, came to view economics very much as Veblen did. Both felt that the conventional economics of their time was much too narrow and abstract to provide a satisfactory interpretation of the real economic world. Like Veblen, Commons took the economic system to be an evolving process, which had passed through a number of stages of development, and which at the time they were analyzing it was in the stage of the "new industrial order." This new industrial order was described by Veblen as "finance capitalism" and by Commons as "banker capitalism." Both agreed that the small-scale

---

[13] Douglas F. Dowd, *Thorstein Veblen* (New York: Washington Square Press, 1966) p. 141.

competitive firm had been replaced in the key industries by the large corporate enterprise, and that the modern industrial economy revealed no tendency to move towards an equilibrium position. They did not agree, however, on the importance of other economic interest groups such as organized labor and the farmers. Veblen believed that these economic interest groups could never successfully challenge the economic power of big business. Commons disagreed with Veblen and was of the opinion that countervailing groups such as organized labor and organized farmers had emerged to challenge the power of the large business units. Commons described these countervailing groups as "protectionist interests." With the decline of the free competitive market system, each major economic interest group found it necessary to organize against other groups, and especially against large-scale business.

The major characteristic of Commons's new industrial system was conflict rather than harmony. If there was to be harmony in economic affairs, it would be a managed and not an automatic harmony. Commons had witnessed the industrial strife, the depressed agriculture and the recurring business cycles of the last two decades of the nineteenth century. He also observed the merger movement, the growth of large oligopolistic enterprises and the development of the public utility industries in the early decades of the twentieth century. He was impressed by the inability of the unregulated private enterprise system to provide sustained employment for the workers, satisfactory returns to farmers, sufficient protection for small businesses and adequate purchasing power for consumers. When Commons turned to the orthodox treatises on economics for an explanation of the existence of these major economic problems and for possible solutions to them, he found that orthodox economics could not measure up to his demands upon it.

Commons tells us in his *Institutional Economics* that his objective was not to do away with the traditional economics of his day but rather to develop "a rounded-out theory of Political Economy."[14] He explained that orthodox economics dealt with the mechanics of the production, distribution and consumption of wealth. His "collective economics" went beyond what in effect was the production or technical economics of conventional economists. Whereas the conventional economists dealt with "man to nature" relations, Commons was

---

[14] John R. Commons, *Institutional Economics* (New York: The Macmillan Company, 1934) p. 6.

concerned with "man to man" or cultural relations. The modern industrial system, which was the object of Commons's scientific interest, is a complex of bargaining, managerial and rationing (by the state) transactions which does not satisfactorily dispose of scarce economic resources, and which consequently does not adequately meet individual and collective needs. Since the industrial system did not realize its full economic potential, and did not provide each major economic interest group with what it believed to be a fair share of the national income, the obvious need according to Commons's interpretation was for a program that would create a managed, harmonious equilibrium in the nation's economic activities.

Commons was a product of the American Mid-West, untouched by Marxian or other radical influences. Unlike Veblen, Commons was an optimist who believed that the American economic system could be reconstructed with the aim of improving its operations without changing the essentials of private business enterprise. His underlying social philosophy was the solidarism which became so popular at the turn of the century as a substitute for the radical Marxist philosophy. The solidaristic philosophy was pluralistic rather than dualistic. Solidarists like Commons did not accept Veblen's division of the economy into two main classes, the vested interests and the workers. Instead they observed that there was a plurality of classes — big business, small business, organized labor, organized farmers and a variety of less well organized consumer groups. It was Commons's position that, although these various classes were in conflict over many economic objectives, nevertheless they all had a realization of enough common interests to make it possible for them to collaborate in improving the functioning of the new industrial system. The problem, as Commons saw it, was to find new institutional arrangements that would eliminate the evils of "banker capitalism" and convert it into "reasonable capitalism."

In the early years of his career as an economist Commons was primarily interested in the labor problem. He felt that much of this problem was due to the fact that orthodox economics treated labor as a marketable commodity which was to be classed along with the other factors of production. This approach proved to be disastrous in the new industrial system with its large trade unions and collective bargaining procedures, because it ignored what Commons described as "industrial goodwill."[15] This goodwill was based on a

---

[15] John R. Commons, *Industrial Goodwill* (New York: McGraw-Hill, 1919) pp. 19-20.

psychological relationship between the employer and his employees. Commons explained in his work on *Industrial Goodwill* (1919) that industrial goodwill is as important as the factors of production recognized by conventional economists. Prior to 1929 Commons had hoped to see the nation's labor problems solved by having it adopt new institutional arrangements which would create the necessary "industrial goodwill" between business and labor. He recommended the use of labor contracts, better labor legislation, personnel departments, shop committees, industrial commissions and an overall permanent National Joint Conference of Capital and Labor. Commons's institutional innovations can be summarized as a series of proposals to establish an industrial government which would seek to substitute "class collaboration" for "class struggle."

Commons and Reasonable Capitalism

The Great Depression of the 1930's awakened Commons to the realization that the labor problem was only one of the many problems associated with American capitalism, and that the labor problem could be solved only by solving the larger problem of banker capitalism. Commons explained that this type of capitalism, which had developed after 1885 and was dominant when the Great Depression struck in 1929, had three major defects. It stabilized "scarcity profits" but not "efficiency profits"; it was unable to prevent recurring periods of depression; and it was unable to maintain full employment. The large business enterprise was a going concern that maximized profits not by improving efficiency and enlarging production and employment, but by elevating scarcity over efficiency and thus restricting output. In spite of all the efforts of large-scale business enterprise to stabilize the economy it was still plagued by the vagaries of the business cycle. In Commons's opinion the most serious problem of the capitalist system was its failure to provide sustained full employment. Workers valued employment over peace and liberty, and if the western democracies were to compete successfully with fascism and communism, they would have to find some way of maintaining full and steady employment.

After 1885 the decline of the free competitive market as a device for providing guidance for the economic system led to the spread of conflicts among the nation's major economic interest groups. In the absence of a strong positive government which might have provided economic guidance, the Supreme Court was called upon to prevent the exploitation of workers, farmers and consumers by big business.

According to Commons's interpretation the Supreme Court became a faculty of political economy which domesticated banker capitalism through a series of court decisions that preserved the general welfare. Farmers were protected from exorbitant freight rates, workers were guaranteed reasonable working conditions, and consumers were shielded from exploitation by the public utilities by decisions of the Supreme Court which upheld the constitutionality of fair rates of return on investment in public utilities as determined by state public utility commissions.

In this manner "judicial sovereignty" as exercised by the Supreme Court provided guidance for the new industrial order in the absence of adequate guidance from either the market mechanism or the federal government. By 1929, however, the industrial system had become so complex the Supreme Court found it increasingly difficult to guide the economy. After 1929 the federal government became more aware of its responsibility as an agent for the guidance of the nation's economy. Judicial sovereignty was then replaced by "administrative sovereignty."

Under Commons's administrative sovereignty the guidance of the economy came more and more from administrative agencies, many of which were established in the early 1930's. During the New Deal there were added to previously established agencies such as the Interstate Commerce Commission (1887) and the Federal Trade Commission (1914) new agencies such as the Federal Power Commission (1930), the National Labor Relations Board (1935), the Securities and Exchange Commission (1934) and the Federal Communications Commission (1934). These regulatory agencies combined legislative, judicial and executive functions when they investigated economic activities and issued orders to contending parties with the aim of resolving economic conflicts. Commons envisioned a revitalized Congress, stirred to action by voluntary associations representing business, labor, agriculture and consumers, which would lay down broad legislative guidelines for the conduct of administrative agencies. In this situation the Supreme Court would be concerned only with the maintenance of due process. Commons's administrative sovereignty would supplement the guidance that was provided by the private market mechanism to the end that a more "reasonable capitalism" would be established. Where the private market system could not assure reasonable economic practices and reasonable economic values, the administrative agencies of the government would step in to assure the public that reasonable practices and values would prevail. It was Commons's expectation that under "reasonable capitalism" production and employment would be stabilized at a full employment level, that inflation would be curbed, and that business enterprises would be more concerned with making profits by being efficient and enlarging output than by limiting production and exploiting non-competitive advantages.

Commons's approach to the problem of how to deal with the depression of the 1930's was quite distinct from the approach of those economists who felt that the key issue was how to control fluctuations in private investment. It was Commons's position that the depression was to be attributed mainly to a scarcity of gold and an inadequate supply of money. Since the money supply had not increased in step with the growth of the economy, consumers were unable to purchase what was being produced, prices fell and the foundation was laid for a depression. Commons's remedy for the depression took the form of recommending different ways of enlarging consumer purchasing power. These included the issuance of fiat money by the government to finance relief payments, an easy credit policy on the part of the Federal Reserve System and a federal unemployment insurance program. It was argued by Commons and other "monetarists" such as George F. Warren and Frank A. Pearson that a larger money supply would increase consumer buying and restore prices to a level that would maintain prosperity.

Commons's monetary approach to the depression was in marked contrast to the approach of Wesley C. Mitchell and John M. Clark. Both Mitchell and Clark put much more emphasis on fluctuations in private investment than on changes in the money supply as a major cause of the depression. Commons's contribution to the problem of coping with the depression was not in the realm of theory. His contribution was to point out the need for collective action if the deficiencies of the private enterprise system were to be corrected. This had been his message in the thirty years prior to the Great Depression. Starting with his work on labor, public utility and tax problems at the turn of the century, Commons never ceased to emphasize the importance of collective action in control of individual economic behavior. The new industrial order after 1885 had opened the door to collective action on the part of business, labor, agriculture and consumers. What was needed to handle the problems of the new industrial system successfully was more collective action under the sponsorship of the state and federal governments. This collective action would take the form of institutional innovations such as new administrative agencies, unemployment insurance and old age pension schemes, shop committees and industrial councils. If "reasonable capitalism" was to be established, Commons pointed out that there would have to be a considerable modification of the institutional framework of the private enterprise system. Like Veblen, Commons called for institutional experimentation and innovation, but he was not prepared to carry this innovation anywhere nearly as far as Veblen was willing to carry it. In the years of the New Deal Commons's pragmatic, collective approach with its quite limited outlook was favorably received in government circles.

Common's Concept of Economic Science

In developing his collective economics Commons takes the "transaction" as his starting point. He definies a transaction as a legal-economic relation between two or more persons which looks towards the future. Commons explains in *Legal Foundations of Capitalism* (1924) that transactions together constitute a flow or process in which they merge into one another and become collective or institutional in nature. The three types of transactions, namely, bargaining, rationing and managing transactions, unite to form "going concerns" such as corporations, trade unions, trade associations and farm co-operatives. The most important going concern is the business corporation which is composed of the "going plant" and the "going business." The going plant is concerned with efficiency and the production of useful goods, whereas the going business is concerned with scarcity and the accumulation of scarcity or money values. Commons's study of transactions is carried on with the aid of five explanatory principles which condition, limit and direct the complex of transactions comprising the capitalist system. These principles are the principles of "efficiency," "scarcity," "working rules," "futurity" and "sovereignty." Working rules are customary ways of carrying on economic activity. These working rules of the going concerns may emphasize efficiency and the creation of economic or use values. Or they may emphasize scarcity and the creation of market values or financial assets. The capitalist system is oriented towards change and a dynamic future during which the scales may be tipped in favor of an economy of economic abundance or in favor of an economy emphasizing restricted output and the maximization of financial returns or scarcity values. Where there is no overall state guidance the direction that the economy takes is determined by the outcome of the power struggle among the nation's major economic interest groups. The state can influence this power struggle by using its sovereign power to eliminate conflicts among economic interest groups and to provide guidance for the economy. The state's rationing or directing power can override the bargaining and managerial transactions of corporations, trade unions, trade associations and other going concerns when these transactions do not result in a "reasonable" type of capitalist economy.

Commons explains that what distinguishes his collective economics from traditional analytical economics is his concept of futurity. The economic system as viewed by traditional nineteenth-century economists and their twentieth-century followers had no future other than the equilibrium position towards which it was supposed to be automatically moving. The economic system, as Commons sees it, is a process with a future during which the economic system may be reconstructed. His collective economics stresses the dynamic and purposive qualities of an economic system based upon uncertain expectations relating to future production and consumption. Commons's economics emphasizes the fact that the dynamic American economy is open not only to the possibility of great risks and hardships for many participating individuals, but also to the possibility of continuously improving the living standards of the masses. Commons emphasizes the importance of the collective efforts of the nation to make the best of a world of limited resources. Individual wills are congealed into a form of collective volitiency or will-to-action. Collective volitiency leads to collective action of many forms which are designed to control individuals at their work of disposing of scarce human and natural resources. In this situation economics becomes less a matter of "individual economy" and more a matter of "political economy."

Commons's political economy is an amalgam of economics, political science, ethics, jurisprudence, history and psychology. His transactions went far beyond the simple exchange relations found in the market place. In rounding out economics he pushed far beyond market economics. For example, he made the valuation process a cultural process which included market valuation but which went beyond market values to consider "reasonable values."[16] The latter values are determined by the courts which pragmatically consider the interests of all parties involved in the conflict over what a reasonable value is. Commons does not deny the existence of market values.

---

[16] Ben B. Seligman, *Main Currents in Modern Economics, Economic Thought since 1870* (New York: The Free Press of Glencoe, 1963) p. 175.

What he does is to broaden the concept of value to include values not determined in the market place. In other words, he added a negotiational theory of value to the market value theory of the conventional economists. This is another example of how he rounded out the science of economics or broadened its scope. Like Veblen and other institutionalists Commons considered economics to be a cultural science that studied the economic aspect of human culture or that aspect of culture concerned with the provision of material goods.

Wesley C. Mitchell's Quantitative Economics

Of the institutionalists who came after Veblen none was closer to the founder of American institutionalism than Wesley C. Mitchell, who had sat in Veblen's classes at the University of Chicago. Mitchell must have been greatly impressed by the contrast between the orthodoxy of J. Laurence Laughlin and the heterodoxy of Thorstein Veblen. Although we can see the influences of both economists on his work, it was Veblen who left the deepest imprint on Mitchell. The latter was well aware of the contributions of the conventional economists of his time, but he was not prepared to work within the framework of the established "analytical" or "marginalist" economics. Mitchell was very critical of the psychological theory underlying neo-classical economics and also of the view of the economic system held by the neo-classicists. He believed that an adequate interpretation of the real economic world required the introduction into economic analysis of the recent contributions of social psychology. It also required an evolutionary approach to the study of the economic system.

Mitchell takes the position in his article on "The Prospects of Economics" (1924) that economics, like other social sciences, is a "science of human behavior."[17] What distinguishes economics from other social sciences is that it deals with the aspect of human behavior which is concerned with the provision of goods and services. Since economics is a science of human behavior, it is very essential to have a sound and realistic theory of human behavior, if the real economic world is to be satisfactorily interpreted. Mitchell found the rationalistic and hedonistic psychological theory of the conventional economists of his time quite unsatisfactory. He was convinced

---

[17] Wesley C. Mitchell, "The Prospects of Economics," in *The Trend of Economics*, edited by R. G. Tugwell (New York: Alfred A. Knopf, 1924) p. 25.

that the introspective analysis of utilities and disutilities could not throw much light on the nature of economic behavior. Mitchell's psychological approach was behavioristic and objective. He did not deny that men were to some extent rational, and operated in part according to the principle of the economic calculus. It was Mitchell's position that man is a social product whose behavior is largely shaped by the values and the institutions of the society in which he lives. Human behavior should therefore be studied within the framework of an evolving set of social and economic institutions. Some of these institutions and their related values induce men to act in what are regarded as socially desirable ways, whereas other institutions and values lead men to act in a socially undesirable manner. In Mitchell's opinion the neo-classical economists erred when they took man to be an independently rational creature who used his reason without being influenced by the value and institutional systems surrounding him.

Mitchell's psychological theory emphasized the behavioristic and objective aspects of human behavior. The proper way to study economic behavior was to examine it objectively as it appeared in the real world. Mitchell did not follow Veblen in emphasizing the instinctive basis of human behavior, because instincts cannot be objectively analyzed. Mitchell did not deny that man has biological drives or impulses, but he analyzed these drives only as they appeared in the form of observable human behavior. He wanted not only to observe human behavior, but also to apply the statistical method to it. His desire to handle large masses of behavioral data led him to adopt the statistical approach that we see so well developed in his studies of the business cycle. It was Mitchell's view that economics could make no further progress until it analyzed economic behavior both objectively and quantitatively. By the time that Mitchell turned to his economic studies early in this century he believed that the orthodox economists had gotten about all that they could from their introspective approach to the study of economic behavior.

As has already been indicated Mitchell was very dissatisfied with the conventional economists' view of the economic system. He observed that their view was not only static and cross-sectional, but was also out of date since it applied largely to a competitive system that was rapidly disappearing in the early decades of this century. Mitchell substituted a dynamic process view of the American economy for the mechanistic, equilibrium view of Alfred Marshall and other orthodox economists. Like the orthodox economists, Mitchell also analyzed "the current working" of the economic system, but he placed this current working within the framework of "the cumulative changing of economic processes."[18] Mitchell did not dispense with current, cross-sectional analysis of the economy. Instead he updated the cross-sectional analysis of the orthodox economists so that it included a study of the large corporations which were responsible for the severe fluctuations in economic activity. Also he analyzed the current cross section of the economy in relation to the evolving capitalist system. In effect he sought a marriage of the marginalist economics of Alfred Marshall and John Bates Clark and the evolutionary economics of Thorstein Veblen and Werner Sombart. His aim was to enlarge the scope of economics by viewing the economic system as a process with a past, present and future.

If economics was to be more than a "system of pecuniary logic, a mechanical study of static equilibria under non-existent conditions," Mitchell asserted that the science had to be grounded in objective data that would enable the economist to test the validity of his generalizations about the economic system. It was therefore necessary to make widespread use of the quantitative or statistical method of handling economic data. In furthering this objective Mitchell worked for many years with the National Bureau of Economic Research which was dedicated to the quantitative study of business cycles and related matters. It was not that Mitchell was unaware of the value of deductive or qualitative analyses, although many of his critics have asserted that he seemed to be moving in the direction of reducing economics to mere quantification.[19] What Mitchell objected to was the excessive abstractionism of neo-classical economics and its failure to provide a firm inductive basis for what passed as "pure theory." He was opposed to both the construction of "grand systems" of economic generalization and mere fact gathering. His "analytic description" was designed to avoid the errors of both excessive deduction and excessive induction. Mitchell may properly be criticized for what he failed to achieve with his "analytic description" of business cycles, but not on the ground that he was a rank empiricist.[20] Mitchell was well aware that "Qualitative distinctions

[18] Wesley C. Mitchell, "Human Behavior and Economics," *The Quarterly Journal of Economics*, Vol. XXIX, November 1914, p. 37.

[19] Joseph A. Schumpeter, "Mitchell's Business Cycles," *The Quarterly Journal of Economics*, Vol. XLV, November 1930, pp. 151-158, and T. C. Koopmans, "Measurement without Theory," *The Review of Economic Statistics*, August 1947, pp. 161, 163, 172.

[20] Ben B. Seligman, *op. cit.*, pp. 198-200.

must remain basic in all their [economists'] work." Mitchell believed
that detailed, quantitative studies of the business cycle would enable
economists to have a better understanding of the qualitative aspects
of the money economy. He felt that in the early decades of this
century there was more to be gained from quantitative than qualitative economic analysis. His inquiries might be "more intensive and
tamer" than Veblen's broad speculative studies, but in Mitchell's
opinion this was the way to advance beyond Veblen on the path that
the latter had staked out.

Mitchell's Analysis of the Business Cycle

Mitchell's general view of the economic system was borrowed
in large part from Veblen. Like Veblen, Mitchell took the economic
system to be an evolving process which contained two subprocesses,
the making of money and the making of goods. These two subprocesses were harmoniously related in the standard economics textbooks of Alfred Marshall, F. W. Taussig and other conventional
economists, who largely ignored the phenomenon of the business
cycle. In Mitchell's view the main feature of the economic system
was the failure of money making and goods making to be harmoniously related, as was indicated by the recurring depressions and
the heavy social costs of these depressions. The conventional economists of Mitchell's time regarded the business cycle as a temporary
deviation from an equilibrium position of the economy, which was
prevented from going too far from this equilibrium position by the
economy's self-correcting forces. For the conventional economists
equilibrium was the normal economic condition of the economic
system, and each phase of the business cycle was a temporary ab-
normal condition. Mitchell reversed this conventional economic view.
He asserted that the business cycle was a normal condition in the
money economy, and equilibrium was only a temporary situation
through which the business cycle very quickly passed. Mitchell was
convinced that the business cycle was a special feature of the
capitalist era from 1875 to 1929. It was not necessarily a permanent feature of the capitalist system of producing and distributing
goods. Writing in 1927 in *Business Cycles: The Problem and Its
Setting*, Mitchell explained that it was conceivable that the four-
phase business cycle that he had described in 1913 could disappear,
if the overall nature of economic organization was changed. He was
prophetic on this point because this is what actually happened when

welfare capitalism replaced *laissez-faire* capitalism after 1929, and the nineteenth-century type of business cycle disappeared.

The essentials of Mitchell's business cycle analysis were presented in his classic 1913 study *Business Cycles*. According to his interpretation the business cycle was a self-generating oscillating movement of the business system which went through the four phases of prosperity, recession, depression and revival. Each phase of the cycle contained within itself factors that would lead to the succeeding phase. For example, in the upswing of the cycle in the revival phase various factors such as the increased demand which spread from one industry to another, the "epidemic of optimism" and the lag of costs behind prices would react upon one another in a cumulative manner to provide an upward momentum that would convert revival into prosperity. At the end of the prosperity phase other factors such as the elimination of the lead of prices over costs, the exhaustion of excess bank reserves, and the accumulation of inventories would react upon one another in a downward cumulative manner until prosperity was followed by recession. Although Mitchell was able to construct a pattern of a typical business cycle, he pointed out that no two cycles were alike. Since there were many economic factors at work during the four phases of the business cycle, Mitchell could find no single main cause of the cycle. Instead of one cause he found many conditions that led to the recurrence of the cycle. He therefore substituted a pluralistic interpretation of business cycles for the monistic interpretations of many of his predecessors in the study of business cycles. If there was one factor that received special attention from Mitchell it was fluctuations in profits and rates of return on net worth. Depression turned into revival when orders for new equipment and inventories improved the profit prospects of businessmen. Likewise during revival the more rapid increase in prices than in costs enhanced profit prospects and spread an optimistic outlook among businessmen. It was the eventual decline in profit prospects, as prices levelled off and costs crept up, that weakened the momentum of the prosperity phase of the business cycle. But changes in profit prospects were associated with many other factors such as changes in bank reserves, interest rates, employment, wage rates, population, sales volume and various other endogenous factors, so that no one factor could be selected as *the* cause of the recurring business cycle.

When he wrote his *Business Cycles: The Problem and Its Setting* in 1927 Mitchell proposed to write another volume that would summarize his theorizing about the business cycle. He never wrote this proposed volume, and his *What Happens during Business Cycles*, which was published posthumously in 1951, did not contain his final views about the nature and causes of business cycles. It appears that Mitchell's pluralistic approach to the business cycle was so broad in its coverage that he was never able to refine his vast statistical studies to the point where he could draw from them a satisfactory theoretical treatment of the business cycle. He provided many insights which later gave rise to such theoretical constructs as the principle of acceleration, which was developed by John M. Clark, and the concepts of leading and lagging time series which became the basis for short-run business forecasting. Later economists have observed that much of present-day business cycle theory can be found in embryonic form in Mitchell's work.[21] Even if he had been disposed prior to the end of his career in 1948 to present a theory of the business cycle, Mitchell would have found that the regular self-generating business cycle which he had analyzed in 1913 had by 1948 lost many of its fundamental characteristics. By 1948 the regular four phase business cycle had become no more than an irregular succession of periods of business expansion and contraction. By this time the role of the government in economic affairs had become so important and the functioning of the economy had become so different from what it had been in the years 1875-1929, that much of Mitchell's early economic analysis was no longer applicable to the post 1929 economic situation.

Mitchell and National Economic Planning

In his 1913 work on *Business Cycles* Mitchell distinguished between "broad changes of economic organization" and "lesser changes."[22] The "broad changes" included such changes as the growth of big business, the integration of industry, the spreading of organized labor and the development of monopoly control. Mitchell realized that these large changes could eventually alter the structure and functioning of the whole economy as it moved along the path of industrialization. Under the impact of these changes an old era of capitalist development such as *laissez-faire* capitalism could be

[21] A. F. Burns, editor, *Wesley Clair Mitchell: The Economic Scientist* (New York: National Bureau of Economic Research, 1952) pp. 93 ff, and M. Friedman, "Wesley C. Mitchell as an Economic Theorist," *Journal of Political Economy*, Vol. LVIII, December 1950.

[22] *Business Cycles* (Berkeley: University of California Press, 1913) p. 583.

replaced by a new era of capitalist development such as welfare
capitalism. Such a long-run development could greatly affect the
nature and operation of the business cycle. "Lesser changes" included
only those changes which occurred in each of Mitchell's four phases
of the business cycle. The bulk of Mitchell's economic analysis is
concerned with the lesser changes that create the momentum in each
cycle phase. Although as early as 1913 Mitchell had called attention
to the emergence of the large business corporation, the "centralization of economic power," the merger movement and the progress
of industrial technology, in the years 1913-1929 he did not direct
much of his attention to these developments, with the result that he
sought to develop a theory of the business cycle and not a theory of
industrialization. Since he analyzed economic developments over the
years 1875-1948, he had the opportunity to move beyond business
cycle theory, as Thorstein Veblen and Werner Sombart did, to develop a theory of capitalist development or of industrialization. After
1929 Mitchell did move beyond business cycle theory, but he did
not go very far in developing a theory of capitalist development or
industrialization. His work in this area is quite fragmentary.

Early in the 1930's Mitchell became convinced that the only solution to the problem of how to prevent fluctuations in business activity
was some form of national planning, which would at the same time
preserve the private enterprise system. As early as 1913 he had
called attention to the growth of planning within business enterprises and their lack of coordination. Up to 1929 he had hoped to
secure more harmony between money making and goods making by
such limited devices as a better banking system, a stabilized dollar,
employment exchanges, a public works program and more and
better information for businessmen. Mitchell had always felt that the
money economy had to have some kind of social control, if its
undesirable features were to be eliminated. By 1933, when he made
his report to the Research Committee on Social Trends, he had
come to the conclusion that "To deal with the central problem of
balance, or with any of its ramifications, economic planning is called
for."[23] Mitchell never recommended any detailed planning program.
He called for the establishment of a national planning board which
would advise the Congress and prepare the way for the adoption of
a national planning program. He did not inquire into the problem

---

[23] Report of the President's Research Committee on Social Trends, *Recent
Social Trends in the United States* (New York: McGraw-Hill Book Co., 1933)
p. xxxi.

of how a national plan would be constructed, or what kind of organization for planning would be necessary. By 1948 France, the United Kingdom, the Netherlands and the three major Scandinavian countries were well launched on national economic planning programs. If Mitchell was aware of these West European experiments in national economic planning, he did not draw upon them to support his own views about planning.

In his 1913 study on *Business Cycles* Mitchell had criticized the "planlessness" of production. The trouble with the economic system, he said at that time, was that it was guided by no "large human purpose." He pointed out that "If the test of efficiency in the direction of economic activity be that of determining what needs are most important for the common welfare and then satisfying them in the most economical manner, the present system is subject to further criticism. For, in nations where a few have incomes sufficient to gratify trifling whims and where many cannot buy things required to maintain their own efficiency or to give proper training to their children, it can hardly be argued that the goods which pay best are the goods most needed."[24] Mitchell went on to explain that an economic system which was guided by the "artificial" aim of "pecuniary profit" would fall far short of reaching the ideals of public welfare. It was his view that prospective profits should not be eliminated as a guide to business leaders. Instead private profit making should be regulated or controlled so that it would advance and not jeopardize public welfare. The uncontrolled market system did not always bring about a close correspondence between personal and social utilities. Too many goods with high personal and low social utility were being produced. It was Mitchell's observation in his article on "The Backward Art of Spending Money" (1912) that, contrary to what the standard economics textbooks said, consumers were not as well informed as were the producers, and were far from being rational in their buying habits. In a money economy dominated by the pecuniary motive consumer welfare would suffer, unless some "large human purpose" was introduced into the nation's economic affairs. By 1935 Mitchell was convinced that this large human purpose could be provided only by some kind of democratic national planning.

Mitchell's interest in national planning turned his attention to the problem of determining the content of the economic welfare which would be maximized by a planning program. He explained that it

---

[24] *Business Cycles*, p. 39.

was not the role of the economist to determine what should be the content of economic welfare. This content should be a reflection of the desires of the majority of the people. Economists, however, can help to make the production process more rational by throwing light on the consequences for economic welfare of following different lines of economic action.[25] Mitchell believed that it is possible to set up some tentative, objective criteria for the measurement of economic welfare concerning which there could be secured a consensus of public opinion. In other words welfare can be made objective and definite in relation to such basic matters as minimum requirements for food, clothing, shelter, sanitation, education and health care. It is Mitchell's position that it is possible to set up some quantitative standards with regard to these fundamental elements of human welfare. Beyond these minimum requirements it is more difficult to define the content of economic welfare. It is clear to Mitchell, however, that the "good life" requires a more equitable distribution of the national income, more economic security, freedom from the fear of technological unemployment and more freedom to share in the economic abundance that the economic system can produce.

Mitchell's View of Economic Science

Mitchell had a functional view of economic science. Like John Dewey, he believed that ideas were essentially plans of action. Economics has the "social value" of enabling mankind to cope more easily with various economic difficulties. Mitchell wrote that "In economics as in other sciences we desire knowledge mainly as an instrument of control. Control means the alluring possibility of shaping the evolution of economic life to fit the developing purposes of our race. . . . Always the center of our interest lies in the changes that have taken place in economic behavior, the changes that are now taking place, the changes that may take place in the future."[26] Mitchell did not see in the world around him the economic equilibrium that appeared so prominently in the writings of conventional economists. If the disequilibrium that he saw was to be removed, there would be a need for new institutional arrangements such as a national planning board and a national planning program, which he had proposed. In Mitchell's opinion it is the responsibility of

---

[25] Simon Kuznets, "The Contribution of Wesley C. Mitchell," *Institutional Economics: Veblen, Commons, and Mitchell Reconsidered* (Berkeley: University of California Press, 1963) pp. 111-112.
[26] "The Prospects of Economics," *loc. cit.*, p. 25.

economists to point out the direction in which institutional change should go, if money making and goods making are to be harmoniously related.

Mitchell must be credited with placing business cycle analysis on a firm empirical foundation, which it had lacked prior to his 1913 study of business cycles. His work in this area provided many new insights of which, however, others were to make more use than he did. Mitchell's work in this area would doubtlessly have had a longer lasting theoretical significance, if he had penetrated the "money surface of things" more deeply than he did. Had he concentrated his attention on the major significant factors at work in the business cycle such as saving and investment, and had he paid more attention to the behavior of income recipients and investors, Mitchell's work could have anticipated much of the macro-economic analysis that came after 1935.

Mitchell's main deficiency relates to his treatment of what Veblen called the drift of the business system. Mitchell was interested in much more than the cyclical fluctuations of the business system. His ultimate concern was with the evolving economic process in the period 1875-1945 and the "broad changes" which were at work altering the structure and functioning of the evolving industrial system. These changes, related to scientific progress and technological change, had during his lifetime converted *laissez-faire* capitalism into welfare capitalism, and, according to Mitchell, pointed in the direction of some kind of planned capitalism, presumably along the lines of the indicative planning which has emerged in Western Europe since 1945. Mitchell presents his analysis of the evolving industrial system in a very sketchy manner. He failed to tie together his interest in the "large corporation, dominant in business today," "the continuing forces — science and economic change," "the integration of industry," the "organization of labor," "the centralization of power" and the "extension of monopoly control." In short Mitchell did not develop a theory of the process of industrialization and the logic inherent in this process, which would have provided a receptacle for his many insights into the working of the money economy.

Mitchell's work was in a number of ways an advance beyond Veblen.[27] He supplied an empirical basis for the analysis of the modern industrial economy which was lacking in Veblen. Furthermore he provided an interpretation of the evolution of the American

---

[27] Joseph Dorfman, *The Economic Mind in American Civilization*, Volume IV, 1918-1933, pp. 375-377.

economy which was more realistic than Veblen's interpretation. Unlike Veblen, Mitchell was convinced that the American economy had the capacity to change enough to ensure its survival for an indefinite period. On this point Mitchell agreed with John R. Commons, J. M. Clark and other institutionalists. Also Mitchell was more restrained than Veblen in his criticism of orthodox economics, and was more careful to point out that institutionalism would not dispense with many of the building blocks of conventional economics. It was always Mitchell's hope that his quantitative economics would help to bridge the gulf between Veblen's evolutionary economics and the orthodox economics of the standard textbooks.

J. M. Clark's Social Economics

No post Veblenian institutionalist was more original in his theorizing about the evolving economic process than John Maurice Clark (1884-1963). Clark's concepts of overhead cost, social costs and social values left a deep imprint on economic thought as it developed over the past half century. Neo-classical economics had reached its zenith when Clark came on the academic scene. He completed his graduate work at Columbia University in 1910 just three years after his father John Bates Clark had published his *Essentials of Economic Theory* (1907). The economics of the older Clark was similar to that of Alfred Marshall. Both of these orthodox economists developed a "static economics" which explained the operations of a competitive economic system with an inherent tendency towards equilibrium. Both the elder Clark and Marshall had intended to write a second volume on "dynamic economics," which would explain those aspects and forces of the real economic world that had been left out of their volumes on static economics. Neither John Bates Clark nor Alfred Marshall ever got around to writing their promised second volumes on dynamic economics. To do so would have required changes in basic assumptions relating to the nature of human behavior and of the economic system, which neither the elder Clark nor Marshall was able or willing to make.

The economics of John Bates Clark, Alfred Marshall and other orthodox economists in the early years of this century was an economics of variable costs in contrast to John M. Clark's economics of overhead costs. The economics of variable costs applied to a small-scale competitive economy in which overhead or fixed costs played a minor role. Most of the costs per unit of output of the small-scale competitive firms were variable costs in the form of labor and raw material costs since overhead or capital investment in the small competitive firm was not large. In addition capital investment in the competitive economy of the neo-classical economists was highly mobile and responsive to profit changes in various industries. In the competitive world of John Bates Clark and Alfred Marshall self-correcting forces preserved the tendency towards equilibrium. Selling prices were kept close to costs of production so no surplus profits could be secured in the long run. Since it was assumed that producers met consumer preferences, consumers got what they wanted, and consumer wants were therefore not "manufactured" or created by producers. Entry and exit from each industry were unhindered, no surplus productive capacity existed, and there was no discrimination among buyers. Market prices were good measures not only of personal but also of social utility. A high price meant that a good had both high personal and high social utility. In the competitive economy of the neo-classical economists there was no discrepancy between business and social efficiency. When a businessman made a profit, he met consumer wants and so contributed to social welfare. Efficiency in competitive profit making went hand in hand with contributing to society's economic welfare. Social efficiency was but the sum of the individual efficiencies of many small competitive firms, just as social utility was said to be the sum of many individuals' utilities.

The economic system that was discussed in Alfred Marshall's *Principles of Economics* (1890) and John Bates Clark's *Essentials of Economic Theory* (1907) was not the kind of economic system that John M. Clark observed when he wrote his doctoral dissertation on *Standards of Reasonableness in Local Freight Discrimination* (1910). By this time large-scale industry had come to occupy the core of the modern industrial economy, and small-scale competitive enterprise had receded into the background. In the areas where large-scale industry operated, entry into the industry was frequently very difficult for newcomers, surplus productive capacity persisted and selling prices remained well above average unit costs of production. Furthermore, surplus profits were not eliminated in the long run, buyers were subjected to discrimination and consumers did not always bring their wants into the market place. Instead through advertising producers "manufactured" many of the wants of consumers. Finally J. M. Clark observed that there was a wide discrepancy between business or commercial efficiency and social efficiency.

J. M. Clark did not wholly repudiate the static economics which his father had passed on to him. He was well aware of the contributions of the long line of economists from Adam Smith to John Bates Clark. J. M. Clark felt, however, the need to move beyond static economics to dynamic economics, if he was going to be successful in explaining the new industrial world that scientific progress and technological change had created after 1875. Clark was quick to perceive that developing a dynamic economics was not simply a matter of adding dynamic economics to the already existing static economics. If a dynamic economics was to be developed, it would be necessary to reconstruct economic science in a number of fundamental ways. There would be a need to work out a new theory of social organization, and a need to make new assumptions with regard to the nature of human behavior and the nature of the economic system.

Clark abandoned the theory of social organization running through the work of the neo-classical economists, which took society to be a harmonious scheme of human relations in which human behavior was mainly individual behavior, and in which conflict or friction was automatically washed away. In the neo-classical view social organization was in essence static and social forces automatically preserved its equilibrium. J. M. Clark followed the pragmatic philosopher John Dewey and the eminent sociologist Charles Horton Cooley in taking society to be an evolving process in which collective action dominates individual action, conflict rather than harmony prevails among social groups and disequilibrium rather than equilibrium is the usual state of affairs. Although individuals and groups have conflicting interests, they have enough "collective intelligence" to work out ways of resolving their conflicts. There is no guarantee, however, that they will have the necessary urge to make the adjustments required for the construction of an harmonious society. Unlike the neo-classical economists who took social harmony as a given datum, Clark regards social harmony as a goal that can be achieved only by the use of social intelligence and by collaboration on the part of society's major economic interest groups.

Clark was quite unsatisfied with the psychological theory underlying the conventional economics of his time. He was very critical of what he regarded as the excessively individualistic and introspective nineteenth century psychology, which had been accepted by the neo-classical economists. Clark's psychological theory takes the individual to be a struggling being in a dynamic historical process rather than a contemplative rational being who inhabits a world of economic and social equilibrium. Human behavior, while it has a rational element in it, is also of an impulsive and habitual nature. Man is an impulsive individual who is greatly influenced by his environment, and who enjoys the getting of a good as well as the consuming of it. Consumer wants, as Clark explains them, are tendencies to "action with a feeling-value attached" to them. The consumer does not always come to the market place with self-created wants. On the contrary his wants are to a great extent determined for him by the environmental forces of the market place. Furthermore, he is an activist who is vitally concerned with the conditions of production and consumption. But the effort to be rational can be fatiguing, and for this reason consumers have recourse to habitual behavior when they enter the market place. It was Clark's position that the orthodox marginal-utility theory of consumption was an extreme case of oversimplification.

Overhead Costs, Social Costs and Social Values

Clark also renovated the view of the economic system held by the neo-classicists. He explained in *Studies in the Economics of Overhead Costs* (1923) that the economic system is a "dynamic social organism, rather than a static mechanism with an endless uniformity of perpetual motion."[28] He goes on to point out that the economic system as a process does not "tend to any complete and definable static equilibrium." While economists may discuss a temporary equilibrium between supply and demand in a competitive market, or while they may talk about the equilibrium position of a business firm in terms of maximizing profits, they can discover equilibrium in the whole economic system only by freezing the forces that make for change, development and disequilibrium in the real economic world. This Clark refused to do. Since he wanted to address himself to the major problems of the real economic world, he wanted to develop a view of the economic system that would lead him towards and not away from the real economic world.

The industrial economy that Clark investigated in the first half of the current century was the product of scientific and technological progress and the mechanization of industry. By 1923 Clark was analyzing the dynamic industrial economy, a "New Leviathan," which the unending string of inventions of the past century and a

---

[28] J. Maurice Clark, *Studies in the Economics of Overhead Costs* (Chicago: University of Chicago Press, 1923) p. ix.

half had brought into being as the "unintended byproduct of man's cultural evolution." The New Leviathan had a core or heartland of large industrial enterprises surrounded by smaller business enterprises. What Clark did was to analyze the new industrial economy from the supply and demand points of view. On the supply side he found major deficiencies which he attributed to the impact of the large overhead or fixed costs of the industrial corporations. In the absence of cooperation corporations with large overhead costs turned to cutthroat competition in order to drive out competitors. Later through collusive efforts they restricted output and secured surplus profits. In periods of prosperity large corporations overinvested in response to rising consumer demand, and sought to make as much profit as possible in order to offset the lean periods of depression. Having a short-term rather than a long-term approach to business affairs, the large corporations contributed a great deal to the recurring imbalances of the economic system.

It was at this point in his economic analysis that Clark introduced his novel concept of overhead costs. He observed that businessmen regarded labor and raw materials as variable costs, which could be reduced in periods of depressed business by cutting down employment and the purchase of raw materials. The businessman assumed no responsibility for the upkeep of workers and producers of raw materials such as farmers, miners and lumbermen. He did, however, maintain his own overhead in the form of industrial plant and equipment. Clark asserted that from the social viewpoint labor and raw materials producers are overhead costs just as are private plant and equipment, and should be maintained just as private plant and equipment are maintained. If business did not maintain workers and raw material producers by assuring them continued incomes, then society would have to do so or suffer the losses coming from a deteriorated labor force and sick extractive industries. Clark went further with his concept of overhead costs to say that the whole industrial system could be regarded as an overhead cost for which provision should be made by society. If the industrial system is not properly maintained, it slips into depression with its large social cost of unrealized national income.

Clark also called attention to the "unpaid" or "social costs" which are not included among industry's actual costs of production. These unpaid costs include such items as the pollution of air and water and other forms of environmental deterioration caused by the production processes of modern industry. Since these social costs are not included among the costs for which private industry makes provision, they are borne by society. Private industry is not held accountable for the adverse consequences of these unpaid social costs for personal health and income-earning capacity. Since private business accounting makes no provision for these unpaid costs, Clark proposed that a social accounting should be developed which would reveal the full costs of industrial production by adding unpaid social costs to paid private costs. It was Clark's position that more of the burden of unpaid social costs should be borne by private industry, which should make more effort to prevent the deterioration of the natural and social environment.

Clark also observed some major deficiencies on the demand side of the market mechanism of the modern industrial economy. The large industrial corporation is in a position to manipulate consumer demand to its own advantage. By means of advertising it is in a position to canalize the "underlying tendencies" of human nature with the result that consumer wants are "manufactured" just as are the commodities produced to satisfy these wants. Not only are consumers induced to buy what corporations produce, but also consumers are induced to buy goods that appear to have a high utility to the consumer but which have a low utility to society. In the competitive markets price was a good measure of both personal and social utility. But this was not the case where the market system, dominated by large-scale corporations, was no longer competitive.

Clark finds that the modern industrial economy is deficient because it takes inadequate account of social values. He explains in "Toward a Concept of Social Value" (1936) that unlike market values, social values have no price tags on them. They include such "inappropriables" as scenic beauty, wilderness areas, our historical heritage as revealed in various artifacts, clean and attractive cities, and unpolluted air and water. Since social values cannot be appropriated by private business, they are of no concern to businessmen. Even worse, the production of private market values results in the destruction of social values, unless businessmen are restrained by society. Clark distinguishes between market valuation and social valuation. Unless these two valuation processes are harmonized, market values will be produced at the expense of social values. An increase in the supply of market values may be accompanied by a reduction in the supply of social values. A proper coordination of the market and social valuation processes would enlarge the total supply of both market and social values. Just as private financial accounting has no concern with social costs, it also takes no account of the social values destroyed by the private production process. Clark envisages a social accounting that would include all costs both private and social, and all values both private and social. Such full or complete accounting would give a better understanding of what the economy is actually producing and at what costs.

Clark's social accounting is related to his concept of social efficiency. He drew a distinction between business or commercial efficiency and social efficiency. Business or commercial efficiency is the efficiency of the individual business enterprise in making profits. Social efficiency is the efficiency of the economic system in producing "human" or "social" values. These values are values that contribute to community welfare as well as to individual welfare. Whereas in a purely competitive economy the self-correcting forces of supply and demand keep business and social efficiency closely related, in the modern industrial economy a discrepancy between these two types of efficiency has appeared. Since the self-correcting forces of the competitive economy that existed before 1875 have been greatly weakened, the only way to eliminate the discrepancy between commercial and social efficiency, to prevent the imbalances that periodically occur and to make social accounting effective is, in Clark's opinion, to adopt a program for the social control of business.

Clark's Social-Liberal Planning

Clark's first prescriptions for the control of the economic system were presented in his *Social Control of Business* which was published in 1926. At that time he saw the problem as one of making a piecemeal attack on various parts of the economy that needed regulation, because they were beyond the reach of the competitive forces of the market place. After 1929 Clark came to the conclusion that the economic system had failed in its main task of "energizing production." Social control now called for the treatment of an "organic malady" which took the form of the business cycle. The time for piecemeal regulation was over. What was now needed was a coherent overall attack on the recurring business cycle. Clark explained in *Strategic Factors in Business Cycles* (1934) that a strategic factor was one that not only significantly influenced the course of business activity, but was itself subject to social control. According to Clark's analysis of the business cycle the two most strategic factors were producers' goods in the form of industrial plant and equipment and durable consumers' goods such as houses and automobiles. The crucial business activities to be controlled in order to reduce economic fluctuations were investments in industrial plant and equipment and expenditures on houses and automobiles. It was at this point in his analysis that Clark developed his concept of "business acceleration." He explained that in a period of prosperity a small percentage increase in consumer demand could cause a large percentage increase in the demand for industrial plant and equipment. The derived demand for capital goods would increase very rapidly, because businessmen would not only replace worn-out equipment, but would also order new equipment to take care of the increase in consumer demand. The magnified or accelerated demand for industrial equipment would bring a boom to the industries producing industrial equipment, which would in turn increase wages and consumer buying. In this manner the upward movement of the economy would receive a strong impetus toward a more rapid acceleration. When the rate of increase in consumer demand began to decline, the upward movement would be reversed, since the producers' goods industries would be faced with a very large decline in orders for new industrial equipment.

Clark's solution for the problem of business acceleration and the accompanying economic instability was the regularization of investment in industrial equipment and of the purchase of houses and automobiles. If capital budgeting was to be adopted, businessmen would have to change their patterns of behavior and their outlook. They would have to take more account of their "long-run and collective interests." No one industry can act alone and be successful with regard to capital budgeting. What is necessary, in Clark's opinion, is some form of collective action such as voluntary national economic planning. Clark saw no possibility of establishing a completely competitive economic system. Nor was he interested in seting up a "completely collectivist system." He favored a third course of action which would preserve the main features of the existing capitalist economy, but which would establish a "social constitution for industry." This social constitution would be the basis for a program of national economic planning designed to "eliminate undesirable fluctuations of industrial activity and to make reasonably free use of our powers of production to support an adequate standard of living, on a sound and enduring basis."[29] Clark described his

[29] J. M. Clark, "Economics and the National Recovery Administration," *The American Economic Review*, March 1939, Vol. XXIV, p. 23.

proposed national economic planning as "social-liberal planning."
In this planning a "social budget of supply and demand" would reveal the extent of the nation's productive powers and the private and
public demands which these productive powers could satisfy. Clark's
planning was of an overall, indirect nature. There would be no
direct controls imposed on the business system. Only indirect monetary and fiscal controls would be used to achieve the goals of the
national plan. Clark's planning proposals did not envision a large
increase in the role of government in economic affairs. He explained in his well-known article "Toward a Concept of Workable
Competition" that there are forces in the economic system that will
make it unnecessary for the government to assume the burden of
doing something about every departure from the model of perfect
competition.[30] Also the whole planning program was to be on a
voluntary basis. Unless the nation's major economic interest groups
freely collaborated with the government Clark's social-liberal planning could not succeed.

Clark was very tentative about his planning proposals. He was
well aware that planning of the American economy was not around
the corner. He realized that it would require much educational effort
to get the support of many of the nation's economic interest groups
for a national planning program. Nor could he guarantee success
once such a program was launched. His planning proposals were
an appeal to make the great economic experiment that would either
substantiate or invalidate his views about the feasibility and desirability of national economic planning.

Clark's Concept of Social Economics

Clark's social economics studies the current economic situation
within the framework of the evolving economic process. The economy is studied both statically as a cross-section and dynamically as
an evolving series or chain of cross-sections which together constitute the economic process. Clark's synthetical social economics includes three types of analyses: (1) an analysis of the principle of
exchange as it works out in the market place, (2) an analysis of
the economic system as an evolving cultural process and (3) an
analysis of the nation's aims which provide guidance for the economic system. The analysis of the principle of exchange is con-

---

[30] J. M. Clark, "Toward a Concept of Workable Competition," *The American Economic Review*, Vol. XXX, No. 2, June 1940, p. 256.

cerned with short-run equilibrium situations in competitive markets and in the operations of individual firms. The analysis of the evolving economic process reveals no overall equilibrating tendencies. While for some analytical purposes the economist may construct equilibrium models of the market system or the individual business enterprise, there is no equilibrium model of the economic system as a dynamic evolving cultural process in which scientific progress and technological change have major disruptive effects.

Clark explains that the ultimate problem of all social science is society's scheme of values, how they originate, what influences them, how they may be altered and how they may be achieved. The problem of social values has an economic aspect which should be the main concern of economists. The economic problem is how does the economic system in disposing of scarce resources enable society to achieve its values, or prevent society from securing these values? Clark defines his social economics as a study "of the way economic forces work, and a study of the economic efficiency—or inefficiency —which results."[31] The efficiency with which he is primarily concerned is not the private efficiency of profit making but the social efficiency of contributing to the achievement of society's values or goals. The effort to achieve these social goals becomes an effort on the part of the people to establish what Clark describes as "moralized economic communities." Clark's strong pragmatic bent leads him to assert that economics should play a large role in the building of these communities.

Clark occupies a place somewhere between the broad generalizations of Veblen and the strong empiricism of Mitchell. Clark avoided the speculative sweep of Veblen's analysis of the "drift" of business enterprise, and also the statistical foraging among large masses of economic data that Mitchell carried on. Unlike Veblen, Clark was optimistic about the possibility of making the private business system serve the general welfare. He had more faith than did Veblen in the "collective rationality" being used to achieve a harmony between business and social efficiency. Clark was more willing than was Mitchell to push beyond the limits of statistical analysis. He used Mitchell's earlier statistical spade work to develop his concept of business acceleration. Clark was also more energetic than Mitchell in cultivating the somewhat nebulous areas of social costs and social

---

[31] J. M. Clark, "The Socializing of Theoretical Economics," *The Trend of Economics*, p. 85.

values. He was better prepared than either Commons or Mitchell to write a general treatise on the nature and scope of economics from the institutionalist point of view. Unfortunately he never got around to tackling this important job. Had he done so he would have presented a clearer view of his synthetical "social economics," and at the same time he would have given more substance to what he described as "the rather elusive movement known as 'Institutionalism.'"

Rexford G. Tugwell's Experimental Economics

Rexford G. Tugwell, one of the younger post Veblenian institutionalists, was born in the same year (1891) that Veblen wrote his first essay on an economics topic. When Tugwell graduated from the University of Pennsylvania in 1915 he went out into a world that was being rudely shaken from its nineteenth century complacency. He witnessed the great economic adjustments of the First World War period, the succeeding era of international disorganization and false prosperity and after 1929 the agonizing efforts of many nations to preserve their free enterprise economies and their democratic ways of living. The First World War had demonstrated how productive "the massing of effort in common enterprise" could be. The postwar years, however, revealed how difficult it was for the nation to realize the full potential of its economic system on a sustained basis. It was not long before Tugwell came to see that the American economy was a "going system" in which private and public welfare were far from being one and the same thing.

Tugwell's understanding of the nature of the economic system was shaped in large part by the views of one of his economics professors at the University of Pennsylvania, Simon N. Patten, whose economics was in many ways very similar to Veblen's cultural economics. Patten took the economic system to be an evolving process which had reached a new industrial stage in the last quarter of the nineteenth century and the first quarter of the twentieth century. As a result of the changes in industrial technology that occurred in the second half of the nineteenth century, the competitive system was giving way to new cooperative methods of meeting the economic problems of the day. The major economic interest groups were being forced by the pressure of economic change "to accept the discipline of the new industrial regime."[32] Since the basic characteristics of the

---

[32] Simon N. Patten, *The New Basis of Civilization* (New York: The Macmillan Company, 1912) p. 77.

new machine age fostered cooperation rather than competition, the individualistic competition of the first three quarters of the nineteenth century was being rapidly transformed into the cooperative activity of the new industrial age.

Patten explained that the new industrial economy was potentially a very fruitful economic system, but its potential surplus was not secured because of a conflict between man's work habits and his predatory drive. The new industrialism held out great promise of a rising standard of living for the masses, but society suffered from a cultural lag which prevented this promise from being realized. Patten explained that since 1860 there had been an "economic revolution," but no "intellectual revolution" which would have altered the restrictive and predatory attitudes of businessmen. This lag between the changes in the economic system and in the mental attitudes of businessmen would have to be eliminated before a new "cooperative economic society of the future" could be established. Patten was convinced that such a society could be organized, because human nature had two characteristics which had been ignored by orthodox economists. These two characteristics were the exploratory and cooperative aspects of human behavior. It was Patten's view that, although man is acquisitive, he is also exploratory and cooperative, and can hold his acquisitive drive in check by giving vent to his cooperative impulse. His exploratory nature will lead him to work out new institutional arrangements for releasing the economy's large productive potential. Also man's cooperative nature will enable him to work collectively to plan the construction of the cooperative economic society of the future.

Patten differed from Veblen on two main points. First, he substituted a pluralistic view of society for Veblen's dualistic view. This meant that Patten did not analyze economic activity in terms of a struggle between two contending classes. Instead he observed conflicts among a number of classes. Secondly, Patten did not believe that class conflicts would destroy the capitalist system and replace it with a fascist or socialistic system. Patten's "cooperative economy" of the future was to be a new stage in the evolution of the capitalist system in which cooperation would replace conflict, not in a Marxian classless democracy, but in an "interclass democracy" in which the surplus derived from private property would be shared equitably by all classes.

Tugwell accepts Patten's basic views relating to the nature of the economic system and of human behavior. He agrees with Patten that man is an exploratory and cooperative individual who can create new institutions in an experimental way, and who can control individual action with various forms of collective action. All this fits in with Tugwell's position that man can adjust to the new age of planning into which Tugwell believes we are moving. Tugwell also shares Patten's interest in making economics a realistic, experimental social science. He deplores the excessive abstractionism or "conceptualism" which engulfs orthodox economics. While it is essential to develop analytical concepts, Tugwell asserts that it is more important to show how these analytical devices may be used to explain the new industrial system, and to show how its major problems can be solved.

Tugwell's Theory of Economic Development

Tugwell looks upon the historical process as a cyclical movement in which eras of cultural equilibrium are followed by eras of cultural disequilibrium in a never ending series. After a period of cultural equilibrium has been established, the time comes when man's restive and exploratory nature makes him dissatisfied. He then turns to new institutional arrangements and new values in search of which the old cultural equilibrium is destroyed and replaced by a transitional period of cultural disequilibrium. It is Tugwell's view that since the latter part of the eighteenth century mankind has passed through a period of widespread cultural change which is now leading us to another epoch of cultural equilibrium in the not-too-distant future. Tugwell explains that we are moving "toward our apotheosis, the golden age of the machine. . . . The passivity of nature will have its way again for a time. There may be an interim, a period of comparative adjustment, and something like peace."[33] The era from 1875 to 1929 was a period of economic development during which the industrialization which had begun in the second half of the eighteenth century would be brought to a high level of maturity. In Tugwell's opinion we were in the 1930's entering an era of "economic maintenance" during which the main problem would be to derive the maximum benefit from a mature industrial economy. This would not be an easy task because, although it may have been said that "industry" had come of age, the same was not true of "business."

---

[33] Rexford G. Tugwell, "Experimental Economics," *The Trend of Economics*, p. 375.

Tugwell explained in his *Industry's Coming of Age* (1927) that, while industry had become mature, business was still in an adolescent stage. He pointed out in the late 1920's that business continued to be guided by attitudes and policies that failed to recognize the fact that industry had become mature. Industry in the heartland of the economy had become large scale, and was unable to achieve its full production potential because of the obstacles placed in its way by outmoded business attitudes and policies. Tugwell explained that there is a contradiction between the logic of industry and the logic of business. By a cultural or social logic Tugwell means the way in which an institution or a complex of institutions necessarily functions or develops as a consequence of the impact of the forces or factors at work in the institution and its environment. The logic of industry or of technological advance calls for mass production, low unit costs of production, low prices, mass sales and mass consumption. The logic of business, however, in the modern industrial society points in the direction of restricted output, high unit costs of production, prices high enough to create surplus profits, restricted sales and limited consumption. In our "mongrel" or mixed economy "market coordination" has been in large part replaced by "corporate coordination" which, however, has failed to remove the discrepancy or conflict between the logic of industry and the logic of business. The few hundred large corporations that dominate the economy endeavor to protect themselves from the instabilities of the business system by accumulating large corporate surpluses in the form of undeclared dividends or retained earnings. These "liquid reserves" prevent the translation of technological progress into lower unit costs and lower selling prices. It is Tugwell's position that the liquid surpluses of large industrial corporations are a major economic problem, because these surpluses enable corporations to expand or contract their capital investment programs without any control being exercised by either the private capital market or by the government. Such corporate investment results in periods of overinvestment or underinvestment, and creates serious economic instabilities. According to Tugwell's interpretation those individuals who insist upon the right to make profits fail to accept the responsibility of stabilizing private investment and of maintaining the continuity of society's producing, selling and consuming operations. Tugwell asserts that it is at this point in the industrial system more than at any other point that some kind of social control is needed.

Tugwell's Social Management Program

It is Tugwell's general thesis that the new industrial system, which developed after 1875, had by 1929 demonstrated its lack of adequate economic guidance. With the disappearance of the largely competitive economic system after 1875 the competitive forces of the free market mechanism were no longer strong enough to provide automatic guidance for the nation's economy. The guidance that accompanied the new corporate coordination was unable to provide the economic stability, sustained economic growth and fair sharing of the national income that the general population demanded. Since the large industrial enterprises did not provide satisfactory economic guidance, it was Tugwell's opinion that there was a need for a new pattern of government. In 1935 Tugwell called for the abandonment of the "policeman doctrine of government" with its negative approach to the role of the government. What was needed was a new doctrine of government which would assign to the government a positive role in the directing of the nation's economic activities. Tugwell recommended a fourth directive branch of government which would be independent of the executive, judicial and legislative branches.[34] Composed of representatives of all the nation's major economic interest groups with long terms of appointment, the directive branch or national economic council would have only educational and advisory functions. The directive branch, free from the pressure of coping with short-run problems and the demands of politics, would be in a good position to take a long view of the problems of the evolving industrial system. It would educate the public and advise the Congress about the need to establish a national policy for future economic guidance, which would seek to subordinate the interests of private economic groups to the larger general welfare.

The national economic guidance recommended by the directive branch of government would take the form of national economic planning. In Tugwell's proposed planning program each industry would establish its own industrial planning agency on a voluntary basis with representatives of employers, workers and consumers. A central planning board representing the various industries and the government would serve as a mediating and integrating body with the responsibility of coordinating the plans and policies of the vari-

---

[34] Rexford G. Tugwell, "The Fourth Power," *Planning and Civic Comment*, Part II, April-June 1939, p. 10.

ous industries. The two major economic activities that the central planning board could not leave to the subordinate industrial planning agencies would be the investment in plant and equipment and the determination of prices. Tugwell explained in "The Principle of Planning and the Institution of *Laissez-Faire*" that the powers of private corporations to determine their own investment and price policies were incompatible with the operation of the modern industrial economy in a way that would maximize general welfare. Government regulation of corporate price and investment policies would be designed to make the logic of business enterprise adjust to the logic of industry or technological advance. This regulation would lead the large corporations to pass more of their productivity improvement on to consumers in the form of lower prices, would prevent the excessive accumulation of corporate retained earnings and would help to stabilize the economy by stabilizing the investment programs of the large corporations. Although Tugwell would preserve the private enterprise system, he calls for a reconsideration of the nature and role of private property and of the incentive to private profit making. His industrial planning program would result in a relocation of economic power, transferring it from the large business enterprises to the weaker economic interest groups which would be allied with the government in the national planning program.

Tugwell's national planning program would combine planning for industry and for agriculture. His plan for agriculture would reduce the number of cultivated acres to only those acres required to meet the nation's agricultural needs. Some acreage would be permanently withdrawn from cultivation and converted into forest or park land. Other land would be placed in a land bank until it was needed for cultivation. All that the government would have to do would be to provide some guidance in the selection of crops. Surplus labor in the agricultural sector would find employment in the expanding industrial sector. It is Tugwell's view that agricultural planning cannot be successful until industrial planning has been carried out successfully, because only then would industry provide a stable demand for all agricultural products and also a demand for the surplus labor in the agricultural sector.

Over the years from the First World War to the Great Depression of the 1930's Tugwell's main concern was with eliminating the lags and obstacles that prevented the new industrial economy from realizing its full production potential. It was the objective of his national planning program to reconstruct the institutional framework of the nation's economy so that its productive powers would be fully released. Once this was done two other objectives could then be realized. Workers could be guaranteed economic security by providing full employment on a lasting basis. Also each family could be assured a health-and-decency standard of living as a minimum. The achievement of these goals would not require blueprint planning. Tugwell's planning proposals may be summarized as an effort to carry scientific management to the still higher levels of social management. He regards his planning proposals as an extension of American economic experience and not as something that breaks with American traditions.

Tugwell unites his concepts of the logic of the industrial system and the logic of economic reform. The logic of the industrial system points in the direction of mass production, low unit costs of production, low selling prices and mass consumption. If the logic of the economic system is to be allowed to work itself out, the economic system will have to be reconstructed by adopting new institutional arrangements and new economic attitudes. According to Tugwell's interpretation the logic of economic reform points in the direction of a cooperative movement on the part of business, labor, consumers and the government to establish a national planning program on a voluntary basis. The logic of economic reform does not specify the details of any planning program. It does suggest, however, that both a return to a *laissez-faire* competitive economy or the establishment of a highly collectivized economy are not in conformity with industrial trends in the western democracies.

Tugwell's Views on the Nature and Scope of Economics

Tugwell defines economics as "the discovery and orderly stating of particular problems and the suggestion of solutions—the problems, being roughly, but not closely, defined as those having to do with our ways of getting and using a living." We see in this definition Tugwell's strong pragmatic bent. He defines theory in general as "sustained thought about some difficulty of practice." When he applies this generalized concept of theory to economic theory, Tugwell explains that economic theories have their origins in the psychological difficulties created by attempts to improve the material welfare of mankind. Current economic theory is sustained thought about economic phenomena which deal with immediate problems. It is to be distinguished on the one hand from "economic principles" which merely explain things as they are, and on the other hand from economic doctrines "which are economic principles that have passed into history." Tugwell does not dispense with the economic principles and economic doctrines of the orthodox economists. What he objects to is the tendency of these economists to underemphasize economics as an instrument which should be used to enlarge economic welfare. In Tugwell's opinion economics in the hands of orthodox economists becomes too much of a defense of the *status quo* and not enough of a challenge to improve the economic system.

Tugwell shifts attention from the economics of the market place to the economics of the whole system concerned with the production and distribution of goods and services. The problems which he investigates are the problems that have come out of the process of industrialization. Since the economic process is but a part of the larger social or cultural process, it is Tugwell's position that the economic system and its problems cannot be effectively analyzed unless economists proceed on the basis of a satisfactory theory of the cultural process. When analyzing the cultural process, Tugwell does not uncover any laws of cultural development. Instead he develops the concept of a logic of cultural development. According to this concept cultural development is not a purely random affair which can only be described by the social scientist. On the contrary cultural development has a shape or pattern which is determined by the factors operating in the social situation in which the development occurs. Given a cultural situation in which there is an intricate institutional framework, conflicting interest groups, conditions favorable to scientific progress and technological advance and men with an exploratory and experimental nature, scientific and technological progress will provide a continual impetus to cultural change, and men will attempt to solve their problems through some form of collective action. Applying the same analysis to economic development Tugwell uncovers no laws of economic development, but instead a logic of economic development in which technological change has a major role, and which points in the direction of some kind of collective action such as national planning to solve the problems created by the maturing of the capitalist system. Given a mature industrial system with its large-scale production, conflicting economic interest groups, and an active government which is prepared to provide guidance for the nation's economy, the logic of economic development would not call for the restoration of a highly competitive, self-regulating economy. Instead the logic of economic development, as Tugwell sees it, indicates that the solutions of the advanced industrial economy's problems will be secured, if at all, by new institutional arrangements and new mental attitudes that are favorable to the achievement of economic reform and reconstruction through some form of national economic planning.

Veblen had laid the foundation for a theory of economic development with an emphasis upon technological change as the prime mover in this development. Commons, Mitchell and Clark failed to extend Veblen's contributions in this connection. They did not come forth with a well-developed concept of the logic of economic development. Had they done so, they could have more effectively answered their critics who asserted that Commons, Mitchell, Clark and other institutionalists never got beyond fact gathering and description when they were investigating the evolving economic system. The same criticism could not be made against Tugwell who emphasized the importance of going beyond mere description to develop a logic of economic development with its subsidiary logics of the industrial system, the business system and economic reform. As we shall see, Tugwell's contribution along this line has been further developed by the post 1945 neo-institutionalists. Tugwell's concept of the logic of the economic system constitutes the core of his theory of the economic process, which in turn provides a general framework for his analysis of the current functioning of the industrial system and of its various problems.

Gardiner C. Means's Administrative Economics

The large industrial corporation was a matter of great interest to all post Veblenian institutionalists as well as to Veblen. This was not unusual since the large corporation was the product of the scientific progress and technological change that came in the last quarter of the nineteenth century. The emergence and growth of the large business corporation after 1875 was a major feature of the process of industrialization which was a main concern of the pre-1945 institutionalists. No institutionalist of this period displayed as much interest in the operations and significance of the large industrial corporation as did Gardiner C. Means. After examining the economic, legal and political significance of the large corporation in the 1920's and early 1930's, Means arrived at the conclusion that the developments in this area could be best described as a "corporate revolution." A. A. Berle, Jr. and Means explained in *The Modern Corporation and Private Property* (1933) that the large-scale corporate enterprise of the 1930's was so fundamentally different from the small-scale competitive enterprise of the nineteenth century, that orthodox interpretations of prosperity and depression were inadequate in the 1930's. It was Berle and Means's message to a befuddled world in 1933 that the economic problems of the time would probably not be solved in a satisfactory manner, until the equilibrium economics of Alfred Marshall had made way for the new "administrative economics."

Means observed that in the corporate capitalism of the 1930's there were two forces at work, the one a centrifugal force tending to spread the ownership of corporate wealth among a growing number of stockholders, and the other a centripetal force tending to centralize control over corporate wealth in a decreasing number of directors' hands. Means called attention to the fact that by 1932 only 200 of 300,000 non-financial corporations controlled almost one-half of all the non-financial corporate wealth, and received 43 per cent of the annual net income of all non-financial corporations. This rise of corporate capitalism was accompanied by some major changes in the structure and functioning of the industrial system. These changes included the separation of the ownership and control of corporate wealth, the distortion of the profit system since corporate profits went in large part not to the corporate managers but to the stockholders, the narrowing of the free market system as administered prices replaced free competitive prices and the reduction of consumer control of the production process as large corporations came to manipulate demand by means of forceful advertising and salesmanship activities. Furthermore, the new "corporate absolutism" had come to challenge even the authority of the state to regulate its economic affairs. Until 1930 there had been "an abdication of the state" as a guiding factor in economic activity. In the years prior to the Great Depression the large industrial corporations had narrowed the influence of the market mechanism, had molded the complex of laws, rules and customs to suit their own purposes and had shaped the nation's economic, social and political goals so that they would conform with narrow commercialized ends. The problem, as Means saw it in the 1930's, was to render the corporate absolutism innocuous so that corporate capitalism could serve the interests of the general public.

Means points out in *The Modern Economy in Action* (1936) that the modern industrial system in which the large industrial corporation operates is quite unlike the competitive economic system in which the small unincorporated firm formerly functioned. He explains that the competitive economic system of the first three-quarters of the nineteenth century was an economy in which deviations from any equilibrium situation were soon eliminated by self-correcting forces. For example, a tendency to oversave in a largely competitive economy would soon be corrected by declines in consumer goods prices and interest rates which would make saving and investing less profitable. More saving would mean less consumption and hence a decline in consumer goods prices. As savings increased interest rates would fall and would discourage saving. Any tendency for lower interest rates to encourage investing would be offset by lower consumer goods prices, which would discourage businessmen from investing and enlarging their output. Any deviation from a balance between saving and investing at a full employment equilibrium level would be soon corrected and the balance would be restored. In the new industrial system dominated by large industrial corporations self-correcting forces have been replaced by self-reinforcing forces. Deviations from equilibrium or balanced situations are not quickly corrected. Self-reinforcing forces sustain the deviations for lengthy periods of time during which national income, production and employment fall to very low levels where they may remain for quite some time, unless public policies are adopted to restore the economy to a full employment level.

Means explains that a purely competitive economy tends to realize its full production potential, because small competitive firms are pushed to the most efficient point of operation by the competitive market forces. Each firm will expand its operations until the extra or marginal costs of producing the last unit of output are just covered by the selling price. A small competitive firm can hold back production only at the risk of being eliminated by its competitors. Means points out that there is no such tendency to the realization of the economy's full production potential in the modern industrial society. The large industrial corporations pursue a restrictionist production policy, which maximizes surplus profits rather than output and social utility. They expand production only to the point where marginal unit cost equals marginal unit revenue, and consequently stop producing much earlier than would a competitive producer. In this situation a large discrepancy develops between the industrial system's potential output and its actual total output.

Means goes on to explain that, besides restricting output, the large industrial corporation distorts the nation's income distribution pattern by giving investors "disproportionately high profits." The large corporation's price and production policies are designed to create large surplus profits which are much larger than are needed to reward investors for assuming the risks of investing in corporate equities. Furthermore, surplus or excess profits result in an imbalance between saving and investing, because those individuals who receive excess profits tend to oversave. Means explains in *The Modern Economy in Action* (1936) that in the mixed economy of today with its inflexible consumer and producer goods prices and its sluggish interest rates a tendency to oversave is not checked by self-correcting forces in the form of declines in prices and interest rates. When savings, drawn from surplus profits in prosperous periods, become excessive, consumption is curbed at the very time that production is expanding. Furthermore, when saving becomes excessive, inflexible selling prices make investment unattractive, because markets cannot be expanded by lowering prices. When a tendency to increase saving is not followed by an increase in investing, then consumption, production and employment decline. These downward tendencies are reinforced until at a lower national income saving and investing are once more in balance. The original tendency to oversave, instead of being offset by self-correcting forces, is supported by self-reinforcing forces which support the original imbalance until a lower national income corrects the imbalance between saving and investing.

Many policies and programs have been adopted with the aim of regulating the price and production policies of the large industrial corporations. These include control through government ownership, government regulation without public ownership, the formulation of price and production policies by industrial councils and the influencing of industrial policies by labor unions and cooperatives. While these devices for the control of industrial price and production policies have been useful, they all suffer from the same deficiency. They do not look at the economy as a whole or suggest remedies that take into consideration overall adjustments covering the entire economic system. They are not concerned with the larger issue of "steering the economy so as to make it yield to the American people the best living that is technically possible." As he shifts his attention from partial to overall solutions to the problems of the modern industrial system Means becomes firmly convinced that there is a pressing need for overall national planning. He observes not only that the overall economic coordination and guidance once

supplied by the automatic forces of the competitive system are absent
from the modern industrial economy, but also that there is no hope
of restoring any simple automatic economic coordination. According
to Means's interpretation the only way out of our economic difficulties is to supply the necessary coordination and guidance of
economic activity by adopting some form of indicative, voluntary
national economic planning.

Means's National Planning Program

It is Means's position that the market mechanism of the industrial
economy needs to be supplemented by administrative action on the
part of the government. The market mechanism with its many rigidities or inflexibilities cannot alone provide the coordination and guidance required for a satisfactory functioning of the industrial system.
The market mechanism operating alone creates imbalances between
selling prices and unit costs and between saving and investing. It
also fails to keep the economy on the path of sustained and adequate
economic growth. If the economy is to achieve the balance and
growth that general welfare demands, the government must be prepared to modify the inherited system of economic policies which is
no longer appropriate to the structure of the modern industrial
system. Some economists recommend that the inherited economic
policies be preserved and that the structure of the economy be
altered by breaking up big industry and restoring a competitive system. Means does not agree with the pulverization school of economists who would recreate a *laissez-faire* competitive economy. He
would preserve the large-scale structure of the industrial system and
alter the inherited system of economic policies to meet the needs of
the new industrial system. He would do this by adopting a national
economic planning program that would facilitate or supplement
the working of the private enterprise system. Such a program would
be an extension of the business, resource conservation and regional
planning already being carried on.

In Means's national planning program planning would be carried
on at three levels. At the top national level a planning agency would
be concerned with the growth of gross national product and the
various demands coming from households, businesses and government for the national product. The first step in the establishment
of a national economic plan would be to develop production-con-
sumption patterns or a national economic budget, which would
show the nation's production potential and the various possible de-

mands for this output potential in a plan period. The national planning agency would deal with matters affecting the whole economy such as the distribution of investment among the various industries and the elimination of bottlenecks in the production process. At the next level planning would be carried on within each industry where industry planning boards with representatives from business, labor, consumers and the government would agree upon price schedules and production quotas with the aid of industrial codes as was done under the National Industrial Recovery Administration in the depressed 1930's. An effort would be made to secure agreement among the members of each industrial planning board with respect to prices and production quotas for the industry that would be in the best interest of consumers, workers and producers. At the level of the individual business enterprise each firm would operate within the framework of the plan for the industry. As far as possible economic control would be left in the hands of individuals and corporate enterprises. The planning program would be directed mainly at the large industrial corporations in the core of the economy. There would be no need to plan the affairs of the small-scale competitive industries in which the free market forces still play an effective role. The national planning program would be primarily concerned with the price and production policies of the large business enterprises. When the large-scale core of the economy was planned, the rest of the economy with its small-scale business enterprises could be expected to fall into line of its own accord.

It is the purpose of Means's national planning program to create a managed equilibrium. When this equilibrium was achieved there would be an optimum use of the nation's economic resources. An optimum use of the nation's resources would be a full, balanced, and efficient use of these resources. Means explained in *The Structure of the American Economy* (1940) that this optimum use of resources would be secured when "there would be no unemployment of men or machines. . . . The resources going into different uses would be in balance with each other and in relation to consumers' wants . . . and, finally, in doing any particular job, the minimum amount of resources would be used or consumed consistent with the job to be done."[35] National planning would direct the use of the nation's economic resources to the satisfaction of basic consumer wants. Means estimated in 1935 that sixty-five per cent of consumer

---

[35] National Resources Planning Board, "Toward Full Use of Resources," *The Structure of the American Economy*, Part II, June 1940, p. 5.

expenditures were for basic consumer necessities such as food, clothing and shelter. Since these consumer needs can be met with the standardized products turned out by large-scale corporate enterprises, it would be much easier to plan for an expansion of these products than for an increase in the output of luxury goods.

Means regards national planning as an opportunity to strike a balance between the consumer and producer points of view. With the decline in competition after 1885 consumers were relegated to a secondary role in the nation's economic affairs as direction of the economy came more and more from large-scale producers. Means recommends that the consumer interest should be strengthened not by organizing consumers as such, but by pooling consumer interests drawn from labor unions, farm groups and women's organizations. The government should not attempt to develop a consumer movement that is separate from other economic interests. The consumer interest should represent a spontaneous reaction to economic difficulties on the part of the general public and should develop from the bottom up.

Means's national economic planning program calls for a reconsideration of the relations between government and the major economic interest groups. He disagrees with those who say that we should try to make the government more representative of the "public interest" than of major economic interest groups such as business, labor, agriculture and consumers. Means advocates the frank recognition of the presence of organized economic interest groups and the setting up of formal arrangements which would give adequate representation to these interest groups. Some interests, such as consumers, are now poorly organized and have little representation in the administrative branches of government. What is necessary is that satisfactory channels be made available through which all interests may express themselves. When all economic interest groups are organized and are given an opportunity to express themselves, there will then be the problem of creating an "evenhanded balance" of interests. Means is convinced that such a balance, which is necessary for successful national economic planning, can be established.

Gardiner C. Means's Economics of Control

The contrast between the conventional economics of the period prior to 1939 and Means's "economics of control" cannot be better brought out than by pointing out that what was the special or exceptional case in conventional economics became the general case in Means's economics. Whereas the orthodox economists of the pre-1939 period took the small-scale competitive firm as the norm of economic enterprise and the large-scale corporate firm as the special case deviating from the competitive norm, Means reversed this order. In his analysis the large industrial corporation is the norm of business enterprise, whereas the small competitive firm is no longer typical of the modern industrial society. The large industrial firm operates with a great deal of influence in the crucial core or central area of the industrial economy, while the many small competitive firms function on the periphery of the economy with little impact on its general functioning. What Means does is to reconstruct the orthodox view of the economy in order to provide a new framework of economic analysis in which the large industrial corporation and its operations become the primary analytical concern.

When Means abandons the orthodox view of the economy in which the small competitive firm plays the major role, he also dispenses with the view that the total economy has a tendency to move towards an equilibrium position. Means's hybrid or tripartite economy with its core of oligopolistic and monopolistic enterprise surrounded by a band of middle-size monopolistic competitive enterprise, and this in turn by a band of small-scale competitive enterprise, reveals no tendency to move automatically towards an equilibrium position. On the contrary, the price and production policies of the large industrial corporations guarantee that there will be no overall equilibrium of the nation's economic system. This is so because the price and production policies of the large corporations increase the inflexibilities of the economy, distort the nation's income distribution, create surplus profits and curb production. In Means's economy of administered corporate prices, administered wages, large industrial corporations and large trade unions, very sizeable income inequalities and unorganized and powerless consumers, the basic tendency is towards disequilibrium as revealed in the recurring fluctuations in economic activities. In addition there are the long-run or secular changes which suggest that the heartland of large-scale business enterprise may expand further as the peripheral area of small-scale business enterprise shrinks in size. It is Means's position that technological change points in the direction of a continuation of the trends leading to more collective action in control of individual action, and to a substitution of private and public administration for free market coordination. Means concludes that not only is there no fundamental tendency towards equilibrium in the modern industrial economy, but also the forces contributing to disequilibrium if left unchecked will become stronger in the future as collective action spreads over more of the nation's economy, and the forces of the free market system become weaker.

Like the other post Veblenian institutionalists Means analyzes the economic system in terms of an original or initial state and a future or terminal state. The initial state is the state of the economic system as Means sees it at the time that he is analyzing the current economic situation. He contrasts this initial state of the economy, with its tendency towards disequilibrium, with a future state in which there would be a managed or planned equilibrium. In Means's analysis the economy is a developing process which is moving towards goals or ends determined by those economic interest groups which have the most economic power. Up to 1929 these groups were dominated by big business. After 1929 more power was secured by workers and farmers. It is Means's view that this power shift will continue, and will increasingly favor consumers as well as workers, farmers and small businesses. These groups are interested in securing a stable economy with sustained economic growth and a fair sharing of national income by all economic interest groups. The means by which these goals can be achieved, according to Means's interpretation, is democratic, overall or indicative national economic planning. If the public is to reform the industrial economy successfully, Means asserts that it will have to move towards this planned future state in which the orthodox economists' fiction of an automatically created competitive equilibrium will be replaced by a real managed or planned equilibrium. Means constructed his "economics of control" to enable the public not only to understand the economic problems confronting it, but also to aid the public in its efforts to move towards a future state where the full production potential of the industrial system would be not only achieved but also fairly shared.

Veblen and the Post Veblenians

A survey of the economics of Veblen and the post Veblenians of the 1930's reveals that, while they have much in common, yet there are significant differences in their work. If we turn first to what is common in the work of these heterodox economists, we find that they all have the same views on the definition and scope of economics, and they all adhere to the same general approach to the study of the economic system. Veblen and the post Veblenians defined economics as the study of the evolving complex of institutions concerned with meeting the material needs of mankind. In other words, economics from the institutionalist viewpoint studies the material aspect of our evolving human culture. Since culture is a process, the economic system, a part of culture, is also a process. The economic system is analyzed within the framework of the total culture of which the economic system is a part. Commons, Mitchell, Clark and the other post Veblenians established no precise boundaries for the science of economics. Since they viewed the economic system as a part of the larger social or cultural whole, they felt a need to use the contributions of such related social sciences as sociology, cultural anthropology, social psychology and jurisprudence when they were interpreting economic behavior. Veblen and the post Veblenians were prepared to make use of any data that would throw some light upon the functioning of the maturing capitalist system. They agreed with John M. Clark who asserted that "Unless they have been finally and authoritatively established in some writing which has escaped my notice, I feel free to contend that it is less important to keep inside any traditional limits than to follow our natural questionings wherever they may lead, and do whatever work we are especially fitted for and find undone."[36]

The methodological approach of Veblen and the post Veblenians to the study of the economic system was an evolutionary approach. None of these heterodox economists had the short-run approach of the conventional economics textbook writer who limits his analysis of the economic system to a particular point in time. Some of these heterodox economists had a longer view of economic development than others. Veblen's evolutionary approach carried him back to the Stone Age, while Commons looked back to the eighteenth century. Mitchell, Tugwell and Means were more concerned with the recent past. Both Veblen and the post Veblenians concentrated their attention on the development of the American economy after 1890. During their lifetime the post Veblenians saw the American economy undergo major structural and functional changes as unregulated monopoly or finance capitalism reached its peak during the 1920's, and was rapidly transformed into welfare capitalism during the 1930's. While Veblen and the post Veblenians were always inter-

---

[36] John M. Clark, "Toward a Concept of Social Value," *Preface to Social Economics* (New York: Farrar and Rinehart, 1936) p. 65.

ested in the immediate economic situation, they analyzed it from the long-range point of view. The current economic scene was analyzed within the framework of the evolving economic system. Taking the long-range view meant more than investigating the economy as the product of a long evolutionary development. It also meant inquiring into the trends at work within the economy. Concern with economic trends led Veblen and the post Veblenians to compare the current or initial state of the economy to a future or terminal state towards which the economy was moving, or towards which in the opinion of these heterodox economists it was considered to be desirable for the economy to move.

Besides duplicating Veblen's view of the economic system as an evolving process and his evolutionary approach to the study of the economic system, Commons, Mitchell, Clark and the other post Veblenian institutionalists developed a view of human behavior that was basically similar to Veblen's view. Like Veblen they abandoned the introspective, hedonistic psychology that was so prominent in the orthodox economics of their time. Veblen and the post Veblenians took human behavior to be a social or cultural product in which reason was heavily overlaid by custom and habit. Unlike the orthodox economists, Veblen and the other heterodox economists of the 1920's and 1930's did not emphasize the individualistic and rationalistic aspects of human behavior. Instead they called attention to how frequently in the modern economic world collective action controls individual action, and habit is substituted for reason.

In spite of the fact that the post Veblenians agreed with Veblen on the nature and scope of economics, on the proper approach to the study of the economic system and on the nature of the economic system and human behavior, there are major differences in the work of Veblen and the post Veblenian institutionalists. These differences arise for two reasons. First, Veblen had a different social philosophy from that of the post Veblenians, and, secondly, Veblen and the post Veblenians were looking at the American economic system at widely different points in time. Veblen's social philosophy or interpretation of the social process was strongly influenced by Karl Marx. He accepted Marx's technological interpretation of history, his dualistic interpretation of economic evolution as a struggle between two classes and his view of the inevitable demise of the capitalist system. Veblen did not accept Marx's teleological interpretation of the course of economic development that made socialism the inevitable successor to capitalism. In the same connection Veblen substituted a negative and pessimistic outlook for Marx's positive and optimistic outlook.

The Marxian heritage, which was so prominent in Veblen's social philosophy, is largely absent in the social philosophy that permeates the economics of Commons, Mitchell, Clark, Tugwell and Means. In effect what these post Veblenians did was to substitute John Dewey for Karl Marx and pragmatism for Hegelian Marxism. The social philosophy of John Dewey is pluralistic, optimistic and activist in nature. The pragmatist has not a dualistic but instead a pluralistic approach to his interpretation of the social process. He abandons Marx's class struggle, and puts in its place a struggle of many conflicting groups, which eventually resolve their disagreements not by overturning the existing social system but by reforming it. Hence pragmatists are optimistic and activist in outlook. They are optimistic about the possibility of mankind solving its problems in an orderly, gradualistic and non-revolutionary manner. They are also activists whose enthusiasm for social and economic reform leads them to work for the creation of a more reasonable social and economic system.

This profile of the Deweyite pragmatist is applicable to Commons, Mitchell, Clark and the other post Veblenian institutionalists. They all abandoned Veblen's oversimplified dichotomy between the "vested interests" and "the working population," and analyzed the American economic system in terms of a pluralistic struggle among big and small business, organized and unorganized labor, farmers and consumers. The post Veblenians did not accept Veblen's interpretation of capitalist development with its inevitable demise of the capitalist system. Instead the post Veblenians saw the possibility of saving capitalism by reforming it and by converting welfare capitalism into democratic planned capitalism. Whereas Veblen was negative and somewhat pessimistic about mankind's future, the post Veblenians were positive and optimistic. They all adhered to a functional view of economic science which led them to emphasize the importance of economics as a tool for the reforming of society and the enlargement of human welfare.

Veblen had developed his social philosophy and his theory of capitalist development in the period 1890-1910 when what Commons called "banker capitalism" was dominant, and many of the harsh features of industrialization were ignored by the public authorities. The post Veblenians came a generation later, and concentrated their attention on the demise of "banker capitalism" and the rise of "welfare capitalism." Had Veblen lived through the 1930's he would probably not have altered his social philosophy or his theory of capitalist development. For the post Veblenians, however, with their pragmatic social philosophy, and their outlook shaped largely by the events of the 1920's and 1930's, it was easy to find Veblen's gloomy interpretation of the evolution of the capitalist system unacceptable.

The post Veblenian institutionalists also repudiated certain byproducts of Veblen's economic analyses. As we have seen, Veblen had used instinct psychology to support his dichotomy between "business" and "industry." According to his interpretation the acquisitive instinct played a large role in the behavior of businessmen, while the instinct of workmanship was said to dominate the behavior of the workers. Veblen's cultural dichotomy based on the separation of business from industry or of money making from goods making was given a psychological foundation in the distinction he made between the two instincts of acquisition and workmanship. The instinct psychology, which had found some acceptance in the early years of the twentieth century, was largely abandoned by psychologists when the post Veblenians were making their economic analyses in the 1920's and 1930's. Unlike Veblen, they found no need to refer to instincts when explaining human behavior. Instead they adopted a much more behavioristic approach to the study of human behavior.

The post Veblenians also assigned less influence to technology as a factor shaping human behavior than did Veblen. There is nothing in the writings of Commons, Mitchell, Clark, Tugwell and Means comparable to Veblen's emphasis on the importance of the discipline of the machine process. Veblen's emphasis on the role of the machine in determining human behavior opened him to the criticism that he was an advocate of technological determinism. No such criticism could be levelled against the post Veblenians. In general they paid much less attention than did Veblen to the role of technology in the shaping of human behavior. It could even be argued that the post Veblenian institutionalists paid insufficient attention to the role of technological change in the process of industrialization. Had they paid more attention to the impact of technological change on economic activity, the post Veblenians might have contributed more than they did to the analysis of technological change as a cultural imperative giving shape to the process of industrialization. The post 1945 economists working in the institutionalist tradition, such as Clarence E. Ayres and John K. Galbraith, have met this problem more successfully by adopting a middle position between conventional economists, who ignore the impact of technological change, and economists like Marx and Veblen, who are criticized for overemphasizing the role of technological change in the shaping of the economic and social process.

In his efforts to substantiate his position that orthodox economics needed to be reconstructed, Veblen attacked this type of economics vehemently and with a great deal of bitter satire. The forcefulness of Veblen's criticisms of orthodox economics led his critics to assert that Veblen would do away with inherited economic theory. Although the post Veblenians also differed very greatly from orthodox economists with regard to the nature and scope of economics, they were more careful than Veblen to acknowledge their indebtedness to inherited economics. They admitted that much could be learned about the economic system even though it was taken to be something on the order of a static mechanism. For the post Veblenians it was a matter of not limiting themselves to static economic analysis and of learning more about the economic system of their time by taking it to be an evolving cultural product. The post Veblenians did not see any need to attack the orthodox version of economics with the intensity and forcible expression of views that Veblen had brought to this task. They were never able, however, to dispel the notion held by orthodox critics that Veblen and later institutionalists largely dispensed with conventional economic theory, and had nothing to put in its place. Had they written general treatises on economics both Veblen and the post Veblenians might have been more successful in demonstrating as groundless the view that they dispensed with all inherited economic theory and put nothing in its place.

Neither Veblen nor the post Veblenians developed the theory of the economic process as far as they might have. They did not get much beyond pointing out that the economic process went through various stages of development as the result of the changes in industrial technology, and that the economic process was in a state of disequilibrium because the real product flow and the financial or income-expenditure flow were not harmoniously related or coordinated. Veblen's separation of "goods making" from "money making" reappears in Commons's distinction between "efficiency profits" and "scarcity profits," in Clark's division between "social efficiency" and "commercial efficiency" and in Tugwell's contrast between "mature industry" and "adolescent business." Neither Veblen nor the post Veblenians moved much beyond this point in theorizing about the economic process to develop the concept of the logic of the process of industrialization, which explains the shape or pattern that this process has taken on. As we shall see, the post 1945 economists, who have worked along institutionalist lines, have contributed much more to the development of the concept of the logic of the process of industrialization. According to this concept as worked out by Clarence E. Ayres, John K. Galbraith, Gerhard Colm and Gunnar Myrdal, the logic of industrialization has in the past half century in the western democracies pointed in the direction of a socially directed or planned coordination of the industrial economy's real and financial flows. It is the position of these present day heterodox economists that there is inherent in the process of industrialization a logic of development which makes it possible, but not inevitable, that the economic inequalities among classes and the disequilibrium resulting from the discrepancies between the economy's real and financial flows may be successfully eliminated.

The failure of Veblen and the post Veblenians to develop fully the concept of the logic of the process of industrialization left them open to the attack that their analyses of the economic process did not go beyond a description of this process. As Lionel Robbins put it in his critical observations on institutional economics, "Yet not one single 'law' deserving of the name, not one quantitative generalisation of permanent validity has emerged from their [the institutionalists'] efforts. A certain amount of interesting statistical material. Many useful monographs on particular historical situations."[37] But nothing else, according to Robbins. It was not clear to Robbins in 1932, as it was not clear to other critics of institutionalism, that the institutionalists did not expect to uncover any laws governing the economic process. What Veblen and the post Veblenians were doing was to move towards the uncovering of a logic of economic development or of the process of industrialization. It was their generalizations concerning this logic of industrialization that made their work much more than simple description. They did not, however, make this point clear to the exponents of economic orthodoxy. Nor did they go very far in developing the concept of the logic of industrialization.

---

[37] Lionel Robbins, *An Essay on the Nature and Significance of Economic Science*, p. 114.

Veblen's main criticisms of the American economic system were that it did not make full use of its production potential, and in addition it all too frequently produced goods that did not contribute to the enhancement of the life process. The post Veblenians concurred with Veblen on these two criticisms of the private enterprise system. Clark, Mitchell, Tugwell and Means recommended the adoption of some kind of democratic national planning under which it would be planned to achieve the full use of the nation's productive capacities, while at the same time preserving the private enterprise system. Veblen's socialist planning had the same objective of realizing the economy's full production potential. Like Veblen, the post Veblenians asserted that the private market system frequently produced goods with high personal or individual utility but low social utility. As Mitchell put it, the private market system on too many occasions produced less urgently needed goods in place of necessities. Clark also pointed out that the private market system ignores social values which have no price placed on them. Veblen and the post Veblenians agreed that in the modern industrial economy market price is not always an adequate measure of economic value or value to the community. Veblen had substituted "brute serviceability" or serviceability to the community for the subjective utility of the marginalist economists, and for the abstract homogeneous common labor of Marx as the proper ultimate measure of value. He did not, however, extend his analysis of the value problem very far. Nor did the post Veblenians do much to extend Veblen's analysis of the value problem. Both Veblen and the post Veblenians were moving in the direction of a technological or instrumentalistic interpretation of value such as was later developed by Clarence E. Ayres.

If the popular image of the institutional economist that has prevailed in recent decades in the United States had been based more on the work of Commons, Mitchell, Clark and other post Veblenians than on Veblen's work, this image might have been quite different from what it has been in the minds of much of the economics profession. This image, based on Veblen's work as interpreted by orthodox economists, is, as we have already seen, that of an economist who spurns inherited economics but puts nothing substantial in its place, who may be a sociologist but who can hardly be classed as an economist, who is a misguided advocate of technological determinism, and who has never gotten beyond the stage of writing descriptive monographs. In view of Veblen's major role in the development of American institutionalism it would have been very difficult for the post Veblenians to alter this popular image of the institutionalist, even if they had had a special interest in doing so. Of the five heterodox economists discussed in this chapter only Mitchell may be regarded as a disciple of Veblen. Commons, Clark, Tugwell and Means were not Veblen's students, nor did they display any particular interest in his writings. Consequently they did not get involved in trying to change the image of the institutional economist that came to be accepted by a large part of the economics profession prior to 1945.

Since the late 1930's, and especially since the close of the Second World War, there has appeared a number of economists who have worked along institutionalist lines, but who have drawn their inspiration for the reconstruction of economics from non Veblenian, West European intellectual sources. Prominent among these latter-day heterodox economists are Gunnar Myrdal, Gerhard Colm, and Adolph Lowe. Even in the United States a new generation of heterodox economists, represented by John K. Galbraith and taking little or nothing directly from Veblen's work, has made its appearance. It is quite clear that much of the criticism directed against Veblen has no relevance to the work of Myrdal, Colm, Lowe and Galbraith. It is for this reason that it is appropriate to refer to these present-day heterodox economists as "neo-institutionalists" to distinguish them from the "old" institutionalists generally associated by the economics profession and others with Thorstein Veblen.

Just as the course of economic development left Ve` ulen in its wake, a similar fate has befallen the post Veblenians of the 1930's. The main concern of their economic interpretation was with the mass consumption economy that had developed in the United States in the 1920's and 1930's. Since 1945 the American economy has moved into the next developmental stage of the "service economy," in which the main issue is the provision of private and public services rather than durable consumer goods. Two complicating factors in this new economic era are the population explosion and the postwar technological revolution. The problems associated with the new importance of public or collective services, the large increase in population, and the impact of the automated and computerized industry on society have focused attention on the public sector of the nation's economy and the role of government in economic and social affairs. The institutionalists of the 1920's and 1930's were mainly interested in how to prevent depressions and how to stabilize economic activity at a full employment level. For Mitchell,

Clark, Tugwell and Means the main issue was the "social control of business." Now that the private enterprise system has been fairly well domesticated, the main issue for economists who today work in the institutionalist tradition is what Gunnar Myrdal has called the "challenge to affluence," or what John K. Galbraith refers to as the preservation of the "quality of human life." While institutionalists since Veblen's time have always been concerned about the impact of the business system on the quality of human living, the emergence of the new "service economy" has given this issue a new significance in the second half of the current century.

CHAPTER III

THE INSTRUMENTAL ECONOMICS
OF CLARENCE E. AYRES

Clarence E. Ayres is today the best-known member of the group of economists who are generally described as institutional economists. For almost half a century, as a member of the academic world, Ayres labored to bring to students and the general public his views concerning the nature of economic reality and the need to develop a new way of comprehending this reality. What Ayres has sought to do has been to substitute the institutionalist way of thinking about the economic world for the orthodox or conventional way of thinking about this world which originated with the French Physiocrats and Adam Smith, and which has been preserved in orthodox or standard economics up to the present.

In Ayres's opinion there is a very pressing need to pass on to the economics profession and to the public the institutionalist way of thinking about the economic system. As he sees the problem, the future progress of mankind depends upon our sloughing off the myths, traditional beliefs and mores which prevent us from making further progress in constructing a more productive and reasonable society—what Ayres has described as a Creative Society. In developing the new or institutionalist way of thinking about the economic world Ayres relies very heavily upon the work of Thorstein Veblen and John Dewey. After receiving his doctorate in philosophy from the University of Chicago in 1917 Ayres devoted the next thirteen years to the field of philosophy where he espoused the cause of pragmatism. Even before he turned to economics in 1930 Ayres was already acquainted with the work of Thorstein Veblen, since there was a very close connection between Veblen's institutionalism and Dewey's instrumentalism. Ayres is a self-acknowledged follower of Veblen. Although he has taken from Veblen his general approach and some of Veblen's interpretation of the evolving economic system, it is in Dewey's work that Ayres found the inspiration to go beyond Veblen. This is especially the case in connection with the problem of value. Ayres's technological or instrumental theory of value, which is his main contribution in the field of economic theorizing, owes more to Dewey than to Veblen.

In turning from philosophy to economics in 1930 Ayres did not forsake philosophy. On the contrary, he looked at economics from the point of view of a philosopher who was deeply indebted to John Dewey and his pragmatic philosophy. In the first three decades of the current century Dewey had embarked upon a reconstruction of philosophy which involved the substitution of pragmatism or instrumentalism for the standard common sense or idealist philosophy of his time. Likewise, Ayres since 1930 has been engaged in the reconstruction of economics. For Ayres this has meant a substitution of institutionalism for the inherited orthodox or standard economics. It has been Ayres's position that the fundamental defect of standard economics is that it is based upon an inadequate pre-Deweyian philosophy. Orthodox or standard economists have a mistaken way of looking at the economic world because their economics is constructed on an outmoded philosophical foundation. In Ayres's view economics, if it is to be a realistic science that correctly explains the nature of the economic system, must be reconstructed on a new philosophical foundation. Ayres finds the definition of economics, the view of the economic system, the explanation of economic progress and the analysis of the value problem by standard economists from Adam Smith to John M. Keynes to be quite unacceptable.

The Philosophical Foundations of Orthodox Economics

Ayres explains that orthodox economics was largely developed at a time when philosophy was under the influence of thinkers who had a static and rationalistic approach to the study of human affairs. These philosophers, going back to Plato and Aristotle and continuing up to the advent of John Dewey's philosophy of pragmatism around 1900, had a dualistic approach to the study of reality. They separated human experience or the actual daily round of events from what was alleged to be a more uniform and ultimate scheme of things lying behind the flux of actual human events. The behind-the-scenes scheme of things was asserted to be perfect, changeless and the reflection of some Ultimate Reason or eternal spirit. This classical philosophical approach takes society to be fundamentally changeless and static. There is no inner spring or factor at work in the world which is an independent source of dynamic change, and which would, if it existed, necessarily push the world along an evolutionary path. According to the interpretation of classical philosophers science or knowledge accumulates but does not change the underlying essential world order of things.

According to this static and universalistic approach of the pre-Darwinian and pre-Deweyian philosophy, individuals are at bottom passive and contemplative. Since the world is basically changeless and a perfect reflection of some rational order of things, individuals do not have to be exploratory or innovatory. The purpose of knowledge is to explain the world and not to change it. Science is not forward looking in the sense of being concerned with human problems that need to be solved. Knowledge is not the power to change things, but only the understanding to explain things. What is important in human behavior is not emotion but reason. Men are essentially rational creatures who passively contemplate an unchanging world. The duality of the messy actual world and the behind-the-scenes clean perfect world is reproduced in the individual in the form of a separation between "body" and "mind." The body is material and the source of emotions, while the mind is mental and the source of reason. In some strange, unexplained way in pre-Deweyian philosophy the body is associated with the actual imperfect world, whereas the mind is the bridge to the changeless, perfect world. Truth and value are absolutes which the rational mind contemplates as products of the world of ultimate reason lying beneath or above the untidy and disorderly actual world that our eyes see.

Ayres explains that it is the pre-Deweyian rationalistic philosophy that has nurtured orthodox economics from the eighteenth century up to the present. Orthodox economists have persisted in searching for the world of equilibrium lying behind the actual economic world of conflict, strife and flux. Standard economists cling to an assumed dualism between the untidy, disorderly actual economic system and a hypothetical orderly and rational economic order. To be sure, present day orthodox or standard economists accept this dualism in a much more sophisticated way than did Adam Smith and other classical economists. Today standard economists no longer believe that the world of economic equilibrium is guided by an Ultimate Reason or Invisible Hand. Nevertheless, the most recent and widely used principles of economics textbooks continue to indoctrinate students with the view of an imaginary world of perfect equilibrium which is the starting point for all economic analysis. Although exceptions to this perfect economic world are noted, the exceptions are never permitted to wipe away the lingering idea that behind the actual economic system there is something more fundamental, more universal, more orderly and more rational than what the real world displays.

The Philosophical Foundations of Ayres's Instrumental Economics

Ayres, like John Dewey, has made a major break from classical nineteenth century philosophy. Following Dewey, Ayres has abandoned the dualism that runs through standard philosophy. Dewey takes society to be a life process in which there is no such thing as a dualism between what is seen and what is behind the scenes. There is no changeless, static or orderly process behind the life process of mankind. The life process is just what it is—people in the process of acting, experimenting, accumulating scientific knowledge and altering the actual scheme of things with the aim of improving social well-being. All is unity. Biologically mind and body are inseparable, and likewise, from the pragmatic philosophical point of view, there is no separation between what is mental and what is material.

Dewey goes on to explain that the life process of mankind has two main features or aspects—the institutional and the technological aspects. The institutional aspect of the life process relates to customary modes of behaving and acting, which are backward looking and concerned with values embedded in social tradition. The institutional aspect of the life process is static and concerned with the preservation of inherited beliefs, class distinctions and status arrangements. The technological aspect of the life process is concerned with tools, scientific knowledge and experimentation. As Ayres has put it, science is the knowing aspect of technology, and technology is the doing aspect of science. Dewey explains that science and technology are innovatory and forward looking, and they bring about changes in the physical world which in turn erode the institutional arrangements of the life process. There develops a clash between "inherited institutions" and contemporary scientific and technological tendencies, which results in a modification of the institutional structure of the life process.[1] Dewey points out that it is "the task of future philosophy to clarify men's ideas as to the social and moral

---

[1] John Dewey, *Reconstruction in Philosophy* (New York: Henry Holt and Co., 1920) p. 26.

strifes of their own day [resulting from the clash between the institutional and technological aspects of the life process]. Its aim is to become so far as is humanly possible an organ for dealing with these conflicts." Having this view of philosophy, Dewey would agree with William James that "philosophy is vision" and not the contemplation of eternal verities.

According to Dewey's interpretation the life process is a process of change and development. Experience is a matter of doing and adapting to the changing environment. Adaptation involves reconstruction of the environment and a search for ways of improving social well-being. Human intelligence is "the purposeful energetic re-shaper of those phases of nature and life that obstruct social well-being." [2] Thought and action are forward looking and open the door to the idea of progress. The life process, acting under the influence of scientific and technological change, develops in the direction of an enlarged social well-being. As a pragmatist Dewey is an optimist. Change is inevitable but a particular outcome of change is not inevitable. Dewey does not argue that human progress is inevitable. He does assert that the possibility of social progress is inherent in the life process, and he is optimistic about the possibility of realizing this social progress as a by-product of scientific and technological progress.

Dewey's views about the nature of the social world drew heavily from the prior work of Charles Peirce, William James, Georg Hegel, Charles Darwin and Karl Marx. He also appears to have been significantly influenced by Thorstein Veblen who was born only two years before Dewey, and who was associated with the latter on the faculty of the University of Chicago in the early years of the current century. Dewey has said of Veblen that "I always found Veblen's own articles very stimulating and some of his distinctions, like that between the technological side of industry and its 'business' aspect, have been quite fundamental in my thinking ever since I became acquainted with them." [3] Unlike Dewey, Veblen was not interested in the reconstruction of philosophy but instead in the reconstruction of economic science. In reconstructing economics Veblen had occasion to question the philosophical foundations of the inherited, conventional economics of his time. He also brought a new philosophical approach to the work of reconstructing eco-

---

[2] *Ibid.*, p. 51.
[3] Quoted by Joseph Dorfman in his *Thorstein Veblen and His America* (New York: The Viking Press, 1934) p. 450.

nomics. He was never very explicit or systematic, however, in his treatment of this problem. Ayres views his own work on the reconstruction of economics as a more systematic effort to show the impact of the new pragmatic philosophy upon economic thinking.

It is clear that Ayres is heavily indebted to both John Dewey and Thorstein Veblen, a fact that he readily acknowledges. Like Dewey and Veblen, Ayres takes the life process of mankind to be his main consideration and point of departure. Ayres states that "Doing-and-knowing, science-and-technology, is the real life process of mankind. This is the process from which modern industrial civilization has resulted, and it is the process in terms of which men have always judged things good and bad, and actions right and wrong."[4] We shall see that Ayres goes on to analyze the polarity between backward-looking inherited institutions and forward-looking science and technology, and between the imaginary world of myth, legend, inherited beliefs and traditional mores and the real or genuine world of reflective thought, scientific experience and technological progress. As with Dewey and Veblen, so also with Ayres his analysis is directed towards the conflict between these two incompatible processes or worlds and the adverse consequences of this conflict for economic life. Since, like Dewey and Veblen, Ayres believes that science has a function to perform, namely, to contribute to race survival, Ayres is moved to point out how the conflict between inherited institutions and the developing technology can be reduced with the aim of enlarging the general welfare.

Ayres's Theory of Culture

Ayres's approach to the analysis of the functioning of the American economy is indicated by his definition of economics. In *The Industrial Economy* (1952) he explains that "Economics is the study of the economy."[5] Ayres's concept of the economy is quite different from the classical concept which viewed the economy as a static system which, under the influence of market forces, gravitates towards a condition of equilibrium. In place of this static, non-evolutionary view of the economy Ayres substitutes a view which takes the economy to be an evolving, dynamic process in which there is no tendency towards an equilibrium. Instead there

---

[4] C. E. Ayres, *Toward a Reasonable Society* (Austin: The University of Texas Press, 1961) p. 15.

[5] C. E. Ayres, *The Industrial Economy, Its Technological Basis and Institutional Destiny* (Boston: Houghton Mifflin Co., 1952) p. 1.

is an adjustment of institutional arrangements to underlying technological conditions, an adjustment, which, however, is so incomplete as to leave at present a considerable imbalance between the institutional and technological aspects of economic activity.

Ayres's analysis of the economy does not proceed primarily on the level of the individual as do the analyses of standard or orthodox economists such as Lionel Robbins. Robbins reduces economics in the ultimate to an analysis of individual choice among alternative uses of scarce resources for the satisfaction of given wants.[6] Robbins views the economy as the sum of the actions of individual businessmen, workers and consumers. Ayres's analysis of the economy proceeds on the level of the "generalization of culture."[7] Instead of analyzing the economy in terms of individuals, Ayres examines the economy as a cultural process which contains forces that are independent of individuals. The most important of these forces is scientific and technological change. For Ayres the economy as a cultural process has an existence that is independent of the individuals who participate in its affairs. Ayres's central purpose as a scientist is to understand the economy as a whole. He shifts the center of attention from the individual as a choosing person to the whole economy as an evolving process in which individuals as a collective unit or body seek to cope with the problem of using scarce resources to serve culturally determined wants or needs. This does not mean that Ayres ignores individual economic behavior. Instead he regards all such individual behavior as cultural or social behavior, and so analyses individual behavior within the framework of culture viewed as a process.

Underlying Ayres's theory of the economy is a theory of culture. Culture is an "organized corpus of human behavior" which exhibits two aspects; namely, the institutional (or ceremonial) aspect and the technological aspect.[8] The institutional aspect of human culture includes all the institutions based on legend, inherited beliefs, mores, status and the hierarchical ordering of society. This part of human culture is inhibitory in nature. It is resistant to change and development. It is restrictive and backward looking, and seeks to preserve existing class arrangements and restrictions.

---

[6] Lionel Robbins, *An Essay on the Nature and Significance of Economic Science*, p. 20.

[7] C. E. Ayres, *The Theory of Economic Progress* (Chapel Hill: The University of North Carolina Press, 1944) p. 112.

[8] *Ibid.*, p. 95.

The technological aspect of human culture includes scientific know-how, skills and tools. At the heart of technology are found science and innovation. There is a propensity of tools and skills to proliferate. New combinations of tools are being developed continuously. It is for this reason that Ayres asserts that it is the peculiar characteristic of technology that it is developmental in nature. Ayres calls attention to what he describes as the principle of technological progress. New technological developments, new combinations of devices or tools, are "bound to occur." Once the steam engine was developed, the steam-propelled locomotive was bound to follow, sooner or later. There is thus a logic of technological development. Given certain tools and skills, new combinations of these tools and skills are bound to occur within the framework of existing tools and skills. But there is nothing teleological about technological development. No particular invention is bound to occur, but the proliferation of tools and skills in general necessarily takes place and in an accelerating manner.

The proliferation of tools and skills is greatly helped by the cross-fertilization of cultures. For centuries Chinese culture was stagnant as technological progress came to a standstill. When tools such as printing blocks, the compass and gunpowder were exported from China, and paper, the decimal system and science were exported from the Islamic world to Western Europe, these tools and skills were combined with the frontier institutions and atmosphere of Western Europe to create a dynamic progressive culture. Much of the technological superiority of Western Europe after the Crusades can be attributed to the cultural cross-fertilization of that area.

Ayres's theory of culture is associated with a technological interpretation of cultural development. Changes in the technological basis of human culture shape the institutional superstructure in the long run. Since the institutional structure is resistant to change, the adaptation of institutions to the changing technological foundations of culture is slow and associated with much conflict between those individuals whose status and hierarchical social position are threatened by technological change and those individuals who stand to gain from new institutional arrangements. The cultural process is continuously affected by the lag between institutional and cultural change. We have social, economic and political problems because outmoded institutional arrangements become obstacles which must be removed before a satisfactory adjustment between the institutional and technological aspects of our culture can be achieved.

Ayres's Theory of Human Nature

Ayres's theory of human nature stresses the fact that man is a social product. His beliefs, attitudes and wants reflect the impact of the cultural environment and the social forces at work within that environment. Ayres observes that "A separate individual is a phenomenon unknown to experience."[9] Furthermore, Ayres does not accept the position of conventional economists that man has an "inner nature" which is above and beyond cultural influences, and which determines his wants and values. According to Ayres the concept of an inner nature underlying man's behavior is a relic of the time when philosophers and social scientists held the view that "body" and "mind" are separate entities with mind being more substantial and fundamental than body. According to this outmoded philosophical view man's inner nature is a reflection of his mind. If the investigator wants to understand man's wants and values, he has to indulge in an introspective analysis which is supposed in some inexplicable way to reveal man's basic wants and values. Such an interpretation of how man comes to express his wants pays no attention to the cultural milieu in which people live and from which, according to modern psychologists and other social scientists, they derive their wants and values.

Ayres repudiates the introspective, individualistic explanation of human behavior which still dominates the theory of consumer behavior of standard economists, who reduce the theory of consumption to an explanation of man's "primary wants" in terms of some introspectively determined concept of utility or consumer satisfaction. Ayres asserts that man has no "inner original nature" untouched by cultural forces. On the contrary all human wants and values are social or cultural in origin. Man is not a passive contemplative creature. Rather man is an active, problem-solving individual who is endowed with a "creative intelligence." This intelligence is an instrument for solving human problems and providing more individual and social well-being.

The world is not perfect. Man is born into a culture which is full of imperfections. Besides being an intelligent individual, man is a creature of custom and habit. He too frequently accepts the tradi-

---

[9] *The Theory of Economic Progress*, p. 91. Quoted by Ayres from C. H. Cooley, *Human Nature and the Social Order* (1902).

tional beliefs and values passed on to him by the institutional complex of the social system. Human behavior directed by inherited beliefs and attitudes and not by the appeal to scientific evidence is frequently irrational behavior. It is for this reason that Ayres states that human purposes and goals have always been in large measure irrational.[10] Since society's institutional complex is resistant to change and backward looking in its beliefs, attitudes and values, it becomes an obstacle to behavior that could enlarge individual and social well-being. Problems emerge when men try to handle current problems with outmoded beliefs, mores and values. Fortunately for man he has the means of overcoming the institutional obstacles to social progress. He can use his creative intelligence to appeal to science and technology in his effort to eliminate outmoded beliefs, attitudes, mores and customs. He can cut through the cake of custom with the aid of science and technological progress to secure an adjustment of the institutional process to the underlying technological process. He can wipe away the "institutional dust" to reveal the "real" or "technological values" which contribute so much to the enlargement of individual and social well-being.

The Interpretation of American Capitalism

Ayres observes that the capitalist economy, being a part of western culture, is a part of that evolving culture process. The economy as a process has passed through a number of phases or stages and is now at the stage of "financial capitalism." During the evolution of the capitalist system the industrial revolution has had the effect of substituting large-scale for small-scale enterprise in many industries, and of replacing the single proprietorship with the corporate enterprise. In recent decades the government has had to intervene on a wide front because of the failure of finance capitalism to stabilize the economy and to secure adequate economic growth and employment.

According to Ayres's interpretation, the American economy is a combination of two economies, a "price economy" and an "industrial economy." The price economy, which today dominates the industrial economy, is concerned with financial matters such as money, prices, sales, contracts and all the financial arrangements the ultimate concern of which is "money power." Those individuals who participate in the activities of the price economy believe in the

---

[10] C. E. Ayres, "Piecemeal Revolution," *The Southwestern Social Science Quarterly*, Vol. XXX, No. 1, June 1949, p. 15.

"creative potency" of money, savings and capital as a financial fund. They attribute the economic progress of the nation to the use of money power as expressed through saving and investment. Inequality of incomes makes saving possible, saving gives rise to investment and investment makes economic growth possible. Savings or funds invested in capital are alleged to have a "creative potency."[11] The accumulation of money is taken to be the mainspring of economic progress by the business class and the owners of private capital. The possessors of money power never attribute economic growth and progress to the progress of science and technology. They do not look upon capital as physical equipment which is constantly being improved as a result of scientific and technological progress. The "financial overlords" of the price economy look upon capital primarily as a fund of money which comes into existence only through private saving, and which is uniquely creative.

In Ayres's view the price economy is an institutional complex that is based on "ceremonial behavior"; that is to say, behavior which is related to the social establishment or entrenched authority and privilege which are supported by custom and mores[12]. This institutional complex is a power system of status and mores backed up by inherited myths, legends and attitudes relating to property, classes and class distinctions. The myth of the purely competitive economy is maintained by those in possession of money power because it enables them to operate behind a façade of free private enterprise. It also enables them to oppose government intervention in business affairs, and to argue against the social obligations of private property ownership. The price economy as an institutional complex is static in outlook, resistant to change and backward looking. The ceremonial behavior associated with the price economy is frequently wasteful and archaic. It retards technological progress and restricts national output. It elevates "price" over "technology," and in so doing becomes an obstacle to the maintenance and advancement of what Dewey called the "life process," or what Ayres describes as social well-being.

Ayres's "industrial economy," which is akin to Veblen's process of goods making, is in his view more fundamental than the "price economy." The industrial economy is a technological economy the central concern of which is science, tools and skills to be used for the production of goods and services. Whereas the price economy

---

[11] *The Theory of Economic Progress*, p. 56.
[12] *Ibid.*, p. 45.

is essentially a "power system," which asserts that money is a creative force, the industrial economy is a production system which takes
technology to be the only truly creative force in the American economic system.[13] In the industrial economy capital is looked at in its
real sense as a piece of physical equipment, which is an instrument
of economic progress. Whereas the ceremonial behavior of the
price economy is static and inhibitory of change, technological activity is developmental and open to change. The industrial economy is
antipathetic to traditional beliefs and attitudes, class status and class
distinctions. Technological change is constantly undermining the
institutional basis of the price economy and forcing the price economy to adjust to the industrial economy. Already owners of corporate property have been largely dispossessed of the management
of their property, and the government has assumed responsibility
for directing the economy and providing full employment. But the
process of adjustment of the price economy to the industrial economy
is far from being complete. What is needed to complete this adjustment, according to Ayres, is a new way of thinking which will find
the essential meaning of the economic system not in "price" but in
"technology."

Price and Technological Values

Ayres points out that the two economies, the price and industrial
economies, give rise to two different concepts of value. The price
economy is the source of what Ayres calls "price values," the values
established in the market place.[14] According to conventional economics price is the locus of value and the guide to economic welfare.
Price is taken to be a measure of exchange value, which is the
power to command other goods in exchange. If a good comes to
command less of another good in the market, the price of the first
good falls in comparison with the price of the second good. In this
connection "value" means "price ratio." Some economists push their
analysis beyond exchange values and price ratios to consider use
value, the essence of which is said to be utility. For these economists
the foundation of value is in utility or use value which is related to
man's inner nature. Since "utility" and "man's inner nature" are
matters that can be approached or considered by the economist only
introspectively, sophisticated orthodox economists are inclined to
take wants as given or primary data which do not need to be

---

[13] *The Industrial Economy*, pp. 127-129.
[14] *The Theory of Economic Progress*, p. 226.

analyzed. For these economists value is closely related to price with the result that value is a function of price. Value is somehow derived from price. Value is at bottom a matter of price and not a technological phenomenon. Economics from this orthodox point of view is essentially a science of price, and the essence of the economic system is found in price relationships.

In Ayres's view it is an illusion to believe that price measures or reflects real or genuine value. The illusion arises because price makes value seem very definite and quantifiable. There is no way of measuring the utility which underlies the value that price is presumed by conventional economists to measure. Ayres points out that if price quantifies value it quantifies vice as readily as virtue, anti-social as well as social goods. Orthodox economists try to escape this dilemma by taking wants as given or primary data not open to analysis. Ayres explains that "prices do not measure real values but only quantify the judgments of people made antecedent to their price transactions. Whether those judgments are wise or foolish is determined not by the pricing mechanism but by their relation to the technological life-stream."[15] Ayres distinguishes between "price values" and "real" or "technological values." Price values are frequently ceremonial or pseudo values. The values behind prices in the market system of finance capitalism are values that reflect traditional mores, money power, class or hierarchical status and distinctions and outmoded beliefs and attitudes. In modern capitalism use value or what has utility for an individual, Ayres explains, is not determined by some esoteric inner nature of mankind. On the contrary what is useful or valuable to an individual is determined by the cultural milieu in which he lives. In our highly commercialized society it is the backward-looking, change resistant institutional complex based on traditional mores, beliefs and attitudes that determines what an individual considers to be a use value. Consequently, Ayres asserts that the values behind prices in finance capitalism are largely "unreal," "ceremonial," "fancied" or "pseudo" values that do not contribute to the preservation and advancement of the life process of mankind.[16] Price values are what Veblen described as pecuniary values or consumer superfluities.

---

[15] *Ibid.*, p. 227.
[16] By the term "ceremonial," which is borrowed from Veblen, Ayres means something relating to entrenched authority which is supported by custom, mores and status, and which is further buttressed by the performance of some ritual.

They are frequently the highly-advertised products that the upper income groups purchase, and which the lower income groups sometimes purchase as a matter of emulation or "keeping up with the Joneses."

Ayres asserts that the kind of values that the price economy is concerned with are in large part ceremonial or fanciful and not contributory to the advancement of social well-being. There are more fundamental values than price values which are the concern of the industrial economy or the technological process. These are the real values which contribute to the efficient working of the technological system on which life depends. Price or institutional values are grounded in myth and traditional belief. Technological values are grounded in science and technology. Ayres points out that "the technological process is itself the locus of value."[17] This means that the criterion of value is not some immeasurable ultimate subjective utility, but instead it is objective technology. If one wants to find out if a good or a value is "real" in the sense that it contributes to the general welfare, he turns not to the introspective concept of utility but to the technological process. Bread is a real value because science and technology prove to us that bread maintains the life process. Heroin used as a source of personal stimulation is not a real value because science and technology reveal how it undermines the life process. For Ayres the only criterion to which mankind can turn in determining what is or is not a "real" value is science and technology. The technological criterion of value is a pragmatic criterion which can be subjected to the test of scientific evidence obtained from observation and experiment. Any other criterion of value such as utility introspectively related to the inner nature of man, or myth, tribal legend and inherited mores, is unrelated to the technological process, and cannot be subjected to the pragmatic test of scientific evidence. As Ayres puts it, "Human values do not derive from the universe at large. . . . Genuine values derive from the life process of mankind, a process to which every man is committed by virtue of already being a man."[18]

In his analysis of the value problem Ayres goes behind the price system to consider the concept of use value. Orthodox economists have always paid little attention to value in use because it is said to be purely subjective, and therefore not amenable to scientific analysis. This approach to use value, in Ayres's opinion, is wrong.

[17] *The Theory of Economic Progress*, p. 211.
[18] *Toward a Reasonable Society*, p. 15.

Value in use takes on a new significance when "use" is related to the technological process. Value in use is then no longer a matter of personal or subjective whim or fancy when "use" or "usefulness" is considered in terms of being scientifically or technologically useful for sustaining the life process. In Ayres's own words, "For every man the real and valid judgments of economic value are those he makes between purchases, judgments of value in use as economists once said, tested and verified by the way things work in the continuous effort of existence. . . . For every individual and for the community the criterion of value is the continuation of the life-process—keeping the machines running."[19]

Prominent among the technological, real or genuine values with which Ayres is concerned are economic abundance, equality, freedom, security and excellence. The technological process as it has worked out through the Industrial Revolution has created conditions in which these values have been made available to the general public. The fundamental value upon which all other values are established is economic abundance, "the progressive multiplication of all good things." This value is intimately associated with the technological process and improvement in it over the decades, and has already been achieved in the United States. The Industrial Revolution introduced a competitive *laissez-faire* economy in which consumer and occupational freedom became well established. Equality, "the progressively wider participation of all in all good things," also stems from the technological process.[20] The Industrial Revolution destroyed feudal rank and class. It has largely eliminated the servant class and placed women on a more equal footing with men. The value of security is now also more widely enjoyed by mankind. Until recently life even in the western world was highly precarious. The chief hazards were famine, disease and war. Technological progress has made the population in large sections of the world free from famine and disease. Social security systems have reduced personal hazards very significantly. Personal security is still threatened by the possibility of catastrophic warfare. But there is also the possibility of using "technically efficient organization for mutual advantage" to reduce the hazard of war.

A fifth value of interest to Ayres is the value of excellence which is a matter of taste, beauty and truth. In the modern industrial economy quantity does not have to be achieved at the sacrifice of

[19] *The Theory of Economic Progress*, p. 230.
[20] *Toward a Reasonable Society*, p. 241.

quality. It is erroneously argued by some individuals that mass production cannot be accompanied by good taste, that things have to be rare to be excellent, and that steel and concrete are inherently ugly and bigness is necessarily vulgar. Ayres describes these views as the elitist theory of excellence to which he does not subscribe. He argues that "there is nothing about the quantitative potency of the industrial economy that is necessarily debasing."[21] Where mass production has been accompanied by bad taste, it is frequently the case that the producers have made no effort to maintain or improve the quality of their output. Technological progress is not the enemy of quality in output. Each age can find artistic expression with the aid of new raw materials such as steel, concrete and plastics and with new technological processes. No age has a monopoly on excellence. Those individuals who find excellence only in the culture of the past have a mystical, backward-looking approach to the problem of excellence. The elitist theory of excellence is based on cultural nostalgia and "outright ancestor worship." The technological approach to excellence is forward looking. It asserts that the new industrial society, with its vast increase in scientific knowledge, automation and computerization, need not be a society without excellence. No one can effectively deny that on occasion quality has been sacrificed to quantity in the newly emerging industrial society. But this, according to Ayres's interpretation, is because we have allowed those who possess money power to dominate economic activity. Ayres would have those who possess "cultural power," namely, scientists, technologists, educators, artists and philosophers, replace those who have money power so that in the new industrial society the quality of economic life would be continuously improved. The "industrial way of life" which gave rise to an Albert Einstein and a John Dewey would then continue the quest for excellence which received such an impetus in the days of ancient Greece from a Plato and an Aristotle.

Ayres explains that all values are interrelated. There is a unity of values which derives from the fact that all values are a function of science and technology. All values are related to the same basic criterion, which is a science-technology criterion. A value is a value because it is life sustaining, and it is life sustaining because it is in conformity with, or a reflection of, the technological system upon which all life depends. Having more of a particular value does not

---

[21] *Ibid.*, p. 240.

always mean having less of another value. Securing economic abundance does not mean a loss of freedom; achieving equality does not lead to less security; and excellence does not preclude abundance. On the contrary, freedom is a necessary condition for the securing of economic abundance and equality. It is only where men are secure that they can enjoy freedom, equality and abundance. And only free men in an affluent society can come to enjoy a life of excellence. It is wrong, therefore, in Ayres's opinion, to argue that more security means less freedom, more equality means less abundance, or more abundance means less excellence.

In making a distinction between what he describes as "price" or "unscientific" values and "technological" or "real" values Ayres does not propose to do away with the price system. He proposes to maintain the price system but also to have prices in the market place reflect real, technological values and not the ceremonial or fanciful values that prices have been reflecting in the modern capitalist system. By transferring the guidance of the private enterprise system from the "financial overlords" and other possessors of money power to those individuals who are representative of the sciences and the arts, Ayres would make certain that the kinds of goods that are priced and sold in the private markets would also be the types of goods that would meet his technological or scientific standard. In other words the private price system would be cleansed of those ceremonial, unscientific and backward-looking influences, beliefs and attitudes that inhibit the improvement of the life process of mankind.

The Concept of Economic Progress

Ayres emphasizes the point that economic thinking has always embodied a concept of progress which has been related to the value problem. It is for this reason that Ayres describes economics as "the science of value." He explains that progress is inseparable from the value problem because progress involves the achieving of more real or technological values. Progress must be thought of in terms of the advancement of science and technology, and is therefore a function of science and technology. Progress is not a movement towards any given "end" such as maximum utility or satisfaction. For Ayres there are no generalized ultimate values or ends such as maximum satisfaction somehow related to the inner aspirations of mankind. Ayres asserts that modern science has put an end to this introspective approach. In his analysis progress is not an end but rather "Progress is the continuation of this [the life] process" with the aid of advancement in science and the creative arts.[22] Progress is achieved as the institutional barriers to scientific and technological progress are removed. As science and technology progress, there is a need for society's institutional complex to be adjusted to the new technological basis of society. The further the boundaries of inequality, ignorance, superstition, coercion and injustice are pushed back, and a more "reasonable society" is established, the more progress is achieved. Progress is then made by substituting real or technological values for ceremonial or price values. As these pseudo or fanciful price values are replaced by genuine or real values the life process is nourished and enriched. Society comes to enjoy greater economic abundance, full employment, greater economic freedom and equality and an economic life of higher quality. Progress in essence means the achievement of a life of greater excellence.

Ayres calls attention to the fact that the cultural process is not teleological. It has no predetermined end. There is no guarantee that we will continue to make progress in improving our culture, in cutting down superstition, entrenched privilege and status, coercion and injustice. Much remains to be done before we complete the building of that "reasonable society" which is the goal of the American people. Real values, Ayres explains, will never wholly supplant institutional or fanciful values. But as real values come more into their own, the life process will become more rational than it is at present. Ayres asserts that all our experience points in this direction. In recent centuries democracy has become more firmly established, church and state have been separated, science and technology have progressed and we have moved closer to economic abundance. Past experience makes Ayres optimistic about the possibility of achieving a more rational and hence more reasonable society.

The Deficiencies of the American Economic System

Ayres explains that achieving economic progress depends first upon realizing the full potentiality of the industrial system by securing a high rate of economic growth, and secondly upon making certain that the people are able to obtain the goods and services of high quality that they would like to have. The finance or monopoly

---

[22] *Theory of Economic Progress*, p. 242.

capitalism that reached the highwater mark of its development by 1929 was unable to guarantee the American people an adequate and sustained flow of high quality goods and services. Ayres published his first major study of the American economic system, *The Problem of Economic Order*, in 1938 after he had observed this economic system passing through the worst depression it had ever experienced. In this study Ayres presented an interpretation of American capitalism which was to be elaborated in his subsequent publications, *The Theory of Economic Progress* (1944), *The Divine Right of Capital* (1946) and *The Industrial Economy* (1952). Ayres explained in his 1938 study, *The Problem of Economic Order*, that the 1930's had witnessed a crisis in the development of the capitalist system. Monopoly capitalism had failed to provide a satisfactory guidance for the nation's economy as was evidenced by the serious depression of the 1930's. Following John A. Hobson, Ayres developed an underconsumptionist interpretation of the economic difficulties of the 1930's. It was his view that the breakdown of the American economy was primarily the result of a deficiency in mass purchasing power.[23] In the prior period of prosperity personal incomes had increased at differential rates, the incomes of the upper income groups growing much more rapidly than the incomes of the low income groups. As a consequence of these differential income growth rates the upper income groups saved more income than was needed for the investment required by the prevailing economic growth rate. Eventually mass production was not matched by mass consumption and the depression ensued. Thus in Ayres's opinion the main problem of capitalism is the maldistribution of income. Within the capitalist system there is a paradox, "the paradox of industrial potency and social impotence."[24] On the one hand the capitalist system is potentially a very productive system, but on the other hand it is unable to realize fully this production potentiality or potency because of a recurring lack of mass purchasing power.

In searching for the reason for the discrepancy between mass production and mass consumption and the breakdown of the capitalist system in the 1930's, Ayres arrived at the conclusion that the deficiencies of the capitalist system resulted from the dominance of pecuniary considerations over technological considerations. The

---

[23] C. E. Ayres, *The Problem of Economic Order* (New York: Farrar and Rinehart, Inc., 1938) p. iv.

[24] *Ibid.*, p. 81.

technological process could not provide a large and expanding flow of goods and services on a sustained basis because the nation was dominated by the "dogmas of commercialism." Economists since the time of Adam Smith had made economics largely a study of prices and markets, and had concentrated their attention on price relationships and other pecuniary matters. They had not penetrated to the technological foundation underneath the pecuniary institutions of the economic system. Following the lead of orthodox economists, businessmen, workers and consumers came to view the economy primarily in monetary terms. To most people money was considered to be the main instrument of economic progress. Money was held to be crucial because it was believed that economic progress depended upon the growth of the material equipment of industry, that is to say, upon the expansion of the supply of capital equipment. But this supply of capital was said to be created by the money saving of the upper income groups. Therefore, according to this interpretation accepted by people in general, money power played a crucial role in bringing the modern industrial system into existence. Ayres argues that this kind of false thinking gave rise to the "legend of the creative function of capital [as a fund of money that has been saved]" and of the "mythological potency of capital."[25]

Ayres asserts that capitalism has been a permissive but not an active cause of industrial growth. As an institutional climate it has been favorable to the development of the industrial system. Money making and the accumulation of capital funds, however, have not been the "seeds" from which the industrial system has sprung. In his opinion any such interpretation is nonsense. The modern industrial system is an outgrowth of science, technology and invention. It is the offspring of the machine process and not the money making process. The social dividend or gross national product is not basically dependent on money accumulation, which in Ayres's opinion plays only a secondary or permissive role.

The unfortunate consequence of having the population in general believe that the progress of society depends upon the accumulation of money is that the income distribution system of capitalism has come to be regarded as sacred. Consequently it becomes difficult for those who believe otherwise to eliminate the maldistribution of income and the imbalance between the power to produce and the

---

[25] C. E. Ayres, *The Divine Right of Capital* (Boston: Houghton Mifflin Co., 1946) pp. 66, 86.

power to consume. Ayres observes a strong institutional resistance to transferring enough consumer buying power to low income groups to keep mass production and mass consumption in balance. The upper income classes cling tenaciously to their "functionless saving"—the excess of saving above what is needed to finance economic growth. The consequences of the failure to provide enough consumer buying power to take up the mass production are not only depression but also war as nations seek markets abroad for their domestic surpluses.

The second major deficiency of the capitalist system besides its failure to achieve the full use of its production potential is its failure to produce "the right goods in the right proportions." This is the problem of price or ceremonial values versus real or technological values. In a society where money is power and economic progress is held to depend primarily upon the accumulation of money or savings, the value system of the public is distorted by excessive concern with pecuniary matters. Individuals become status seekers, class distinctions lead to inequality, economic freedoms of the masses are restricted, and consumer goods and services increasingly become superfluities which contribute little or nothing to the maintenance of the life process. The price system becomes an inadequate guide to increased general welfare. The main gatway to economic equality, freedom, justice, security and excellence is abundance of goods and services. Without economic abundance society cannot have a value system that not only sustains the life process but also leads to a life of quality. In Ayres's view of things the elimination of the maldistribution of income in the capitalist system, what Ayres describes as the "wellspring of all economic evil," would serve two purposes, the creation of economic abundance and the establishment of a society of excellence.[26]

Capitalism and Economic Planning

Ayres argues that there must be other ways to deal with the underconsumption of the lower income groups than by tolerating depressions or recessions, or by engaging in war. His solution for this problem is that "deliberate planning must take the place of the planless growth of recent centuries."[27] As early as 1938 Ayres in *The Problem of Economic Order* called attention to the fact that in the United States we have an extensive and complicated industrial

---

[26] *Ibid.*, p. 30.
[27] *Ibid.*, p. 190.

society, and yet no one assumes responsibility for providing overall economic guidance. In the past three decades Ayres's interest in economic planning has been strengthened by the course of economic events. He explains that planning is a function of knowing. As we have accumulated knowledge about how our economy functions, about income and production flows, employment and unemployment, and about the roles of investment and consumption, and as we have added to our supply of national income statistics, we have become better prepared to plan our economic activities. Economic planning, Ayres points out, is "a manifestation of the technological process."[28] The same situation that creates a need for economic planning also creates an array of tools for the carrying out of this planning. Such new tools as gross national product statistics, input-output economics, national economic accounting, national economic budgeting, and flow-of-funds accounting make economic planning more feasible now than in the 1930's. As the technological process undermines society's institutional structure this structure fails to make the necessary adjustments. Planning is then needed to cope with the problems of institutional maladjustment. As Ayres expresses it, "It is this kind of problems—problems resulting from institutional obstruction—that gives rise to economic planning. The over-all problem of economic planning is one of institutional adjustment. . . . The progress of science and the industrial arts is continually altering the physical patterns of social life so as to produce situations contrary to the institutional [ceremonial] practices of the community."[29] It is the aim of economic planning to provide the devices by means of which the technological foundation of social life and the institutional or ceremonial superstructure or practices of the community can be made compatible. It is for this reason that Ayres defines planning as "the process of adjustment to continuing change."

In every age economic planning consists of discovering technical devices that will aid in solving the problems of the age. The critical problem of the current age is the tendency for production to exceed "the propensity to consume." The technical device needed is one that will modify the economy's income distribution mechanism so that the imbalance of production and consumption may be corrected. Ayres wants to add to society's institutional structure a new institution in the form of an income distribution control mechanism that

[28] *The Industrial Economy*, p. 190.
[29] *Ibid.*, p. 192.

will prevent excess saving or oversaving. Such a mechanism would make Say's Law work by insuring that all income earned is spent on either investment or consumption. Ayres "diversionary [income] mechanism" would seek to make certain that aggregate demand is always adequate to absorb aggregate supply at full employment.

Ayres's search for a planning device that will divert income from the oversavers to the underconsumers leads him to consider a number of devices. Deficit financing does not qualify as the desired planning device because it does not eliminate the chronic tendency toward oversaving. It compensates for but does not eliminate this institutional disorder. Public works would not be a satisfactory device for coping with the oversaving problem because, if the oversaving is very large, the public works program would have to be very large and could eventually come to compete with private enterprise. The diversionary income mechanism that Ayres favors is the social security system which he would enlarge in the direction of a "basic minimal income for all which is independent of the performance of any service or the ownership of any property."[30] This arrangement would mean "the perpetual automatic guaranteed consumption of all, regardless of circumstances." Such a guaranteed minimum income plan would be financed by means of the progressive personal and corporate income taxes. These taxes would be used to draw off income from those who tended to oversave. The tax revenue would then be transferred to those who were short of consumer purchasing power. The aim of the enlarged social security program would be to increase the flow of mass consumer purchasing power all the way down to the smallest income, and "ideally, to create income where none at all exists at present."

Ayres's diversionary income mechanism would redistribute private income but not private wealth. To redistribute wealth would require a large change in the whole of society's institutional structure, and Ayres does not recommend any such major institutional change. He is searching for a middle position between the extreme right which opposes any change in the institutional structure, and the extreme left which calls for a wholesale liquidation of the institutional structure of the capitalist system. In proposing a middle position Ayres advocates "pragmatic planning" which is guided by technical and not ideological considerations. Ayres is a gradualist who seeks to save capitalism by making it work better. Ayres's

---

[30] *Ibid.*, p. 272.

proposal of a diversionary income mechanism which would redistribute income would in effect be a "socialization of demand" without a socialization of private property.[31] Under the proposal for a diversionary income mechanism as national income grew the absolute size of the income received by upper income property owners could actually increase. But relative to the total income received by the low income groups, the total income received by the upper income groups would decline.

Economic Planning and the Value Problem

In Ayres's treatment of economic planning there is a higher purpose than providing for economic stability and an increasing social dividend. Planning is related to the problem of values because it is the aim of planning not only to secure a large output of goods and services but also "the right kind of goods in the right proportions." The right kind of goods or values are technological or "scientific" values which have high utility for both the individual and the community. In helping to adjust the institutional superstructure of society to its changing technological foundation planning replaces myth and legend with science, and "ceremonial adequacy" with efficiency in the production of those goods that contribute to maintaining the life process of mankind. Ayres explains that we must plan to avoid those goods that cater to such things as fashion and propriety or decorum. Goods that meet the standards of conventional etiquette or "ceremonial adequacy" meet artificial standards of what is correct in conduct. Such goods do not meet the standards of adequacy for maintaining the life process or for enlarging general welfare. They are not in conformity with technological standards of what is scientifically sound and contributory to race survival.

The right goods or values are also those that contribute to a life of quality or excellence. It is the aim of economic planning to provide the foundation of a life of quality which is economic abundance. Once an affluent economy has been achieved other values such as security, freedom, justice and excellence will be more readily obtained. The unplanned economy with its commercial dogmas and irrational concern for money power cannot lead to the "reasonable society" towards which the public is groping.

Some considerable progress has already been made towards the planned "reasonable society" that Ayres envisions. John M. Keynes

---

[31] *The Divine Right of Capital*, p. 176.

broke with those individuals who believe that saving is always good for the economy, and that more saving is always desirable. Keynes called attention to the need to support aggregate demand with the aid of government spending and various fiscal and monetary measures so that aggregate demand will absorb aggregate supply at a full employment level. But Keynes, in Ayres's opinion, did not go far enough in his analysis of the problems of the capitalist system. Keynes did not point out that the creative potency of money capital was a myth, and that it was science and technology as reflected in physical capital and industrial know-how that had creative potency. Keynes was singularly uninterested in technology as a factor that was reshaping the structure and functioning of the capitalist economy. Ayres accepts Keynes as far as he goes, but he does not go far enough. Keynes has no well-developed theory of economic progress and of the institutional obstacles to progress. Keynes was mainly interested in keeping the economy functioning at full employment, and he expressed little interest in the problem of values. He did not raise the question of production for what? If Keynes had asked the questions that Ayres has asked he might have gone beyond mere "interventionism" to economic planning.

The Destiny of Industrial Society

Ayres points out that we have already made much progress in altering the institutional structure of western societies, and in freeing technology so that it may serve mankind better. There has been a considerable "technologization of the social structure" in which the institutional structure has been successfully adapted to the demands of the changing technological process. The structure of the industrial economy "is becoming less and less a system of status supported by ancient tradition and belief, and more and more an organizational device for getting things done—that is, for operating the machines by which we live."[32] The Industrial Revolution which began not in the eighteenth century but when man first discovered fire, and which has continued up to the present, indicates the probable course of future cultural development. Ayres asserts that there is a destiny that can be read into the history of the industrial economy. Nothing is inevitable but much is probable. The technological revolution is a permanent revolution which carries society forward

---

[32] *The Industrial Economy*, p. 401.

but to no predetermined end. Ayres is optimistic with regard to the future of the industrial system. He argues that industrialism does not necessarily mean a decline in the quality of life, the denial of the worth of the individual, or the defeat of the common man by the industrial-military complex. Affluence is not by definition an evil. On the contrary, it is only in an affluent society that people can throw off the shackles of the institutional past.

Ayres observes that "Better than any previous generation we know what we are doing, and what is good for us." The institutional structure of western society has exhibited a unique degree of adaptability and we should take advantage of this feature of our society. There has in recent decades been a shift from the sacred to the secular, from authority to efficiency, and from status to process. But the transition is by no means complete. We are currently at a turning point in getting a new criterion of value and welfare to replace our outmoded criteria of money power, class distinction and hierarchical status. The new criterion would be the scientific-technological criterion of what contributes to the life process. This new criterion points in the direction of the destiny of industrial society which is "continually greater abundance, increasing stability, continually greater physical and social freedom and a degree of freedom of the spirit such as the world has never known before."[33] Ayres is not a starry-eyed optimist. He warns us that the destiny of industrial society as conceived above is not assured. If we do not correct the deficiencies of capitalism such as its tendency towards a discrepancy between potential full-employment industrial production and actual current consumption, our destiny will be "continued international disturbance" and the likelihood of war. If we are to avoid this destructive destiny, we shall have to adopt a new way of thinking about economic affairs—a way in which the primacy of the technological process is acknowledged and which leads to the substitution of real, genuine and scientific values for fanciful, ceremonial and pseudo values. Ayres concludes what is probably his last book, *Toward a Reasonable Society* (1962), with a defense of industrialism and the industrial way of life which "is a way of life to which modern man has dedicated himself because it is the epitome of the real values which take their meaning from the life process of mankind. And its supreme value is hope—a hope, warranted by past achievements—of a far better life next year for our-

---

[33] *Ibid.*, p. 409.

selves, in the next century for our children's children, and in the next millenium for all mankind."[34]

Ayres's Critique of Orthodox Economics

Ayres is not unaware of the contributions of economists since the time of the Physiocrats and Adam Smith. He explains that "classical political economy was convincing because it achieved a prodigious feat. It found meaning of a sort in the hurly-burly of modern economic life."[35] This meaning was tied in with the concept of the price system or market mechanism. The early economists worked out theories of price, interest, rent and wages and revealed the interconnections between these items in economic life. According to the interpretation of the classical economists it was these interconnections or relationships which together constituted the price system—a system that was said to organize and guide all economic activities. The marginal concept, originating in Ricardo's work, was given broader theoretical significance by Menger, Jevons, J. B. Clark and others and made a part of the theory of the price system. In other words marginalism rounded out the science of economics as it was viewed by Adam Smith and other classical economists. There is no intention on Ayres's part to dispense entirely with the work of the founders and expositors of classical and neo-classical economics. What Ayres objects to are the deficiencies of this type of economics which have been passed on to later generations of economists, and which still greatly influence their work.

These deficiencies of classical and neo-classical economics included taking the existing economic system as it was, without any special concern for its evolutionary development, and treating it as a complex of relationships which is basically organized by the price system. No account was taken of the underlying technological foundation of economic life which did much to shape the business superstructure. Not being aware of both the business and technological processes, which together constitute the economic system, the orthodox economists of the late eighteenth and nineteenth centuries assumed that there was a basic harmony underlying the strife and conflicts observed in daily economic activities. These orthodox economists did not see the disequilibrium between the price system and the industrial system, a disequilibrium which revealed itself in the contradiction between the pecuniary or unreal values created by the

[34] *Toward a Reasonable Society*, p. 294.
[35] *The Theory of Economic Progress*, p. 20.

price or business system and the technological or genuine values produced by the industrial or technological system. As a consequence of these deficiencies in the orthodox view or interpretation of the economic system, the economics of the classicists and neo-classicists became obsessed with prices and other pecuniary matters —with the price or market mechanism—an obsession which, Ayres asserts, has continued to dominate conventional economics up to the present. In other words, orthodox economics has emphasized, and continues to emphasize, the importance of the economy's financial flows to the neglect of its more fundamental real flows. Consequently, for orthodox economists of the past and the present, economics in the final analysis becomes a science of price or wealth.

A further deficiency of orthodox economics arose from the fact that, when price and not industry is taken as the point of departure economic analysis turns to consumers and a vague subjectivistic notion of utility or mental satisfaction. Behind price is demand and behind demand is utility which is asserted by the orthodox economist to be a reflection of wants arising from the inner nature of mankind. Lionel Robbins, the dean of economic orthodoxy, puts the matter very well when he states that "there is but one end of activity—the maximizing of satisfaction [utility.]"[36] Since little can be done, however, with the introspective concept of utility, the orthodox economist promptly proceeds to abandon his subjectivistic notion of utility or satisfaction by stating that "Economics takes all ends for granted."[37] In the hands of the orthodox economists economics becomes only a study of the disposal of scarce resources which have alternative uses. In Robbins's own words, "the subject-matter of Economics is essentially a series of relationships—relationships between ends conceived as the possible objectives of conduct, on the one hand, and the technical and social environment on the other. Ends as such do not form part of this subject-matter. Nor does the technical and social environment. It is the relationships between these things and not the things in themselves which are important for the economist."[38] Not being satisfied with narrowing the boundaries of economics by reducing human wants to "utility," a Platonic absolute or essence beyond inductive scrutiny, the orthodox economist proceeds to wrest the economic system from its cultural (social and technical) moorings by asserting that the method *par excellence* by which economic

---

[36] Lionel Robbins, *op. cit.*, p. 15 fn.
[37] *Ibid.*, p. 31 fn.
[38] *Ibid.*, p. 38

behavior is to be studied is to retreat to the land of the "isolated individual." Again Robbins puts this very clearly by stating that "it is clear that the phenomena of the exchange economy itself can only be explained by going behind such relationships and invoking the operation of those laws of choice which are best seen when contemplating the behaviour of the isolated individual."[39] Present day orthodox economists might not state these issues so clearly or so simply as Robbins does, but in Ayres's opinion orthodox economics as far as its basics are concerned has not moved beyond Robbins's position as originally stated in his well-known essay of 1932.

A further deficiency of orthodox economics in Ayres's opinion is the theory of productivity imputation which underlies the orthodox marginal theory of distribution. According to this theory of distribution labor and capital earn or receive as compensation their marginal contributions. In a competitive market the forces of supply and demand bring it about that each factor of production receives a return equal to its contribution at the margin. Associated with this theory of distribution is the concept of imputed productivity. Labor, capital and entrepreneurial ability are each held to be productive or creative and therefore to be the source of a special contribution to total output. Ayres denies the validity of the concept of creativity of the instruments of production. He asserts that factors of production do not individually "create" product.[40] No one creates anything individually but only as one of a number of factors responsible for total production. Ayres explains that total output is the "causal consequence of the functioning of that society as a whole." To assign agency or productivity to any particular individual or other factor of production is to be the victim of a "myth of creativity." The theory of imputation which assigns specific productivity to labor and capital is a distributive formula which is based on a misconception of the process of production. What makes the modern economy productive is not labor or abstinence but the advanced industrial technology. Behind this technology are research and development which are the principal agents of technological change. And behind research and development are education and pure science.

Ayres raises the question: Why are some people better off than others? His answer is not that those who are better off or receive

---

[39] *Ibid.*, p. 20.
[40] C. E. Ayres, "Ideological Responsibility," *Journal of Economic Issues*, Vol. 1, Nos. 1 and 2, June 1967, p. 6.

larger incomes are more "productive" or "creative" than those who receive smaller incomes. Highly skilled technicians are paid more than unskilled common laborers because they have scarce skills and know-how which aid the technological process, but not because they are individually creative or productive. Technicians and engineers use our accumulated science and industrial technology for which they are not individually responsible, and which enable these technicians and engineers to further the technological process. To say that the market forces give the technicians and engineers what they create or produce at the margin is in Ayres's opinion nonsense. The theory of productivity imputation, however, is not "utterly irrational and obstructive," for, if it were, the economy and the community would have long ago disappeared. The idea that the free market assigns to each factor of production what it creates, even though it is in itself unsound, did perform a service in the late eighteenth and early nineteenth centuries. This false idea encouraged individuals to produce more, and it did give rise to more economic progress than would have occurred if the theories of distribution held in the Middle Ages or in antiquity had prevailed in the eighteenth and nineteenth centuries.

When Ayres finds that the marginal productivity theory of distribution and its associated doctrine of productivity imputation are based on a myth of creativity, he is not dispensing with the marginal principle or concept. No one can seriously doubt the usefulness of the marginal concept in the fields of production and consumption. The marginal concept unrelated to any theory of imputed creativity or productivity is a useful concept to explain some of the behavior of producers and consumers. In the field of production economics the combining of different resources is necessarily related to the concept of marginal units of resources. But all this has nothing to do with the assignment or imputation of specific creativity or productivity to individual factors of production.

According to Ayres's interpretation our distributive system is merely an institutional arrangement. If some get more than others it is because our institutional structure permits this outcome. The rich are rich and the poor are poor not because the rich are very productive and the poor hardly productive at all, but because our "conventional wisdom" induces the poor to accept the institutional arrangements under which the rich get more and the poor get less. We can either change our institutional arrangements drastically so that the rich get less income and the poor more, or we can as in the Welfare State merely tax the rich and transfer income to the poor. It is Ayres's inclination to accept the second arrangement. "We favor the Welfare State because it tends to give the whole community what the whole community creates, and in doing so gives the community the greatest possible encouragement to create more, so that all of us taken together will be better off than anybody has ever been before."[41]

While Ayres does not reject the body of useful concepts and tools with which every economist needs to be equipped before he can effectively carry on an analysis of the current economic situation, he does reject the features or aspects of orthodox economics discussed above. He repudiates orthodox economics as a way of thinking, as a way of interpreting economic behavior, and as a way of handling the problem of values. Ayres deplores the orthodox economist's obsession with price phenomena, his unwillingness to broaden the scope of economics enough to include the technological process, and his failure to grapple satisfactorily with the value problem. He considers to be unfortunate the inclination of the orthodox economists to reduce economics, in its purist form, to mere "economizing" or choosing among alternative uses of scarce resources. When the orthodox economist makes economics the "science of choice," he substitutes a state of the mind for the world of reality. From Ayres's point of view this is the consequence of the orthodox economist's unwitting acceptance of the outmoded subjectivistic philosophy of idealism as the underpinning of his science rather than the new realistic philosophy of pragmatism.

Ayres's Concept of Economics

Ayres does not deny that people make choices among alternative uses of scarce resources as they seek to take care of their wants. He emphasizes the point, however, that choosing among alternatives, or economizing, always goes on within a cultural milieu or framework. Mankind does not live in isolation but rather in cultural association. For Ayres economics is the study of the part of culture that deals with the use of scarce resources to achieve the ends of individuals and groups which are culturally determined. He states that "Modern Western civilization, centering in Europe and America, is conspicuous for the degree of elaboration to which it has carried the organization of the material affairs of life. This, indeed,

---

[41] C. E. Ayres, *op. cit.*, p. 11.

is its distinguishing mark, and it is this which has called into being the 'science of economics.' In a more special and precise sense, therefore, economics is the study of the tremendously intricate and far-flung organization by virtue of which modern Western society gets its living."[42] Essentially economics is then a theory of the economic order or system, or as Ayres puts it, "Economics is a study of the economy." The economist's "chief interest is in trying to make out what sort of thing 'the economy' is, what sort of forces shape and modify its pattern, and what sort of problems it raises that call for community decisions."[43] Ayres explains that all the different economic activities of the nation fit together so as to constitute a "system" or "economic order." Since he is primarily interested in western nations, the economic system or order with which Ayres primarily deals is the capitalist economy. In his hands economics becomes a study of the capitalism which is the main concern of the American people.

Although there is much order in the functioning of the American capitalist system, there is also a great deal of conflict. The basic conflict is between the institutional complex of society and its technological foundation. The institutional complex incorporates the commercial or business process which is concerned with pecuniary or ceremonial values, whereas the technological foundation of society incorporates the science-technological process which gives rise to real, genuine or economic values. This conflict between the commercial and industrial aspects of the economic system brings into being an "unreasonable" society based upon inherited authority, hierarchical status, entrenched privilege, class distinctions and economic inequality and injustice. The adjustment of the business or commercial process to the underlying technology of the economic system is slow, and the lack of adjustment is the source of the maldistribution of income and economic instability. The current economic situation that Ayres analyzes is the initial state of things which he finds before him. He finds this initial or current state of economic affairs to be unsatisfactory in many important ways. At the same time he observes the American people endeavoring to change this unsatisfactory initial state. Socially conscious business, labor, farm and consumer leaders are taking thought about how to improve the current state of the economy. They are looking forward

---

[42] *The Problem of Economic Order*, p. 3.
[43] *The Industrial Economy*, p. viii.

to a future state of the economy in which the institutional super-structure of the economy will be fairly well harmonized with its technological foundation. Various groups in the American community are seeking to plan their economic future and to construct what Ayres has described as a "reasonable society." In such a society real or technological values would replace pecuniary or ceremonial values, and inherited authority, hierarchical status, entrenched privilege and class distinctions would be eliminated.

The economic system is an evolving process which is moving from its current or initial state of economic affairs to some future or emerging state or condition. What can the economist say about this process of movement or development from an initial to a future state of the economic system? Are there any laws of development which can be used to explain the developing economic process? If the term "law" is used to mean some recurring uniformity such as the laws of diminishing utility, of demand, or of decreasing returns which have been worked out in the area of pure economics, then there are no such laws applicable to the development of the economic system. Ayres explains that there are certain broad generalizations or "basic principles" that can be applied to the process of economic development.[44] These generalizations include the observation that the process of economic development is indivisible and irresistible since it is based on a technological revolution that is spreading over the entire world, and that can be indefinitely resisted by no nation. In addition, Ayres asserts that the technological revolution spreads in inverse proportion to institutional resistance, that the most important factor in economic development is the educational level of the community, and that the technological revolution brings its own universal values (real or genuine values) into being to the exclusion of non-universal, irrational or ceremonial values.

The Logic of Economic Development

More important than these basic principles of economic development for throwing light on the nature of the evolution of the economic system is the logic of economic or cultural development which Ayres finds at work in the process of economic development. The logic of cultural development is the course that a cultural process will probably follow because of the influence of various factors at

---

[44] *The Theory of Economic Progress*, "Foreword—1962," Second Edition, 1962, p. xviii.

work in the cultural environment. Cultural evolution is not a blind, directionless, or haphazard development which follows no pattern whatsoever. As Ayres has put it, we cannot deny "any sort of pattern in cultural development. . . . the development of culture exhibits pattern."[45] Culture is not a "sheer hodge-podge conglomeration." He explains that "The inescapable fact is that human experience does manifest a development pattern of some sort. To close one's eyes to it is simply to go blind."[46] What ties together the pattern of cultural development in general and economic development in particular is a logic of development. Ayres explains that the cultural process and other social phenomena have patterns that "come into existence, and grow, and change, by a logic of their own—that is, by processes of quite a different character from that of individual behavior."[47] When the economist turns to the part of the total cultural process which is the economic process he raises the questions: "What are the forces that have shaped the industrial economy and are still shaping it? What is the logic of the process that is manifest in the industrial economy? In short, what does the industrial economy mean, as a social phenomenon?"[48]

The cultural process develops in accordance with its own inner logic which derives from the presence of mankind and certain environmental factors which are cultural imperatives. In any cultural situation these environmental factors function as imperatives or guides which necessarily influence or determine the direction in which cultural development takes place. For example, in a cultural situation where men are living on river banks where reed-type plants grow, it is logical to expect that sooner or later wind musical instruments (flutes or whistles) will be developed. Likewise, where men dwell in wooded areas near bodies of water the logic of cultural development will point to the emergence of dugouts and other means of transportation by water along with navigational aids. It is not inevitable in the above-mentioned cultural situations that a particular type of wind musical instrument or method of water transportation will be developed, but it is highly probable that the development of musical instruments and methods of transportation by water will follow certain logical lines as determined by environmental factors.

---

[45] *The Theory of Economic Progress*, p. 123.
[46] *The Divine Right of Capital*, p. 186.
[47] *The Industrial Economy*, p. 40.
[48] *Ibid.*, p. 42.

Applying the logic of cultural development or evolution to the American economic system, Ayres is able to indicate in a broad kind of way the course this system will probably follow as it moves from its current or initial state to another state in the not too distant future. The cultural factors or imperatives of the current American economic situation are large business enterprises, large trade unions and farm organizations, and a large federal government, all of which possess considerable economic power. Other cultural imperatives are the inhibitory business process and the developing, changing, inherently revolutionary technological process. Ayres's logic of economic evolution points in the direction of further technological change as industrial technology becomes more complex, and a further restriction of the free market mechanism as the major economic interest groups seek to consolidate their power positions. The logic of economic evolution also points in the direction of a larger role for the federal government as it endeavors to reduce conflicts among the major economic power groups, and as it seeks to remove the imbalance between mass production and mass consumption. An enhanced role for the federal government in economic affairs will sooner or later lead to more economic planning as a substitute in part for free market operations. As Ayres sees it, national economic planning will probably be carried on within the framework of the existing capitalist system as it is done in various West European countries today. Under a program for national economic planning the business system or process will be more effectively adjusted to the technological process. Such adjustments will herald the decline of ceremonial or fanciful values and the spread of real or technological values as the logic of economic evolution carries American capitalism closer towards the ideal of a "reasonable society," which is Ayres's future economic state of affairs.

Unlike Karl Marx, Ayres finds no laws of capitalist development leading to the inevitable demise of capitalism and the transition to socialism. Neither Veblen nor Ayres duplicates Marx's interest in the laws of capitalist development. In place of any such laws both Veblen and Ayres substitute a logic of capitalist development which is non-teleological in nature. In the hands of Veblen as with Ayres the logic of capitalist development has no inevitable outcome. Veblen asserted that the demise of capitalism was inevitable, but what came after capitalism was not inevitable. It could be either fascism or socialism. Ayres does not foresee the end of capitalism, and what will be the next stage in capitalist development is uncertain.

Criticisms of Ayres's Instrumental Economics

Orthodox or standard economists' criticisms of Ayres's economics move in three directions. The first line of orthodox criticism asserts that Ayres, like Veblen, repudiates economic theory and puts nothing in its place. According to this criticism Ayres divides the whole of economics into "price theory" (which is bad) and "institutional economics" (which is good).[49] As has already been explained, this criticism arises from a misinterpretation of Ayres's position with regard to micro-economics and macro-economics. For the analysis of some problems such as tax incidence Ayres would find micro-economics very essential, just as he would find macro-economics essential for an analysis of employment policy. Ayres does not repudiate or dispense with the basic concepts or analytical tools of the micro-economist and the macro-economist. What Ayres objects to is their obsession with price phenomena, their neglect of the technological factor in economic life, and their static intellectual underpinning which is derived from the outmoded philosophical position that nourishes standard economics.

A second orthodox criticism of Ayres's economics is to the effect that when he discusses "ends" or "wants" Ayres is a religious moralizer and not a scientist. As one critic phrases it, unlike Ayres, "Orthodoxy [standard economists] does not go behind [human] wants for the reason that it pretends to no omniscient ability to decide what should be wanted."[50] Institutional economists, including Ayres, are criticized on the ground that they do not have a key to the question of what man should want. This criticism is thoroughly groundless because Ayres does not purport to tell the American people what economic ends they should want. Ayres analyzes these people as individuals who have wants which are culturally determined. Individuals who participate in economic activity as producers, workers or consumers are want-bearing individuals. As such they are for Ayres the basic data of economic science which should be analyzed. He analyzes individuals and their wants because these wants affect how they function as participants in economic affairs. Nowhere does Ayres tell people what they should want. He observes that individuals in the United States and else-

---

[49] Benjamin Higgins, "Some Introductory Remarks on Institutionalism and Economic Development," *The Southwestern Social Science Quarterly*, Vol. 41, No. 1, June 1960, p. 17.

[50] Jack E. Robertson, "Folklore of Institutional Economics," *The Southwestern Social Science Quarterly*, Vol. 41, No. 1, June 1960, p. 30.

where want economic abundance, security, equality, freedom and excellence. It is a complete misreading of Ayres's work to say that he tells individuals that they should want these particular "ends" or "values." Why should he? Anyone can observe that, independently of Ayres and all other neo-institutionalists, many people in Western Europe and the United States as elsewhere are openly and vigorously pressing for the satisfaction of these wants or values.

Ayres deplores the position of orthodox or standard economists which leads them not to analyze the various wants that many of the people in Western Europe, the United States and elsewhere now have. Not to analyze these wants and their impact on economic life is from Ayres's point of view quite indefensible. Not to analyze the impact on economic life of the producer-managed wants of consumers which have little or no social utility, or the importance of unsatisfied wants for clean air, pure water, and adequate living conditions would be described by Ayres as nothing less than a serious default on the part of orthodox economists.

A third orthodox criticism of Ayres's economics asserts that Ayres is the victim of a cultural monism which leads him to overemphasize the importance of the technological factor in economic life and to underemphasize the significance of the business system and the businessman. Critics along this line are the victims of the Schumpeterian influence which leads them to agree with Joseph Schumpeter that businessmen are really creative innovators who respond to profit inducements and in so doing improve the economic system.[51] These critics do not accept Ayres's statement that businessmen are only permissively creative while technology is actively creative. Ayres asserts that businessmen under capitalism are a necessary but not a sufficient cause of economic progress. As long as a nation preserves a capitalist system there will be both private property and private business enterprise. Both private property and private business enterprise will be necessary features of the capitalist economy. If they were to disappear the nation's economic system could no longer be described as capitalistic. In the Soviet communist system private property in the means of production and private business enterprise have largely disappeared. What is common to both Soviet communism and American capitalism is large-scale, automated industrial technology. In both types of economic system property relations and forms of economic enterprise are institutional arrange-

---

[51] Manuel Gottlieb, "Clarence E. Ayres and a Larger Economic Theory," *The Southwestern Social Science Quarterly*, Vol. 41, No. 1, June 1960, p. 36.

ments which Ayres regards as secondary or permissive, while industrial technology is primary. Whatever the property and economic enterprise arrangements are, in Ayres's opinion, they can be only indirectly creative or productive, whereas industrial technology is directly creative of national output. Since industrial technology is in Ayres's view primary and therefore more basic than institutional arrangements, he cannot agree with his orthodox critics that under capitalism the business system is on a par with industrial technology as a source of economic abundance and economic progress. Ayres would assert that his work does not suffer from his acceptance of cultural monism. Instead it is his critics who are disadvantaged by a failure to understand the nature of culture and the cultural process.

Instrumental Economics: An Evaluation

Prominent among Ayres's contributions to institutionalism is his clarification of its philosophical foundation. The philosophical position of an economist is important because it determines his intellectual orientation or his way of viewing the world in general and the economic system in particular. Orthodox or standard economics continues to be influenced by the static, common sense, pre-Deweyian philosophy which has had much to do with shaping the intellectual orientation or mental set of the classical and neo-classical economists from Adam Smith to Alfred Marshall. Veblen broke away from the philosophical position of the orthodox economists and replaced their static, idealist philosophy with a pragmatic philosophy. Veblen brought to economics an evolutionary philosophy with a strong pragmatic bent. Born two years before John Dewey, Veblen in his formative years did not have the advantage, as did Ayres, of being able to absorb the philosophy of pragmatism as it took shape in the hands of John Dewey and other pragmatists. It is clear that the modernized version of Hegel's evolutionary philosophy that underlies Veblen's economic thinking is very close to Dewey's pragmatic philosophy. Veblen, however, did not clearly indicate to his readers what the impact of the pragmatic philosophy upon his work was. He did not point out that the pragmatist holds that the universe originated not in order but in flux, that conflict and not harmony is the basic feature of human activity, that thinking and doing are indissolubly associated, that the cultural process has its own logic of development, and that economic values are grounded in science and technology. While Veblen held many views that were close to those of the pragmatists, he never openly embraced the philosophy of pragmatism. This philosophy leads to social activism in the service of humanity. Veblen always remained somewhat equivocal about the role of the scientist as an activist in human affairs.

At times Veblen showed a deep disinterest in the future welfare of mankind. He assumed the pose of a disinterested scientist who did not hold a functional view of his science. At these times Veblen's work appeared to be dominated by an idle curiosity which left no room for the view that economics had a function to perform, namely, to contribute to human welfare. At other times when Veblen was discussing the dichotomy between serviceable and disserviceable institutions, or between pecuniary and economic values, he focussed his attention on how serviceable institutions and economic values could contribute to race survival or the improvement of the life process. Here he came close to the view that economics should be a functional science in the service of humanity. There was a dichotomy within Veblen that pitted the disinterested, misanthropic scientist with no special concern for mankind against the reformer-scientist yearning to improve economic science so that it could more effectively contribute to the welfare of mankind. Veblen died without ever resolving this significant issue.

Ayres openly accepts the philosophy of pragmatism as the proper philosophical foundation of institutional economics. The pragmatic philosophy shapes institutional economics as a way of thinking about the economic world. "Economics," Ayres observes, "is more than a field of inquiry; it is a way of thinking."[52] In his opinion orthodox economics, based on idealist pre-Deweyian philosophy, is the wrong way of thinking about the economic world, whereas institutional economics based on the pragmatic philosophy is the right way of thinking about this world. This latter pragmatic institutionalist way of thinking leads the economist to view the economy as an evolving process in which the technological process plays the dominant role as it moves the economic system towards an abundance of rational and scientifically based values. It is this pragmatic institutionalist way of thinking that causes the institutional economist such as Ayres to regard his science as a functional science in the service of humanity.

A second major contribution of Ayres is his handling of the

---

[52] *The Theory of Economic Progress*, p. 4.

value problem which is closely related to his work on the philosophical underpinnings of institutional economics. One of the least developed parts of Veblen's evolutionary economics was his treatment of the value problem. He made a beginning by contrasting pecuniary or market values with economic or real values. Veblen cut through the orthodox economists' obsession with prices and price values in the search for a more fundamental kind of value. He did not find the orthodox discussion of use value based upon a highly introspective or subjectivistic concept of utility as a very promising lead for the analysis of the value problem. Instead he turned to the concept of use value in the sense of a good that would contribute to race survival or which would "further the life process." Veblen was looking for a location of value other than the price system and for a standard of value other than price. When Veblen asserted that technology or the state of the industrial arts was the strategic factor in the production of goods and services, he came very close to saying that the location of value was in the technological process, and that the criterion of value was technological in the sense that one could determine whether or not a good was a value by subjecting it to scientific or technological tests as to its ability to contribute to race survival or the well-being of mankind.

With regard to the value problem Ayres is much more explicit than Veblen and later institutionalists. He makes the value problem the central concern of economics, and in his hands economics becomes the science of value. Following the pragmatist line Ayres finds the location of economic values in the technological process which operates behind the price system. The standard or criterion of value is not some vague introspective concept of personal satisfaction or utility unrelated to the cultural environment but supposedly related to an imaginary inner nature of mankind, or to what Wesley C. Mitchell described as the "dim inner realm of consciousness."[53] When Ayres states that the criterion of value is technological what he means is that goods can be subjected to scientific laboratory or other tests to determine whether or not they contribute to the general welfare. Bread is an economic value not because it looks good, smells good, tastes good or because the Bible calls it the staff of life. Bread is an economic value because it can be scientifically shown that it has nutritional elements which contribute to race survival

---

[53] W. C. Mitchell, "The Role of Money in Economic Theory," *The Backward Art of Spending Money* (New York: McGraw-Hill Book Co., 1937) p. 173.

or the maintenance of the life process. Tobacco is not a real or genuine economic value, not because it smells, tastes, or looks bad, but because it contains elements which can be scientifically demonstrated to undermine health and so not contribute to the welfare of mankind.

Ayres's position with regard to the value problem has always been that of the institutional economists. Ayres's real, genuine, rational, or scientific values are the same as Veblen's "economic values," John R. Commons's "reasonable values," Wesley C. Mitchell's "urgently needed goods," and John M. Clark's "service values." But these other institutionalists did not deal with the value problem in any exhaustive manner. It has remained for Ayres to complete their work on the value problem, and in so doing to make economics a value-oriented science in the sense that it deals with people who have culturally-determined values which guide or direct their activities. These value-bearing people in the sector of society that is concerned with the production and distribution of goods and services are the objective data that the economist analyzes and interprets. When Ayres makes economics a value-oriented science he converts it into a vital social science that political, social and economic leaders can turn to in their efforts to improve the lot of mankind.

Ayres's instrumental economics is not a normative science. He does not set up norms of conduct to be followed in the world of economic affairs. As a scientist he studies values only as he finds them expressed by individuals who participate in economic activities. The values, fanciful or genuine, that people have are objective data which can be subjected to objective scrutiny by the economist. Ayres's instrumental economics is an empirical, positive science the findings of which are subjected to scientific evidence. When Ayres personally wishes to advocate the acceptance of certain values, he drops his role as a scientist and takes on the role of a reformer. Any economist is free to do this without degrading his work as a scientist. Ayres, like other institutionalists, is interested in economic policy and reform and in making the economic world a better world. This is because he holds a functional view of his instrumental economics, which in itself remains a positive science.

Although Ayres has borrowed the basics of his instrumental economics from Veblen, he has excluded from his own economics various unacceptable parts of Veblen's work. He has found unacceptable Veblen's concept of a primitive utopia of savagery or early stone age in which the instinct of workmanship was supposed to have been given free play while the instinct of acquisition was somehow kept submerged.[54] In Ayres's opinion Veblen's views in this connection represented bad anthropology. In line with modern psychological developments Ayres also dispenses with Veblen's outmoded use of instincts. He also does not accept Veblen's position that close contacts between the workers and the machines will induce them to develop a matter of fact outlook on the world. In Ayres's opinion this is an oversimplified analysis of the impact of the machine process on mankind. As has already been pointed out, Ayres does not accept Veblen's interpretation of the course of capitalist development, and thinks instead in terms of saving capitalism rather than officiating at its demise. Both Ayres and Veblen see economic evolution pointing in the direction of more economic planning, but whereas Veblen's planning would move in the direction of a socialist regime Ayres's planning looks in the direction of a reformed capitalism.

The Limitations of Ayres's Instrumental Economics

What has enabled Ayres to make significant contributions to the development of institutional economic thought has also been a source of limitation or deficiency in his economic thinking. This factor has been his absorbing interest in the relations between philosophy and economics. His abiding interest in the philosophical foundations of economics has taken up so much of his time and energy he has failed to move in directions that would have strengthened his instrumental economics. Ayres does not always clearly indicate his position with respect to orthodox or standard economics. When he emphasizes the limitations of standard economics he gives some of his readers (judging by the reactions of his critics) the false impression that all standard economics is "bad" economics, and that he would dispense with it even as a body of tools or concepts used for analytical purposes. A reading of Ayres's writings very quickly shows that he makes much use of the analytical tools of micro-economics and macro-economics. More detailed statements by Ayres with regard to this matter would have prevented much of this misinterpretation on the part of his readers and critics.

---

[54] C. E. Ayres, "Institutionalism and Economic Development," *The Southwestern Social Science Quarterly*, Vol. 41, No. 1, June 1960, p. 45.

A more serious limitation of Ayres's economics is the atmosphere of detachment that hovers over his work and leads him to give insufficient attention to recent developments in economic science and their application to the major economic problems of the times. For example, one finds in Ayres's work no references to developments relating to econometrics, input-output economics, linear programming, game theory, systems analysis, national economic budgeting and the like. Ayres is harshly critical of mathematical economics, and with respect to some of the so-called refinements in economic theory produced by mathematical economists Ayres stands on firm ground. In some cases he has good reason to fulminate against what he describes as the "esoteric formulas of scholastic orthodoxy."[55] His observation that "in recent decades economic orthodoxy has become increasingly recondite, and professional economists have barricaded themselves from criticism behind the formidable complexities of their trade" carries considerable weight.[56] But condemnation of the excesses of mathematical economists is no excuse for ignoring the progress made in such fields as econometrics, inter-industry economics, linear programming, benefit-cost analysis and national economic budgeting. Where recent developments in these fields are important is in the area of economic policy making, about which Ayres does not have much to say.

Ayres does not ignore issues and policies, but he seems somewhat impatient with them. When he recommends economic planning as a means of solving economic problems, he has little to say about the nature or significance of economic planning. There is no discussion of planning techniques or procedures such as the use of input-output matrices and econometrical models. Nor is there any discussion of the planning experience of such western democratic countries as France, Holland, Norway and Sweden, in which national economic programming or budgeting has been carried on with considerable success. Major issues such as a national incomes policy or the division of resources between the public and private sectors of the economy have not engaged Ayres's attention. He has himself explained that economists' "interpretations [of the economic process] point toward certain policies. Thus every economist is an advocate of the policy that flows, by logical necessity, from his interpretation of the facts. . . . it is a disservice to the interpretation not to give the clearest

---

[55] *The Theory of Economic Progress*, p. 307.
[56] *Ibid.*, pp. 306-307.

possible statement of its logical consequences."[57] Institutional economics must compete with other types of economics in the area of economic policy measures and recommendations. If institutional economists have nothing more to suggest in the area of policy making than what is already being suggested by the Keynesians, then their economics will not command much public attention. Ayres realizes this, and he is prepared to move beyond Keynesian interventionism to national economic planning. His failure, however, to enlarge upon his views in this connection is a serious limitation of his instrumental economics.

The limitations or deficiencies of Ayres's work discussed above do not in any significant way detract from his major contribution which has been to reveal the philosophical foundations of institutional economics. Other economists working in the institutionalist tradition have in recent years offset the deficiencies in Ayres's work. It remains that no other institutionalist has shown as clearly as has Ayres that institutional economics is not only a field of inquiry but also a way of thinking about what Ayres has described as "the larger realities" of the economic world which lie behind the price system of the modern industrial economy. Ayres feels a deep responsibility to inform the public about these realities so that we may all the sooner push beyond the Welfare State to the Creative State with its "happy, healthy . . . well-informed . . . [and] superbly productive community."[58] As a true pragmatist Ayres remains highly optimistic about the future of our industrial economy. The process of the industrialization of the West has by no means come to an end. On the contrary we can look forward to a further industrialization of the modern industrial economy. We are, says Ayres, now living, as a consequence of the technological revolution, in "a golden age of scientific enlightenment and artistic achievement." To achieve further progress along these lines we must not only be prepared for profound cultural changes, but we must also go far beyond the conventional wisdom of economic orthodoxy which is, in Ayres's opinion, a serious impediment to an understanding of the nature of the modern industrial economy.

---

[57] *The Industrial Economy*, p. ix.
[58] "Ideological Responsibility," p. 11.

CHAPTER IV

JOHN KENNETH GALBRAITH'S
ECONOMICS OF AFFLUENCE

In recent years the way in which the American economy functions and its influence on the quality of life have become questions
of widespread popular interest. Serious questions have been raised
not only about the economy's ability to achieve a high and sustained
growth rate and low unemployment, but also about its capacity
for sustaining a way of living that elevates quality over quantity,
and makes the private market system the servant and not the master
of the consuming public. Prominent among the critics of recent
economic trends in the United States is John K. Galbraith. As a
professor at the most prestigious American university, director of
the Office of Price Administration during the Second World War,
editor of *Fortune* magazine, ambassador to India, President of the
Americans for Democratic Action, and adviser to the Kennedy
Administration, Galbraith has been in a unique position to observe
the American economy functioning in war and peace, and to analyze
the flow of academic and non-academic economic thought. Galbraith
is today one of the most widely known American economists,
largely because he has taken his case not to the economics profession
but to the general public. Public interest in Galbraith and his economic views has been stimulated by three widely read products from
his witty and satirical pen—*American Capitalism, The Theory of
Countervailing Power* (1952), *The Affluent Society* (1958) and
The New Industrial State (1967). The public interest in these volumes has been so extensive as to make Galbraith something of a
literary phenomenon with some of his books reaching the top of the
best seller lists. There is no doubt that he has sparked the interest and intrigued the minds of businessmen, workers, politicians
and even housewives, who in ordinary circumstances pay little attention to what economists have to say. He has raised economic discussion to a public level not witnessed before in the current century.

In order to understand Galbraith's "qualitative economics" one must first inquire into the two basic preconceptions that dominate his economic theorizing. These preconceptions relate to his concept of social and economic reality and to his theory of human behavior. The economic and social reality with which Galbraith is concerned is an evolving process subject to continuous change. Economic reality is not a static set of circumstances but is, instead, a flow of circumstances in a constant state of flux. Ever since his first major publication, *Modern Competition and Business Policy*, appeared in 1938, Galbraith has been mainly interested in interpreting the changing economic reality or "the real world," which he asserts is not the world analyzed in economics textbooks and refined economic treatises.[1] The real economic world is taken by Galbraith to be an emergent thing which, like Alfred N. Whitehead's "event," incorporates the past, present and future. Economic reality is not a static entity that can be caught frozen on the glass slide of a biologist or within the conventional limits of some mathematical formula. Other economists have dealt with parts of economic reality but have ignored the "movement" or "larger change" which runs through all the real economic world. Galbraith explains that after a period of time he became primarily interested in "a much greater and very closely articulated process of change."[2] The key to an understanding of Galbraith's economics of opulence or affluence is his concern with technological change and its impact on institutions and the minds of men.

The Role of Technological Imperatives

The active factor that subjects the economic world to constant change is technology which Galbraith defines as "the systematic application of scientific or other organized knowledge to practical tasks."[3] According to this interpretation technology is a cultural force or "imperative" which exists independently of mankind and so has a dynamic or compulsion of its own. In Galbraith's own words technology has "an initiative of its own" which can revolutionize the structure and functioning of the economic system. We live, says

---

[1] H. S. Dennison and J. K. Galbraith, *Modern Competition and Business Policy* (New York: Oxford University Press, 1938) pp. 19-25.

[2] John Kenneth Galbraith, *The New Industrial State* (Boston: Houghton Mifflin Co., 1967) p. vii.

[3] *Ibid.*, p. 12.

Galbraith, in a world of "technological compulsions" which define to a certain extent how men act and how the economic system is shaped. For example, twentieth century industrial technology necessarily leads to the emergence of large-scale enterprises which dominate markets and states, and which call into being "organization men" who help bend mankind to the demands or needs of the large mature industrial enterprises. Technology even rides roughshod over ideology, and gives rise to the same basic "industrial system" in capitalist, socialist and communist societies. There is a "march of events" giving expression to technological progress, which forces essentially the same industrial pattern on all large, advanced countries.[4] Although men are responsible for technological change, accumulated change of this type becomes a cultural imperative with a dynamic of its own. This change then becomes one of the circumstances over which man does not have complete control, and to which therefore he is forced in the long run to adjust. He is faced by "the clear dictates of circumstance," which he may resist, but which in the long run will work their way out.[5] In attaching so much importance to technological change Galbraith accepts a technological interpretation of economic and social development.

The logic of technological change and progress means that, given a certain state of technological progress, economic and other institutions must inevitably take on a shape that is in conformity with the existing industrial technology. Far from being a willy-nilly, directionless movement, economic and social evolution or development moves within broad limits "defined" by technology. It is for this reason that Galbraith states that modern technology defines the structure and functions of large-scale enterprise and also "defines a growing function of the modern state."[6] He summarizes his views on the role of technology with the statement that "It is part of the vanity of modern man that he can decide the character of his economic system. His area of decision is, in fact, exceedingly small. He could, conceivably, decide whether or not he wishes to have a high level of industrialization. Thereafter the imperatives of organization, technology and planning operate similarly, and we have seen to a broadly similar result, on all societies. Given the

---

[4] John Kenneth Galbraith, *The Affluent Society* (Boston: Houghton Mifflin Co., Mentor Book Edition, 1958) p. 21.

[5] John Kenneth Galbraith, *The Liberal Hour* (Boston: Houghton Mifflin Co., 1960) p. 139.

[6] *Ibid.*, pp. 4-5.

decision to have modern industry, much of what happens is inevitable and the same [in all advanced societies]."[7]

Although Galbraith accepts a technological interpretation of the course of human events, he is not a materialist who takes mankind to be a mere pawn of circumstances. After all, it is man who originates, invents and contributes to technological progress. He is a self-active individual who, however, must live in a hard-and-fast environment where technological circumstances have a dynamic of their own. Unfortunately, Galbraith points out, man is resistant to change and on occasion attempts to run counter to the logic of technological progress. In many ways man is a pretty helpless creature before "the massive onslaught of circumstance," which ceaselessly changes his economic system and forces him to make adjustments or pay a heavy price, which he usually does.

Galbraith's Concept of Human Nature

Galbraith's second basic preconception, relating to the nature of human behavior, is closely related to his preconception concerning the essential nature of economic reality. Galbraith takes man to be largely a creature of habit and inherited ideas and attitudes, whose rationality only infrequently comes to the surface. Galbraith's concept of the individual who is representative of mankind is far removed from the traditional economics textbook concept of a rational person exercising free "will and determination." Man is a social product who is most comfortable with inherited ideas and attitudes. He is resistant to the challenge of change and prefers instead "the conventional wisdom." Since any alteration in underlying circumstances is not squarely faced, "we are guided, in part, by ideas that are relevant to another world; and as a further result we do many things that are unnecessary, some that are unwise, and a few that are insane."[8] In its reaction to the real world mankind is dominated by tradition, myth and illusion which substitute an imaginary world for a real world. This occurs because man is the victim of a cultural lag. Since he is unable to adjust his ideas and attitudes rapidly enough to keep them in touch with the changing economic world, he clings to ideas and attitudes that may have had some relevance to the real world in the past, but are now no longer attuned to the real world of the present. Human behavior consequently exhibits

---

[7] *The New Industrial State*, p. 396.
[8] *The Affluent Society*, p. 14.

much irrationality. Men have strong nostalgic attachments to the past, and prefer the old to the new. Businessmen, politicians and even economists have ideas and attitudes that made some sense in the nineteenth century small-scale competitive world, but which are today "obsolete and impalpable." Far from being the rational beings portrayed in the economics textbooks, businessmen, farmers, workers and consumers are misguided individuals who are attacking real problems with outmoded ideas and attitudes. Mythical or erroneous beliefs, such as that free competitive markets still widely exist, that big business is still subordinate to market influences, or that more production is always good, entrap the public and prevent it from understanding and coping with the major economic issues of the second half of the twentieth century. We are, says Galbraith, victimized by a "system of illusions."

Although, as Galbraith asserts, we have a great "horror of new thought," and suffer the consequences of the greatest of vested interests, namely, the myth-racked mind, he is not prepared to write us off as hopeless victims of mental obsolescence. On the contrary, he is optimistic enough to believe that we can be made aware of the fact that we are the victims of a cultural lag, and that this awareness is the first step towards an escape from the crassly commercialized world in which we live. This is the message that lies behind the mordant wit and biting satire met so frequently on the pages of *American Capitalism*, *The Affluent Society*, *The New Industrial State* and other writings.

This analysis of Galbraith's basic preconceptions reveals that his analysis of the ills of modern economic society is based upon the assumption of a fundamental dichotomy between "circumstances" (reflecting technology) and "wisdom" (man's ideas or understanding of the world around him). Galbraith explains that circumstances (or events) and wisdom (or ideas) have lives of their own, and for a considerable period of time may follow independent and different courses.[9] Whereas circumstances or technology open the door to continuous change, ideas are inherently conservative. When man's wisdom or understanding gets out of step with the march of circumstances, he fails to understand the real nature of economic reality and the problems associated with this reality. This is the situation today, according to Galbraith's interpretation, in which we now find ourselves. We are failing to understand the real nature

[9] *Ibid.*, p. 17.

of the modern industrial system and how we are serving its needs rather than having it serve our needs. Our misunderstanding of the modern industrial system is labelled "conventional wisdom" by Galbraith. It is this obsolescent wisdom based on myth and illusion that leads us to approve an economic system which subordinates the quality of life to the mere possession of the maximum quantity of goods. This has happened because "circumstance has marched far beyond the conventional wisdom."[10] It is Galbraith's purpose to expose this discrepancy or dichotomy between "underlying circumstances" and "outmoded conventional wisdom," and to eliminate the cultural lag into which the public has fallen. The need is to create an "unconventional wisdom" in harmony with the underlying circumstances of the modern industrial system. We will then be in a position to understand the real world and to take steps to escape from the dilemma in which as we produce more goods the quality of life goes down. Galbraith's "unconventional wisdom" is derived from his interpretation of the course of American capitalism since the early years of the present century, with special emphasis upon what has occurred since the end of the Second World War. He hopes that his interpretation of American capitalism will wipe away the myth and illusion which prevent people from realizing the opportunity to live a life in which quality takes precedence over quantity.

The American Economic System 1900-1970

Galbraith's interpretation of the American economic system covers the first six decades of the current century during which there occurred "a vast and autonomous transformation" of the nation's economic system as it moved from a "market economy" to an "organized economy." During this period the American economic system passed through the eras of *laissez-faire* and welfare capitalism, and is currently in the era of "guided capitalism." The era of welfare capitalism of the 1930's coincided with the Keynesian Revolution which undermined the inherited Marshallian economics. Keynes asserted that changes in market prices and interest rates no longer operated as self-correcting forces that would keep the economic system at a full employment equilibrium level. He explained that it was quite possible to have an equilibrium between aggregate demand and aggregate supply at a less than full employment level.

---

[10] *Ibid.*, p. 268.

If full employment levels of production and employment were to be achieved, private expenditures would have to be supplemented by public expenditures financed through government bond sales and not tax increases. The main concern of the 1930's was to increase the level of production and employment. Resource allocation was of very secondary significance. One did not worry about how economic resources were being allocated in the private sector, or between the private and public sectors, when millions of workers could not find employment.

Galbraith points out that the situation has drastically changed since 1945. The problem that was of such great national concern in the 1930's, how to raise production to a sustained full employment level, is now no longer the main issue. The western world has not had a serious unemployment problem (except for minority groups) since 1945. The new problem is the allocation of resources between the private and public sectors, or as Galbraith puts it, "an atrocious allocation of resources between private wants and public needs, especially those of the cities."[11] The resource allocation problem introduces the question of national economic guidance, because resources must somehow be directed into those channels that maximize human welfare. This is why the current era of capitalist evolution is described as the era of "directed" or "guided" capitalism. The era of welfare capitalism in the 1930's never raised the issue of guidance because the government's overriding goal was simply more production and hence more employment. Keynes and his followers of the 1930's, and even later, had no special concern with economic resource allocation. This is why Galbraith describes Keynesian economics as obsolete since it never did, and currently does not, make resource allocation and the quality of life the major issues.

The shift from welfare capitalism to guided capitalism and from preoccupation with increased production to concern for resource allocation has since 1945 been accompanied by a technological revolution which has revolved around the scientific advances of recent decades stimulated in large part by war, defense and space exploration. Galbraith explains that our highly intricate and sophisticated technology, based upon advances in physics and chemistry, has given a new prominence to the large industrial corporation.

---

[11] John Kenneth Galbraith, a review of John Maynard Keynes's *The General Theory of Employment Interest and Money*, New York *Times Book Review*, May 16, 1965, p. 39.

The large corporation had already made considerable progress during the 1920's in reshaping the American economy. While advance on the corporate front was somewhat delayed in the 1930's, since 1945 the large corporations have moved rapidly ahead until today some 500 large corporations dominate the nation's economic system. The current era of guided capitalism is the era of the large corporations which, according to Galbraith's thesis, provide a major part of the economy's guidance, and in so doing have dethroned the consumers and even bent the state to their needs. Although the technological revolution has given us an "economy of opulence" or an "affluent society," we suffer grievously from the fact that our opulence or affluence applies only to private goods and not to public goods. The large industrial corporations in the era of guided capitalism see to it that economic resources are poured abundantly into the private sector and only niggardly into the public sector. The result is a highly commercialized society in which "quantity" overrides "quality," and the higher dimensions of life are largely ignored.

The Large Corporation and Technocratic Capitalism

Galbraith observes that economic developments in the United States in the past 60 years have created a dual economy in which a core or heartland of large-scale corporate enterprise is surrounded by an area of middle-size and small-scale enterprise. In this latter area are found small-scale producers, retailers and craftsmen whose activities are competitive in nature. This means that these individuals and firms are subject to control by the market place. Prices are set by the forces of supply and demand, and each enterprise seeks to maximize its profits within the limits set by the free competitive market. Galbraith has no special concern with these outlying competitive areas of the American economy. The focus of his attention is instead on "the heartland of the modern economy," where the five hundred largest corporations which produce close to half of all the goods and services turned out annually in the United States are responsible for nearly all communications, electric power and transportation, most manufacturing and mining, and a considerable share of retail trade and entertainment. It is this heartland of the modern economy with its few hundred large corporations that Galbraith describes as "the industrial system."[12]

The key organization in the core of the modern economy is not

[12] *The New Industrial State*, p. 10.

the large "entrepreneurial" corporation under the control of a single individual but instead the large "mature corporation" whose stock-holders play no active role since ownership and management have long been separated. The management of the mature corporation is a "collective and imperfectly defined entity" which includes a chairman, president, vice-presidents with important responsibilities, and division or department heads. Not only are ownership and management separated, but also management is frequently sepa-rated from decision making. Management, according to Galbraith's analysis, is not the brain of the mature corporation. The "guiding intelligence" or decision makers of the mature corporation embrace all who bring specialized knowledge, talent or experience to group decision making. This group includes specialists in planning, pro-duction, design, marketing, research, data collection and analysis, finance and the like who operate through corporate committees or groups. Those who because of some special talent or experience participate in group decision making are called by Galbraith the "technostructure" of the mature corporation.[13] This new "decisive factor of production" is the association of men of diverse technical knowledge, experience or other talent, which modern industrial tech-nology and planning require. "It extends from the leadership of the modern industrial enterprise down to just short of the labor force and embraces a large number of people and a large variety of talent. It is on the effectiveness of this organization . . . that the success of the modern business enterprise now depends."[14] Since the corpor-ation chairman, president, and other senior officials usually do not have access to the specialized knowledge and information of the technostructure, they are not likely to run counter to the collective decisions of the technostructure. Whereas the board chairman and other top officials appear to the outside world to manage the cor-poration, usually actual decision making lies with the technostruc-ture. The main function of the corporate chairman and other senior officials who are on the periphery of the technostructure is to provide for corporate continuity by hiring specialized talent and organizing the groups or committees in which the members of the technostruc-ture participate.

Galbraith explains that in the current era of guided capitalism the industrial corporation does not seek to become large in order to secure monopoly profits or to enjoy the economies of scale. The

---

[13] *Ibid.*, p. 71.
[14] *Ibid.*, p. 59.

main reason that corporations are driven to enlarge their size is to have the advantages of planning. The large corporation must plan to minimize risk by controlling its sources of supply, the demand for its products, the sources of its capital, and fluctuations in its prices. In order to achieve these goals, in Galbraith's opinion, "there is no clear upper limit to desirable size. It could be that the bigger the better. The corporate form accommodates this need. Quite clearly it allows the firm to be very, very large."[15]

Galbraith emphasizes the point that the large mature corporations are not controlled by the market. Instead the control is the other way around. These corporations control their markets by substituting industrial planning for the operations of independent free market forces. The large corporation cannot afford to operate in a risky market situation. It requires a heavy investment of capital and a long time elapses between the original conception of a new product, its designing and production and its ultimate sale. The large corporation in the economy's heartland seeks both security from risk and autonomy in operation. Through industrial planning the vagaries of the market place are reduced or eliminated. These vagaries arise from the behavior of prices, consumers, trade unions, aggregate demand and the state.

Fluctuating prices are eliminated by large corporations through informal price arrangements, such as price leadership and collective refraining from cutting prices, which are immune from antitrust attack. There is nothing more important to the large corporations than stable prices which make the price interrelations of corporations reliable. The essence of corporate planning is the search for reliability or the absence of risk. Markets for goods and services are assured by sales methods, principally advertising, which assure a loyal patronage on the part of consumers. In the markets dominated by the large corporation power does not lie with the consumer. The "Accepted Sequence" according to which there is a flow of instruction from the consumer to the producer as to what the consumer wants no longer holds. Instead there is a "Revised Sequence" in which the large producing corporation extends its influence forward to shape consumer attitudes and to induce consumers to want what the corporation is prepared to sell. Ordinary physical wants for food and clothing originate with consumers, but psychological wants for non-necessities are contrived by the producing corpora-

---

[15] *Ibid.*, p. 77.

tion and so originate with it. High pressure sales methods not only assure each successful large corporation an adequate share of the market, but also enlarge total sales. Total consumption must move with total production if prosperity is to reign in the core of the economic system. Since Say's Law no longer works, adequate total consumption can be guaranteed only by convincing consumers that everything produced is worthwhile, and that all that is produced should be consumed. The consumers must not question the production goals of the corporations. And, furthermore, consumers must continue to avoid leisure and work a long week, moonlighting if necessary, in order to have enough income to buy what the large corporation induces them to think they want.

Eliminating or severely restricting the market forces of supply and demand and trussing up the consumers is not enough to guarantee the security of the large corporations. What about the stockholders who own the corporations, the bankers who loan funds to the corporations, and the workers who supply labor? May they not in different ways interfere with the rule of the corporation's technostructure? They could do so unless appropriate steps are taken. Galbraith explains that the stockholders are kept satisfied, and therefore harmless, by making certain as far as it is possible, that enough profits are earned to maintain dividends at an adequate level. An adequate level is one that keeps stockholders from complaining about the technostructure's conduct of the corporation's affairs, and threatening to inquire into these affairs. Bankers are held at bay, and thus out of the corporation's activities, by having the corporation earn enough profits to assure a large flow of retained earnings or undistributed profits. These retained earnings then enable the corporation to finance its own capital investment expansion with a minimum use of outside funds. Bankers can only direct the savings of individuals into government bonds, savings and loan certificates, savings accounts, or into the stocks and bonds of those small business enterprises which are unfortunate enough not to be able to manipulate prices so as to secure for themselves an adequate flow of retained earnings, as do the large mature corporations in the economy's industrial core.

Another problem is the trade unions which supply labor to the large corporations. How have the large corporations been able to bring the trade unions into their managerial net? For decades prior to 1945 the large trade unions had vigorously opposed corporate management as they fought to be an equal participant in industry and to secure the maximum returns to labor. Galbraith observes that this situation has changed greatly since 1945. The unions have been shorn of so much of their power they no longer pose a threat to the security and independence of the corporate technostructure. Technological progress and automation have enabled the corporation to substitute white collar workers and machines for blue collar workers. Furthermore, the post Second World War general prosperity and high levels of production and employment make the unions appear less needed by workers. With total union membership no longer expanding, unorganized white collar workers and machines displacing organized production workers in manufacturing, and the full employment philosophy and program making union membership less necessary, the economic power of unions has significantly declined. Furthermore, the large corporations are now more willing than in the past to meet demands for wage increases, especially when they are related to productivity increases. This has taken still more wind out of the unions' sails, and has induced them to be less interested in industrial conflict and more concerned with industrial cooperation. While this cooperation between the large unions and the corporate technostructures is by no means universal or complete, it has in Galbraith's opinion gone far enough to rid the large corporation of insecurity on the labor front. The corporation can now rely upon a labor supply at a reasonable and relatively stable wage level.

According to Galbraith's interpretation there remains one further source of possible interference with the autonomy and free action of the corporate technostructure. This is the state. To be autonomous in the exercise of their economic power and to be secure in the maintenance or preservation of this new-found power the technostructures of the large mature corporations have had to bring the nation's government into line. An important objective that the large corporations in the economy's heartland cannot provide for is a high level of total demand which is beyond the scope of industrial planning. And unless there are stable high levels of production and employment there is no guarantee that the general public will have enough income to buy all that the large corporations want to sell. The experience of the depressed 1930's has demonstrated how governments can prevent depressions and recessions with their declining or restricted levels of employment and income. Keynes explained how an anti-depression policy of tax cuts and increased government expenditures could overcome or prevent depressions and recessions. After 1945 the government and the large mature corporations came to accept the Keynesian proposals for preventing the development of depressions and severe recessions. But, Galbraith points out, the Keynesian program does not work so successfully in preventing booms. In boom periods governments, for political reasons, are unwilling to increase taxes and curb government expenditures enough to prevent prosperity from turning into a speculative boom. In addition, booms lead to inflation because large corporations are prepared to pass on wage increases to consumers in higher prices. This inflation is a further stimulant to speculative booms. The only organization that can curb inflation when there is no slack in the economy is the government with the aid of wage and price restraints. Wage and price guideposts, that seek to keep wage increases in line with increases in output per manhour and to keep prices in general stable, open the door to the possibility of avoiding the excessive booms that inevitably lead to recession and levels of national income and total demand that are not sufficient to enable the public to buy all that the large corporations want to sell.

The technostructures of the large corporations for the most part, according to Galbraith's interpretation, support the Keynesian program for economic stabilization at high employment levels, and also the post Keynesian wage-price program for curbing inflationary developments. To the extent that these programs have been successful in the post war decades, the large mature corporations have enjoyed the economic security that comes with sustained prosperity. Risks and uncertainties in the market place have been further reduced. But one large risk would have remained if the government had not taken care of it. This is the risk associated with large investments in highly sophisticated, advanced research and development which might not prove to be a source of profits. Much of this risk has been eliminated since 1945 by having the government underwrite technological progress in such areas as nuclear energy, space exploration and supersonic transportation. Where they have government contracts and therefore guaranteed markets in these and other areas the large corporations stand to lose nothing if research is not fruitful, and to gain a great deal if it is successful. By passing on the risks associated with technological progress to the government and the public, the large mature corporations eliminate the final major risks associated with markets. In this manner the state has completed the structure of planning initiated by the industrial system.

It might be thought that a close association between government departments and the large corporations would greatly restrict or even eliminate the independence of action or autonomy which these corporations so zealously seek to protect. This has not happened, Galbraith explains, because the state is made to serve the needs of the large corporations. Although the large industrial corporation has become an arm of the state, the state has itself become an instrument of the industrial system. Where large corporations sell to the government, as in the case of weapons, aircraft and space vehicles, the technostructure of these corporations closely advises the government departments. Galbraith asserts that this advice is given with the hope of getting contracts for the war *matériel* the technostructure produces. In other words the government's foreign policy is to some extent determined by or adjusted to the technology of war. Even former President Eisenhower, who was well known for his sympathy for private business, felt constrained to warn the public of the potential danger to government policy that might arise from the industrial-military complex.

Some of the goals of the state such as annual increases in gross national product and stable prices and wages are already in harmony with those of the large mature corporations. But in the area of foreign policy there is room for conflict between the state and the large corporations. Galbraith points out that it is in the interest of the large corporations to support the thesis of inevitable conflict between capitalism and communism. The conflict thesis, if accepted by the state, means more orders and more state supported research for the large corporation. Galbraith argues that monolithic communism has disappeared, and that there is now no reason to postulate an inevitable conflict between the United States and the Soviet Union. Therefore there is less need for a large military budget. There is the ever present danger, however, that foreign policy in the United States will reflect the needs of the large industrial corporations more than those of international harmony. To the extent that this has already happened the private industrial system has caught both the consuming public and the government in its managerial net.

The Consequences of Industrial Planning

What have been the consequences of the rise of the large mature corporations and the shift of economic power to the technostructures that dominate these corporations? What has been the outcome of the industrial planning by large corporations? On the credit side there has been a vast expansion of the supply of goods and services. Galbraith draws attention to the theory that the large mature corporation does not seek to maximize profits.[16] The technostructure, which would not get the maximized profits anyway, is more interested in maximizing sales than profits. The growth in the sales of the corporation contributes more to the corporate image and the prestige of the technostructure than do larger profits and smaller sales. The product designers, production and sales experts, information analysts and other members of the technostructure are motivated to some extent by pecuniary considerations. But after a certain income level has been reached the corporate official as an "organization man" identifies himself with his corporation and its goals. A major goal is a share of the expanding national market for goods and services. More goods can be sold at low prices and at less than maximum profits than at high prices and maximized profits. Of course profits must be large enough to pay sizeable dividends to stockholders and to secure enough retained earnings or undistributed profits to finance the corporation's capital investment program. But profits are not maximized since this would mean losing out in the expansion race to those corporations that place large and expanding sales above maximum profits.

Besides placing a high premium on expanding sales the large mature corporation is technologically oriented. Corporations and corporate officials acquire prestige by being known for their "technological virtuosity." Technological progress facilitates the search for better product design and new products and contributes to the program for expanded sales. Galbraith's conclusion is that in the net the market power of the large corporations is "socially efficient."[17] It has made possible in the United States the world's highest standard of living. This conclusion is at variance with the conclusion of the standard economists. Galbraith does not agree with Paul Samuelson and other standard economics textbook authors who argue that the market power of large corporations (oligopolies) is in the net inefficient, exploits the public, and should therefore be kept at a minimum by rigorous enforcement of the nation's antitrust laws.

On the debit side Galbraith finds that there is much to say against the behavior of the industrial system in recent decades. His

---

[16] John Kenneth Galbraith, "Market Structure and Stabilization Policy," *The Review of Economics and Statistics*, Vol. XXXIX, No. 2, May 1957, p. 127.
[17] *The New Industrial State*, p. 185 fn.

major objection to the way the industrial system has performed is
that this system has bent the consumers and the state to serve its
needs rather than the other way around. The large corporations,
by means of sales expenditures, have been able to manage consumer
demand so successfully that consumers have come unwittingly to
accept the goals of the industrial system as their own goals. As
Galbraith puts it, consumers have become "the mentally inden-
tured servants of the industrial system."[18] The industrial system per-
suades the great 'mass of consumers that all production is good, that
private goods are inherently superior to public goods, and that the
aesthetic dimensions of life are unimportant. Leisure is undesirable
when it prevents consumers from making enough income to buy
the expanding volume of automobiles, household appliances, deter-
gents, cosmetics, mouth washes, deodorants and other products pro-
claimed by commercial television to be absolutely necessary if one is
to aspire to the American image of the ideal male or female. The
industrial "preoccupation with production" becomes the irrational
concern of the consumer.[19] It is taught by the large corporation and
accepted by consumers that increased production always means
increased welfare. It is assumed that the marginal urgency of additional new goods never declines, and that the level of consumer
satisfaction can be maintained indefinitely no matter what or how
much is produced. The urgency of consumer wants is alleged by
the producers never to decline. It is the purpose of sales expenditures, especially on commercial television, to perpetuate this false-
hood by managing consumer demand and creating an endless supply
of "contrived wants" for bamboozled consumers.

In Galbraith's opinion this corporate demand management has two
very unfortunate consequences. First, consumer demand management seriously lowers the quality of life. It commercializes life by
assigning the highest priority to the goals of the large corporations
which exclude the aesthetic and other non-commercial dimensions
of life. Demand management surrounds the "affluent society" with
industrial ugliness. Scenic and architectural beauty, the physical
historical heritage, clean air and water, open green spaces and other
amenities are sacrificed to the expansion of sales. Instead of contributing all it could to the development of better human personali-

---

[18] *Ibid.*, p. 67.
[19] *The Affluent Society*, p. 103. See also John Kenneth Galbraith, "Economics and the Quality of Life," *A Contemporary Guide to Economics Peace
and Laughter* (Boston: Houghton Mifflin Co., 1971) pp. 4-8.

ties the industrial system prevents the full achievement of the good life.

The Imbalance between Private and Public Goods Production

The second adverse consequence of the management of consumer demand or the creation of "contrived" consumer wants is the social imbalance, the lack of balance between privately produced goods and goods provided by the state. We have today an "opulent supply of some things and a niggardly yield of others," and as a consequence "an atmosphere of private opulence and public squalor."[20] Advertised private goods are assigned an absolute priority over such social goods as education, public housing, hospitals, public recreation facilities, aid to the poor and aged, resource conservation, sewage disposal and other much needed public services. Public services should expand with the growth of private production in order to maintain the balance between these two types of goods. Galbraith points out that we have a balance in what the nation produces, with all industries appropriately interrelated as Wassily Leontief's input-output tables show. But there is no balance in what the nation consumes. Consequently "The family which takes its mauve and cerise, air-conditioned, power-steered, and power-braked automobile out for a tour passes through cities that are badly paved, made hideous by litter, blighted buildings, billboards, and posts for wires that should have long since been put underground. They pass on into a countryside that has been rendered largely invisible by commercial art."[21] Since there is no equal time given to the advertising of public services, consumers are not left free to choose intelligently as between private and public goods.

Galbraith goes on to explain that the social imbalance between private and public goods is accompanied by an investment imbalance. The distribution of investment is distorted by the industrial system which puts too much money in ordinary material capital and not enough in personal or human capital. Galbraith asserts that there is a fundamental flaw in our machinery of resource allocation. Large corporations will not invest much in the education of people or in pure research because they are not sure of getting the benefits of this kind of investment. Human development and scientific research give rise to external economies the benefits of which all firms may claim. Furthermore, investment in education and human devel-

---

[20] *Ibid.*, p. 199.
[21] *Ibid.*

opment broadens the range of human wants and lessens the dependence of consumers on the "contrived" wants artificially created by the large corporations. Improved education leads consumers to want more along the lines of travel, music, fine arts, and literary and scientific interests and less of automobiles, alcohol, food, sex, sports and movies. Since such a development would run counter to the goals of the industrial system, private business downgrades investment in education and public services. The leadership of the large corporations seeks to reduce taxes and public expenditures and to persuade the public that a privately spent dollar is always superior to a publicly spent dollar.

Not only does the industrial system impose its value system on consumers, but it also seeks to impose the same values on the state. The large corporations encourage the state to sponsor the idea that any increase in gross national product is good. Although the business leadership opposes increases in public expenditures for civilian purposes, they do not object to increases in military expenditures, since the latter bring large orders for goods and also cause the state to underwrite risky technological advance. The industrial system also makes the educational system serve its needs by encouraging the state to expand the educational facilities for the training of technicians and engineers and to pay much less attention to the training of social scientists, humanists and artists. These latter educational products might challenge a situation in which the industrial system makes the state and the nation's educatioₙal system subservient to the goals of the industrial system.

Galbraith is careful to explain that the subordination of the public and the state to the needs of the large mature corporations in the core of the economic system is by no means complete. Discriminating consumers can still elect to ignore the management of consumer demand. But few consumers do so. Some members of the government are aware of the influence of large corporations over government departments. Also the nation's intellectual community is becoming increasingly aware of the extent to which the values of the industrial system have become the nation's values. Nevertheless, it is Galbraith's general position that the guidance of the nation's economy is very substantially in the hands of the technostructure of the large corporations in the heartland of the economy. In spite of what the popular economics textbooks say to the contrary, consumer sovereignty plays a minor role in national economic guidance. Even the popularly elected government has fallen into the web of industrial planning. National economic guidance comes substantially from the "organization men" who comprise the corporate technostructure. Since these organization men have identified themselves overwhelmingly with the goals of the large corporations, the industrial system "increasingly accommodates men to its needs" and the needs of the industrial system are accorded "automatic priority." In this situation the larger dimensions of life are ignored and the quality of life declines to a low level. This is Galbraith's indictment of the world's largest and most productive economic system.

The Educational and Scientific Estate

Although Galbraith deplores the failure of the American economic system to serve the non-commercial dimensions of life, he is not without faith in the future. His faith and hopes for the future are derived from a paradox or contradiction which is inherent in the functioning of the industrial system. This paradox arises from the fact that in demanding and securing a large supply of scientific talent from the nation's colleges and universities the technostructure has created a growing body of educators and academic scientists who are independent of the large industrial corporations, and who have come to challenge the supremacy of these corporations. In other words, the large corporations have called into being a scientific and intellectual community that could possibly in the long run greatly reduce the power of the technostructure, and make the industrial system serve men's higher uncontrived wants.

Galbraith labels the large group of educators and pure research scientists the "educational and scientific estate."[22] They are closely allied with the broader "intellectual community" which includes writers, artists, philosophers, theologians and journalists. The educational and scientific estate is associated at the edges with the scientists and engineers within the corporate technostructure and with civil servants, journalists, writers and artists outside the technostructure. In Galbraith's opinion the educational and scientific estate is in a very crucial position because the technostructure must turn to it for scientific talent. Also the technostructure needs to maintain a close connection with the educational and scientific estate in order to keep informed about the most recent advances in scientific and technological innovation. The technostructure would like to dominate and manage the educational and scientific estate

---

[22] *The New Industrial State*, p. 286.

as it does consumers, trade unions, stockholders and government departments. The technostructure would like to have the scientific and intellectual community identify itself with the goals of the industrial system. But this has not occurred, and instead of the absorption of this community by the large corporations there has developed a conflict of interests. The educational and scientific estate has come to criticize the subordination of pure research to applied research both on university campuses and in industrial laboratories. It has also objected to the management of individual or consumer behavior by what Galbraith describes as "organized public bamboozlement" with the aid of newspapers, billboards, radio and especially television. Hence the paradox that "The economy for its success requires organized public bamboozlement. At the same time it nurtures a growing class which feels itself superior to such bamboozlement and deplores it as intellectually corrupt. . . . This conflict, in one form or another is inevitable with [industrial] planning. That [planning] requires that the needs of the producing mechanism take precedence over the freely expressed will of the individual."[23] And this is what the educational and scientific estate and the broader intellectual community have increasingly come to criticize and to challenge. It is Galbraith's fervent hope that this criticism can be magnified into a major successful attack on the current supremacy of the large mature corporation.

Capitalism and Countervailing Power

In his *American Capitalism* which first appeared in 1952 Galbraith emphasized the importance of countervailing power as a device that would help to protect the general public from exploitation by those who possess what he described as "original market power."[24] Original market power is monopoly power which enables a seller to exploit those from whom he buys or to whom he sells. When those who are exploited become strong enough to offset original market power by forcing the holder of original power to share the monopoly gains, then those who were formerly exploited come to possess countervailing power. Such power emerged, for example, when the large automobile producers were able to force the steel producers to lower their prices under the threat of the automobile producers constructing their own steel plants. The large

[23] *Ibid.*, p. 294.

[24] John Kenneth Galbraith, *American Capitalism, The Concept of Countervailing Power* (Boston: Houghton Mifflin Co., Sentry Edition, 1956) p. 137.

retail mail order and chain stores acquired countervailing power in their dealings with their suppliers. Both the trade unions and farmers secured countervailing power with the aid of government intervention that forced union recognition upon the employers and protected the farmers with parity price and crop control programs. Galbraith explains that countervailing power is effective only in periods of slack demand when those with original market power are forced to look for customers and are therefore willing, under pressure, to share monopoly gains. In periods of inflation and boom countervailing power ceases to function because demand is running high, sales are abundant and there is no pressure to share monopoly gains with buyers. Threats to buy from other sources of supply are of no importance when a boom is on and there is no or little slack in the economy. When countervailing power can no longer protect the public from monopolistic exploitation during an inflationary period, it is necessary to turn to other means of protecting the public's welfare.

In *American Capitalism* Galbraith argued that the main threat to capitalism was not deflation but inflation. Keynes had taught us how to overcome depressions and recessions, but he had not provided us with the key for solving the problem of inflation. He had shown how demand could be propped up with tax cuts and increases in government spending in periods of deflation, but he had not explained how demand could be successfully curbed in boom times. The failure of Keynesian anti-inflation policy is political and not economic. It is because political leaders are unwilling to raise taxes and cut government spending severely enough that the Keynesian anti-inflation program does not work. In the early 1950's it was Galbraith's view that "it is the sad fact that within the broad framework of democratic and especially of American politics no satisfactory solution [to the inflation and boom problem] does exist. Those [solutions] that are most satisfactory, at least to their authors, are the least consistent with our political traditions."[25] It was Galbraith's position in 1952 that American capitalism could only thrive as long as economic decision making remained decentralized. Recurring wage-price spirals, inflation, booms and recessions would cause the government to centralize price and wage decisions by establishing wage and price controls in peace time as in war time. He concluded in 1952 and again in 1956 that "It is inflation, not deflation, that

---

[25] *Ibid.*, p. 190.

will cause capitalism to be modified by extensive centralized decision. The position of capitalism in face of this threat is exceedingly vulnerable. . . . In any case there is no doubt that inflationary tensions are capable of producing a major revision in the character and constitution of American capitalism."[26]

When Galbraith wrote *American Capitalism* the United States had had no experience with an incomes policy such as has emerged since 1962. In *The New Industrial State* (1967) fifteen years later Galbraith is much more optimistic with respect to the possibility of curbing inflation and cutting off wage-price spirals. Now Galbraith believes that the large corporations and large unions are more prepared to exercise restraint in raising prices or wages. The planning of the large corporations looks forward to stable prices. The progressive increase in output per worker allows for annual increases in wage rates without either higher industrial prices or reduced corporate earnings. Consequently, according to Galbraith's interpretation, workers may in the future be more willing to accept moderate wage increases. In this situation "All that remains is for the state to give a clear initiative in this [wage and price] regulation."[27] This initiative was provided by the Kennedy and Johnson Administrations, and from 1962 to 1965 wage and price guidelines were an accepted part of government policy. While the wage and price guidelines have been less successful since 1965, Galbraith feels that they will inevitably become a permanent feature of the industrial system. The large corporations and large unions are now so intimately associated with the state and its goals there is no other prospect. Wage and price guidelines would complete the planning structure of the industrial system.

For some investigators of the American economic system Galbraith's long-run outlook on price and wage or incomes policy will appear to be excessively optimistic. Certainly the experience with price and wage guideposts in the United States since 1965, in boom and recession periods, is not encouraging. Anyone familiar with the efforts of the West European countries to formulate a satisfactory national incomes policy knows that very little has been achieved since 1945. The euphoria that sometimes hovers over Galbraith's analysis of the American industrial system does not have its counterpart in studies of the industrial system in the United Kingdom,

---

[26] *Ibid.*, pp. 200-201.
[27] *The New Industrial State*, p. 256. See also "Inflation, Recession or Controls," *A Contemporary Guide to Economics Peace and Laughter*, pp. 88-99.

France, Italy, Belgium, the Netherlands and the Scandinavian countries.

The Pursuit of Excellence

Galbraith next asks the questions: Where does our pilgrimage towards quality and excellence take us, and how should it be guided? On the first question Galbraith is quite clear. He states that our pilgrimage should seek more quality or excellence and less quantity. The "pursuit of sales" should be subordinated to the "pursuit of excellence." A life of high quality is one that encourages the development of the human personality and the enlargement of individual well-being. Quality or excellence is to be explained in terms of what Galbraith calls its "dimensions." He would assert and promote "the neglected dimensions of life." These dimensions ignored by the industrial system are threefold: the social welfare, the aesthetic and the freedom dimensions of life. The social welfare dimension includes all that contributes to the health, education and recreation needs of the individual. This dimension of human living requires growing expenditures on public facilities and services in which the industrial system has displayed little interest. It can be served most importantly by improving education which Galbraith considers to be strategic in securing emancipation from the debasing tendencies of the industrial system. This is so for two reasons: first, education provides the understanding and skepticism which are necessary to assure the "systematic questioning of the beliefs impressed by the industrial system"; and, second, education opens the door to a larger range of consumer wants which include the higher, non-commercial dimensions of life. In addition to education the social welfare dimension of life calls for more public housing, better health facilities and services, public clinics and better care of the ill, aged and infirm, improved urban and interurban transportation and rubbish removal and more adequate public recreational facilities and services. All such public facilities and services provided by federal, state or local governments are not closely related to the needs of the industrial system and will therefore be minimized by that system.

The aesthetic dimension of life is Galbraith's special concern. He finds that the industrial system has been particularly effective in planning for ugliness rather than beauty, in alienating the artist and in narrowing "the aesthetic response normal to a society of secure well-being." He asserts that artistic or aesthetic achievement is beyond the reach of the industrial system. More than this, there is a conflict between aesthetic and industrial achievement. Aesthetic goals interfere with mass production and the management of consumers. The large corporation hires teams of scientists but no teams of artists, because the latter, unlike the former, cannot identify themselves with the goals of the industrial system. Unlike the technostructure, artists do not work in committees, and, what is worse from the point of view of the large corporation, artists object to management of their affairs from the outside and insist upon maintaining individual freedom as an important dimension of life. The artist has no preoccupation with the mere production of goods and therefore cannot be of service to the large corporation as it now operates. But in a wealthy nation efficiency can and should to some extent be sacrificed to beauty. Industrial plants can be located where they are least offensive rather than most efficient. Historic sections of cities can be spared the bulldozer. Power lines can be put under the landscape and not on it. Some rivers can be unburdened with dams and power plants in order to preserve their natural beauty. Urban areas can be built or rebuilt to express architectural beauty and not to suppress it. All this could be afforded by the world's wealthiest nation without any serious interruption of the flow of consumer goods many of which are contrived and not what free, independent consumers would choose to purchase.

To meet the problem of giving greater expression to the aesthetic aspect of life Galbraith recommends putting "aesthetic priority" above "industrial priority." This means that a progressive community will eventually substitute the "test of aesthetic achievement" for the "test of production." In this connection the United States could learn much from Western Europe whose products such as furniture, glass, ceramics, leather and metalware are well known for their high standards of design. Also West European standards of land use and housing design could be duplicated with much benefit in many areas of the United States.

The freedom dimension of life is more intangible than the welfare and aesthetic dimensions but not less important. Galbraith emphasizes the point that the large corporation calls for conformity rather than freedom, acceptance rather than skepticism. The large corporations want to make human behavior, whether of consumers, trade unionists or government officials, predictable and therefore subject to management. The monolithic industrial system in absorbing and reducing economic conflict precludes the examination of social goals and so minimizes social introspection. The end result is the suppression of individuality. Galbraith argues that such a system is weak for it is the conflict or pluralism of economic interests that supports the pluralism of political discussion and social thought. It is Galbraith's view that the discontent of recent years among students and intellectuals is a reaction against the suffocating blandness of a society dominated by an industrial system which seeks to crush freedom of expression and individual challenge. If consumers are free from the influence of the persuasive art of advertising, they may reject consumer superfluities. Even better, they might elect to substitute leisure for toil, and thus escape the situation where their contrived wants usually exceed their incomes, and they are forced to turn to consumer installment debt in order to pay for what they are induced by the industrial system to want. The quality of life can be high only when the industrial system serves mankind, and the criteria of good living are determined outside this system and imposed on it. The freedom dimension of life is based upon the freedom to express, to be skeptical about, and to challenge values. This freedom cannot be achieved, Galbraith argues, as long as the nation's educational system, and particularly higher education, is chained to the wheel of the industrial system. The public can escape from the thralldom imposed on it by the industrial system only when it is educated about its subservience to this system and about the qualities of a good life which make room for "leisure, contemplation, the appreciation of beauty and the other higher purposes."

Planning and the Future of Capitalism

How would Galbraith guide the pilgrimage to the land of high quality living? He has already made the first step in this direction by laying the foundation in his writings for a popular understanding of the nature of the industrial system and its trends. He has also explained the nature of a society of excellence where the prime objective would be the development of human personality. Galbraith avers that a life of high quality can be achieved only by eliminating the supremacy of the large mature corporations and by adopting a program of social control and social planning. It is Galbraith's position that the movement of the industrial system is towards more planning. We already have the industrial planning carried on by the large corporations which, as explained before, has sought to protect these corporations from market risks and also to protect their autonomy. This planning has a technological basis in the sense that technological advance has necessarily led to industrial planning. As Galbraith has put it, "Technology, under all circumstances, leads to planning; in its higher manifestations it may put the problems of planning beyond the reach of the industrial firm."[28] This is the situation which now faces us. The planning that Galbraith believes is necessary if we are to eliminate the undesirable trends of the industrial system must go beyond the industrial planning of the large corporations. The logic of technological advance points to the need for some kind of social planning that goes far beyond industrial planning.

Galbraith is not referring here to a program for comprehensive national economic planning such as is found in France, the Netherlands, Norway, Sweden, India and Israel. He accepts private industrial planning within certain prescribed limits. As he explains, "In some places market responses still serve. Over a very large area such responses cannot be relied upon; the market must give way to more or less comprehensive planning of demand and supply. Here, if the industrial system does not plan, performance will be poor and perhaps appalling. . . . There is no natural presumption in favor of the market; given the growth of the industrial system the presumption is, if anything, the reverse."[29] Galbraith would not eliminate industrial planning; instead he proposes to domesticate it and make it serve the needs of society as well as the legitimate needs of the large corporations. It is his view that private industrial planning should be combined with planning in the public sector. Both private and public planning should be carried on within a larger framework of social control whose aim is to achieve a society of excellence.

Galbraith's program for social control and social planning consists basically of planning the overall framework within which the society of excellence would function. It is the state's responsibility to take an affirmative stand and to provide a "framework of order" or a climate that will be favorable to the expansion of public facilities and services, to the achievement of high aesthetic standards, and to the widest possible expression of individuality. Galbraith would not interfere with private industrial planning except to make certain that it was serving the needs of society as well as those of private industry. In the public sector Galbraith proposes to fill certain "planning lacunae" or gaps which our industry-dominated political

---

[28] *The New Industrial State*, p. 20.
[29] *Ibid.*, p. 362.

administrations have ignored to a great extent. More planning is needed for education, health, the conservation of resources, and the development of outdoor recreation and forestry in the eastern United States. The urban housing and land use problems require a public planning authority of adequate power which can acquire land, as is done in Sweden, before it is purchased by real estate speculators. Galbraith also recommends planning for urban and interurban transportation with the aid of one autonomous planning authority that could freely cross city, county and state boundaries.

The general aim of Galbraith's planning in the public sector would be to secure a satisfactory balance between privately and publicly produced goods and services. A balance would be achieved when with a given supply of economic resources no more satisfaction could be achieved by producing more public goods and fewer private goods. Galbraith freely admits that no precise equilibrium can be achieved between the satisfactions derived from public and private goods. Equilibrium in this connection cannot be precise because different people are involved in the use of public and private goods, and also because satisfaction from contrived or managed private wants is being compared with satisfaction from unmanaged public wants.[30] Galbraith points out that the current imbalance between private and public goods is clear, and the direction we should take to reduce this imbalance and eventually eliminate it is obvious.

Galbraith's program for social control would alter the relations between industry and the government, especially in connection with military and defense expenditures. Galbraith does not accept industry's argument that conflict between the Soviet Union and the United States is inevitable. On the contrary, he argues that peaceful coexistence is possible, and so the arms race should be replaced by a scientific and technological race. The state would still underwrite much technological advance but big business would no longer bend the state to its needs and influence both military and foreign policy.

According to Galbraith's proposals the state should also provide the essential framework for artistic effort. State support for the aesthetic dimension of life should be recognized as a major public responsibility that is central and not marginal to life as is now the case. The state should subsidize the arts, devote more funds to instruction in artistic appreciation and enjoyment, and also protect high architectural standards. In Galbraith's opinion only social plan-

---

[30] *The Affluent Society*, p. 249.

ning can eliminate the cultural gulf that now exists between the arts and industry.

Finally, planning for education would be a crucial part of Galbraith's program for social control. The nation's colleges and universities should regain control of their budgets so that the higher educational system would be superior to and independent of the industrial system. The educational system should be a force stimulating skepticism, discussion and emancipation from the adverse influences of the industrial system. This means that the colleges and universities must retain control over the education and research they provide. An educational system that places the development of human personality above the task of providing scientific talent to the industrial system would also be a strong bulwark for the state's plan for human welfare and the aesthetic dimension of life.

Planning and the Intellectual Community

What are the "mechanics of emancipation" by means of which Galbraith's proposals could be put into effect? He is well aware that proposals for social and economic reform are not very significant if there is no way of getting these proposals realized. He believes that his recommendations avoid this difficulty. He is prepared "to identify a mechanism which will assert and promote the neglected dimensions of life against the powerful adaptive motivation of the industrial system. In less formidable language, there must be some political force for accomplishing what the industrial system ignores and, indeed, holds to be unimportant."[31] This political force is the educational and scientific estate in particular and the intellectual community in general. If the monopoly of the industrial system is to be broken, Galbraith asserts that we must turn to the educational and scientific estate for the necessary political initiative. Galbraith is not thinking in terms of the educational and scientific leaders forming a third or independent political party. Instead, these leaders are expected to persuade legislators to accept the goals and ideals of the intellectual community or be replaced by other legislators who do not need such persuasion. Unlike the technostructure of the large corporations, the educational and scientific estate is not required to refrain from direct political action. This estate gains power and adherents from its capacity for social invention. It is prepared to feed upon the widespread dissatisfaction of the nation's youth with

---

[31] *The New Industrial State*, pp. 344-345.

the values of an industry-dominated, computerized and automated society. The educational and scientific estate is well positioned to express skepticism concerning official military and foreign policy and also concerning the goals of the industrial system. Already scientists have emerged since World War II as an independent force which has criticized the military use of nuclear energy. The educational and scientific estate has shown considerable strength in Democratic Party politics in a number of states, and has had a significant influence on foreign policy relating to international disarmament and the possibility of more peaceful relations with the Soviet Union.

Galbraith is not unaware of the limitations of the educational and scientific estate as a political force. Its members suffer from a lack of self-confidence, many of them believing that they have no chance of convincing the general public of the need to be emancipated from subservience to the industrial system. Many members of the educational and scientific estate do not assume any responsibility for improving the quality of life. They suffer from the widespread belief that "Politics is not the business of the intellectual or the artist. Theirs is the purer domain of the spirit and the mind. This can only be sullied by concern for practical affairs."[32] Nevertheless, Galbraith remains optimistic about the possibility of the community of educators and scientists becoming an effective political force. Their numbers are growing at the very time that the New Left is strongly criticizing the goals of the Establishment. Galbraith concludes his thoughts on proposals for the reform of society with the statement that "Yet it is safe to say that the future of what is called modern society depends on how willingly and effectively the intellectual community in general, and the educational and scientific estate in particular, assume responsibilities for political action and leadership."[33]

Galbraith's Interpretation of Economic Trends: An Evaluation

Before going on to the question of Galbraith's views on the nature and significance of the science of economics, it may be worthwhile to review critically his interpretation of the trends in the modern industrial system and his proposals for social control and planning. What Galbraith has worked out in his various writings is an interpretation of the American economic process. His interests are much broader than those of standard or conventional economists who are

---

[32] *Ibid.*, p. 384.
[33] *Ibid.*, p. 387.

primarily interested in the current economic scene in which the main problem is maximizing output or satisfaction from a given supply of economic resources. Like Veblen, Galbraith has interpreted the evolution of the American capitalist system, and again like Veblen he has painted with broad strokes of the brush. He has pushed far beyond the scope of conventional economics to consider such matters as power, technological change and the quality of life. This means that he has moved from the area of the measurable to that of the immeasurable. This immediately presents problems because where the social scientist cannot measure, he cannot be definite or precise. When Galbraith writes about the declining power of the trade unions or the rising power of the corporate technostructure, it is difficult to indicate how far power has declined in the one case and increased in the other. If economic power cannot be measured, generalizations about changes in power relations tend to remain somewhat vague and indefinite. Doubtless there will be critics who will assert that Galbraith has overstated the case for the decline of unionism as a potent force in economic life. Other critics will argue that he writes too facilely about the power of the technostructure. Power relations within large corporations are difficult to pin down, and Galbraith does not provide his readers with any detailed case histories to bolster his position with regard to this issue.[34] The same may be said of his analysis of what he calls the "ministerial" and "communications" roles of the large trade unions operating in the core of the industrial system.

When we turn to Galbraith's analysis of "influence" on or "management" of consumers and the state, we see that it is very difficult to indicate the extent of this influence. This is especially true in the area of industry-government relations. That such influence exists, few would deny. The important issue, however, is not whether or not the influence exists, but rather how extensive and pervading it is. Again Galbraith does not parade detailed case histories before his readers. Indeed, it would be very difficult to document such an influence in a way that would silence many critics of Galbraith's interpretations in this connection.

To some extent Galbraith may be the victim of his own interests. As a social critic seeking to enlighten the general public, he is necessarily limited to broad generalizations. Cold statistical material is poor fare for the layman in economic matters. Detailed and com-

34 Robert M. Solow, "The New Industrial State," *The Public Interest*, Number 9, Fall 1967, p. 105.

plicated case histories are not much better. Such material is usually avoided by the social critic or satirist. It is the sweep of broad generalizations wittily presented that engages the public's attention. Veblen learnt this lesson well, and so has Galbraith. While there was much in Veblen's broad generalizations that was useful in an interpretation of the American economy, it remained for more pedestrian economists such as John R. Commons, Wesley C. Mitchell and John M. Clark to support the Veblenian generalizations (not all of them by any means) with more specific economic analyses. It appears that the same may be said to some extent about the "enlightenment" presented in *American Capitalism*, *The Affluent Society*, and *The New Industrial State*.[35]

Galbraith's thesis in *The New Industrial State* which states that planning by the large industrial corporation in the heartland of the economy has largely replaced the free market mechanism in that area has been vigorously attacked by both academic and government economists.[36] These attacks assert that Galbraith overemphasizes the importance of the large industrial corporation, ignores the extent to which market power in the producers' goods industries has been eroded since 1945, and underestimates the ability of the Federal Government to preserve competition even in the oligopolistic industries. Galbraith's rejoinder asserts that no one can deny that the heartland of the industrial economy is now highly concentrated, and that no economist has proposed any acceptable way of "demerging" the existing highly concentrated industries. Even though the government prevents any further concentration of industrial market power, Galbraith sees no prospect of eliminating the very extensive industrial market power that now exists. To some extent Galbraith and his critics are not arguing about the same things. Galbraith is concerned with the existing large core of industrial concentration. His critics are dealing with recent and future trends with regard to industrial market power, which could limit the further expansion of this power. As far as Galbraith is concerned he feels that the main issue is the current very extensive

---

[35] R. L. Heilbroner, *The New Republic*, Vol. 157, July 8, 1967, p. 26, and Robert M. Solow, "The New Industrial State," *The Public Interest*, p. 101.

[36] The criticisms of Walter Adams, Willard F. Mueller, and Donald F. Turner are presented in *Hearings before the Subcommittee of the Select Committee on Small Business, United States Senate, Planning, Regulation, and Competition*, 90th Congress, 1st Session, Washington, D.C., June 29, 1967.

spread of industrial market power, and how this power must be domesticated if we are to survive in a "civilized fashion."[37]

In addition to the oversimplification of issues that some critics may find in Galbraith's work, others may object to what they regard as an overemphasis on the role and importance of technological change. Some interpretations of Galbraith's work might lead to the conclusion that he believes that technological change will inevitably result in the creation of a society of cultural excellence. The linkage would be as follows. Technological change has inevitably led to the development of an industrial system in which the large corporation plays the dominant role. The industrial system needs a supply of specialized, technical talent for its large-scale operations. This need then gives rise to an educational system that supplies scientists and other specialists. In the expanding colleges and universities there necessarily develops a community of educators and academic scientists who challenge the supremacy of the industrial system, and this intellectual community then becomes a political force that destroys the supremacy of the large corporations and ushers in a society of cultural excellence. When this happens technological change has then worked out its full impact.

The weak link in this chain of technological inevitability is the political role of the community of educators, academic scientists and other intellectuals. Galbraith is careful to point out that the success of the intellectual community as a political force is by no means assured. He has expressed considerable skepticism about the political future of the educational and scientific estate. With regard to their possible political success he remains skeptical but hopeful. This being the case, he holds to no doctrine of technological necessity with regard to the future shape of our society. For Galbraith there is no external guarantee that the educational and scientific elite will be our saviors.

Galbraith is also criticized on the ground that he has a preconceived notion of the good life that he would impose on consumers.[38] It is suggested by some of his critics that he is merely substituting his own brainwashing of consumers for the brainwashing done by the large corporations producing consumer goods. Other critics assert that Galbraith's educational and scientific elite would be like Plato's philosopher-kings in his ideal Republic who presumed to

---

[37] *Ibid.*, p. 7.
[38] Irving Kristol, "Professor Galbraith's 'New Industrial State'," *Fortune*, July 1967, p. 195.

tell the general public what was good for them. Both criticisms arise from a misreading of Galbraith's interpretation of consumer behavior. He would leave all decisions as to what goods and services contribute to the good life to be settled in the final analysis by the general public. He does not guarantee that consumers will make these decisions wisely. What he wants is to have consumers fully informed as to the consequences of their decisions and how these decisions are made. The general public may accept or reject the standards and advice of the educational and scientific elite. Galbraith is optimistic enough to believe that the public will accept this guidance knowingly and willingly.

Some may also object that there is not much in Galbraith's work that is original. When referring to the work of other economists Galbraith has said that "I have drawn on their work, quantitative and qualitative, at every stage; I could not have written without their prior efforts."[39] He explains that in their specialized works economists have dealt only with parts of economic reality and changes in these parts. It has not been the usual practice of economists to look at economic reality as a whole, and to consider all the major changes affecting this whole. What Galbraith has done has been to combine the specialized works of economists and to end up with more than these specialized works contained. In other words, as he puts it, his interpretation of the real economic world and its trends is more than the sum of the interpretations of its parts. What is his contribution that is more than the sum of other economists' partial interpretations? It is, in brief, that as we have moved from a poor to an affluent society, businessmen, labor leaders, politicians, and even most economists have failed to make the adjustments in their thinking that would enable them to replace our affluent but uncouth society with a society of human excellence. In the latter kind of society, if achieved, the industrial system would become a diminishing part of life, economists would no longer be the "highest arbiters of social policy," and aesthetic goals would then be paramount.

Galbraith's Planning Proposals: An Evaluation

To some of Galbraith's readers his proposals for achieving a society of excellence are the least satisfactory part of his analysis of the evolving industrial process. Galbraith is at his best when he is exposing the deficiencies of the modern economy. He is much more

---

[39] *The New Industrial State*, p. 402.

comfortable wielding the scalpel that exposes the diseased inner organs of the industrial system than when he is carrying the unfurled banner of economic and social reform. He invites criticism in this connection by turning in on himself and stating that "On the whole, I am less interested in telling where the industrial system is going than in providing the materials for consideration of where it has arrived."[40] With this approach to policy and programs it is not surprising that Galbraith's recommendations for improving national guidance and achieving a higher level of social and individual well-being remain somewhat tentative and, to some critics, somewhat superficial. Galbraith's general answer to this problem, as has already been explained, is more social control and planning. He finds that much of the planning already being done is worth continuing. Private industrial planning for economic stability and technological progress, Keynesian regulation of aggregate demand, Kennedy-Johnson wage and price guidelines, and planning in the public sector receive Galbraith's approval.[41] He would add more planning in the public sector, especially at the state, county and local levels, and more government support for the arts.

This planning *mélange* of the old and the new takes no account of the recent improvements in the science and art of national planning as it is carried on in the United Kingdom, France, Belgium, the Netherlands, Italy and the Scandinavian countries. These countries have discovered that it is essential to have all major economic interest groups participating in the planning process. National social and economic priorities have to be quantified in terms of their demands on the nation's gross national product. Decisions have to be made as to the division of the economic resources going into the public and private sectors. In Western Europe all this requires organization and procedures in the form of a national economic coun-

---

[40] *Ibid.*, p. 324.

[41] *Hearings before the Joint Economic Committee, Congress of the United States, January 1965 Economic Report of the President, Statement of John Kenneth Galbraith*, Part 2, 89th Congress, 1st Session, Washington, D.C., Feb. 24, 1965, pp. 10-33.

Galbraith's 1969 proposals for the revitalization of the Democratic Party included proposals for a guaranteed annual income for the poor, price and wage controls to curb inflation, higher personal income taxes, bloc grants of financial aid from the federal government to the large cities, public ownership of low income housing and urban transportation systems, and public urban land ownership. Galbraith's economic program is presented in *Who Needs the Democrats and What It Takes to Be Needed* (New York: New American Library, 1970), pp. 64-75.

cil representing business, labor, agriculture, consumers and the government; planning boards on the national and other levels; and annual and long-term national economic budgets that project gross national product and the national priorities that absorb this product.[42] None of this crops up in Galbraith's planning proposals. He apparently feels that the existing political and governmental structures and procedures in the United States do not have to be extensively altered for the task of effective social control and planning.

The only essentially new ingredient in Galbraith's planning program is a new political force in the shape of the educational and scientific estate and the larger intellectual community. To many who are closely associated with the community of educators and academic scientists there is little if any prospect of this community ever becoming a significant political force that could lead the pilgrimage to the land of excellence in human living. At best the nation's intellectual community might indirectly stimulate organized labor, organized farmers and organized business to want a society of excellence so strongly as to plan for it, as is being done today in the Scandinavian and other West European countries.

Galbraith's Critique of Conventional Economics

In the course of enlightening the general public with regard to the undesirable trends of the industrial system Galbraith has found it necessary to criticize severely what he describes as "conventional" or "standard economics." This is the kind of economics found in the most widely read textbooks used for the instruction of students and other "innocents." Galbraith's attack on the inadequacies of standard economics was muted until the publication of *The New Industrial State* where he tells us that, just as John M. Keynes used the orthodox economics of A. C. Pigou as a point of departure for his disagreement, so likewise Galbraith uses the standard economics of Paul A. Samuelson (and of Robert Dorfman to a more limited extent) as the kind of economics that needs to be renovated and made more realistic. It is not Galbraith's intention to do away entirely with standard economics. On the contrary he finds much in standard economics that is worthwhile. His main objection to the economics

---

[42] An analysis of the use of national economic budgets in Western Europe since 1945 is given in Allan G. Gruchy, *Comparative Economic Systems, Competing Ways to Stability and Growth* (Boston: Houghton Mifflin Co., 1966).

of the standard textbooks is that it is the victim of a cultural lag and consequently does not adequately explain the real economic world. As he puts it, "The problem of economics . . . is not one of original error but of obsolescence."[43]

Textbooks like Samuelson's *Economics* still emphasize the importance of an economic world in which consumers are sovereign, private industry is subject to control by the market, and the primary aim of the producer is profit maximization. The standard textbooks concentrate their attention on the millions of small producers in agriculture and industry instead of the few hundred large corporations in the industrial core of the economy. Consequently inadequate attention is paid to consumer demand management, corporate price control and non-profit maximization, and industry-government relations. It is Galbraith's contention that conventional economists are aware of the emergence of the large corporation but they largely ignore it, and so do not integrate it into their economic analysis. As he expresses it, "So economic instruction concedes the important and then discusses the unimportant."[44]

It is Galbraith's view that conventional economists continue to theorize as if the poor society of the nineteenth century were still with us. They continue to say that human wants which are insatiable reflect human needs. Therefore our prime concern should be with increasing gross national product. Since wants are said to be original with the individual and consumers are held to be free to decide what they want to buy, any increase in production is good. Furthermore, since quality can be largely taken for granted, quantity of output is the prime test of good economic performance.

This view of the economic world found in the popular standard economics textbooks is, in Galbraith's opinion, not only unrealistic and outmoded but in addition very harmful. Besides preventing students and the public from understanding the real industrial system of today, conventional economics aids the large corporations in their efforts to make the public serve the needs of the industrial system rather than the reverse. Why does a large section of the economics profession, and especially the successful textbook writers, cling to an unrealistic view of the economic world and therefore fail to inform their readers of the undesirable trends of the modern industrial system? The explanation is by no means simple. A main reason for

---

[43] *The New Industrial State*, p. 215.
[44] *Ibid.*, p. 46 fn.

the unrealistic analyses of the standard economists is that they have a static, mechanistic view of the economic system. They study the American economic scene but not the American economic process. Since they pay little attention to technological change and economic development, economics and economic doctrines tend to become "traditional" and "sanctified." A lag then develops between what exists in the real economic world and what is discussed in the textbooks. The development of this cultural lag is stimulated by other conditions. Standard economists seek to simplify economic life so that it can be analyzed in terms of mathematics and symbolic logic. To take into account technological change and new institutional developments, such as the rise to supremacy of the large industrial corporations, would complicate economic analysis very much. Economic reality, Galbraith explains, is complex and untidy. Economists who insist upon using investigational techniques that require simple, tidy phenomena will end up with a neat but irrelevant science of economics. For this reason Galbraith concludes that the motives that direct the technostructure of the large corporation, such as the desire for the expansion of sales or for the achievement of technological superiority over competitors, "are not easily adapted to the simplifications of mathematics and symbolic logic. Scientific truth in economics [as understood by standard economists] is not always what exists; often it is [instead] what can be handled by seemingly scientific [mathematical] methods."[45] It is much simpler to run counter to reality and to assume, as the standard economists do, that what motivates the managers of the large corporations is primarily the maximization of profits. This suits the "convenience" and "vested" interest" of the economics profession which fervently clings to an oversimplified interpretation of economic life. From their point of view, Galbraith explains, "Better orderly error [oversimplification] than complex truth."[46]

Another factor accounting for the deficiencies of conventional economics, and one that is particularly disturbing to Galbraith, is the close association of this type of economics with the modern industrial system. He contends that conventional economics is the servant of the society that nurtures it. It is not surprising therefore that standard economics instruction rather systematically "excludes speculation on the way the large economic organizations shape social attitudes to their ends. Nor is the service less important for being

---

[45] *Ibid.*, p. 146.
[46] *Ibid.*, p. 62.

rendered, in the main, in innocence and in the name of scientific truth."[47]

Since standard or traditional economics is not much concerned with technological change and economic evolution, Galbraith observes that standard economists are conservative and not innovatory. Since they are engrossed with a phantom economic world in which impersonal forces control the markets and government plays a limited role, standard economists are opposed to the expansion of government regulation and social planning. They have, says Galbraith, come to accept a theology of the market which teaches that a free price is always superior to a controlled or regulated price. These economists are also unwilling to pay much attention to such matters as wage and price guidelines, wage and price boards, economic planning and the role of planning authorities. Analysis and consideration of these matters are opposed because they would broaden the scope of economics and would reduce it to the level of political science, where there is nothing like the highly determinate, mathematical analysis of the standard economists. Prices or wages that are influenced by the government are untidy and do not fit into the precise and logical diagrams of the standard economist. It is therefore more convenient for the standard economists to ignore these complex and untidy data than to give up their precise but oversimplified version of economics.

Galbraith considers Keynes's economics to be a great advance on Alfred Marshall's and A. C. Pigou's economics. But the world has changed significantly since Keynes's *General Theory of Employment Interest and Money* appeared in 1936. Time has taken its toll, and now Keynesian economics is the new orthodoxy. Keynes constructed "a new body of conventional wisdom, the obsolescence of some parts of which, in its turn, is now well advanced."[48] In the 1930's the main matter of critical concern was the size of total production and not its composition. More production meant more employment, and it was Keynes's chief interest to show how production could be raised to a full employment level. He explained in *The General Theory* that it was the volume and not the direction of investment that was important. More investment would result

---

[47] *Ibid.*, p. 167. See also John Kenneth Galbraith, "Economics in the Industrial State: Science and Sedative, Economics as a System of Belief," *The American Economic Review*, Vol. LX, No. 2, May 1970, pp. 469-478.

[48] *The Affluent Society*, p. 25. See also "How Keynes Came to America," *A Contemporary Guide to Economics Peace and Laughter*, pp. 58-59.

in more production and more employment.[49] Any production, even leaf raking or pyramid building, would increase employment. The direction of production or the ways in which resources were allocated were unimportant when mass unemployment was the issue. Furthermore, Keynes said that when full employment was reached Alfred Marshall's economics would take over, and the free market could be relied upon to allocate resources in accordance with consumer preferences.[50]

Galbraith points out that in the most important area of the modern industrial system, the large-scale manufacturing sector, Marshall's free market is largely gone for good. Furthermore, the main issue today is not the amount of total output but instead its composition. The production problem has been solved but not the problem of the rational use of output. The Keynesian conventional wisdom continues to direct attention primarily to the single goal of increased output. Keynes's preoccupation with enlarging total production has not only become obsolete, but has also passed on the infection to the economics profession and the makers of government policy. These Keynesian views that were so fertile and relevant in the 1930's have now become sterile and obsolescent.

Galbraith's Economics of Excellence

What would Galbraith do to make economics a more realistic and therefore more useful social science? His thoughts along this line are presented in a very revealing addendum to *The New Industrial State* entitled "An Addendum on Economic Method and the Nature of Social Argument."[51] Galbraith pays high tribute to the many economists who have escaped from the narrow confines of conventional economics, and who have realistically studied the large corporation, price theory, decision theory, the large trade union, industry-government relations and other special features of economic life. He points out, however, that while scientific specialization is a convenience, it can also be a source of error. This is true because the specialist fails at times to go beyond his special interest with the result that he denies himself knowledge that can be had only outside his own area of investigation. Unless the contributions of specialists are fully integrated in a general analysis, the full

---

[49] John M. Keynes, *The General Theory of Employment Interest and Money*, p. 379.

[50] *Ibid.*, p. 378.

[51] *Ibid.*, pp. 401-412.

value of the specialists' work is not realized. For example, the many specialized studies of different aspects of the large corporation until recently suffered from a lack of integration and so have not even yet been fully assimilated into the main body of economics. "What is avoided [by specialists] is reflection on the consequences of putting them [specialized studies of individual developments affecting large corporations] all together, of seeing them as a system. But it cannot be supposed that the principal beams and buttresses of the industrial system have all been changed and that the structure remains as before. If the parts have changed, so then has the whole."[52] Galbraith regards his own work as a step towards a more integrated theoretical analysis. He believes that his study of the modern industrial system not only complements but also illuminates the work of many economic specialists. In his opinion the work of the generalist and that of the specialist are both equally necessary.

What Galbraith is suggesting is that we need a new comprehensive interpretation of the economic system to improve upon the standard presentation found in economics textbooks. This new look at the economic system would take this system to be an evolving process. Economics would then be a study of the changing process by means of which mankind secures a supply of goods and services to meet its various needs. In Galbraith's hands economics becomes a theory of the economic system or process, or more particularly, a theory of evolving American capitalism with special attention being paid to the current era of "organized capitalism." In this respect Galbraith differs from Alfred Marshall and John M. Keynes, both of whom were mainly concerned, not with the evolving economic system, but with the existing economic scene of their day with a stable unchanging technology. In his general approach to economic studies Galbraith duplicates the approach of Thorstein Veblen and later institutionalists who took as the object of their investigations the evolving capitalist system with its rapidly advancing technology.

While there are laws or principles that apply to a static economic situation where change has been ignored, there are no laws of development that apply to the total evolving industrial system. Nor does Galbraith look for any such long-term evolutionary uniformities that would apply to all evolving economic systems. In place of laws of economic development Galbraith uncovers a logic of industrial development or evolution. This logic shows that, given certain

---

[52] *Ibid.*, p. 395.

technological advances, the shape of the industrial system will be consistent with these advances. There is an internal consistency in the evolving economic process which must be understood if one is to understand the real economic world. Whereas Karl Marx looked for the immutable laws of economic development, Galbraith uncovers the impact on economic life of technological imperatives. What provides unity in his study of the complex of interlocking economic changes is his logic of industrial development. It is this logic that converts mere description into scientific interpretation and unites the various parts of his analysis of the modern industrial system.

Like Veblen, Galbraith takes technology and technological change as the point of departure for his analysis of the evolving industrial system. Technology is the point at which he breaks into the evolving industrial system. Galbraith's large "matrix of change" deals with all the major interlocking changes affecting the industrial system. Galbraith, however, does not pay equal attention to all sectors of the economy. His theory of American capitalism has much more to say about industry than about agriculture or trade unionism. Like Veblen, W. C. Mitchell, John M. Clark and Gardiner C. Means, Galbraith is primarily concerned with the large corporation, the "master institution" of Veblen's analysis. Like the institutionalists, Galbraith takes the large industrial corporation as the norm of business enterprise which should replace the norm of small-scale competitive enterprise about which so much is said in the standard economics textbooks.

All economists who study the economic system as an evolving process compare the current or initial state of the economy with some future state. The initial state of the economy is the condition of the economy as the economist sees it before him. Since he is interested in altering or improving this initial state, at some point his analysis turns to a consideration of a future different state where economic arrangements may be altered to achieve certain goals. Veblen, Mitchell, Clark, Means and other institutionalists incorporated both current and future states of the economy in their analyses. Their future state was some kind of a planned economy with variations from Veblen's soviet of technicians to Clark's social-liberal planned economy.

Galbraith likewise has his initial and future states of the economy. He compares the industrial system as he finds it around him with the industrial system as he would like to see it in the future. As in the case of the institutionalists he proposes to alter his initial state of the industrial system with the aid of a program of social control and planning. His future state of the industrial system would be a planned economy in which the logic of industrial evolution would be harnessed to the needs of a society of excellence. Consumer sovereignty would be reestablished with the aid of the intellectual community. The state would no longer be in the service of the large industrial corporations. Production would be subordinate to the broader non-economic dimensions of life, and the gap or discrepancy between "technology" and "conventional wisdom" would be removed.

The question may be raised, how universal is Galbraith's theory of the industrial system? Is it a theory that relates to all types of economic systems such as the capitalist, democratic socialist and communist systems? Does the title of his book, *The New Industrial State*, refer to the kind of state to be found in all advanced industrialized countries, or is he writing primarily about *The New American Industrial State?* It is quite clear that the United States is uppermost in Galbraith's mind as he analyzes the new industrial state. The illustrations and statistics of his analysis relate primarily to the American scene. When he delivered the Reith Lectures, however, before a British television audience in 1966 and presented a synopsis of *The New Industrial State*, Galbraith said his thesis about the industrial system applied to Great Britain as well as to the United States. In his references to socialist and communist countries, while developing his convergence thesis, Galbraith asserts that the logic of industrial evolution is working its way out in the Soviet Union and in socialist India as well as in the United States. This logic is bringing these different economies closer together with respect to their economic structure and functioning. In this way one may regard Galbraith's theory of the industrial system as a universal theory. As soon as one moves, however, into a more detailed analysis of institutional arrangements, ruling elites, and cultural heritages with their nationalistic leanings, the universal aspects of Galbraith's theory of industrialism recede into the background. His theory of the industrial system then becomes a theory of the American industrial system. Galbraith's work is not primarily in the field of comparative economics. The comparative aspect, while present, is subordinate to a profound interest in the evolving American economic system. One reads his books not to understand the Scandinavian, British, French, West German and Soviet economies, but rather to get an incisive, and one might say moving, account of the evolution, present status and future prospects of the world's most productive economic system.

The Function of Economics

It might be thought by some of his critics that Galbraith has gone beyond the boundaries of his science and has brought up value issues that have no place in a scientific discussion. It is not Galbraith's intention to confuse the roles of the scientist and the moralist.[53] He does not seek to impose his own value system upon the public, nor does he propose to tell the people what they should want. He attacks conventional economists on the ground that they help prevent the public from getting what it wants, or might want if it were free to choose the goods and services that it desires. As things now stand, in Galbraith's opinion, the economics profession aids the large corporations in bamboozling the public. When economists, Keynesians included, teach that all production is good (because the market system is alleged to be free and therefore consumers are sovereign) and that more production is always good, they simply aid the large industrial corporations in managing consumer demand and in imposing their value system on the public and the government. The large corporations publicly agree with the conventional economists when the latter say that impersonal forces govern the market and that consumers are free to make their own choices, but these corporations know that the conventional economists are wrong in their views about markets and consumers. The large corporations, Galbraith points out, hide behind the façade of conventional economics. Since much of the economics profession, the conventional part, has the same value system as have the large corporations (such values as that production is always good and that the more production the better), this segment of the economics profession indirectly, and perhaps unwittingly, through the large corporations imposes its distorted value system on the general public.

Although the conventional economists do not intend it, it is they and not Galbraith who help prevent the public from determining or freely giving expression to their own value system. It is the conventional economists who support the view that consumers should avoid

---

[53] In his review of Galbraith's *The New Industrial State*, Robert M. Solow incorrectly describes Galbraith as a moralist who seeks to impose his own values on the general public. As a scientist Galbraith analyzes the industrial system to show how it prevents people from getting what they would want if they were free from advertising and high pressure salesmanship and were able to choose what they want. See Robert M. Solow, *op. cit.*, p. 108.

leisure, and should continue to work in order to earn enough income to purchase the goods that the high pressure salesmanship of the large corporations induces them to buy. Furthermore, it is the conventional economists who support the large corporations in subordinating aesthetics to economics, and beauty to utility. It is the objective of Galbraith's program of social planning to free the public from domination by the large corporations, and to enable the public to pursue whatever goals it decides are in its opinion worthwhile. In the final analysis the arbiter of what is good, aesthetic and worthwhile is the public, and not the economics profession. It is Galbraith's aim to make economics a useful tool and not an obstacle to achieving a society of excellence. As an economist and scientist it is not Galbraith's function to set up standards of the good and the beautiful. This is the function of artists and philosophers who must secure the approval of the public. But it is Galbraith's purpose to see that the economy provides the material foundation of the values that a society of excellence considers to be desirable. It is also his purpose to make the science of economics an aid and not an obstacle, as he believes it now is in the hands of conventional economists, to the achievement of a way of living in which quality is not smothered by quantity. As he puts it, individual "well-being is not adequately improved if problems associated with collective need are unsolved and if this progress involves an unacceptable commitment to the technology of war."[54] In the final analysis it is the public, and the public alone, that will decide when and how these problems will be met. Galbraith hopes that his economics of excellence will aid the public in handling these crucial issues successfully.

---

[54] John K. Galbraith, "A Review of a Review," *The Public Interest,* Number 9, Fall 1967, p. 118.

CHAPTER V

GUNNAR MYRDAL'S ECONOMICS
OF INTEGRATION

Among European economists none is better known today in the United States than the eminent Swedish economist, Gunnar Myrdal, whose extensive contacts with the American scene began in 1929 when he visited the United States as a Rockefeller Fellow. Myrdal's reputation in the United States was first widely established by his sociological study of the American Negro which was published in 1944 under the title of *An American Dilemma, The Negro Problem and Modern Democracy*. It was not unusual that Myrdal should have made this excursion into the field of sociology. Like the American institutionalists Myrdal takes economics to be a cultural science with no precise boundaries. From Myrdal's holistic point of view economics is a study of problems in the use of scarce natural and human resources which are brought to the attention of economists by historical and current developments and by the interests of the general population. In the study of these problems Myrdal asserts that the economist should have reference to any data, psychological, sociological, historical or economic, that throw light on the problems under investigation. Myrdal's main interest has been the analysis of the developing economic process and the movement towards more fully integrated or planned economies in the western world and elsewhere. In developing the theory of the emerging integrated economy Myrdal found it necessary to free himself from the conventional Swedish economics to which he had been introduced as a student after the First World War. He found the theoretical core of the conventional *laissez-faire* economics of the first three decades of this century to be very inadequate as the basis for an interpretation of the "era of sustained abnormality" which came after 1914 and which has continued to the present.[1] Myrdal observed that the conventional

---

[1] Myrdal provides an outline of his intellectual development in the "Postscript" to *Value in Social Theory* (London: Routledge and Kegan Paul, 1958) pp. 237-262.

economics of the years 1900 to 1929 was narrowly conceived, static, excessively subjectivistic, and burdened by inherited preconceptions which made it an inadequate device for the interpretation of the economic realities of the post 1929 world. Myrdal attacked not only the relevance of conventional economic theory but also the philosophical and methodological approaches of the orthodox economists who constructed this theory. He did not dispense entirely with traditional economic theory. On the contrary he accepted many basic economic concepts developed by his predecessors, but added to them. He kept many of the basic concepts or "bricks" but rebuilt the theoretical structure of his science. Eventually he found himself replacing conventional or orthodox equilibrium economics with a new economics of integration oriented around the concept of a cumulative process of development.

In developing his economics of integration Myrdal on frequent occasions left the academic environment to participate in the world of real events. He became an expert adviser to the Swedish government during the depressed 1930's; he served on many committees and commissions investigating economic and social problems; he was active in helping to construct the Swedish social security system; he served as a representative of the Swedish Social Democratic Party both in the Parliament and as a cabinet member; and he participated in international affairs for a decade as the Executive Secretary of the United Nations Economic Commission for Europe. In more recent years he has been actively engaged in studying the problems of the underdeveloped countries. It is this extensive contact with the actual problems of both the mature and the newly developing countries that has nourished Myrdal's strong empirical bent, and provided a realistic foundation for his integrative economics.

Myrdal's Concept of the Evolving Social Process

An understanding of Myrdal's concept of the social process is fundamental to an explanation of the kinds of economic studies that have engaged his attention. Myrdal explains that it is the purpose of social science to explain the nature of "social reality." For some purposes it is useful to regard social reality as a form of equilibrium. This is the case when the economist is investigating the current economic situation which may be regarded as a cross-section of the economic process. The economist may be interested in the equilibrium conditions that prevail in the current market for a commodity, service or factor of production such as capital. Or the economist may be concerned with a short-run analysis of the business system in which fluctuations between prosperity and recession occur. In this situation the economist may investigate the disequilibrium condition of the economic system and the factors at work or the policies designed to restore some kind of equilibrium of the economic system. When, however, the economist is concerned with what Myrdal describes as "broad issues," he takes the economic system to be a part of the evolving social process. Social reality in general and economic reality in particular are a complex of social relations that is moving along a path of change and development. The ultimate purpose of the economist is not to study the current economic situation or short-run fluctuations in economic activity. Myrdal states that "the rational purpose of study and thought must be to find out where we are heading."[2] If social reality is an evolving complex of human affairs, the social scientist should be interested in its past, present and future. Such an approach will throw light on the path which the developing social process is following, the human needs that it is meeting or not meeting, and the prospect that this process will change in such a manner as to fulfill human wants in the future.

When the social scientist looks upon the social system as a developing process, he finds it important to explain the factors which give rise to the evolution of the social process and the manner in which these factors operate. In Myrdal's analysis the development of the social and economic processes comes about as "the result of modern technology . . . together with its cultural, social, economic and political consequences."[3] It is technological change as revealed in the progress of science and in the improvement of industrial technology that acts as the mainspring of social and economic evolution. But technology does not operate alone. It is embedded in an historico-cultural complex which provides a framework or setting for technological change. Technological change is accompanied by political, social, religious and other types of change. Developments on the domestic and international fronts of a country have much to do with the pace and impact of technological change. Since 1914 we have lived in what Myrdal describes as a "crisis-ridden world." Technological change has combined with wars, depressions and economic and social revolutions to alter the ways of living in the western world

---

[2] Gunnar Myrdal, *An International Economy, Problems and Prospects* (New York: Harper and Brothers, 1956) p. 314.

[3] *Ibid.*, p. 300.

very significantly since 1900. In the western world the momentum of the social process has been derived from economic progress which in turn has been the outcome of scientific and technological progress.

Myrdal's Theory of Cumulative Causation

In order to explain how technological and industrial change causes the economic process to evolve or develop Myrdal has developed his theory of circular cumulative causation.[4] This theory of change originated as an explanation of cumulative economic causation in the work of the well-known Swedish economist Knut Wicksell, who played a large role in the development of Myrdal's economic thought. In his work on monetary theory Wicksell abandoned the static equilibrium concept used by conventional price theorists in favor of a labile or dynamic equilibrium concept.[5] In the general equilibrium concept of orthodox price theory a deviation from equilibrium would set in motion self-correcting reactive forces that would correct the deviation and restore the original static price equilibrium. In Wicksell's dynamic concept of equilibrium a deviation from the original monetary equilibrium would set in motion self-reinforcing, reactive forces that would result in a cumulative movement in the same direction as the primary deviation. In Wicksell's analysis of monetary phenomena a deviation of the money rate of interest from the equilibrium or natural rate of interest could cause a cumulative increase or decrease in production or investment which would go on until no further investment gains or losses were incurred, and the conditions for monetary equilibrium were again restored. The dynamic element in Wicksell's concept of equilibrium was to be found in the deviation from equilibrium which brought about a self-accelerating or cumulative process before equilibrium was again restored.[6]

Myrdal took Wicksell's concept of dynamic equilibrium and converted it into a general theory of social change which was first presented in his classic study of the negro problem in *An American Dilemma*, and then applied to economic problems in such later works as *An International Economy* (1956), *Rich Lands and Poor*

---

[4] Gunnar Myrdal, *An American Dilemma, The Negro Problem and Modern Democracy*, Appendix 3, "A Methodological Note on the Principle of Causation" (New York: Harper and Brothers, 1944) pp. 1065-1070.

[5] Knut Wicksell, *Interest and Prices* [*Geldzins und Guterpreise*] (London: Macmillan and Co., Ltd., 1936) p. 92.

[6] Gunnar Myrdal, *Monetary Equilibrium* (Reprints of Economic Classics; New York: Augustus M. Kelley, 1962) pp. 32-34.

(1957), *Beyond the Welfare State* (1960), *Challenge to Affluence* (1962) and *Asian Drama* (1968). Myrdal's theory of circular cumulative causation is an explanation of the dynamics of the causal relations among the various factors in a social or economic situation. This theory asserts that an original or primary change will cause secondary reactive changes which will reinforce the primary change and cause the social process to move further in the same direction taken by the primary change. For example, a decline in the health of a low-income sector of the labor force which reduces labor productivity will decrease wages and depress living conditions, which will further reduce the health or well-being of the workers and cumulatively lead to a still further decline in labor productivity. The primary change, a decline in worker health, gives rise to secondary factors which in a circular fashion reinforce the primary change to cause a cumulative downward movement in worker productivity. In a developing country in the take-off stage an increase in real gross national product may improve worker productivity and living conditions which in turn further increase real gross national product, and cause the newly developing country to move along a cumulative upward path. The primary change, an increase in real gross national product, is reinforced by secondary factors in a cumulative upward process. The significant elements in Myrdal's theory of social change are the primary change, the circular reinforcing secondary changes, and the upward or downward cumulative process.

As we shall see, much of Myrdal's interpretation of the emergence and evolution of the welfare state revolves around his interpretation of the unfolding of a "dynamic social process of cumulative causation," as the western economic system moved from feudalism through mercantilism and *laissez-faire* capitalism to the modern welfare state. Likewise, Myrdal applies his theory of circular cumulative causation to the problems of the newly developing countries where the cumulative process has much difficulty in moving upward.

The Goal-Directed Social Process

Myrdal is not only interested in the factors or forces that give momentum to the social process and in the process by means of which these forces exert their influence on the course of social and economic development. He is also interested in the fact that the social process is to some extent a goal-directed process. Myrdal does not accept the determinist philosophy of history according to which history is a blind destiny determined in advance and independently of mankind. The social process is not a blind process that is being pushed along the path of cumulative development for which man has no responsibility. On the contrary man is a value-creating individual who sets up goals or ideals which he seeks to achieve. Myrdal points out that "The future is not a blind destiny but is, instead, under our responsibility. We have the powers to analyze the facts and to establish rationally the practical implications of our ideals. We have the freedom to readjust our policies and, thereby, to deflect and change the trends."[7] When the social scientist examines the social process, he observes that people have goals and wants which greatly influence how they function in the social process. For example, in the welfare state of the western world the people want full employment, a rising standard of living, equality of opportunity for all, economic freedom and a fair sharing of national income. In order to achieve these goals the people have approved a restructuring of the formerly *laissez-faire* capitalist system and an extensive modification of how this system operates. According to Myrdal, a part of the data that economists should analyze are the goals which people actually have and which are very influential in determining the structure and functioning of their economic system.

The cumulative process through which social reality passes is guided to some extent by human wants and ideals. It is impossible to grasp the nature of this reality fully unless the social scientist includes the study of human wants and ideals in his study of the social process. It is for this reason that Myrdal states that "There is no way of studying social reality other than from the viewpoint of human ideals. A 'disinterested social science' has never existed and, for logical reasons, cannot exist."[8] The social scientist, however, does not impose his wants, ideals or value judgments on the community or nation that he is analyzing. What he does is to investigate the role and influence of the wants, goals and ideals of the communities which he is studying.

The Evolution of the Welfare State

Myrdal's scientific interests have been concerned with economic activity over the entire world. He observes that the world is divided into three large orbits or spheres of influence; namely, the western orbit which includes mainly the so-called "rich lands" of North-

---

[7] *An International Economy*, p. 335.
[8] *Ibid.*, Appendix, p. 336.

Western Europe and North America, the communist orbit dominated by the Soviet Union and mainland China with their satellites, and the third orbit of developing countries in Asia, Africa and Latin America. Myrdal, himself a product of the "rich lands," is primarily interested in the western orbit and the somewhat dependent orbit of underdeveloped countries. The western and underdeveloped spheres are closely related by trade and aid. In these two orbits Myrdal observes the spectacle of rich countries like the United States, Canada, Australia, the United Kingdom, Sweden, France and West Germany growing richer, while the large number of newly developing countries are growing relatively poorer. It is Myrdal's position that the rich countries are failing to meet their obligations to aid the newly developing countries in ways that will assure their success in achieving adequate levels of economic growth and social progress. Myrdal observes the rich countries of the western world perfecting their welfare states, while at the same time there is no world welfare state. On the contrary Myrdal observes a paradox in that the domestic or internal forces in the rich western nations that have given rise to the national welfare state have at the same time been inimical to the development of a world welfare state. National solidarity in the various major western democracies has not led to international solidarity with the result that the outlook for political, social and economic advance in the many underdeveloped countries remains bleak and unpromising.

The welfare state found in the western world is the end product of a long economic evolution. This evolution falls into three divisions. After the feudal era the mercantilist state emerged and dominated Western Europe until the second half of the eighteenth century. The mercantilist state was followed after about 1750 by the liberal state which flourished for a little more than a century. The foundations of the welfare state in North-West Europe were largely laid after the turn of the century in the decades 1900-1930. Since World War II the edifice of the welfare state has been brought close to completion, especially in the Scandinavian countries, the United Kingdom, West Germany and other continental countries. Myrdal explains that the mercantilist or pre-liberal state of the period 1500-1750 was an authoritarian state that was organized mainly to protect the vested interests of the upper classes. With suffrage severely restricted, and hence little participation by the majority of the people in political affairs, the pre-liberal state was not in any sense a welfare state. The liberal state of the period 1750-

1900 was important because it laid the foundation for the western ideals of equality and liberty. Both the natural rights and utilitarian philosophies, which flourished in the eighteenth century and nourished the new science of political economy, emphasized the doctrine of equality based upon equal innate human capacities. The liberal or *laissez-faire* state of the period 1750-1900, however, was essentially an undemocratic state, since universal suffrage was not obtained until after 1900 in many western countries. The modern welfare state could not emerge until the workers secured the right to vote. It was the democratization and urbanization of the western nations after 1900 that prepared the way for the emergence of the welfare state. Mass education and the decline of the *laissez-faire* market economy contributed further to the erosion of the nineteenth century liberal or *laissez-faire* society of Western Europe.

Myrdal analyzes the evolution of the twentieth century welfare state in terms of an irreversible cumulative process which developed after 1875 as the liberal state was slowly eroded under the pressure of national and international developments. The technological and industrial change which came after 1875 inaugurated an era of economic progress which was to transform the liberal or *laissez-faire* state into the welfare state. Technological and industrial change converted the nineteenth century free market economy into the twentieth century integrated economy. After 1900 major economic power groups were established in industry and agriculture. Trade associations, trade unions, consumer cooperatives and farmers' organizations greatly restricted the area of the free market. The growth of big industry was accompanied by the combining of small-scale enterprises in business, commerce and agriculture as a matter of self-defense. The emergence of economic power in one sector of the economy led to the development of countervailing power in other sectors of the economy.

The primary factor of technological and industrial change, which led to an increase in real output and a rising standard of living and which moved the western nations in the direction of economic progress, was accompanied by other factors that reacted in such a way as to accelerate technological and industrial change and to push society further along the path of economic progress. These factors were the increasing rationality of human behavior, the democratization of society, the spread of mass education, the expanding participation of the masses in public policy determination and the development of a more egalitarian society.

Myrdal explains that there is an inherent tendency in western civilization for the attitudes of people to change and to change in the direction of more rational behavior. As civilization advances people become less conformist and less inhibited. During the Victorian era people were non-experimental and unsophisticated. This was the era of widespread conventionalism. With the progress of science and the spread of mass education a typical cumulative process of circular causation was set in motion. Changes in people's attitudes towards the conformist Victorian society and the shocks from events such as the First World War and the depression of the 1930's led people to accept a larger role for the state in economic affairs. These developments caused individuals to become less conformist and more experimental in outlook, and hence still more "economically rational" and sophisticated. The whole social system was made to move in a cumulative way further towards "a general rationalization of attitudes" than anybody could have originally foreseen.[9]

The cumulative drive towards the welfare state was strengthened by the democratization of the nation's political process which shifted political power to the masses, and prepared the way for a larger participation by them in the determination of the direction of social and economic change. The spread of mass education, the development of a more egalitarian society with the aid of minimum wages, social security and better housing, and the widespread urge for achieving a rising standard of living were additional factors that reinforced the initial technological and industrial change leading to economic progress. These many factors reacted in a circular manner upon one another, and together accelerated the upward movement to higher levels of living. External factors such as the progress of the Soviet Union and the cold war have created an interest on the part of the western democracies in the problem of economic development. But the main factor giving rise to their continuing urge for economic expansion and rising levels of income and well-being is, in Myrdal's opinion, the "bustle for development" which has its origins in western culture. With the whole communications industry inducing individuals to buy an endless flow of consumer goods, the rich nations strive more diligently than the poor nations to improve their standard of living.

---

[9] Gunnar Myrdal, *Beyond the Welfare State, Economic Planning and Its Implications* (New Haven: Yale University Press, 1960) p. 36.

The Organizational State

Myrdal describes the modern welfare state as an "organizational state." Individual action has since 1900 been increasingly replaced by organized or collective action. The nineteenth century small-scale atomistic economic order has now been replaced by a large-scale integrated economic system. Myrdal explains that "a powerful but state controlled infrastructure of collective organizations has come into being." These collective organizations such as industry associations, employers' associations, producer and consumer cooperatives and confederations of trade unions are coming more and more to function like public authorities. They cooperate with the state in laying down norms of behavior and they share the responsibility for establishing short and long term economic settlements. Wages, prices and profits are now frequently settled by various collective bargaining arrangements among employers' associations, confederations of trade unions and farmers' organizations with the central government providing "an umpire service." The multilateral collective bargainings among these economic power groups have made many supply and demand curves in a sense "political."

As the organizational state developed after 1900 it was increasingly called upon to intervene in economic affairs. If it had not intervened the conflicts among business, financial, labor and agricultural groups would have given rise to a downward cumulative process of circular causation. It is Myrdal's thesis that, as industrialization spread after 1900, intervention steadily increased to the point where there was a need to coordinate the large unplanned complex of state intervention. When this need for the coordination of the large volume of state intervention was recognized and accepted by the public, national economic planning was introduced in the Scandinavian countries, the United Kingdom, France and other continental countries. The cumulative upward moving economic process necessarily converted the welfare state into a planned state. Unlike Soviet economic planning, the national planning of the North-West European countries was an unplanned development. The intervention that preceded national planning was also unplanned. The spread of the intervention that was later to lead to national planning was caused by violent international crises such as the First and Second World Wars and the Great Depression of the 1930's. Before the onslaught of these major crises the old automatic scheme of international economic relations based on the gold monetary standard crumbled, and was replaced by a poorly coordinated and managed state intervention on the international front.

The international factors leading to an increase in the volume of state intervention were supplemented after 1900 by a large variety of domestic national factors pointing in the same direction. Reference greatly the supply and demand for commodities and services. the emergence of large economic power groups in a position to influence greatly the supply and demand of commodities and services. The necessity for the central government to act as an economic umpire, the concern for a more egalitarian society, the demand for a fairer sharing of national income and the effort to provide full employment inevitably led to a great increase in the volume of government intervention and the need for some kind of coordination of this intervention. As Myrdal sees it, planning is the outcome of a process of cumulative causation. The first acts of intervention were applied to the play of the market forces which could no longer provide economic stability, high economic growth and full employment. Additional factors at home and abroad, discussed above, increased the volume of intervention and reinforced the primary or original intervention in the market place. In this manner the movement towards more intervention became accelerated. As the system of intervention became more complex, contradictory and confused the need for a "rationalizing coordination" of all schemes for intervention was impressed upon the central government.

Myrdal defines national economic planning as coordination. It is a coordination of all important public economic and social policies with the aim of "bringing the economy of a country to function in accordance with the majority interests of all citizens."[10] The national planning of the western democracies, unlike the blueprint comprehensive planning of the communist countries, is of a compromise character. It is pragmatic, non-comprehensive and not politically ostentatious. Western national economic planning has nothing to do with fixed production targets for industries or firms. It relates instead only to broad aggregates such as gross national product and private and public consumption and investment. Taking Sweden as his planning model Myrdal explains that national planning in the welfare state proceeds on the basis of annual and four or five year projections of gross national product and its private and public con-

---

[10] *Beyond the Welfare State*, p. 6.

sumption and investment uses. These projections, which are national economic budgets, project national priorities in the form of annual economic growth rates, the amount of gross national product to be devoted to public and private investment and the level of public consumption. These budgets show how national priorities and economic policies are coordinated in order to achieve the national goals.

Myrdal explains that the fiscal budget plays a secondary role in the national economic budget. The revenues and expenditures of the fiscal budget are adjusted to secure the priorities set forth in the national economic budget. Myrdal asserts that the Keynesian view of the fiscal budget as a device to be used to offset business fluctuation is now outmoded. The Keynesian countercyclical budgetary policy was useful only in the era of state intervention which in Western Europe has now been replaced by the era of national planning. Under national planning economic fluctuations are greatly reduced and the fiscal budget is no longer primarily a countercyclical device. Instead it becomes largely a set of items that are to be analyzed as a part of the national economic budget.

The planned economy of the welfare state does not do away with private enterprise. Instead it supplements and facilitates the private business system. Apart from the few key industries such as transportation, power production and communications which are nationalized, the major portion of output in the planned welfare state continues to come from privately owned and operated business enterprises. In Sweden, Norway, France and the United Kingdom only a few key industries have been placed under public ownership. Nor does the welfare state eliminate the market mechanism. Although prices in the advanced welfare state tend to become "political prices" which are significantly influenced by the multilateral negotiations of private economic interest groups, nevertheless the price mechanism is preserved. What the planned welfare state does is to transform the price mechanism into an efficient instrument for national economic planning. The mechanism becomes a device for the achievement of the national goals set forth in the national budget of the welfare state.[11]

The Planned Welfare State

The overall purpose of national planning in the welfare state is to

---

[11] Gunnar Myrdal, "The Trend towards Economic Planning," *The Manchester School of Economic and Social Studies*, Vol. XIX, No. 7, January 1951, p. 37.

throw light on "the direction of the whole national economy."[12] Establishing this direction is the result of a compromise on the part of the various economic power groups. It is for this reason that Myrdal states that national planning in the welfare state is of a compromise nature. He sees in the modern industrial society a convergence of political attitudes. Political parties in the enlightened welfare states of Western Europe no longer disagree concerning the general desirability of redistributional reforms, education and public health programs, progressive taxes, social security or the public ownership of some key industries and banks. Industries and banks in the West European democracies are so extensively regulated they may now be said to be "socialized," and nothing would be gained by formally nationalizing them. Debates among political parties in what Myrdal calls the "advanced welfare states" are less on broad issues and more on the detailed arrangements for securing generally agreed upon national goals. The outcome of the convergence of political attitudes is a "created harmony" of interests and opinions among the great majority of the voters. This created harmony is to some extent concealed by the professionals in the various political parties and in major economic interest groups such as employers' associations, trade unions and farmers' organizations. These professionals have an interest in preserving their organizations and their jobs. Consequently they have to give the impression that the conflicts of opinion and interest among people and parties are larger than they actually are.

The created harmony of the welfare state is quite unlike the automatically created "liberal harmony" of the *laissez-faire* or liberal state. The created harmony is a managed harmony that comes about because people and organizations strive to achieve it. Whereas the liberal harmony of the *laissez-faire* state was created by market forces, the created harmony of the welfare state is in large part the product of non-market forces. Consequently the emergence of the welfare state's created harmony must be explained in terms of the increasingly rational formation of people's attitudes, the gradual democratization of political power and the continued economic progress which has made mutual generosity on the part of the nation's major economic power groups possible.

Myrdal points out that the people in the western democracies accept the welfare state because it is not imposed on them from

---

[12] *Ibid.*, p. 72.

above. It is the outcome of a social process in the directing of which the people have an important role. People feel free under the welfare state because they participate in determining its nature and direction. Participation leads to a solidarity of interests and an identification with the goals of the welfare state. The more people participate at the local governmental levels and in the affairs of the major economic interest groups the less need there is for central government regulations and direction. There is always the danger of excessive centralization of governmental activities in the welfare state. Myrdal draws attention to the fact that there are no minimum wage laws, no compulsory arbitration and no closed shop arrangements in Swedish factories. Because participation is so high in employers' associations and trade unions, the Swedish government has little need to regulate industrial relations. These and other economic problems are worked out at the local level so that there is a minimum of government regulation at the national level.

One of the major deficiencies of the welfare state is what Myrdal calls the "malaise of non-participation" in the affairs of political parties, private economic organizations and local governments. When these organizations were fighting for the acceptance of the welfare state, individuals eagerly participated in the activities of these organizations. But when the fighting stage was over, member participation dropped dramatically. The disease of non-participation is especially bad in the United Kingdom, the United States, Canada and Australia. In the long run the success of the welfare state depends upon effective participation and control by the public.

The Welfare State: The Next Phase

Myrdal finds the welfare state far from perfected. The first deficiency of the welfare state is its overcentralization. There is a great need to "debureaucratize" the welfare state by having the central government responsible only for the major features of national policy in such areas as foreign trade, taxation, labor legislation, social security, education, health and defense. In addition the state should continue to regulate banking, transportation, communications and other public utilities, and to provide an umpire service for activities at the sectoral and local levels. Within this general framework economic interest groups and local governments should settle their problems through cooperation and collective bargaining. The welfare state would then take on the appearance of a "grass-roots" democracy.

A second deficiency of the welfare state is the persistence of a "power oligarchy" of top leaders in business, politics and other sectors of society. This power oligarchy or Establishment benefits from a tax system that is not adequately progressive, and from its control of the newspapers and other mass communications media. The rich have undue political influence and can improperly sway mass opinion on public issues. Consequently private spending is pushed to the neglect of public spending for high priority national purposes. In Myrdal's opinion the only way to make the public "propaganda safe" so that it will not be misled by the private power oligarchy is to educate the public to the abuses of its power by the oligarchy.

A third major deficiency of the welfare state is its inflationary bias. The welfare state has a high pressure economy in which there is little slack in the form of unutilized labor or capital. The multilateral discussions concerning wages, profits and prices have not yet been sufficiently well coordinated with the increases in incomes which are in line with the increases in productivity. The welfare state cannot tolerate inflationary developments without attempting to control them because of the adverse effect of inflation on the distribution of real incomes and on the direction of investment and consumption. Efforts to suppress inflation necessitate many direct controls which lead to the misallocation of resources and the development of many inflexibilities in the nation's economy. Efforts to eliminate inflation with the aid of monetary and fiscal measures have not been successful because the rigorous application of these measures would create large-scale unemployment. No welfare state has yet found a way to combat inflation successfully. The Scandinavian countries have had considerable experience with multilateral negotiations about wages, prices and profits under state guidance, but as yet no way has been found to prevent the inflationary consequences of these negotiations. Myrdal would tackle the inflationary bias of the welfare state by securing a better understanding among the nation's major economic interest groups of the reasons for inflationary developments. This means raising the general level of economics education and improving the participation of people at all levels in the welfare state. In particular people need to be educated to grasp the truth that increasing money incomes faster than productivity is improved is damaging to everyone in the country. In the "industrial democracy" that the welfare state seeks to establish it is assumed that businessmen, workers and farmers know this and act responsibly. In addition Myrdal observes a need for strong and effective consumers' organizations to counterbalance the producers' organizations. One of the major weaknesses of the planned welfare state has been the inadequate consumer countervailing power. The state cannot substitute for weak consumer organizations because if it did it would then no longer function as an umpire. It is Myrdal's conclusion that much remains to be done to bring the welfare state closer to perfection.

It is Myrdal's view that the national economic planning found in advanced welfare states like Sweden, Norway, the Netherlands and the United Kingdom is not a matter of choice for welfare states in general. To the contrary, in his opinion, it is probably their destiny.[13] By asserting that it is the destiny of the welfare state to adopt a planned economy Myrdal is not duplicating the teleological view of the orthodox nineteenth century economists that the economy is moving automatically towards a predetermined competitive equilibrium. In Myrdal's view of the future nothing is inevitable. Nor is the future state of the economy automatically predetermined. It is Myrdal's position that no future state of the economy is guaranteed and that mankind must struggle to achieve whatever goals it sets up. It is also his position that a further evolution of the industrial economy of the western democracies is probable and that such a development, if it occurs, will follow a path indicated by the logic of development. There is a logic of development in the cumulative process of causation through which the western democracies are passing. This cumulative process is spreading the complex of state interventions over such a broad area of the modern industrial economy that it is logical to expect there will be a strong pressure to coordinate these interventions with the aid of a national economic planning program. Man being a self-active, experimental creature, if he is active long enough, must necessarily come to terms with the logic inherent in the upward moving process of cumulative causation that points in the direction of the planned economy of the advanced welfare state.

The American Welfare State

Myrdal has had close contacts with the American economy since the 1930's. He has been a keen observer of American social and economic developments, especially since the early 1940's when he

---

[13] "The Trend towards Economic Planning," p. 40.

made his study of the negro problem and published his now classic
*An American Dilemma, The Negro Problem and Modern Democ-
racy* (1944). He has observed that Sweden and the United States,
his "two spiritual fatherlands," are more similar than any other two
countries not only in the achievement of high standards of living
but also in social and economic values. Nevertheless there are major
differences between Sweden and the United States. Myrdal describes
Sweden as an advanced welfare state which, while far from being
perfect, is much ahead of the United States which cannot yet be
described as an advanced welfare state. It is the Swedish welfare
state with its planned economy that Myrdal takes as his yardstick
for comparisons with the United States. The major difference between these two countries is that the Swedish economy is a well
planned economy whereas the American economy has made only
rudimentary progress along this line. On the welfare front the
United States lags considerably behind Sweden. Myrdal is very
much concerned about the failure of the United States to move faster
and further on the planning front, because he fears that the failure
to plan American economic activities more extensively and successfully than is now done may weaken America's role as a world leader.
Myrdal is greatly impressed with America's potential for world
leadership, and would like to see this potentiality fully realized for
the benefit of all countries.

Myrdal calls attention in *Challenge to Affluence* (1962) to the
major weaknesses of the American economy which are sapping the
strength of the United States and seriously interfering with its role
as a world leader. These weaknesses include the slow and unsteady
rate of economic growth, excessively high unemployment, poverty,
inflation and the imbalance in the international financial position
of the United States.

Myrdal points out that the United States has not enjoyed the high
and steady economic growth achieved by most of the West European democracies since the close of the Second World War. The
United States in 1961-1968 had an average annual per capita economic growth rate of 3.4 per cent that compared favorably with the
growth rates of the West European countries. In years of recession
such as 1969 and 1970, however, the growth rate of the United
States falls much below that of West European countries. According to Myrdal's interpretation of post war developments and discrepancy between American and West European economic growth
rates is to be attributed to the failure of the United States to adopt

the activist programs of the governments in Scandinavia, West Germany, France and other West European countries. These activist programs include a new pattern of economic development which incorporates a much more watchful and directive economic policy on the part of the government. In Myrdal's opinion it is not enough in the United States to seek to eliminate recessions and to stabilize the economy. Rather the government should plan its economic policies with the aim of "pushing the economy into an entirely new pattern" of development and growth.[14]

The American low and irregular economic growth rate has been accompanied by an excessively high unemployment rate. Although many individuals in the United States enjoy continuous employment and a high standard of living, there is a large minority that does not have these advantages. Myrdal explains that a better grasp of the seriousness of unemployment in the United States would be had if the official statistics included those individuals working only part time and those who drop out of the labor market and do not seek jobs when they are scarce. Writing in 1962 Myrdal felt that economists and political and other leaders tended to be too near-sighted with regard to the unemployment problem. This outlook led them to overemphasize the cyclical aspects of the unemployment problem to the neglect of its structural aspects. In Myrdal's opinion the United States could benefit by adopting some of the features of the Swedish unemployment policy which stresses the importance of selective anti-unemployment measures to increase labor mobility and to aid declining industries, localities and regions. Closely associated with the unemployment problem in the United States is the poverty problem. With one-tenth of the American people officially recognized as living in poverty, unemployment and poverty cannot be eliminated and high and steady economic growth cannot be achieved until more equality of opportunity and a wider sharing of national income are secured. As Myrdal sees these problems, success along these lines cannot be had until the tax burdens on low income groups are reduced, unemployment benefit payments are increased, pensions are raised closer to what they are in Sweden (two-thirds of a worker's wages earned in his best years), a comprehensive national health service is adopted, trade unions are opened to the mass of

---

[14] Gunnar Myrdal, *Challenge to Affluence* (New York: Pantheon Books, 1962) p. 5.

poor workers, rural poverty is reduced and an enlarged public sector provides more schools and hospitals, better housing and better city planning.

Inflation and the deterioration of the American international financial position are related problems. Even without full employment the United States has at various times since 1945 suffered from strong inflationary pressures. Any policies that would lead to higher economic growth rates and less unemployment would create a high pressure economy and make the inflation problem even worse. In this connection Myrdal points to two major deficiencies of American economic policies. The first deficiency is the tendency for the regulatory authorities to rely too heavily on general monetary policies when grappling with the inflation problem. Monetary measures are clumsy and hit the economy indiscriminately when they are of a general nature such as a change in interest rates or in bank reserve requirements. Myrdal asserts that more reliance should be placed in the United States on fiscal policies of a flexible nature, as in Sweden, where personal income tax rates can be easily and quickly changed, and tax free investment reserves built up out of private company profits can be readily adjusted in a countercyclical manner. Myrdal goes on to explain that American anti-inflationary policy would be more effective if collective bargaining over wages were to be placed on a more rational basis. He calls attention to Swedish experience with centralized collective bargaining which has prepared the way for achieving less inflationary wage developments than under a highly decentralized system of collective bargaining such as prevails in the United States. Centralized collective wage bargaining under government direction would make it possible to curb the inflationary wage rounds that are experienced in the United States in boom periods. There is also a great need in the United States for an improved institutional infrastructure which would make room for more effective employers' associations and centralized trade union organizations capable of speaking for all of organized labor.

In these and other ways the government in the United States would be in a better position to maintain a watch over the economy's cost-price structure and its relation to the economy's external sector. The government should be interested in price as well as wage developments. Myrdal suggests that the American government should abandon its fruitless fight against monopoly, and should endeavor instead to work with big business and to share in controlling its administered prices as is done in the Scandinavian countries. There is a great need in the United States for more government guidance of the price- and wage-determining processes. This guidance should, however, extend to the whole economy so that policies and programs for economic growth, unemployment, poverty and inflation control, and external balance can be effectively integrated. What the United States needs for this purpose, in Myrdal's opinion, is an overall plan for the development of the economy as a whole. Such a plan would be a framework for government economic policies and also a basis for private business planning. It would require the construction of national economic budgets which would provide projections of the expanding gross national product and its distribution among alternative private and public consumption and investment uses. Alternative projections would present the nation with a choice among different growth rates and patterns. Myrdal feels that the use of long-term national economic budgets or gross national product projections would make government and business decisions that shape the future of the nation's economy more rational. National economic budgeting or programming in the United States should be the special concern of the Council of Economic Advisers supported by the major economic governmental departments. Myrdal states that this national programming should also be the concern of American universities and independent research institutions. At present this is not the case because there is a general tendency to nearsightedness among economists and government leaders. Too much attention is paid to the next recession and not enough to long-term or secular developments. America focuses its attention upon "the immediate, the concrete, and the experimental" to the neglect of "the long view."[15]

Myrdal points out that in the social sciences, as in other sciences, the United States has been singularly uncreative. It has had to rely upon Europe for its philosophy and theory, and for "the comprehensive grip of things and events." In economics American dependence upon English economic thought from Adam Smith to John M. Keynes has been heavy. Myrdal observes that "Even at the universities and other research institutions studies in terms of the long-range future are neglected, except in regard to population and resources.... It is difficult to avoid the reflection that neglect by...

---

[15] *Ibid.*, p. 87.

American universities and other research institutions of the long-range prospects of the American economy as a whole and the undue concentration on short-range issues — or . . . often on timeless and by any standards less important terminological questions and un-worldly constructs [i.e., mathematical models]—is partly responsible for the failure of my distinguished and numerous fellow economists to disseminate more economic understanding among the American people [about the long-range prospects of the American economy.]"[16] This myopic bias of the American economics profession is a serious obstacle to an understanding on the part of the general public of the need for national economic planning. Another major obstacle to the acceptance of national planning in the United States is the position with regard to this issue taken by the business community. Myrdal finds that the strong opposition of business to national planning is at bottom irrational because an understanding of long range trends is essential for sound business planning as well as for government planning.

Myrdal believes that much of the opposition in the United States to the idea of national planning would evaporate if the kind of national planning that he thinks would be appropriate for the United States was more effectively brought to the attention of the American people by economists and political and ᵒther moulders of public opinion. What Myrdal recommends is the kind of national economic planning that has emerged since 1945 in Sweden.[17] Swedish national economic planning is much less regimented or government dominated than French national planning. French planning involves too much *dirigisme* or regimentation which de-rives from the extensive economic controls in the hands of the government. Furthermore neither private economic interest groups nor the French parliament have much to say about the general shape of the French national economic plans. Swedish national planning is of a much less *dirigiste* or restrictive form than is French planning. Swedish planning leaves a greater role for adjustments of

---

[16] *Ibid.*, p. 88.

[17] Similar planning is carried on in Norway and Denmark. Unfortunately Myrdal does not give his readers much of an understanding of how national planning operates in Sweden and other Scandinavian countries. An analysis of Swedish and Norwegian national economic planning is provided in Chapters 13 to 18 in Allan G. Gruchy, *Comparative Economic Systems, Competing Ways to Stability and Growth*, pp. 274-418.

the nation's economy freely made by private business. There is a much smaller nationalized industrial sector in the Swedish economy than in the French economy. Also Swedish planning is more responsive to the goals of the general public and the parliament. Sweden has managed to avoid some of the excessive centralization of the planning activities as they are carried on in France. Bigger government in Sweden under national planning has not meant bigger bureaucracy. Planning in Sweden has not resulted in the proliferation of detailed economic controls, but instead in more overall direction of the nation's economy in which the citizens and the parliament participate. Swedish national planning is a highly decentralized form of national planning which is based upon a considerable unity of outlook among the nation's major economic interest groups and a high degree of cooperation by these groups in the construction and carrying out of the five year national economic plans.

Myrdal is quick to admit that there are many factors which would make the adoption of even the mild democratic Swedish type of national planning very difficult in the United States. The lack of the parliamentary system of government in the United States impedes cooperation between the Executive and the Congress. The working rules of the Congress favor the conservative element in the Congress. The large influence of the rural vote, the low level of city government and the lag in developing an independent non-political civil service are inimical to the development of an interest in national economic planning. Furthermore, the lack of a democratic balance in the nation's institutional infrastructure brings it about that business power which does not look with favor upon national planning is not adequately offset by the power of trade unions and consumers who are more favorable towards national planning. In Myrdal's opinion the only way to overcome these obstacles to the adoption of national planning in the United States is to educate the general public to a better understanding of American economic problems and of the need for some kind of national planning to handle these problems effectively. It is particularly up to the economics profession to be more concerned with long term economic projections and programs and to carry on research in this field. This work would not only provide a more rational basis for national economic policy formation but would also have the wider function of educating the general public about the need for national planning.

The World Welfare State

Myrdal points out that the next logical step beyond the individual or national welfare state is the world welfare state. In the latter state the same values that people seek in the national welfare state would be sought on the international level. In the Welfare World all nations would seek liberty or a democratic way of life, equality of opportunity among nations, and a spirit of brotherhood or international solidarity that would lead rich countries to share their economic abundance with the poor underdeveloped countries. All nations would gain from the international cooperation that would lead to international economic stability and progress. Unfortunately, the nations of the world are very far from achieving a world welfare state. Myrdal draws attention to the fact that the world is divided between a small number of rich countries with very high levels of average real income per head and a large number of poor countries with very low levels of per capita real income. The upper class group of rich nations includes the United States, Canada, Australia, New Zealand, the United Kingdom and the northern fringe of continental European democracies which are located in the temperate zone and are frequently well supplied with natural resources. The large number of poor or lower class countries are found in the Middle and Near East, Africa, South Asia and Latin America (except Argentina and Uruguay). Not only is there a wide economic gap between the rich and poor countries, but this gap has been increasing in recent decades. The rich industrialized countries are continuing to industrialize more rapidly than the poor countries.

Myrdal explains that the very forces that support the national welfare states operate adversely to the establishment of a Welfare World. Since 1914 there have been two contrary processes at work, one process leading to national integration and the spread of the welfare state within each of the rich nations and the other process leading to international disintegration and the impoverishment of the newly developing nations. In the rich nations there has been an upward cumulative process that has reduced or eliminated inequalities among regions, occupations and individuals. As the mature nations in Western Europe and North America have become industrialized and economically well off there have developed in each rich nation an intense feeling of national solidarity and a spirit of mutual generosity. Under government intervention and later national planning the free play of the market forces has been severely restricted with the result that major economic inequalities have been eliminated as the welfare state has been established. Unfortunately the individual welfare state is nationalistic and inward looking. Planning is in essence national. It can control domestic developments but not international developments. In the face of uncontrollable international crises the individual welfare state becomes protectionist in outlook.

There are in the rich countries two main obstacles to the development of a world welfare state, the one institutional and the other psychological. The institutional anti-internationalist bias of the national welfare state arises from the fact that there are many large economic interest groups that have been established to protect the interests of domestic businessmen, farmers and workers, but there is no large domestic interest group to fight for the world welfare state. The psychological obstacle to the establishment of a world welfare state takes the form of negative attitudes on the part of the citizens of the rich countries towards the outside world. People in rich countries have a strong feeling of national solidarity which is antipathetic to any ideal of international solidarity. These two major obstacles will have to be overcome before a new and wider "concerted harmony" among rich and poor nations can be created. Myrdal explains that what is needed is international planning that will coordinate the national planning of the rich and poor countries. There is a great need for international planning to bring an end to the international disintegration which shows no signs of diminishing. The world's poor nations have since 1945 undergone a Great Awakening which has led them to demand a share in the economic progress, liberty and equality of opportunity enjoyed by people in the rich countries.

The Poor Newly Developing Countries

Myrdal is not very optimistic about the possibility of closing the economic gap between the rich and the poor nations. Whereas it was relatively easy to remove many of the economic inequalities within the rich nations, it will be much more difficult to reduce or to eliminate inequalities in the international economy. It is Myrdal's main thesis with regard to the problem of the poor underdeveloped countries that "because of circular causation a tendency toward inequality is inherent in the unhampered play of the [domestic and international] market forces, and particularly so when the general level of development [in a country] is low."[18] According to this interpretation market forces in the international economy work out to the benefit of all nations only when they are at the same level of industrialization. When rich industrialized nations trade freely with poor non-industrialized or weakly industrialized countries, the poor countries are pushed by market forces into a downward cumulative process leading to economic stagnation and a low standard of living. This result is brought about by what Myrdal describes as the "backwash effects" of international trade.[19] These backwash effects are the secondary consequences of trade between rich and poor nations which are adverse to the economic development of the poor nations. The backwash effects are the source of a contractionary momentum which leads to a declining economy in the poor underdeveloped country. When a rich industrialized country with large-scale industries exports manufactured goods to a poor country, the small-scale industry and handicrafts of the latter country are unable to compete successfully, and without tariff or other protection they decline or disappear. A downward circular cumulative process of causation sets in. As the small-scale industry of the poor country declines, industrial external diseconomies develop. The demand for skilled workers declines, the credit system of the country is weakened, people turn more to agriculture and urban culture suffers. These interlocking factors work to push the poor underdeveloped country further down the path of underdevelopment and international economic inequality. If nothing is done to arrest this downward cumulative process, the poor country approaches the minimum level of a subsistence economy which is marked by stagnation and a subsistence level of living.

Meanwhile the rich industrialized countries are enjoying the favorable "spread effects" of international trade which are the source of an expansionary momentum. As the rich country's industry exports and expands, industrial external economies increase, labor is shifted from low productivity agriculture to high productivity industry, the demand for skilled workers increases, education and health are improved, urban centers expand and culture in general flourishes. The cumulative upward process is reinforced in its momentum by these interlocking factors. Further industrialization

---

[18] Gunnar Myrdal, *Rich Lands and Poor, The Road to World Prosperity* (New York: Harper and Brothers, 1957) p. 56.
[19] *Ibid.*, p. 27.

and economic progress ensue. In the unregulated international economy the free play of the market forces causes the rich nations to become richer as the poor nations become poorer. Within the poor nations economic inequalities tend to increase rather than decrease. If a rich nation establishes an enclave in a poor developing country which has no plan to offset the adverse effects of trading through the enclave, the backwash effects of establishing the enclave may have a very adverse impact on the poor country's development. The enclave will drain the few educated and skilled workers and artisans from other parts of the country. The poor country's savings will gravitate towards the foreign enclave. Transportation will be provided to accommodate the enclave and not the country's hinterland. The country's hinterland will become only a source of raw materials or agricultural products. As a result of the cumulative downward process of causation the inequality between the enclave and the rest of the country will increase. Even in a poor underdeveloped country where there are no foreign enclaves the spread effects of international trade may be much weaker than its backwash effects. In a rich country after a certain high level of economic development has been reached, rapid and sustained progress becomes almost automatic. The momentum created by earlier strong spread effects neutralizes any backwash effects. The reverse is true in a poor country where the dominant backwash effects neutralize any spread effects.

The remedy that Myrdal suggests for eliminating the international economic inequalities suffered by the poor underdeveloped countries and for offsetting the backwash effects of international trade is national planning. In these countries the state should plan to interfere with the free play of the market forces in order to give an upward push to the social process. The aim of this planning would be to remove "the stale and rigid social structure" and to seek to establish greater flexibility in the entire economic and social fabric. Since underdeveloped countries usually lack a sense of national solidarity, Myrdal asserts that these countries should encourage a "safe and sound" or "rational" nationalism that will unite the masses and inspire them to support the objectives of a national planning program. The main purpose of the national plan would be to strengthen the spread effects of development impulses in order to start off a cumulative upward moving process of economic growth. Such planning would not be carried on in accordance with the criterion of private industrial profits, but instead in conformity with the criterion of "social extra-profit yields."[20] This means that the national plan would curb consumption and increase the amount of investment especially in the public sector. Social capital in the form of roads, public power plants, railroads and educational and health facilities would be enlarged with the aim of improving the foundation of the nation's productive powers. Such plans would provide more and not less room for private enterprise.

National planning in poor underdeveloped countries would have to be accompanied by rigorous economic controls. Domestic industry would be protected from foreign competition by tariffs. Exports in some situations would have to be subsidized. A major problem to be dealt with would be the wide fluctuations in the prices of primary products exported by the underdeveloped countries. Rigorous foreign exchange control would be necessary to prevent the flight of capital and the waste of foreign exchange on non-essential imports. National planning in underdeveloped countries calls for land reforms not only as a precondition for raising productivity in agriculture, but more importantly as a means of destroying the class structure of a stagnating society. Likewise reforms in education and health would not only improve the productivity of the population, but would also psychologically recondition individuals and the whole society so that they would be more rational in their motivation. National planning in underdeveloped countries has to be based on a policy of "utmost austerity." Social security on a broad scale can be adopted only after average income per head rises much above what the underdeveloped countries can hope for in the coming decades. The success of national planning in the newly developing countries in the long run depends upon the adoption of programs for the control of human fertility.

Myrdal points out that the success of national planning by underdeveloped countries depends to a great extent upon the cooperation of the rich countries. These countries can aid the poor countries in three major ways. They can keep their domestic markets open to the underdeveloped countries even though the latter pursue a policy of tariff protection for their own domestic markets in order to protect their young industries. The rich nations can also cooperate with the poor countries in establishing international programs for the stabilization of the world prices of the primary products exported by the underdeveloped countries. The rich countries must

---

[20] *Ibid.*, p. 91.

seek to override the natural inclination to obtain internationally traded primary products at the lowest possible prices. Finally, since there is no hope of restoring the free international capital market of the pre-1929 period, the rich countries should take steps to enlarge the flow of private capital to the newly developing countries. This can be done where the rich countries are prepared to guarantee the safety of their citizens' investments in the underdeveloped countries. Cooperation between the rich and poor nations should be supplemented by cooperation among the poor nations themselves. Many of the poor nations of the world are too small to pursue an industrialization program effectively by themselves. Wherever it is feasible the newly developing nations should form regional associations or common markets. These associations would greatly increase the bargaining power of the underdeveloped countries in their relations with the highly industrialized countries.

Myrdal is somewhat pessimistic with regard to the future of the world's underdeveloped countries. The internal difficulties faced by these countries are very large. The world's rich industrialized countries are slow to recognize their responsibilities with regard to the development of a world welfare state. In addition the many international organizations established since 1945 for the purpose of aiding the newly developing countries and improving the international economy have not been very successful. The General Assembly and the Economic and Social Council of the United Nations, the International Labor Organization, and the Food and Agricultural Organization have been largely discussion forums and platforms for national propaganda.[21] Other organizations such as the International Monetary Fund and the International Bank for Reconstruction and Development have not fulfilled the high hopes of the countries which established them. But there can be no turning back. The international ideal of a world welfare state continues to struggle for expression. The only solution for the reduction of the international disintegration which continues to plague the world, in Myrdal's opinion, is to be found in educating people to be internationally minded. People must be made to realize that mutual consideration and generosity are to the advantage of all countries. Unfortunately people in general are not yet psychologically prepared for international cooperation. The future of the world depends

[21] Gunnar Myrdal, *Realities and Illusions in Regard to Inter-Governmental Organizations*, L. T. Hobhouse Memorial Trust Lecture, No. 24 (London: Oxford University Press, February 25, 1954) p. 28.

upon eliminating the psychological lag between the nationalistic attitudes and negative impulses of people on the one hand and world circumstances calling for international cooperation on the other hand. What is needed, Myrdal concludes, is a "will to reach a compromise" which would be the foundation of a new and wider "concerted harmony" in the form of a world welfare state.[22]

Myrdal attacks the orthodox or classical theory of international trade on the ground that its assumptions are unrealistic.[23] This theory assumes that each trading nation has free competitive domestic markets, and that the whole international economy is constantly moving towards an equilibrium. According to orthodox international trade theory there is an equalization process at work in the international economy which enables all nations to share the fruits of technological progress and productivity improvement. Productivity improvement in advanced industrialized countries is supposed to lower the prices of manufactured goods exported to underdeveloped countries. These latter countries, according to orthodox free trade theory, gain by importing lower price manufactured goods and by selling primary product exports at high prices. Technological progress and productivity improvement would thus raise the standard of living in both the advanced industrialized countries and the poor underdeveloped countries. Any development in the advanced industrialized countries would call forth a reaction or development in the underdeveloped countries that would sustain the balance or equilibrium of the whole international economy, and all trading countries would stand to gain from this equilibrium.

Myrdal agrees with Raul Prebisch that the basic assumptions of orthodox international trade theory are not in conformity with the facts of the real economic world.[24] The advanced industrialized trading nations do not have free competitive domestic markets but instead have markets dominated by large industrial enterprises and large trade unions. Also developments in one sector of the international economy do not stimulate opposite reactions in other sectors so as to maintain the equilibrium of the international economy. Productivity improvements in the industrialized trading nations are

---

[22] *Beyond the Welfare State*, p. 286.

[23] Gunnar Myrdal, *Development and Under-Development*, Fiftieth Anniversary Commemoration Lectures (Cairo: National Bank of Egypt, 1956) p. 10.

[24] United Nations, Economic Commission for Latin America, *The Economic Development of Latin America and Its Principal Problems*, by Raul Prebisch, New York, 1950.

not exported through lower prices for manufactured goods because the large oligopolistic industries and large unions manage to keep these prices high and also to keep the gains of technological progress for themselves. But even worse, productivity improvements in the underdeveloped countries are syphoned off by the rich industrialized countries. Since the underdeveloped countries have competitive domestic markets and few trade unions, productivity improvements in them result in lower prices for primary product exports which are to the advantage of the industrially developed countries. Instead of inequalities between the advanced industrialized countries and the underdeveloped countries disappearing, as orthodox international trade theory would have it, such inequalities have increased.

It is Myrdal's view that orthodox international trade theory reflects the same inherited predilection for equilibrium which dominates orthodox economics in general. The equilibrium of the international economy is merely an extension of the equilibrium that is supposed to prevail in the domestic markets of the trading nations. The free trade doctrine is a corollary of the assumption of the harmony of interests which is used as a justification for non-intervention in the international economy. It is Myrdal's position that orthodox international trade theory was developed in the early nineteenth century by the world's rich advanced nations in the light of their special interests and to justify the *status quo*.

The Special Case of South Asia

In 1968 Myrdal capped his career as a social science researcher with the publication of his encyclopedic three volume work, *Asian Drama, An Inquiry into the Poverty of Nations*.[25] In his *An American Dilemma* published in 1944 Myrdal had analyzed the race problem in the United States, and had stimulated the American public to consider the gravity of this problem and the pressing need to cope with it. In a similar vein Myrdal in 1968 turned his spotlight on the persisting problem of poverty in South Asia, and indicated to the intelligentsia in that region the necessity of meeting this problem before any kind of satisfactory development could be

---

[25] Published in 1968 by the Twentieth Century Fund in hard cover and in paper cover by Pantheon Books. All references in this chapter are to the paper cover edition by Pantheon Books.

achieved.[26] Myrdal takes each South Asian country to be a social system which is guided by a set of value premises, which he summarizes in the term "modernization ideology." This ideology, which dominates the upper strata of South Asian society, leads each country in that region to seek to achieve such goals as a rise in labor productivity, higher levels of living, social and economic equalization, a united and integrated national community, national independence and democracy at the grass roots.

In each South Asian country there are six major factors or "conditions" that Myrdal finds are causally interrelated. A change in any one of these six factors causes changes in the others. These six factors are output and incomes, conditions of production, levels of living, attitudes towards life and work, institutions and policies. Changes in these six factors may cause an upward or downward cumulative movement in the social system. Myrdal defines development as "the movement of the whole social system upwards" out of poverty and towards higher levels of living. An increase in national income per head is a rough indicator of development, but since development is a "human problem" it cannot be adequately measured in purely economic terms. Development can also be measured in broader terms of attitudinal and institutional advancement with regard to such matters as health, education, land reform, fiscal justice, population control and honesty and efficiency in public administration. By broadening his concept of development Myrdal places the economic problems of development in a wider social setting. In doing so he believes that he is working out "a more realistic approach to the problems of underdevelopment, development and planning for development."[27]

Myrdal's basic thesis in the *Asian Drama* is that the various countries of South Asia have not progressed very far in achieving

---

[26] As an appeal to the intellectual elite of South Asia Myrdal's *Asian Drama* in its current form is much too long (in his own words "the length is abominable") and is unnecessarily burdened with many digressions. The main digression, which is on the methodological problems of economics, is not designed to stir popular interest in the economic, social and political problems of such underdeveloped countries as India, Pakistan, Burma, Ceylon and other countries in South Asia. What is needed is a one volume work that highlights problems, issues and solutions relating to development in South Asia as comprehended by Myrdal. This need has been met with the publication of Myrdal's *The Challenge of World Poverty, a World Anti-Poverty Program in Outline* (New York: Pantheon Books, 1970).

[27] *Asian Drama*, Vol. 1, p. 29.

a developmental take-off, and that their prospects for reaching such a goal are quite poor. It is his position that, whereas the social matrix of the western industrialized countries has been permissive of economic and social development, this has not been true in the case of South Asia. On the contrary the social matrix of the South Asian countries has presented serious obstacles to the progressive development of these countries. In the western countries during the nineteenth century the growth of industry was accompanied by improvements in education, health, urban living and the administration of government, which further stimulated industrial expansion. Industrial expansion was supported by changes in modes of living, attitudes towards life and work and economic and social institutions that reinforced the original advances in industry, and thus contributed in a circular manner to the upward cumulative movement that eventually established the welfare state. The reverse is true of the South Asian countries. Efforts to establish industry there and to spark an upward cumulative movement have not been reinforced by favorable developments with regard to modes of living, attitudes and institutions. Instead industrial expansion and economic development in general have been hemmed in by anti-rational attitudes and a rigid and traditional social structure. The spread effects of industrial expansion have been so limited in their impact that they have been unable to eliminate the stagnation that is so widespread in South Asia.

When analyzing development in South Asia Myrdal centers his attention on India which of all the South Asian countries has progressed the furthest in the practice of national planning, but which except for Pakistan has the lowest per capita gross national product of all the South Asian countries, and whose per capita gross national product is growing at the low rate of a little more than one per cent a year. Myrdal describes India as a "soft" state which has not been able to impose on its people the social and economic discipline that is required for successful developmental planning. Indian planning has been too gradualistic and too piecemeal, and so has failed to achieve the great push needed to lift it out of the "Rip Van Winkle world" that is so inimical to economic and social development.[28] The Indian planners, drawn primarily from the nation's upper social strata, have not succeeded in removing the major barriers to rapid development. The great mass of the population are victims of a

---

[28] *Ibid.*, Vol. II, p. 710.

survival mindedness that keeps their aspirations at a very low level. With survival their constant concern, Indian villagers do not aspire to rise above their customary low level of living. Furthermore among the upper strata of Indian society there is an aversion to manual work which draws support from the educational and caste systems. These anti-rational, traditional attitudes of both the lower and upper classes are major obstacles to achieving a high level of economic and social development in India.

Myrdal observes that in the villages the caste ridden and inegalitarian social structure delivers most of the benefits of government aid to those who need them the least. Land reform has not been carried out vigorously enough to alter the inherited patterns of land ownership and tenancy significantly with the result that widespread share cropping that is not conducive to the best use of the land continues to be practiced. Sanitation remains in a primitive condition, and facilities are inadequate for the attainment of a satisfactory level of health and the effective control of population growth. The educational system continues to emphasize "general" rather than "technical" education. Many children fail to complete their primary or secondary education, and those that do so suffer from what Myrdal describes as "miseducation," an education that emphasizes general education and so fails to train students for professional and technical work. Among the upper classes this miseducation gives rise to the problem of the "educated unemployed" who are unemployed because they have an aversion to doing manual work of any kind. The tax system fails to spread the tax burden equitably and leaves the door open to much evasion and corruption. Another major institutional obstacle to development in India is the inefficient and weak administration of government at all levels.

In Myrdal's opinion India can break out of its traditional stagnant social system and advance along the path of rapid development only when its major attitudinal and institutional obstacles are eliminated. To do this will require something of a social revolution backed up by forceful national planning. The right kind of national planning would eliminate the contradiction between India's modernization ideology and its unwillingness to impose the economic and social discipline that is necessary to put its modernization ideals into practice. Myrdal sees no probability that India will adopt the Chinese Communist totalitarian type of national planning. since the democratic tradition is so well established in that country. But the democratic planning that India needs is quite different from the kind of planning that India has carried on since the end of World War II. In Myrdal's view Indian planning should be more revolutionary and less gradualistic than it has been since 1945. What is needed is a "big push" on many fronts to lift the Indian economy out of its traditional and backward condition. Vigorous planning should be carried on in a coordinated manner on many fronts at the same time. This planning should be aimed at reducing the underutilization of labor which is the source of a national waste of immense proportions. Land reform that would abolish share cropping and enable the peasants to own their land would help to overcome the villagers' survival mentality and to increase the impact of economic incentives. Since the nation's labor force is expected to continue to increase at an annual rate somewhere between 2 and 3.5 per cent until the end of this century, it is Myrdal's position that India's agricultural policy should stress the importance of adopting labor intensive production techniques. Absentee landlordism should be abolished, and progressive cultivators should be enabled to reap the full rewards of their enterprise and labor. Improved health services would increase school attendance and would raise labor efficiency. A reorganized educational system would eliminate miseducation and substitute the "usefully employed" for the "educationally unemployed." An effective birth control program would offset the reduction in morbidity and in the mortality rate so that the benefits of economic growth would no longer be cancelled out by uncontrolled population growth. An improved and more effectively administered tax system would reduce tax evasion and provide for a more equitable distribution of the national tax burden.

What Myrdal hopes to see established in India and the other South Asian countries is a form of welfare capitalism in the private sectors of these countries. With land reform, improved transportation, better technical education and the villages brought more and more into the money economy much more of the nation's economic activity could be carried on through the private market system than is now the case. This would reduce the administrative burden on the planning authorities who could then direct their attention to the public sector and the overall guidance of the nation's economy. As Myrdal sees the problem, India should change from a "soft" to a "strong" state which is prepared to impose the necessary discipline on its people to secure satisfactory land reform and effective birth control. An archaic land tenure system and uncontrolled population growth can negate any progress made in the industrial sector by keeping this sector as an enclave in a largely traditional and backward society. The spread or development promoting effects that come with industrial development such as the growth of a managerial class, the enlargement of the supply of skilled workers, the development of rational economic attitudes and the stimulation of subsidiary industries cannot work their way out through the economy and cannot give rise to an upward cumulative movement if most of the economy remains depressed by a "rigid and inegalitarian social structure." Myrdal points out that when modern large-scale industrial enterprises are brought into competition with traditional crafts and other non-modernized producing units the slight increase in demand for labor coming from the new modern industrial enterprises is more than offset by reductions in the demand for labor in traditional manufacturing. During India's early development phase he would restrict new modern industry to the production of exports and import substitutes so as not to depress the traditional craft industries.

Myrdal attributes many of the inadequacies of Indian national planning to the influence of western economists who not only train many of India's economists, but who also serve as advisors to the Indian planning authorities. Western growth economists adopt a simplistic position with regard to the problem of development which leads them to overemphasize the role of capital investment as the "engine of development." Myrdal explains that the general position of these economists is that more capital investment will lead to industrial expansion which in turn will automatically induce the necessary changes and adjustments in education, health, population control and public administration to guarantee the desired developmental take-off and cumulative upward movement towards more adequate levels of living. This approach of the western economists which leads them to overemphasize the importance of capital investment also causes them to pay inadequate attention to the non-economic factors that are obstacles to national development. Even those economists who have improved their overly simplified capital output growth models by enlarging investment to include "investment in man" do so by incorporating in their models an aggregate expenditure figure for education and health, but they fail to specify the kinds of educational and health improvements that are needed for sound national development. In Myrdal's view this "financial" approach to the problem of investment in man merely covers up the need for basic changes in India's educational and health systems.

There are so many factors involved in national development in South Asia that Myrdal finds there is now available no mathematical model that is a suitable guide for analyzing the problems of national development and for making recommendations on how to stimulate it. All existing models he finds are overly simplistic, and while they have some relevance to the growth problems of mature industrial economies, these western growth models are much less useful to anyone who is concerned with the developmental problems of underdeveloped countries. Myrdal observes that the Harrod-Domar growth models and their variations have two deficiencies which make them of limited value for any analysis of development in South Asian countries. These deficiencies he describes as "misplaced aggregation" and "illegitimate isolation."[29] By misplaced aggregation Myrdal means the use in growth models of broad or aggregate concepts such as total output, total investment and total consumption which abstract from "the very facts that matter most." Misplaced aggregation is excessive aggregation that distorts economic reality by submerging the concreteness of facts and real problems in a sea of all encompassing summation. For example in an underdeveloped and somewhat stagnant economy like that of India it is more important to know *who* consumes and *what* he consumes than to know how total consumption has changed. Also it is more important to know *where* investment occurs and *what* supplementary investment is required to support the initial investment than to know how much is added to total capital investment.

Illegitimate isolation results when economic growth models are constructed on the basis of a few variables without regard to other variables with which the few variables are closely related in the real world. For example to isolate capital investment from attitudes and institutions that are essential for the effective use of this investment is one of the main forms of illegitimate isolation. An economic growth model that suffers from misplaced aggregation and illegitimate isolation is of little help in explaining the growth problems of an underdeveloped South Asian country where the complexity of concrete details should be studied and not ignored by dealing in broad aggregates, and where all relevant variables must be subjected to analysis if the nature of developmental problems is to be fully revealed. In Myrdal's opinion economic growth models of the Harrod-Domar type when applied to the underdeveloped economies

---

[29] *Ibid.*, Vol. III, Appendix 2, pp. 1951-1956.

of South Asia become merely an excuse for glossing over the real problems of development in these economies.

Myrdal explains that "Models are useful, however, only if they focus on relationships that are important for understanding reality and strategic for purposes of policy. Otherwise, instead of serving as thought-therapy and as guides to the formulation of relevant questions, they themselves cramp the mind; rigor petrifies into rigidity. Broadly speaking, this is our accusation against the model-thinking that has been applied to economic planning in South Asia and is reflected in the structure of the plans."[30] Myrdal is careful to point out that his criticism of overly simple growth models is not to be construed as a criticism of "the use of all models in economic analysis and policy-making." He is not on principle averse to the use of economic models. What he objects to is the use of highly unrealistic and overly simplified mathematical models which ignore data that cannot be quantified, and whose claims to quantitative precision cannot always be substantiated. Myrdal explains that "Models are essential aids to clear thinking. Indeed, all thinking in terms of systematic functional relationships between variables is model-building and model-using. . . . The first virtue of models is that they can make explicit and rigorous what might otherwise remain implicit, vague and self-contradictory. Even if a model is totally unrealistic, it may . . . serve as a kind of thought-therapy, loosening the cramped intellectual muscles, demonstrating the falsity or doubtfulness of generalizations, and suggesting the possibility of an interdependence previously excluded. The most justifiable claims for the use of economic models are the modest ones that they are cures for excessive rigidity of thought and exercises in searching for interdependent relationships."[31] But to go further and say that the oversimplified economic growth models of the Harrod-Domar type offer an explanation of the essential nature of economic and social development in South Asia cannot be justified. All too frequently, Myrdal points out, these conventional growth models make it easy to avoid the difficult task of studying reality in all its complexity.

Myrdal goes on to explain that the western economic growth models that have thus far been developed are not comprehensive enough to explain fully the "necessary and sufficient conditions of development." He states in the *Asian Drama* that he stopped short

30 *Ibid.*, Vol. III, Appendix 3, p. 1963.
31 *Ibid.*, pp. 1962 and 1963.

of "intensive model-building" because the parameters and variables of growth models cannot yet be defined with sufficient precision to warrant relying heavily on these models when one is analyzing the developmental problems of a region like South Asia. Myrdal therefore turns from mathematical model building to the "institutional approach which focusses the study of underdevelopment on attitudinal and institutional problems."[32] Instead of abstracting from the modes of living, attitudes and institutions of India and the other South Asian countries, Myrdal includes these factors in his analysis of development along with such economic factors as saving, investment, employment, production and aggregate output. Myrdal's institutional approach does not dispense with the inherited body of economic theory. On the contrary his institutional approach relies upon traditional economic tools, rigorous conceptual analysis and description, but in addition it goes further to include relevant noneconomic psychological and institutional factors. Myrdal's institutional approach results in an amalgam of facts, logical analysis and intuitional grasping of the significance of the total economic and social situation.

Myrdal explains that "the central idea in the institutional approach is that history and politics, theories and ideologies, economic structures and levels, social stratification, agriculture and industry, population developments, health and education and so on, must be studied not in isolation but in their mutual relationship."[33] In other words, Myrdal suggests that one can grasp economic reality satisfactorily only by viewing "economic problems in their total demographic, social, ideological and political setting." This holistic or totalistic approach used by Myrdal raises the question of how wide is the setting in which economic problems are to be placed for analysis. What are the limits or boundaries to the study of economic reality? Myrdal's answer as given in his earlier writings and repeated in *Asian Drama* is that all the factors or conditions that are relevant to the study of an economic problem such as development should be included within the scope of the institutional approach. A relevant factor or variable is one that improves our understanding of economic reality, a matter that can be determined only pragmatically by seeking to uncover "the very facts that matter most."

---

[32] *Ibid.*, Vol. III, Appendix 2, p. 1864.
[33] *Ibid.*, Vol. I, Preface, p. x.

Myrdal emphasizes that his institutional approach is not an indulgence in "loose thinking" as is claimed by conventional economists. He explains that the institutional approach is just as demanding of the economist as is the conventional approach. Just like the conventional approach the institutional approach "imposes the demand that theories and concepts be logically consistent as well as adequate to reality." Nor is the institutional approach limited to qualitative analysis. Myrdal asserts that the goal of scientific investigation must always be to quantify the facts and the relationships among facts as far as it is possible to do so. But seeking this goal of the quantification of facts is not a license to ignore economic and social data that cannot yet be quantified, to fail to pay attention to the concrete details of economic and social reality by turning to excessive aggregation and to oversimplify a human problem by concentrating on too few economic and social variables.

Some critics of Myrdal's *Asian Drama* assert that he is weakest when he comes to a consideration of concrete ways of stimulating economic and social development in South Asia. One critic of Myrdal's work states that "the positive thesis of his book is singularly vague."[34] While Myrdal makes a number of specific policy recommendations with regard to such matters as land and tax reform, population control, the improvement of the educational and health systems and aids that may be given by the rich nations to the poor nations, he remains somewhat vague with respect to the questions of how the attitudinal and the institutional obstacles to development may be removed, and how the nation can proceed in becoming less of a "soft" state and more of a "strong" state that would be prepared to impose on the people whatever economic and social discipline may be called for by the modernization goals. Myrdal's failure to be more specific about how the various South Asian countries may be transformed from stagnant, traditional countries to progressive, rapidly developing nations can be attributed in part to his use of the institutional or totalistic approach to the study of development. This approach causes him to consider so many different factors relating to development it becomes difficult at a later point to suggest policy recommendations that cover the wide array of variables included in his analysis. In addition his deep pessimism concerning the future of South Asia doubtlessly

---

[34] K. S. Krishnaswamy, "Some Thoughts on a Drama," *Finance and Development*, Vol. 6, No. 1, March 1969, p. 48.

has hindered his search for solutions to the problems of development. Some critics maintain that Myrdal's pessimism with regard to the future development of South Asia underestimates the possibilities of increasing exports to the developed countries and also of increasing agricultural production with the aid of new technologies, especially the new varieties of seeds when combined with fertilizers and the necessary water supply.[35] These critics also argue that Myrdal overemphasizes the importance of the land tenure and caste systems as obstacles to development.

In any evaluation of the *Asian Drama* one should keep in mind Myrdal's purpose in carrying out this study. He explained in the preface that "This book aspires to do little more than speed up the reorientation of economic and social research on South Asia. In this situation my findings can only be suggestive and tentative, and I expect that they will soon be lost like the memory of a variation of a melody in a mighty fugue of thinking and research which will proceed and never reach a finale." In *Asian Drama* it was Myrdal the scientific investigator who prevailed over Myrdal the social reformer. In the light of the hugeness of the problem of development in South Asia Myrdal was content with putting this problem in what he regarded as the right perspective, and largely leaving to others the matter of finding detailed and practicable solutions to this problem.

By 1970 Myrdal felt that it was necessary to take account of the criticism that he had failed in the *Asian Drama* to develop fully the policy implications of his study of poverty in South Asia. He answered this criticism in 1970 by publishing *The Challenge of World Poverty, a World Anti-Poverty Program in Outline* which provides a comprehensive summary of the main policies needed to speed up development in India and other underdeveloped countries. Many of these policies had been referred to in the *Asian Drama* but no effort had been made in this earlier study to emphasize the policy implications to be drawn from it. In his new study which he regards as a continuation of the *Asian Drama* Myrdal analyzes the policy problem from the viewpoints of both the underdeveloped and the developed countries. He explains that from the viewpoint of the underdeveloped countries the main concerns should be to eliminate the underutilization of the labor force and the impoverishment of the

---

[35] See for example George Rosen's review of *Asian Drama* in *The American Economic Review*, December 1968, Vol. LVIII, pp. 1397-1401.

masses. In Myrdal's opinion this can be done only through adopting fundamentally radical reforms relating to land ownership and tenancy, education, population control, government administration and the control of corruption. All these reforms if carried out would lead to a modernization of India that would draw upon the energy of the revitalized masses in the rural and urban areas. Myrdal emphasizes the point that most of the effort to achieve a more satisfactory development must come from the underdeveloped countries themselves. This will require a new national pattern of power relations among classes in which the power of the upper class oligarchy would be replaced by the power of the masses. In other words, before satisfactory development can occur in India, there must be a social and economic revolution that has the active support of the masses. Whether such a revolution is to be achieved peacefully or through the use of force remains a question for which Myrdal has no answer. He observes that the social sciences provide no basis for making any scientific forecast with regard to this matter. All that Myrdal sees is a "spectrum of alternatively possible political developments" and he is not prepared to forecast what will actually happen in India and other underdeveloped countries.

Myrdal's Economics of Integration

As our analysis of Myrdal's theory of the welfare state shows, he has been primarily interested in interpreting the evolution of the whole economic system as a part of the evolving social process. While in the early part of his career Myrdal revealed an interest in certain aspects of standard economics, it is not the economics of the market place or of the fluctuations in economic activity that has absorbed most of his attention. Myrdal has a much broader and longer term approach to economics than that of standard economists. His holistic approach takes the economic system to be an evolving process which is changing its structure and functioning over time. Economic systems are institutional complexes which are undergoing a process of development. He raises such questions as what has been the pattern of development of the country's economic system, and what are the alternative directions in which the economic system may move in the near future? Myrdal seeks to grasp the nature of the evolving economic system in the western democracies where the private enterprise system has been significantly changed in the past half century.

In order to understand economic reality the economist has to have a framework of interpretation or "a particular manner of looking at things."[36] Facts do not exude meaning by themselves. They come to mean something only when they are organized within some theoretical framework. As Myrdal puts it, facts must be approached with a "broad vision of what the essential facts are and the causal relations between them." There must be a logically coordinated attempt to understand economic and social reality as a whole. In a sense the basic approach or broad theoretical framework of the social scientist is *a priori* or constructed before all the facts have been investigated. Facts and theory are interrelated and neither comes first. Facts have no meaning without a general framework of interpretation and no such framework can be valid unless it is based on facts. What each social scientist constructs is "the model of models" which functions as a guide in the selection and interpretation of facts.

When Myrdal turns to the interpretation of the evolving economic system he abandons the inherited interpretative framework of standard economists. In the equilibrium approach of these economists there persists the notion that the forces operating in the economic system are moving it towards some kind of stable equilibrium in which a change of any kind very quickly generates a countervailing change which neutralizes or offsets the first change. The underlying concepts of the standard or orthodox "model of models" are stable equilibrium, countervalence and self-correction. Myrdal's "model of models" or framework of interpretation is markedly different from that of standard economists. In Myrdal's interpretative approach the economic system is taken to be a process the momentum of which does not lead to any stable equilibrium. A change in the economy does not lead to self-correction or countervalence but instead to self-reinforcement of the original change and further movement in the direction taken by the original change. Whereas in standard economics the free market mechanism is the device by means of which self-correction and eventual equilibrium are supposed to be achieved, the reverse is true in Myrdal's integrative economics. In his analysis the forces of the market place, if unregulated, support the movement towards self-reinforcement, imbalance and disequilibrium. In Myrdal's view the social process is a cumu-

---

[36] *Rich Lands and Poor*, p. 133. See also *Asian Drama*, Vol. I, p. 6, and Gunnar Myrdal, *Objectivity in Social Research* (New York: Pantheon Books, 1969) pp. 6-19.

lative movement in which any balance that might be achieved between self-correcting and self-reinforcing forces is unstable and not the natural outcome of the play of the forces operating within the process. The momentum of a social process can carry it upward towards a higher state of integration or downward to a lower state of disintegration. Where the social process is stagnant the forces leading to integration and disintegration are for the time being in balance.

Myrdal's theory of economic evolution is general in nature. It applies equally well to countries moving upward to higher levels of integration and to countries moving downward to lower levels of disintegration. In Myrdal's general framework of interpretation the forces leading cumulatively to integration or disintegration are substituted for the equilibrating forces assumed by standard economists to be operative in the modern economy. When he is analyzing the economic systems of the western democracies Myrdal is concerned primarily with the forces leading to economic integration. An integrated economic system is one in which all the parts are related in such a way as to create a harmonious whole. Such an integrated economy is not the product of the free private market place. On the contrary it is Myrdal's position that an integrated economy can be achieved only when the forces of the private market mechanism are subjected to government controls. He explains that the momentum of the economic systems in the western democracies has since 1900 carried them from a condition of low per capita real income to affluence. If the private enterprise system had not been subjected to increasing intervention and regulation at the same time that the nation was becoming affluent, great inequalities among individuals, classes and economic regions would have persisted, and the achievement of national integration would have been greatly delayed. It is Myrdal's position that the unregulated market mechanism in the modern industrial economy draws the skilled manpower and other resources to the expanding regions of the country only to weaken further the economies of the less favored regions. Furthermore, inequalities between individuals and classes in the absence of government intervention are enlarged where the unregulated market mechanism and laissez-faire government policies direct an undue share of the national affluence to the nation's Establishment.

The movement towards an integrated economy would have had little success if the private enterprise system had been allowed to continue to provide direction for the nation's economic activities. As has already been explained, the increasing affluence, the democratization of political power, the spread of mass education and the expanding role of government all combined to domesticate the private enterprise system in the western democracies and to make it the servant of the public. Profit maximization was placed relatively low on the priority list of national goals. Economic progress and increasing affluence made the Establishment willing to accept progressive taxation, social security, mass education, enlarged public health programs and the provision of aid to depressed economic regions. As government intervention in the private market place increased, the momentum of the integrative process became accelerated. The goal of a managed equilibrium or "concerted harmony" of interests was most closely approximated in countries like Sweden, Norway, Denmark and the Netherlands where after 1945 government intervention was broadened into national planning. It is in these countries that national integration has reached the highest levels.

In Myrdal's integrated national economy the government does not eliminate private enterprise or the price mechanism. On the contrary the private enterprise system is preserved as the main source of goods and services. What changes as the economy becomes more effectively integrated is the role of the private market mechanism as a force guiding the development of the nation's economy. In Myrdal's words the private profit-making system becomes the servant and not the master of the general public. Ultimate decisions with regard to major issues such as the redistribution of national income, the elimination of inequalities among individuals and classes and the selection of backward economic regions for development are no longer left to the Establishment and the private enterprise system. The central government, representing the people, is a more powerful force than private enterprise. Today in the well integrated society private enterprise must adjust to the demands of the government. The government supplements and directs the private enterprise system. As Myrdal has explained all important prices and wage rates are "political" in the sense that the price and wage determination processes function only under central government guidance. The impersonal competitive forces of the market place have now largely disappeared in the modern industrial economy, and have been replaced by the forces exerted by organized economic interest groups and by the central government. In the new power situation of the welfare state private enterprise is the junior partner and the central government the senior partner. The central government decides what portion of the nation's economic resources will go into the public sector and what portion will go into the private sector. Private enterprise endeavors to influence this division of economic resources in favor of the private sector. Since private enterprise controls the newspapers and other communications media it is in a strong position to curb the public sector and to influence the public in favor of private production over the production of public goods and services. In countries like Sweden and Norway the state control of radio and television broadcasting has weakened the influence of the upper class Establishment in economic matters. Even in these countries, however, newspapers are still primarily privately owned and a source of great private power and influence.

Besides being in a very strong position to influence the division of resources between the public and private sectors, the government in a well integrated society has an important function to perform in the guidance of the price and wage determining processes. This does not mean that the central government directly controls individual prices and wage rates. On the contrary the government intervenes only at strategic times and places to offer guidance to organized business, agriculture or labor. Some staple prices such as the prices of bread, milk, meat and utility services are frequently controlled in the West European integrated economy but the bulk of key prices and key wage rates are negotiated or administered prices and wage rates. In this situation private enterprise and the private market mechanism are in a secondary position. The basic ultimate decisions with regard to the use of the nation's scarce economic resources for the securing of national economic goals are made by the central government and the voters supporting it.

Values and Economic Science

When an economist focuses his attention on the evolving economic system he cannot avoid observing that the people who participate in the affairs of the evolving economy have various goals, ends or values which they seek to achieve. Evolution or development in the modern society is always toward some stated goals or ends that the community wishes to achieve. When Myrdal analyzes the welfare state he observes that the people want to achieve economic abundance, equality of opportunity to become skilled and productive, freedom in the choice of occupations and the use of personal incomes, a fair sharing of the national income among classes and economic regions and a solidarity of national interests that induces individuals and economic groups to accept policies and programs that are not to their own immediate benefit. The economic process is a goal directed process which can be fully explained, according to Myrdal, only by analyzing the people's goals and their impact upon the process. Businessmen, farmers, workers and consumers are value creating or value carrying individuals who are a part of the data of economic science. Organizations of businessmen, farmers, workers and consumers are also value creating and value carrying groups which are likewise a part of the data of economic science. People's wants, values or strivings are important facts which must be recognized by the social scientist if he is to interpret social reality satisfactorily. As Myrdal words it, "I consider it realistic to seek to account in a methodologically satisfactory fashion for all the facts. People's strivings [goals or values] are, indeed, among the most important social facts and they largely determine the course of history."[37]

Myrdal points out that there is a close connection between economic and political processes. The economic goals of individuals and organizations are embedded in the platforms of political parties which seek to aid people and groups in their efforts to achieve such economic goals as abundance, equality and liberty. When political parties are successful in taking over the nation's government, the government may become a major influence in the guidance of economic affairs, as in the case of the modern welfare state. Governments intervene in economic affairs with the aid of fiscal, monetary, price and wage policies. In the more advanced welfare states they plan the growth and development of the nation's economy with the aid of annual and long term national economic budgets. These budgets set forth the nation's economic and social goals which in turn reflect the goals of the general public. People in some cases have different and conflicting goals or values, and there is therefore a certain indeterminateness within the field of goals or values. This indeterminateness or vagueness, however, relating to goals, ends or values is limited by the fact that all goals or values are culturally determined. They are the product of a culture with a unity that limits the vagueness and conflicts of goals or values. In every culture

---

[37] *An International Economy*, p. x. See also *Asian Drama*, Vol. 1, Ch. 2, pp. 49-69.

Myrdal finds "a certain community of valuations" which implies that people can usually agree on certain general valuations or goals such as, in the well-integrated welfare state, equality of opportunity, liberty in economic affairs and a fair sharing of the national real income.[38]

Myrdal explains that the social scientist objectively analyzes the values of the people who are participating in the affairs of the economic system that is under investigation. Each social scientist has his own system of values of which he should be aware, and which he should distinguish from the value system of the economy he is investigating. As a scientist the economist does not impose his values upon other people. He is more objective, however, if he is aware of his own values and does not permit them to influence his investigation of other people's values. There is no such thing as a value free social scientist or a "disinterested social science." Myrdal objects to the efforts of conventional economists to dismiss the value problem by taking goals or values as given data, and by defining concepts in what is alleged to be an objective or value free way. Terms such as equilibrium, pure competition and utility are value loaded terms the attainment of which remains desirable to the orthodox economist no matter how far he attempts to retreat into a world of pseudo-scientific objectivity. It is Myrdal's position that social and economic reality cannot be satisfactorily studied except from "the viewpoint of human ideals" or values. Social science differs from natural or physical science in that the data of social science (centering in people, groups and classes) are value bearing data, whereas the data of natural science (cells, molecules, protons, etc.) are not value carrying data.

Myrdal explains that values or goals are not "right" or "wrong," "valid" or "invalid." Any quarrel or disagreement among people over values cannot be settled by an appeal to the facts. The rightness or wrongness of values, ends or goals is only a matter of who has the power to make his values dominate society. In the nineteenth century it was the business class that imposed its values on society with the result that the economic system was directed in such a way as to satisfy upper class values. Since 1900 with the increasing democratization of western societies the general population has secured more political power and has gradually substituted its values or ends for those of the aristocratic upper class or Establish-

---

[38] *An International Economy*, Appendix, p. 337.

ment which prior to 1900 had enough political power to impose its values upon the nation. The economic system operates for the purpose of producing goods and services to meet the needs or wants of those individuals and groups that are in a position to dominate the culture. Today in the advanced welfare states it is the common man's values that give direction to the evolution of the economic system. These values are determined by mass association which gives rise to the desire for equality, freedom and brotherhood. It is these values that give the common man his direction. If we are to explain the economic behavior of the general population in the well integrated welfare state we have to inquire into the values or ends that motivate people.

The economist as a scientist does not judge values. Instead he analyzes the consequences for the national output of goods and services of the values held by certain people. Some values such as class distinctions, an aristocratic, hierarchical ordering of society and the cultivation of ceremony and status to the neglect of technological advance hold back improvement in labor productivity and the enlargement of gross national product. Other values such as a democratic ordering of social relations, greater economic equality and the cultivation of a spirit of brotherhood make people more productive and increase the rate of economic progress. Today nationalism as a value prevents international cooperation and planning, delays the economic progress of underdeveloped nations and is an obstacle to the expansion of world gross national product. Internationalism as a value could contribute much to the building of a world welfare state. As a scientist the economist does not propose internationalism as a value or end that nations, especially the rich ones, should adopt. What the economist does is to explain how internationalism could promote world economic growth and welfare.

Values or ends are cultural products which change under the pressure of changing circumstances. Technological advance and industrial progress alter the circumstances in which people make a living. Other factors such as wars and severe economic crises change the underlying circumstances to which our culture and value systems respond. It was the shift from the small-scale competitive economic system of the nineteenth century to the large-scale largely non-competitive economic system of the twentieth century that undermined the sway of upper class values in Western Europe and the United States after 1900 and eventually brought about the substitution of the common man's values for those of the upper classes as society's guiding values. The First and Second World Wars and the Great Depression of the 1930's with its accompanying international and domestic crises contributed to the interest in government intervention and planning and to the emergence of less aristocratic and more socialized values.

Myrdal's Concept of Economic Science

The function of the economist according to Myrdal is to explain the nature of economic reality—the world of economic events. He views economic reality as a "dynamic process" and not as a "static balance." The evolving economic process or system is that part of culture which provides goods and services to meet the needs of individuals and groups some of which have more power than others to determine whose wants are to be satisfied. The economic process or system has two major features: it is an emergent or evolving institutional complex, and also it is a cultural complex that is based upon a conflict rather than a harmony of individual and group interests. When Myrdal analyzes the economic system he observes that there are three areas of scientific interest: the current economic situation, short-term cyclical or fluctuating trends of the economy and the long-term or secular development of the economy. When he investigates the current economic situation, the economist is interested in a cross section of the evolving economic process. In this situation he investigates all the current aspects of production, consumption and investment, economic activities which are largely funneled through the private market mechanism. Closely associated with the analyses of current economic activities are the analyses of short-term fluctuations in these activities. Since the current economic situation may be leading to an expansionary boom or recession, economists are concerned with the economic outlook or the short-run prospects of the economy.

The third field of interest to economists, and the one that has absorbed Myrdal's attention, is the long-term or secular development of the economic system. Here the economist investigates the factors bringing about changes in the structure and functioning of the economic system. Also he raises the question of what direction the evolving economy is taking. Since the economic process is a part of the larger cultural process, there are many non-economic factors of a political or social nature that have some impact on the development of the economic system. It is for this reason that Myrdal declares that social sciences "are essentially only an element of our

culture and share its fate."[39] If the culture is democratic and pro-
gréssive, the development of the economic system is aided by the
presence of positive, growth-fostering cultural factors such as a
stable democratic government, high educational and health standards and a broad based social security system. Where a people's
culture is dominated by an aristocratic, backward looking upper
class Establishment, the evolution of the economic system meets
large institutional and psychological obstacles. An explanation of
the course of development followed by an economic system must
therefore, in Myrdal's opinion, take "non-economic" as well as
"economic" factors into account. Myrdal abandons the conventional
boundaries of economics as they are viewed by orthodox economists.
Since "concrete problems are never simply economic, sociological,
psychological or political," the traditional division of the social sciences has no correspondence with social reality. When studying the
long-term developmental trends of the economy Myrdal abandons
the distinction between non-economic and economic factors influencing development, and writes instead about "relevant" and "irrelevant" factors, or "more relevant" and "less relevant" factors.[40] The
idea that theoretical economic analysis can be restricted to the inter-
actions of "the economic factors" is unacceptable to Myrdal for the
reason that such an idea leads to an unrealistic view of the real
economic world. Myrdal draws attention to the fact that the non-
economic factors are dynamic and normally react in a disequilibrating way. Consequently when the economist opens the door to
non-economic factors in his secular analysis of economic activity,
he abandons the equilibrium assumption and replaces it with a
dynamic cumulative non-equilibrating view of the long-term development of the economic system. This is precisely what Myrdal does
in developing his broad based type of economics.

Myrdal accepts the fact that the equilibrium approach is useful
to some extent when the economist is analyzing the current and
near future economic situation. But this is only because the economist in this situation has only a partial view of economic reality.
If he were to broaden his outlook to take in the long-term trends at
work in the economy, the economist at this point would have to drop
the equilibrium assumption. It is for this reason that orthodox or conventional economists concentrate their attention on the current eco-

---

[39] *Ibid.*, p. 306.
[40] *Rich Lands and Poor*, p. 10. See also *Asian Drama*, Vol. 1, p. 42.

nomic scene and the next short-term movement of the economic system. Since they have a strong predilection for the equilibrium assumption, they are unwilling and unprepared to take a "long view" of the economy. It is the long-term or secular evolution of the economy that is of critical importance, because it alters the structure and functioning of the economic system and determines how this system operates currently and in the short run. The daily and short-run functioning of the western economies has changed very greatly during the past half century as the free market economy has been replaced by the integrated economy of the welfare state.

Myrdal's integrative economics is a broad gauged cultural or social economics as opposed to the narrow "analytical" economics of the conventional economists. This does not mean that Myrdal would dispense with analytical or equilibrium economics. To the contrary he finds that there are many economic concepts or theories which, like "building stones" or "bricks," can be salvaged from the structure of inherited equilibrium economics. He explains that "In economics, as in social theory generally, old thoughts are rarely discarded altogether, and no ideas are new and original."[41] It is the "big structure" or design of traditional economics that Myrdal cannot accept. It is his view that economic theory in general has "never been developed to comprehend the reality of great and growing inequalities and of the dynamic processes of underdevelopment and development." It is Myrdal's objective to create an economics that will fill this gap. In doing so he has made use of a framework of interpretation or way of viewing things based on the concept of a dynamic process, he has freed himself from the predilection of inherited economics to assume that the economic system is moving towards an equilibrium and is dominated by an automatically created harmony of interests, and he has broadened the scope of economics to include any data that are found "relevant" to the study of economic phenomena. Myrdal does not fuse conventional economics and his own integrative economics to form some kind of a joint product. Instead he includes what he finds useful in conventional economics within a non-equilibrium framework to create an unconventional kind of economics. He is convinced that his integrative economics provides "a more realistic and relevant economic theory" with which to explain the dynamic real economic world.

---

[41] *Ibid.*, p. 162.

Myrdal's Criticism of Conventional Economics

Myrdal has been a severe critic of inherited orthodox economics ever since he first wrestled with the metaphysical foundations of economic orthodoxy in *The Political Element in the Development of Economic Theory*, which he published in 1929. In his formative years Myrdal became a critic of the *laissez-faire* economics that was dominant in Sweden in the first three decades of this century. He found the disequilibrium analysis and interventionism of Knut Wicksell (1851-1926) much more to his liking than the "rather uncompromising *laissez-faire* attitude" of David Davidson (1854-1942), Gustav Cassel (1866-1944), Gösta Bagge (1882-1951) and other proponents of *laissez-faire* economics.[42] Myrdal came to economics in an era of prolonged disequilibrium, dating from the First World War, for which the inherited *laissez-faire* economics was anything but appropriate. Myrdal and other young economists of his generation felt a great need to liberate themselves from the intellectual domination of mature economists who, according to Myrdal, had constructed an elaborate body of economic theory which did not explain the real economic world of the years 1914-1929. What Myrdal wanted in these years and later was a less speculative and more realistic economics than the inherited conventional economics. Myrdal attacks conventional or orthodox economics by pointing to the weaknesses of its philosophical foundations. He was led to this mode of attack through his contact with the philosophical work of Axel Hägerstrom (1868-1939) whose philosophical scepticism raised questions about how social scientists go about comprehending social reality. It became clear to Myrdal that economists and other social scientists see the world of facts around them through their own preconceptions about the nature of things. To understand the work of an economist one must first understand his intellectual orientation, mental set, *Weltanschauung* or framework of interpretation in the light of which he selects his data and problems for analysis. The economist's world view or way of comprehending things is made up of a number of preconceptions or predilections with regard to the nature of the external world. Applying this critical approach to the work of conventional or orthodox economists, Myrdal finds that the preconceptions guiding the work of these economists are no longer useful in any effort to grasp the nature of today's economic realities.

[42] Gunnar Myrdal, *Value in Social Theory*, pp. 239-252.

Myrdal explains that present day conventional economists are much more sophisticated in their treatment of equilibrium economics than were their predecessors. Nevertheless there linger in the work of current conventional economists inherited preconceptions or predilections which determine the basic shape or nature of their economic theorizing. The three main inherited preconceptions are related to the concept of equilibrium, the notion of a harmony of interests and an anti-state or pro-*laissez-faire* bias or inclination. These inherited intellectual predilections lead conventional economists to assume that, although the real economic world may be in a state of disequilibrium, nevertheless it is moving towards a state of equilibrium. Although Alfred Marshall, Knut Wicksell and John M. Keynes made theoretical advances by departing to some extent from the inherited notion of stable equilibrium, nevertheless the concept of some kind of equilibrium remained basic to their theoretical work. Likewise the assumption of a fundamental harmony of interests, which is a natural or intrinsic condition in the social and economic world, continues to have a strong hold on the minds of many orthodox economists. Similarly, the anti-state bias or *laissez-faire* inclination, which originated with the philosophy of natural law and utilitarianism in the eighteenth century as a protest against state domination, remains as a subtle influence to color the responses and attitudes of conventional economists. The anti-state bias is also an anti-organization or anti-collectivist bias. It leads the economist to analyze general welfare in terms of the sum of the welfare of individuals and not in terms of the collective aspects of general welfare.

Myrdal is very impressed with the power of tradition in most theoretical speculation and especially in the economic field. Economists remain under the influence of general ideas or predilections that have been inherited from the early period when their science was being developed. The power of tradition gives rise to a "traditionalism of theory" which makes orthodox economists slow to work in directions that open up new vistas. This power also gives a conservative bias to the scientific theorizing of conventional economists who tend to come to the conclusion that everything will work out well if the natural forces of the market are permitted to operate freely. There is a drive in the orthodox economist, originating in his inherited preconceptions, that leads him to seek refuge in the simplicity of the *laissez-faire* model of the economy. Myrdal finds that the conservative bias of orthodox economics is strongly supported by the fact that economic theory is a "rationalization of the inter-

ests and the aspirations of the milieu where it grew."[43] Orthodox
economics is more representative of the views and interests of the
private Establishment than of the common man. Myrdal finds that
orthodox economics tends to be "escapist" in that it has ignored the
equality issue. It has little to say about the poverty issue or the
problems peculiar to underdeveloped countries. Myrdal asserts that,
although orthodox economics was established in the eighteenth
century on the basis of egalitarian ideals derived from the philosophy
of natural law and utilitarianism, this economics in the hands of the
middle and upper classes in wealthy nations like Great Britain and
the United States became a defense for the preservation of inequalities at home and abroad. A "realism of conservatism" that developed
among conventional economists led them to select data and problems
that reflected their inherited predilections for accepting the notions
of stable equilibrium, harmony of interests and the superiority of
individual action over collective or state action.

The inherited predilections of conventional economists have, in
Myrdal's opinion, led them to limit the scope of economics so severely
as to deny to them the possibility of fully grasping the nature of
the real economic world. Standard *laissez-faire* economics, and
Keynesian economics as well, is described by Myrdal as "near
sighted." This is especially true in the United States where economists focus their attention upon the immediate and the short-run
aspects of economic activity. The "general tendency to nearsightedness" leads conventional economists to consider what is happening
immediately and what is going to happen next.[44] Economics in the
hands of these economists is oriented away from "the broad issues
to petty, short term problems." Scanty attention is given to the
secular development of the economic system in which a prominent
role is played by technological change. It is not surprising therefore that orthodox *laissez-faire* economists and Keynesians, who
have little to say about the forces shaping the economy over the long
run, should be concerned with little more than what is happening
now and in the months ahead. It is only when economists like
Myrdal inquire into the nature of economic development that such
notions as stable equilibrium and harmony of interests are found
not to reflect the nature of the real economic world.

Myrdal points out that orthodox economics tends to become "technical economics" rather than "social economics" as the result of the

---

[43] *Rich Lands and Poor*, p. 135.
[44] *Challenge to Affluence*, p. 87.

assertion of orthodox economists that their science deals with "means" but not "ends." When Lionel Robbins and his many orthodox followers take ends or goals as given, and state that economics deals only with alternative ways of securing these given goals, they refuse to analyze the impact of people's ends or values on their economic activities. Economics as cultivated by orthodox economists then moves close to production or technical economics which is primarily concerned with problems of allocation and efficiency. Instead of being viewed as an evolving process, the economic system is taken to be a static production or output machine. Human wants or values and the state of the industrial arts are ignored by being taken as given and the way is opened to apply the inherited notions of equilibrium and harmony of interests. By taking goals and the state of the arts as given, the conventional economists lock themselves into a theoretical system from which what Myrdal calls "the long view" or "the comprehensive grip of things and events" is conveniently excluded, but only at the cost of not fully comprehending the nature of the real world in which equality, equilibrium and harmony of interests are not the natural outcome of the free play of unregulated private market forces.

Myrdal's Social Reformism

Up to now we have been looking at Myrdal as a scientist not only analyzing the course of economic events but also probing the intellectual foundations on which the science of economics rests. His scientific efforts have been buttressed by a deep interest in social and economic reform.[45] His attack on conventional or orthodox economics, while couched in scientific terms, originates in his great concern about what he calls the "equality issue." Myrdal explains that this issue, "the right of all persons to equality of opportunity independent of race, religion and creed, social status and nationality," is at bottom a moral issue. People, especially in the rich nations, preach one thing and practice another. On the plane of general valuations people accept the ideal of equality of opportunity but they deny it in practice. And orthodox economists, representing the Establishment or middle and upper classes albeit unwittingly in most cases, and especially prior to 1900 before the welfare state

---

[45] Myrdal's reformist tendencies were stimulated by the serious problems of the depressed 1930's. In 1934 he and Alva Myrdal published *Kris i befolkningsfrågan* (Crisis in the Population Question) followed by *Population, A Problem for Democracy* (Cambridge: Harvard University Press, 1940).

made its appearance, gave support to this widely practiced escapism. Myrdal's moral fervor is especially evident in his study of the negro problem in *An American Dilemma, The Negro Problem and Modern Democracy*, and in his later writings on the problems of the underdeveloped nations. As Myrdal sees this problem of inequality, it has been largely eliminated in the rich welfare states of Western Europe and North America. But this is not the case in the international economy where equality is more conspicuous by its absence than its presence. Here Myrdal finds widespread exploitation and a great lack of concern on the part of the developed rich nations. When he drops his role as a scientist and takes on the outlook of a reformer Myrdal roundly condemns the "narrow nationalism" of the developed rich nations which prevents them from accepting the underdeveloped nations as equals. In the concluding sections of *An International Economy* Myrdal discusses the "logic of tragedy" by which is meant the tragic situation in which the cold war has absorbed so much of the energy and resources of the rich nations that they do not look favorably on engaging in international cooperation to aid the underdeveloped countries. He expresses his fear that this trend in international affairs will continue somewhat indefinitely with unforeseeable bad consequences for the western world.

In spite of his pessimistic attitude towards achieving international equality of opportunity Myrdal is not a fatalist. He does not subscribe to the deterministic philosophy which closes the door on purposeful human action. He argues that it is possible to translate ideals into practice, and in doing so to direct economic and social trends towards rationally established goals. Myrdal's reformism in the 1930's centered his interest in problems of depression, unemployment, social security and population growth. As an expert adviser to the government and active participant in public affairs Myrdal contributed a great deal to the development of social engineering in Sweden and to the construction of the comprehensive social security program for which Sweden is so well known. Since he believes that international equality of opportunity can be fully achieved only with a more enlightened citizenry in the various countries of the world, Myrdal's reformist efforts since World War II have been concerned with the wide dissemination of knowledge about the need for a more widespread and vigorous international idealism. As a reformer Myrdal is a solidarist who believes that it is possible to unite all the western developed and the underdeveloped countries in a workable international solidarity. Myrdal's solidarism repudiates any idea of a Marxian type class struggle between the rich developed and the poor underdeveloped countries. Just as class struggles have been washed away in the modern democratic national welfare state, Myrdal remains optimistic about the long-run possibility of eliminating international economic conflicts in the world welfare state.

Myrdal is less critical of the domestic policies and programs of the advanced welfare states than he is with regard to their international economic policies. Nevertheless he is conscious of some disturbing trends in these welfare states. He observes in both Sweden and the United States the spread of a materialistic "Babbittism" which exaggerates the importance of material welfare and vitiates the quality of life from the economic point of view. This is especially true in the United States where a considerable part of the population lives in what Myrdal has described as a "rather vulgar affluence" based on satisfying personal needs stimulated by high pressure advertising. Such an affluence is in conflict with "the Puritan ideals of high thinking and prudent living." Myrdal agrees with John K. Galbraith that there is in the United States an excessive concern for privately produced goods and services to the neglect of more urgently needed public goods and services.[46] Some overzealous interest in material goods has also affected the Swedish people. Another disturbing trend in Sweden and the United States is a creeping tendency towards conformity in views. Too much of a premium is being placed on people conforming with established views and values and too little tolerance is allowed for dissent. A rich advanced welfare state is prone to become intolerant of venturesome dissent. In an advanced welfare state affluence which is a worthwhile value in itself may be achieved at the sacrifice of other very desirable values. For this reason Myrdal is prepared to keep the value system of the advanced welfare state under constant review with the aim of modifying those values that might lessen the quality of life.

The Economics of Integration: An Evaluation

One of the major contributions of Myrdal's treatment of economic science is to call attention to the need for all economists to be criti-

---

[46] Gunnar Myrdal, "Adjustment of Economic Institutions in Contemporary America," in Carey C. Thompson (ed.), *Institutional Adjustment, A Challenge to a Changing Economy* (Austin: University of Texas Press, 1967) pp. 80-81.

cally aware of themselves as scientists. He emphasizes the need for economists to be aware of the origins of the mental outlook or general framework of reference that they bring to the study of economic data. Economists should be alert to the basic preconceptions or predilections that they may have borrowed from earlier economists, and which are crucial in determining how they approach or grasp economic reality. A satisfactory and comprehensive grasp of reality may require that they get rid of many of their inherited predilections, or their "heavy ballast" as Myrdal calls it, before they are in a good position to comprehend economic reality. Since the economist's general framework of interpretation is also the basis for his selection of data, and selection implies preference or valuation, the economist should be aware of his own system of values. By emphasizing the role of values in economic analysis Myrdal draws attention to the desirability of having economists bring to light their hidden preferences or values. Objectivity is achieved not by hiding values but by revealing and taking account of them.

A second major contribution of Myrdal's integrative economics is to call attention to the fact that in the final analysis economics is a cultural and not a natural science, a "social" and not a "technical" science. Myrdal's economics emphasizes the importance of broadening the scope of economics to include all factors that have a significant influence on the structure and functioning of the economic system. Traditional or conventional economics is too prone to narrow the scope of economics so that economics becomes technical and nearsighted rather than social and farsighted. Technical or pure economics has a valid role to play but its role is subsidiary and not primary. Since the economic system is a part of culture, Myrdal asserts that the study of the economic system should in the final analysis be social or cultural in nature.

A third contribution of Myrdal's social economics is his emphasis on the importance of integration in economic life. Increasingly in the modern industrial economy the interest of economists is shifting from equilibrium to integration as the importance of private markets declines and the central government comes to assume a larger role in economic affairs. In the small-scale competitive economy the role of government was very small and the market mechanism was effective in providing direction for economic activities. With the appearance of large private economic power groups and the decline of the market as a regulator of economic activities, the central government has taken on a larger role as a guiding factor in economic affairs.

Guidance is provided by the government through the overall planning or coordinating of the nation's economic activities. In the rich developed nations this economic integration is designed to provide equality of opportunity, economic freedom and a solidarity of interests among the people. In the poor developing nations planning or integration seeks to set off a cumulative upward movement towards higher levels of real income and economic progress. In both cases in order to explain the process of economic evolution or development it is necessary to move beyond equilibrium analysis to center attention on the planning or integrating of economic activities. Equilibrium analysis is useful for an explanation of current and short-run economic developments, but when the economist turns to long-run or secular economic developments it is necessary to set aside the equilibrium approach and to turn to the integrative approach. In Myrdal's opinion the key concern in analyzing the economic world of the twentieth century should be with integration and not equilibrium.

Over the years Myrdal has concentrated his attention on the secular trends towards more integrated national and international economies. He has had relatively little to say about an analysis of western economic systems from a short-run point of view. He has written no general treatises in which he might have integrated short-run and long-run economic analyses. For many readers Myrdal's work remains somewhat discursive. He ranges over many issues—the sociology of knowledge, the philosophical foundations of economics and other social sciences, methodological issues, the nature and scope of economics and the theory of economic development and underdevelopment. The discursive nature of Myrdal's work can be attributed in large part to his strong empirical bent. In some ways he has reacted excessively to the metaphysical bent of the orthodox *laissez-faire* economics that dominated the academic scene in Sweden in the years 1900-1929. He rejected the subjectivistic value theory of his orthodox academic predecessors but made little effort to replace it with a more objective and realistic value theory, as has Clarence E. Ayres with his technological theory of value. Doubtlessly Myrdal's long absences from the academic environment made deep inroads into the time available for theorizing on a general plane.

In spite of these limitations Myrdal's economics remains a strong challenge to economists of a more orthodox stripe who cannot see beyond the next recession, and who persist in casting their economic analysis, even of the most recent econometric variety, in an equilibrium mold. Myrdal's criticisms of conventional economics are similar to those made by the members of the American neo-institutional school. Like the latter, he would make economics a truly cultural science. He would abandon the artificial boundaries prescribed for economics by conventional economists, and open the door to a more interdisciplinary approach. Like the American neo-institutionalists Myrdal takes economic systems to be what they are, namely evolving cultural processes. And he raises the same fundamental questions that the neo-institutionalists raise: What is happening to the economic system, where is it probably going and what are the effects of secular trends upon economic activity today and tomorrow? Myrdal would agree with the neo-institutionalists that unless we have some idea of where our economy is going, we cannot act as rationally today or tomorrow as we would like to act.

CHAPTER VI

GERHARD COLM'S ECONOMICS
OF NATIONAL PROGRAMMING

A feature of the guided capitalism of today that distinguishes it from the welfare capitalism of the 1930's is the special interest in many circles in national economic programming which is a method of quantifying the nation's economic goals so that economic policy-making may be placed upon a firm quantitative basis. After World War II the major economic problems of the 1930's, such as low production, economic stagnation and mass unemployment did not reappear. New problems such as how to achieve a high and sustained rate of economic growth and how to allocate the nation's economic resources in order to maximize human welfare made their appearance after 1945. There were two different reactions among economists to these new problems. The post war Keynesians recommended the usual contracyclical program of curbing booms and offsetting recessions by making appropriate adjustments in taxes, interest rates and government expenditures. The government's main job was considered to be the provision of a favorable climate for economic growth by stabilizing aggregate demand. The rate of economic growth and the allocation of resources were to be largely left to private enterprise. Post war Keynesians usually refrained from having the government announce a specific economic growth rate (annual increase in gross national product) as a national goal. They explained that they wanted a "high" economic growth rate, but they gave no quantitative content to the goal of a high rate. In addition, the post war Keynesians wanted an optimal allocation of economic resources but again made no effort to quantify any such optimal distribution. In general the private market system was left free to establish an annual growth rate and to make an allocation of economic resources within the broad limits of a government program of restricted intervention. This post war Keynesian approach to the problems of growth and allocation was fol-

237

lowed in the United States, Canada, Australia, West Germany and in the United Kingdom after 1951 when the British Labour Party was replaced by the Conservative Party.

Most of Western Europe turned to a different, non-Keynesian approach to the problems of economic growth and resource allocation. This was the national economic programming approach adopted by the United Kingdom (from 1945 to 1951 and from 1964 to 1970), France, the Netherlands and the Scandinavian countries. Each of these countries felt it to be desirable to move beyond the Keynesian approach and to quantify growth rates and the national priorities to which economic resources would be allocated. This was done by constructing and publishing annual and four or five year national economic budgets which set forth specific annual growth rates or increases in gross national product and the uses of this product as determined by agreed-upon national priorities. With all major economic goals quantified and projected in the national economic budget economic discussion and economic policy making could be carried on with reference to quantitative guide lines. During the war years 1939-1945 governments in the United Kingdom, the United States and Sweden had demonstrated the usefulness of national economic budgets in guiding economic activity towards the wartime national goals. National economic programming with the aid of national economic budgets had proved its worth on both sides of the Atlantic, and there were many economists and government officials who believed that national economic programming could be as useful in peacetime as it had been in wartime.

This conviction about national economic programming led to its adoption as official government policy in the United Kingdom, France, the Netherlands, Denmark, Norway and Sweden very soon after 1945. In the United States there was a strong movement for the continued use of national economic programming after the war. In April 1945, a number of economists in government service during the war years issued a report on *National Budgets for Full Employment* which was a call for the extension of wartime national programming into the post war peace period.[1] This report made use of a five year national economic budget to reveal in quantitative form the growth rate and resource allocations that would contribute to full employment by 1950. The first version of the Full Employment Bill (which in 1946 became the Employment Act) envisioned

---

[1] National Planning Association, *National Budgets for Full Employment*, Planning Pamphlets Nos. 43 and 44, Washington, D.C., April 1945.

the federal government constructing annual national economic budgets and using them as a basis for the formulation of full employment policies. Such major federal government organizations as the Department of Commerce, the Department of Labor and the Bureau of the Budget expressed an interest in national economic programming in the postwar years.

Prominent among the economists who were interested in national economic programming in the early post war years was Gerhard Colm, who had spent the war years in the Bureau of the Budget. Colm has maintained his interest in national economic programming over the past quarter of a century and has become known as one of the most knowledgeable individuals in this special area of economic analysis. His work as an economist for the Bureau of the Budget and the Council of Economic Advisers and as chief economist of the National Planning Association in Washington, D.C., has kept him in close contact with the kinds of public and private problems to which national economic programming can be applied. Since 1945 Colm has been one of the foremost advocates of national economic programming as an aid in the achievement of a high and sustained economic growth rate and an efficient and balanced allocation of the nation's economic resources.

The Emergence of Guided Capitalism

Colm's interest in national economic programming is very closely related to his interpretation of the current stage in the development of capitalism. He observes that the economies of the advanced western countries have passed through "many historical stages."[2] During these evolutionary stages the capitalist system has made adjustments to the demands of technical progress although not without considerable delay and friction. The American economic system since 1800 has passed through two stages, and is currently faced with the problems of a third evolutionary stage. The evolutionary stage prior to 1875 was a *laissez-faire* period in which the economy functioned without much government guidance or regulation. The economic system was governed by "market automatism" which in theory was supposed to eliminate all conflict among economic interests. After 1875 the state and federal governments found it necessary to intervene in private economic affairs on a broadening front.

---

[2] Gerhard Colm, "Is Economic Planning Compatible with Democracy?" *Essays in Public Finance and Fiscal Policy* (New York: Oxford University Press, 1955) p. 295.

A new stage or era of "unplanned intervention" now made its appearance. In this era powerful groups of industrial and agricultural producers became established as the free competitive markets began to recede. An inconsistency between actual government policy and the prevailing ideology of *laissez-faire* became evident as small scale business enterprise gave way before big business. In the years 1875 to 1929, however, this inconsistency was covered up by the very considerable economic progress that was achieved. The situation changed after 1929, however, when economic expansion came to a standstill, and the federal government was forced to intervene in the private sector of the economy on an unprecedented scale.

In the 1930's organized economic interests turned to the federal government for protection from the vicissitudes of the disrupted market place. The government extended aid to large and small business, organized labor, farmers, and various middle-class interests. Government intervention, however, remained unplanned. Its aim was "*political* equilibrium in the democratic society rather than the shaping of the economic process according to a predetermined pattern."[3] There arose a very pressing need for a coordinated economic policy to cope successfully with the destructive forces of deflation and stagnation, but this need was never recognized by the Roosevelt Administration.

In Colm's view of the American economy there is a large core or heartland in which one hundred of the largest manufacturing corporations account for 35 per cent of the total sales of all manufacturing enterprises. These large corporations are very important in the most dynamic industries. Although there is heavy concentration in the industries of the economy's core area, there are many thousands of competing enterprises outside this area. Also, most employees still work in small scale industries of low concentration. The large industrial corporations possess a great deal of economic power which is not always used to the advantage of the public. Colm points out, however, that the large industrial corporations are forced to operate in the consumers' interest to a considerable extent by intra-industry and inter-industry competition, and also by the corporate urge to expand sales in order to secure a growing share of the national market. The economic power of the large corporations is still a matter of great public concern since it leads to the elimination of price competition, the creation of obstacles to the free entry of new firms, the imposition of conformity and uniformity

---

[3] *Ibid.*

on corporate employees and through ingenious mass advertising and sales promotion to a "possible corruption of taste" and "cultural recession."[4] Colm also calls attention to the fact that the economic power of large corporations opens the door to the possibility of political power being wielded by these corporations.

Colm remains optimistic about the possibility of having the large industrial corporations serve the national interest. The new concern of corporate management for a good public image, the continued surveillance of the behavior of large corporations by the government, the pressure of technological progress and the competition among corporations for markets serve to keep the large corporations in line. In addition, there is the influence of other major economic interest groups such as organized labor and organized farmers. Colm has a pluralistic interpretation of the functioning of the American economy. As he puts it, "The United States now seems to be approaching a situation in which neither business, labor, farmers nor government has disproportionate influence. Each sector is vigorous, dynamic and powerful, but each recognizes that it will be curbed if its actions adversely affect the general welfare."[5] In this situation the role of the government is one of leadership and not domination. There is the possibility of the mutual collaboration of the government and the major economic interest groups in an effort to make the "emerging economic and social system" a workable system that successfully unites "individual freedom and social responsibility." As we shall see, it is this pluralistic view of the American economy that underlies and gives support to Colm's proposals for guiding the economy with the aid of national economic programming. This programming would not be possible without the cooperation of all major economic interest groups.

The Problems of Guided Capitalism

The transition from *laissez-faire* capitalism to guided or directed capitalism since 1929 has been accompanied by much technological progress and a rising standard of living. Yet at the same time as we have moved into an "age of plenty," we are confronted with the growing fear of economic instability and the danger that the quality of life may be deteriorating. Colm emphasizes that although the

---

[4] Gerhard Colm and Theodore Geiger with the assistance of Manuel Helzner, *The Economy of the American People*, Planning Pamphlet No. 102, National Planning Association, Washington, D.C., 1958, p. 106.

[5] *Ibid.*, p. 68.

technological revolution of recent decades has greatly increased our productive potential, we have failed to make the institutional changes that would assure our utilizing this potential. We are still suffering from severe economic fluctuations, persistent price rises and the spread of structural rigidities throughout the economy. As yet we are unable to prevent the development of unbalanced economic relationships. There is nothing in the working of the present day American economy that automatically guarantees balanced wage-price-profit and investment-consumption relationships. On the contrary, according to Colm's interpretation, the guaranty is that the unregulated large-scale private enterprise system will generate wage-price-profit and investment-consumption imbalances.

In some ways more serious than the economic imbalances associated with the current phase in the evolution of American capitalism is the cultural paradox that is developing in the wake of the "coming phase of industrial society." The cultural paradox is that as the supply of economic goods increases, the quality of life decreases. This is what Colm described in 1958 as the problem of "the quality of life in an age of quantitative material abundance." He explains that we cannot "take for granted that our expanding economy will automatically provide the particular goods and services which will make the greatest contribution to the most urgent national objectives and the general welfare."[6] The unregulated private enterprise economy directs too much of the nation's scarce economic resources to the production of private goods and services and not enough to the production of public goods and services. As a consequence public capital facilities and services such as schools, hospitals and roads at the local level have become obsolete or inadequate. They have failed to meet the needs of the growing population and the expanding industry. Another consequence of moving into the new age of abundance is that the complexity and interdependence of the modern industrial system places a premium on conformity and uniformity at the expense of individual creativity. The "organization man" who will not disturb the smooth operation of the large corporation is much preferred to the "creative man" who resists the pressure to conform and who advocates unconventional ideas. The innovatory human capacities that nourished change and contributed to the growth of large-scale enterprise are no longer tolerated by that enterprise.

---

[6] *Ibid.*, p. 81.

An equally important problem is the relation between economic abundance and leisure. The spread of automation and rising productivity make possible a shorter work week and more leisure. But leisure for what? Is the increased leisure to be used for more personal fulfillment, or is it to be used to consume the products which large corporations induce people to buy through mass advertising and ingenious sales promotion methods. Colm raises the question as to whether or not western civilization is culturally prepared for substantially shorter hours of work and longer hours of leisure. If it is not so prepared, the remedy does not lie in the hands of the large industrial corporations, one of whose aims is to produce more and expand sales. Rather it is found in the nation's educational system which should not only train more and better scientists and skilled workers, but should also "develop the individual's potentialities for participating in the expanding opportunities for cultural growth and for constructive recreational activities in the approaching age of abundance."[7] It is Colm's conclusion that the use of expanded leisure should be determined by society and not by the industrial system which places a premium on quantity of production to the neglect of the quality of life. As Colm sees the problem, maintaining or improving the quality of life in an age of economic abundance is something that requires social engineering or planning. Consequently the coming age of abundance will also be an age of democratic planning.

From Keynesian Interventionism to National Planning

Since 1945 the American economic system has entered the evolutionary stage with which Colm is primarily concerned, the era of "planned economic policy." The kind of planning that has been carried on in the United States since 1945 is far from being the kind of planning that Colm believes is necessary to achieve our major economic and social goals. In spite of the efforts to bring some coordination into the field of economic policy making since 1945, in Colm's opinion, the American economic system has failed to make all the necessary adjustments to the demands of "modern technical conditions."[8] The Employment Act of 1946 was designed to modernize the nation's economic policy making procedures, and to bring more coordination into policy making. This Act requires

---

[7] *Ibid.*, p. 107.

[8] "Is Economic Planning Compatible with Democracy?" *Essays in Public Finance and Fiscal Policy*, p. 301.

the setting up of a full employment goal and a statement of the steps that are needed to achieve this goal. The Act created a Council of Economic Advisers in the Executive Office of the President and a Joint Economic Committee of the Congress to review the work of the Council and to make recommendations to the Congress. The Act requires the President to transmit to the Congress an *Economic Report* that sets forth the full employment goal for the coming year and the policies and legislative changes required to accomplish the full employment goal.

In Colm's opinion the Employment Act of 1946 is "a mandate for planning."[9] The Act calls for the setting up of national goals and the presentation of a statement as to how these goals may be achieved. Since the United States had no peacetime experience with national planning, the Congress did not specify any planning procedures. It felt that no planning procedures should be frozen into the Employment Act, and that it would be better to develop these procedures experimentally. Colm points out that 22 years after the adoption of the Employment Act no mechanism for planning has been worked out. The Council of Economic Advisers has used some planning concepts such as projections of gross national product and estimates as to how consumption and investment might be affected by changes in tax policy. The Council, however, has not made use of published annual and long term national economic budgets which constitute the core of all national economic planning procedures.

The reason why the passage of the Employment Act did not result in the national economic programming which Colm feels is essential for the good working of the American economic system is that the administration of the Act was taken over after 1953 by economists and government officials of a Keynesian persuasion who had no interest in national economic programming. In the early years of the execution of the Employment Act there was some prospect that the Council of Economic Advisers would publish national economic budgets setting forth national economic goals. This was especially true after Leon H. Keyserling became the Chairman of the Council in 1949. At this time Colm was on the economics staff of the Council. The *Economic Report* for 1950, prepared under the direction of Keyserling, incorporated a five year national economic

---

[9] Gerhard Colm, "Economic Planning in the United States," *Zeitschrift des Instituts für Weltwirtschaft*, Band 92, Heft 1, Weltwirtschaftliches Archiv, Hamburg, 1964, p. 40.

budget for the years 1950-1954. This budget showed the projected annual growth of gross national product during the five year plan period and the projected division of gross national product among private and public consumption and investment uses in 1954. Gross national product was projected to grow at a rate (3 per cent per annum) that would provide full employment, and private investment was projected to increase more slowly than private consumption because the consumption-investment balance had been upset by the very high rate of private investment in the early post war years.

This first step towards national economic programming was aborted by the outbreak of the Korean War in June 1950. The economy was soon placed on a wartime basis and concern with national economic programming as a publicly declared program quickly evaporated. When the war was over in 1953 the change in political administration placed the Council of Economic Advisers under the control of Keynesian economists. After 1953 the Council, even with the change in political administration in 1960, never again published a national economic budget or showed any interest in national programming. In the Kennedy-Johnson Administrations the Council of Economic Advisers made 5 and 10 year projections of gross national product, and estimated the possible gap between actual and potential gross national product in the future. Gap economics is a refinement of Keynesian economics, and is no substitute for the economics of national economic programming.

It is for this reason that Colm concludes after almost a quarter century's execution of the Employment Act that the American economy is not in any way a formally planned economy, and that the potentials of the Employment Act as a means of introducing planning have not yet been realized. National planning of one form or another has been adopted in all West European countries, except West Germany, but the United States remains outside the area of planned economies. Colm regards national economic planning or programming as an adjustment of mature industrialized countries to the demands of modern technology.[10] In an economy in which industry is dominated in many lines by large scale oligopolistic enterprise, agriculture is highly protected by governmental programs and all major economic interest groups are highly organized and vocal, it is difficult to secure an efficient and balanced operation of the economy. The private market mechanism is unable to carry the

---

[10] *The Economy of the American People*, p. 148.

full burden of providing for a smooth operation of the nation's economic system. In Colm's opinion the private market mechanism needs to be supplemented by government action so that the national economic goals may be secured. The modern industrialized economic system no longer automatically gravitates toward a full employment equilibrium in which resources are efficiently allocated to meet consumer preferences. Even the out and out Keynesians agree with this diagnosis.

The only important argument is: How shall the private sector of the economy be supplemented? The Keynesian prescription is to have the treasury and the central bank manipulate taxes, interest rates and government spending in order to stabilize expanding aggregate demand. The public component of aggregate demand would take care of public needs and the private component would service private consumer needs. Various regulatory bodies, especially the Federal Trade Commission and the Antitrust Division of the Department of Justice, are to make sure that industrial concentration is kept at a minimum and every effort is made to preserve competitive markets. All this, it is hoped by the Keynesians, will prevent recessions, sustain economic growth at an adequate level, stabilize prices, provide full employment and bring about a fair sharing of the national income.

There is considerable doubt in certain quarters that this compensatory and manipulative program of the Keynesians in academic and political circles will ever achieve the national goals referred to in the prior paragraph. Thus far the United States has not been fortunate enough to have no recessions, to enjoy high sustained economic growth, full employment and stable prices and to secure what all interest groups would agree is a fair sharing of the national income. No major West European countries have relied only on the Keynesian program for achieving economic abundance. Even West Germany with its highly concentrated industry, its very active big business-big banker complex and its docile trade union movement can hardly be described as a fertile ground for Keynesian experiments in supplementing private enterprise. Colm shares the views of many West European economists and government officials that, while there is much in Keynesian economic policies and programs that is useful in the effort to achieve growth and stability, advanced industrialized nations have to go far beyond the Keynesian prescriptions if they are to achieve their economic goals. In other words, the solution to our major economic problems, in Colm's opinion, lies in national economic programming which absorbs much of the Keynesian program but which does not rest there.

The Concept of the National Economic Budget

The essence of Colm's national programming is found in the national economic budget. The concept of this budget is derived from a view of the economic system in which this system is made up of two basic flows, the real and financial flows.[11] The real flow is the flow of goods and services from the nation's farms, factories and service-producing enterprises. The real flow is measured by the nation's total production or gross national product, and consists of all the new goods and services annually produced and marketed or added to inventories. The other flow of the economy is the financial flow which can be viewed either as national income earned or income spent. This income-expenditure flow is closely associated with the economy's real flow. The national income is earned by people and property used in the production of the real flow of goods and services. Income earned is returned to the economic system or process by being spent on goods and services coming out of the real flow.

The basic problem in any economic system is to keep the real and financial flows in harmony or meshed together. If the two flows are successfully meshed or coordinated, then what is produced annually is bought up or consumed. If the real flow of goods and services provides work for all who want to be employed, and if the income earned from real production is fairly shared, then the economy is well on the way to meeting the nation's needs. According to the theory of a perfectly competitive economy, the real and financial flows are automatically meshed by the free market system. All who want to work find work and are recompensed in accordance with their marginal contribution to the nation's product. In the early nineteenth century when the United States had a largely competitive small-scale economy, the real and financial flows were harmonized fairly adequately by the free market mechanism. After 1875 as the economy shifted from a small-scale to a large-scale basis, and the free market was obstructed by the exercise of market power by large corporations and large unions, the meshing or coordination of the

[11] Gerhard Colm, "The Nation's Economic Budget, A Tool of Full Employment Policy," *Studies in Income and Wealth, Conference on Research in Income and Wealth*, Volume Ten (New York: National Bureau of Economic Research, 1947) p. 89.

nation's real and financial flows became less and less satisfactory. The evidence of a growing discrepancy or gap between these two flows was recurring depressions and recessions, large scale and chronic unemployment, retarded economic growth and price instability.

When a satisfactory meshing of the real and financial flows was far from being achieved during the 1930's, attention was directed to the problem of trying to measure the real and financial flows and the discrepancies between them. This movement gave rise in the late 1930's to the development of national income accounting based upon national product and income accounts. The combined national product and income accounts, known as the national economic accounts, measure annually the real flow or gross national product, and also show the expenditures, private and public, for the goods and services that make up the gross national product. For example, the 1970 national economic accounts for the United States show a gross national product for that year valued at $976.8 billion. In the same year expenditures for this total product valued at $976.8 billion were $616.8 billion for private consumption expenditures, $139.4 billion for private business investment expenditures, and $220.6 billion for government expenditures at the federal, state and local levels.

A national economic budget is a projection of the national economic accounts into a future period. An annual national economic budget shows projections or estimates of gross national product and the private and public expenditures for this product for the coming year. A four year national economic budget shows the same information about gross national product four years hence. A full employment four year national economic budget would show the gross national product needed four years in the future to keep the estimated total work force fully employed. Such a budget would also project the private consumption, private business investment and government expenditures for the full employment gross national product that would be needed to sustain a full employment, balanced economy. The national economic budget in effect shows how the nation's real flow (gross national product) and its financial flow (expenditures on gross national product) would be harmonized or meshed in some future year in order to achieve a full employment, balanced economy.

The national economic budget is not a forecast of the size of the gross national product and the various expenditures on it in some future period. Instead, this budget is a projection of the government's goals with respect to gross national product and expenditures on it. Colm explains in relation to national economic budgets that "Their main feature is that they reflect [national] objectives and state policy goals."[12] They project the government's objectives with regard to the desired economic growth rate, full employment and balance between consumption and investment expenditures. In other words the national economic budget is a means of expressing the nation's economic priorities in quantitative form.

In showing the national economic objectives in quantitative form the national economic budget becomes a basis for economic policy making. As Colm expresses the matter, the national economic budget is "a tool of quantitative theoretical analysis" on the basis of which economic policies are constructed.[13] It is used to direct "the productive resources of the nation towards the highest priority national goals." The government's fiscal, monetary, spending, price and other policies can be related to the quantified objectives set forth in the annual and long term national economic budgets. Since output and expenditure goals are quantified, policy discussions are made more concrete. The effect of any proposed policy or program on the nation's real and financial flows can be expressed in quantitative form. This facilitates discussion and agreement among various major private economic interest groups and the government.

The meshing or coordination of the real and financial flows observed in a national economic budget is a managed or planned harmonization of these two flows. It is quite unlike the harmonization that would automatically develop in a perfectly competitive economy. The equilibrium projected in the national economic budget is a planned equilibrium that the government hopes to achieve by supplementing the private market mechanism.

The National Economic Budget in Western Europe

Colm draws attention to the fact that both annual and four or five year national economic budgets have been widely used in Western Europe since 1945. The British Labour Government published in the years 1947-1951 an annual *Economic Survey* which incorporated national economic budgets which set forth national eco-

---

[12] "National Economic Budgets," *Essays in Public Finance and Fiscal Policy*, p. 247.
[13] *Ibid.*, p. 249.

nomic goals and the steps to be taken to secure these goals. National economic budgeting has reached its highest levels of development in the Netherlands, Norway, Sweden and France where annual and long-term national economic budgets have been used continuously since 1947. All four nations have published annual or longer term budgets, and have worked these budgets into the fabric of national economic life. In the United Kingdom where national economic budgeting was abandoned by the Conservative Party in the years 1951-1962, this budgeting was restored by the Conservative Party in 1962 when an effort was made to duplicate the national budgeting being practiced in France. In recent years both Belgium and Italy have found it useful to turn to national budgeting as a device for achieving a balanced, expanding economy.

In all these countries the standard procedure has been to establish a national budget office or agency which is assigned the responsibility for constructing the annual and four or five year national economic budgets. These offices work closely with the ministry of finance and the central bank in the coordination of economic policy on the basis of the national economic budget. A very important feature of national economic budgeting in Western Europe is the effort to secure the cooperation of the major economic interest groups in the construction of the budgets and in using them as a basis for national economic guidance. In the United Kingdom the National Economic Development Council, with representatives from business, labor, the public and the government, was established in 1962 for the purpose of advising the government on matters relating to national economic programming. In France the Economic and Social Council performs the same function. In the Netherlands and Sweden economic councils have been organized for the same purpose. In some countries such as Norway cooperation between the government and private economic interest groups in the area of national economic programming is carried on in an informal manner. In all countries of Western Europe where national economic budgeting has become thoroughly well established, the need to secure the cooperation of organized business, labor and farmers, if the budgeting is to be successful, has been well demonstrated.

National Economic Programming and Indicative Planning

Colm's ultimate objective is a kind of "indicative planning" such as is carried on today in France, Japan and some of the Scandinavian countries. He realizes, however, that there is no immediate prospect of any such planning being adopted in the United States. He points out that in this country there is a widely held view that planning is a device, used by socialist and communist countries, that is not appropriate for a private enterprise system. In the United States governments and large business enterprises plan their affairs, but they are unwilling to admit that the whole society should plan its activities. Furthermore, even if there were no strong objections to national economic programming, the American economy is not ready for it. This programming, Colm points out, can be successful only in what in France is referred to as an *économie concertée*—a concerted economy. This is an economy in which all major economic interest groups and the government are prepared to act cooperatively in constructing and carrying out a national economic plan. Concerted or overall national economic planning requires a high degree of collective action on the part of businessmen. They must be well organized so that those business representatives who participate in the national planning process, and in the determination of the long term production and investment goals for the various industries, can speak for their particular branch of industry, and can induce the other business firms to accept the government's national plan. The national plans become self-enforcing in France and Japan because the various private industries are confident that the government will be successful in achieving the planned economic growth rate. The government's long term national plan has an "announcement effect."[14] When the plan is presented to the public, business firms for the most part accept it and make their individual plans in accordance with the objectives of the national plan. This cooperative reaction makes the national plan successful as long as the government has a record of being successful in executing its plans.

Colm does not expect to import in a detailed way the specific planning program of any West European country. He realizes that each country that plans does so within its own institutional framework. The national planning arrangements of a country necessarily reflect the special features of this framework. The one universal feature, however, of all national economic planning programs is the use of annual and longer term national economic budgets. It is impossible to plan in any overall formal way without using such a budget which sets forth the nation's economic priorities in quantified form. If the term "planning" is used very loosely, then all major

---

14 "Economic Planning in the United States," p. 43.

nations may be said to plan, because they have goals and some arrangements for trying to accomplish these goals. This use of the term "planning" does not lend itself to any useful or significant analysis of the problems of national planning. National planning occurs in a significant way only where this planning is to some extent formally structured, and where national economic budgets are used as the hub of the plan structure.

With respect to the future of national economic programming in the United States Colm is optimistic. He asserts that "the increasing use of economic projections [in the United States] for business investment decisions moves in the same direction as indicative planning."[15] He is convinced that eventually more planning on a national level will be tried in the United States, and that gradually we will move into some kind of planning along French, Japanese and Scandinavian lines. Already considerable progress towards a "planned market economy" in the United States has been made. "Program planning" which includes planning for specific public needs such as health, education, national security, water, transportation and urban renewal is already well established. "Business planning" which is oriented to anticipated markets at some time in the future is also well established. Both program and business planning make use of long term gross national product projections as benchmarks or reference points for individual plan projects. Although program and business planning are not overall or general planning, they must both take account of the development and progress of the whole economy. Government departments and business enterprises must relate their individual plans to the growth of population, the expansion of the economic system and the increasing demands on the nation's natural resources. This is done by projecting both population and economic growth for the plan period. Projections of gross national product are especially important in this connection. It is the long term projection of gross national product that provides the link between the whole economic process and program and business planning.

National economic planning, or what Colm describes as "economic-policy planning," in the United States has up to now not duplicated the progress of program and business planning. Unlike program and business planning which are partial in nature, Colm's "economic-policy planning" deals with the planning of the economic system as a whole. This type of planning has both "performance"

---

[15] *Ibid.*, p. 43.

and "achievement" or priority goals. Performance goals include such objectives as full employment, a desirable rate of economic growth, adequate price stability and equilibrium in the nation's current balance of international payments. These national objectives relate to the overall performance of the economy and have no special concern with the allocation of resources, which as far as performance goals are concerned, are assumed to be utilized in an efficient and balanced manner.

In addition to the concern with the overall performance of the economy, there is the question of resource allocation. This is the problem of achievement or priority goals which raises the question of full employment for what? There are many priority goals competing for the nation's productive resources. An effective national plan provides mechanisms which aid the establishing of a priority list for competing goals such as national defense, space exploration, education, health and foreign aid. The national economic council, which is an essential feature of an effective national plan, provides a forum where the nation's major economic interests and the government can jointly discuss the relative merits of competing national goals. In this work of establishing a priority system for national goals the representatives of business, labor, farmers and consumers on the national economic council can call upon scientific and technical experts in the areas under consideration for advice in determining priorities. Consistency among priorities is secured by making sure that all public and private goals do not demand total resources that exceed the total resources available to the nation. These public and private goals if properly planned result in expenditures for the nation's total output or gross national product which should not exceed total output. It is in this connection that the national economic budget is useful, because it enables the national economic council and the government to quantify national achievement or priority goals, and to make them consistent with the nation's private goals and the total available supply of economic resources.

Colm explains that in the United States some progress has been made in the planning of performance goals by having the Council of Economic Advisers make annual and long term projections of gross national product. From 1953 to 1960 during the Eisenhower Administration the earlier efforts of the Council of Economic Advisers under the direction of Leon H. Keyserling to introduce national planning were abandoned. The Chairman of the Council during the Eisenhower Administration argued against making gross national product projections on the ground that they committed the government to a specific annual economic growth rate. The argument went on to say that the public would expect the government to achieve the projected annual increase in gross national product, and that the public would criticize the government if it failed in this connection. With the change in political administration in 1960 the Council of Economic Advisers abandoned the head-in-sand approach of the Eisenhower Council and turned to the publishing of five and ten year gross national product projections. These projections have been used to show what rate of economic growth would provide full employment with reasonable price stability and a favorable balance in the current international payments account. Specific fiscal, monetary, government expenditure, wage-price and other economic policies have been formulated with the hope of achieving the performance goals associated with the projections of gross national product.

Colm points out that, although a mechanism (gross national product projections) has been devised for the planning of performance goals, nothing similar has been done for achievement or allocative goals. Planning for allocative goals is an outgrowth of program planning which is concerned with the allocation of resources in the public sector. Planning for allocative or achievement goals, or "priority planning" as Colm describes it, goes beyond program planning because it is concerned with the allocation of all productive resources to goals in both the public and private sectors of the nation's economy. As has already been explained, allocative or priority planning to be effective requires the joint participation of all major economic interest groups in plan formulation and execution. It also requires the use of national economic budgets which translate national economic priorities into public and private expenditures for specific shares of the nation's gross national product.

In the United States the determining of national economic priorities is at present a very uncoordinated activity on federal, state and local government levels. At each level of government economic priorities are established by a democratic process which includes the activities of government officials, popularly elected legislators and lobbyists for special interests. This priority determining process is a push-and-pull affair in which open and hidden influences play major roles. In recent years there has been a growing interest in the problem of determining priorities among goals competing for the nation's productive resources. Legislators and appointed government officials have made more use of scientific and technical experts and new procedures such as program planning and systems analysis in the work of establishing priorities. Not much progress has been made, however, in handling the problem of how, ultimately, decisions are made as to what national economic goals shall be placed ahead of other goals, and how far each high priority goal shall be carried. On the federal level the Congress and the President and his cabinet have the final responsibility for establishing national priorities. In theory the Congress and the President with his cabinet cooperate in the process of determining priorities. But under the check and balance theory of government the Congress and the President remain at arm's length in their consideration of national priorities. The President does not construct a national economic budget to reveal to the Congress how his proposed priorities would draw upon the nation's total economic resources. The Congress itself has no way of constructing its own national economic budget to provide it with an overview of the whole scheme of public and private economic goals, and how they are related to the country's limited supply of natural and human resources.

Under the current poorly structured way of determining national priorities in the United States even the presidential cabinet has a much less important role than do the cabinets in the West European countries with parliamentary systems of government. Unlike their counterparts in these countries the American cabinet members are not chosen from among individuals elected to the Congress, and they are therefore not in a good position to present their case for national priorities to the Congress. In addition, in some administrations, as in the Kennedy Administration, the presidential cabinet infrequently meets as a joint body, and is therefore not well prepared to discuss the national priority problem. In this situation the Secretary of the Treasury and the Director of the Office of Management and Budget, who are in a crucial position with regard to appropriations recommended by the President, have more influence in the priority-determining process than their official positions would seem to warrant. All this could be remedied, in Colm's opinion, by making the President's cabinet more active in a priority-determining process based upon the use of national economic budgets constructed for consideration by the cabinet, the Congress and the public.

Colm's Proposals for National Economic Programming

Colm is a gradualist with respect to the adoption of national economic programming in the United States. He is well aware of the current obstacles to the widespread acceptance of this programming. Nevertheless, he has been a tireless advocate of national economic programming, and over the past quarter of a century he has frequently testified before government committees on the need for national economic budgets. In addition, he has written extensively on the subject with the aim of educating the public with respect to the usefulness of national economic budgets and the need for some kind of national economic programming. Colm's views along this line are found principally in *National Budgets for Full Employment* (1945), *The American Economy in 1960* (1952), *Long-Range Projections for Economic Growth: The American Economy in 1970* (1959), and *Essays in Public Finance and Fiscal Policy* (1955). The general contours of Colm's theorizing in relation to national economic programming were established in *National Budgets for Full Employment*, which was published at the conclusion of the Second World War.[16]

This study points out that the achievement of full employment after the war required a number of changes in the nation's consuming, saving and investing patterns or relationships. It was therefore necessary, Colm argued, to work out a pattern of economic relationships that by 1950 would balance total demand and total supply at a sustained full employment level. This could be done by constructing a number of "test models" which would show how the American economy might look in 1950 at full employment.[17] A test model is a national economic budget showing the projected full employment gross national product and its distribution in peacetime circumstances among households, businesses and governments at the federal, state and local levels. The National Planning Association study in 1945 presented three peacetime alternative test models or national economic budgets: a government, a business and a standard of living model. In the government model public expenditures were projected to take up an especially large share of the nation's gross national product. In the business model business investment expenditures were emphasized, and in the standard of living model private consumption expenditures were given special weight. In all three cases the projected combined government, business and consumer

---

[16] This study was prepared by the staff of the National Planning Association under the direction of S. H. Thompson with the assistance of E. D. Keyes and V. Coughlan. The study was made with the active cooperation of a number of economists including Gerhard Colm.

[17] *Ibid.*, p. v.

expenditures were large enough to absorb the projected full employment gross national product for 1950. Alternative test models or test national economic budgets were presented in the 1945 study to show different ways of achieving a balance between total demand and total supply at a full employment level. The people and the government in office could decide which of the three models to follow in actual practice. The model or budget chosen would then become a "decision model" which would have official sanction, and would be the basis for concrete economic policy making with the aim of securing full employment, sustained economic growth and price stability.

Table I shows the national economic accounts for the United States for the war year 1944 and Colm's standard of living test model or national economic budget for 1950. The projected pattern of consumer, business and government expenditures for 1950 was markedly different from the actual pattern for the war year 1944. In 1944 as in other war years private consumption expenditures were severely restricted, business investment expenditures for new plant and equipment almost came to a standstill, while government expenditures reached a very high level. In the standard of living test model or national economic budget consumer expenditures were projected to rise to 70 per cent of the 1950 gross national product, having been only 55 per cent in 1944. Business investment expenditures were projected to increase to 14 per cent of the 1950 gross

TABLE I

The U.S. National Economic Accounts for 1944
and Colm's National Economic Budget for 1950
(in billions of 1941 dollars)

Expenditures for gross national product	1944 National economic accounts (actual)	1950 National economic budget (projected)
Personal consumption expenditures	76.0 (55%)	118.4 (70%)
Business investment expenditures[1]	2.0 (1%)	24.0 (14%)
Government expenditures ...	93.2 (44%)	27.6 (16%)
Gross national product	171.2 (100%)	170.0 (100%)

[1] Includes net export surplus.
Source: National Planning Association, *National Budgets for Full Employment,* 1945.

national product, having amounted to only one per cent of the 1944 gross national product. At the same time government expenditures were projected to decrease to only 16 per cent of the 1950 gross national product, having accounted for 44 per cent of this product in 1944. The 1944 American economy was a high government-low private expenditure wartime economy, whereas the projected 1950 economy was a low government-high private expenditure peacetime economy.

Colm's 1945 study emphasized that it would be necessary during the years 1945-1950 to adopt fiscal, monetary, government spending, wage and price and other economic policies that would make possible achieving the desired level and distribution of gross national product in 1950. Through the use of various economic policies the government could influence public and private expenditures so that they would be in conformity with the national expenditure pattern set forth in whatever national economic budget or test model the government would project as a national goal for 1950. The big dangers were that, if appropriate economic policies were not adopted, total demand would not be large enough to absorb the potentially large gross national product in 1950. Or, if total demand was large enough to take up the expanding total supply, this would not occur without inflation. Recessions would then develop and full employment would not be on a sustained basis. A significant conclusion of Colm's 1945 study was that national economic budgeting and related economic policy formulation "will require, for success in a free society, cooperation between and among the private groups and their government."[18]

Colm's National Economic Budget for 1960

Needless to say, the Truman Administration did not accept Colm's post war proposal for national economic budgeting. Instead, the conventional way of moving from a wartime to a peacetime economy was followed. Wartime economic controls were quickly abandoned in late 1945 when the government hoped that a rapid upsurge in production would prevent the development of inflationary pressures. The government also exhorted business and labor to exercise restraint in raising prices or wages. Actual economic developments did not follow the course that the government had called for. The years 1945-1950 were a period of rapidly rising prices. The consumer price index, which was 62.7 in 1945 (1957-1959 = 100)

[18] *Ibid.*, p. 54.

increased to 83.8 in 1950. This was also a period in which an unbalanced economy developed. Private business investment spending expanded so much more rapidly than private consumer and government spending in these years that by 1949 the nation's capacity to produce exceeded its capacity to consume. The outcome was the recession of 1949. Colm's national economic budget for 1950 had projected a balanced economy in which there was more emphasis on consumer and government spending and less on business investment spending than actually turned out to be the case from 1945 to 1950. The *Economic Report of the President* for 1950 called attention to the need for "a sustainable balance, among the various sectors of our economy" in which business investment expenditures would "not be so large as to result in subsequent overproduction in relation to the absorptive capacity of markets."[19] The Council of Economic Advisers' policy recommendation was accompanied by the submission to the President and the Congress of a five year national economic budget for the years 1950-1954. This budget showed how the consumption-investment imbalance could be eliminated in the five year plan period. Neither the President nor the Congress responded favorably to the Council's recommendation for the use of national economic budgeting as a basis for economic policy formulation.

Colm again presented his case for national economic budgeting in *The American Economy in 1960*. In this study, written towards the end of the Korean war, Colm was again concerned with the shift from a wartime to a peacetime economy. The basic problem was to fill the gap after the conclusion of the war when military expenditures would decline, and to place the economy on the path of adequate and sustained growth. Again this meant establishing "a relationship between consumption, investment and government programs which is believed to be sustainable, that is, could be continued over time without causing major maladjustments."[20] Colm explained that there were alternative ways of achieving this relationship that would lead to sustained economic growth. In other words there were different possible combinations of private consumer, private business and government expenditures for goods and services that could result in sustained economic growth. In *The Ameri-*

---

[19] *Economic Report of the President*, January 1950, p. 80.

[20] Gerhard Colm, *The American Economy in 1960*, Planning Pamphlet No. 81, Washington, D.C., National Planning Association, December 1952, p. vi.

can Economy in 1960 Colm presents six different national economic budgets for the year 1960. He projected an annual increase in gross national product of 3 per cent for the years 1952-1960. At this projected rate of increase gross national product would rise from $329 billion in 1951 to $425 billion (in 1951 prices) in 1960. Colm's six alternative national economic budgets showed different ways of distributing the $425 billion gross national product among consumers, businesses and governments in 1960. After examining these six national economic budgets Colm then combined various features of these alternative budgets "in a manner that would give us a feasible and sustainable pattern of economic growth." This combination or seventh national economic budget became his "Adjusted Model," which is reproduced in Table II.[21] This model shows that the aim for the period 1952-1960 was to decrease the share of gross national product going into business investment from 18 per cent in 1951 to 14 per cent in 1960. Also in the same period government purchases were projected to fall from 19 per cent of gross national product in 1951 to 18 per cent in 1960. Personal consumption expenditures, rising from 63 per cent of gross national product in 1951 to 68 per cent in 1960, were projected to change considerably more than the other types of expenditures. As Colm saw the matter, the main problem in the post Korean war period would be to make certain that there was enough purchasing power in consumers' hands in the years 1953-1960 so that they would be able to purchase an expanding share of the growing gross national product.

TABLE II

*The U.S. National Economic Accounts for 1951
and Colm's National Economic Budget for 1960*
(in billions of 1951 dollars)

Expenditures for gross national product	1951 National economic accounts (actual)	1960 National economic budget (projected)
Personal consumption expenditures	208.0 (63%)	291.1 (68%)
Business investment expenditures[1]	58.7 (18%)	58.4 (14%)
Government expenditures ...	62.6 (19%)	75.5 (18%)
Gross national product	329.3 (100%)	425.0 (100%)

[1] Includes net export surplus.
Source: Gerhard Colm, *The American Economy in 1960*, 1952.

[21] *Ibid.*, p. 43.

The achieving of a stable, full employment, growing and balanced economy in 1960 could only be done by making appropriate adjustments in private and public economic policies. Colm's Adjusted Model or national economic budget for 1960 implied a reduction in personal and corporate taxes, greater encouragement of private investment in plant, equipment and housing, larger exports, a moderate increase in non-defense government spending, stable prices and increases in average wage rates equal to the annual average improvement in output per manhour. By relating these fiscal, monetary, government spending, price and wage policies to the national economic budget for 1960 it would be possible to distribute the 1960 gross national product of $425 billion among households, business enterprises and the federal, state and local governments in a way that would result in full employment and sustained economic growth. Some new institutional arrangements, however, might be needed. This was especially the case in the area of price and wage determination.

Colm points out that the full employment economy which is the goal of his proposed national economic programming has an inflationary bias which leads to a wage-price spiral. Fiscal and monetary policies are not effective safeguards against a wage-price spiral because they would have to be used so drastically in the effort to curb inflationary wage and price increases that they would result in an unacceptable level of unemployment. It is therefore necessary to devise other methods than credit and fiscal policies for keeping prices and wages within limits that are consistent with sustained price stability and full employment. In his 1952 study, *The American Economy in 1960*, Colm recommended instituting conferences of nationally known leaders of management and labor which would seek agreement on wage and price policies for a given period. Such agreements would endeavor to set specific figures for desirable average annual wage increases which would contribute to price stability and full employment. Even if no specific figure for desirable average wage increases could be agreed upon, it might be possible to agree upon a range which would narrow the limits within which collective bargaining would move. Colm in 1952 was of the opinion that a more formalized procedure for handling wage and price increases might develop out of the informal discussions of management-labor conferences as has occurred in the Scandinavian countries.

With the change from a Democratic to a Republican administration in 1953 any interest in national economic budgeting that there might have been in government circles disappeared or was soon covered up. In the first year of the Eisenhower Administration it was not even certain that the Council of Economic Advisers would be continued. When it was decided to keep the Council in operation, it was placed under a chairman who was not willing to publish projections of gross national product. In these circumstances Colm's proposal for national economic budgeting fell on stony ground. The years 1953-1960 were not noted for their economic progress. The economy suffered from two recessions. The recession of 1953-1954 was caused by a failure to make certain that private or civilian government spending would fill the gap created by a large drop in military spending in fiscal 1953-1954. The more serious capital goods recession of 1957-1958 was caused by the failure to have the nation's capacity to consume expand as rapidly as its capacity to produce. The very high level of private domestic investment in plant and equipment in 1955 and 1956 was subsequently not supported by a consumer demand that was large enough to purchase at profitable prices what could be produced. There being no adequate national economic guidance from 1954 to 1957, a sustainable relationship among consumer expenditures, business investment expenditures and government purchases did not develop. The gross national product statistics given below show that the distribu-

Colm's Projected and the Actual Percentage Distribution of
Gross National Product in 1960

	Percentage Distribution of Gross National Product	
	1960 (projected) by Colm	1960 (actual)
Consumer expenditures	68	63
Business investment expenditures	14	18
Government expenditures	18	19
	100	100

tion of gross national product projected by Colm was quite different from the actual distribution recorded for 1960. As these statistics show actual consumer expenditures as a percentage of gross national product in 1960 were 5 percentage points below the percentage projected by Colm. At the same time actual business investment expenditures as a percentage of gross national product were 4 percentage points larger than the percentage projected by Colm for

1960. Where business investment expenditures take up 18 per cent of gross national product, we have a rate of investment which in Colm's opinion necessarily creates surplus productive capacity and brings on a recession. In terms of Colm's projection of the uses or distribution of gross national product the actual distribution in 1960 was not sustainable, and could not contribute to the achievement of full employment. The actual 1960 distribution of gross national product was, according to Colm's analysis, "a faulty distribution which would have to redress itself through a recession."[22]

Colm's National Economic Budgets for 1965 and 1970

Towards the end of the Eisenhower Administration Colm again made a study of long range national economic budgeting. In *Long-Range Projections for Economic Growth: The American Economy in 1970*, he presented a number of eight and twelve year national economic budget projections. The eight year projections covered the years 1958-1965 and the twelve year projections the period 1958-1970. In each case alternative budgets in four categories were constructed: high consumption, high investment, high government and high and low defense models. These various models or budgets indicated the general pattern of what could reasonably be expected to happen in the nation's economy in the decade of the 1960's. For each period Colm chose a budget or model which indicated what in his judgment would be a feasible and sustainable course for the nation's economy to follow in the budget period 1958-1970. These judgment models or national economic budgets are presented in Table III. As compared with the actual United States national economic accounts for 1957 these budgets show that Colm projected a relative increase in the proportion of gross national product taken up by private consumer expenditures and a relative decline in the proportion taken up by business investment expenditures. In all his national economic budget projections from 1945 on Colm pointed to the same basic problem which was the need to secure a workable balance in the distribution of gross national product among households, businesses and governments. In the case of each projection the solution proposed was the same; namely, to curb business investment expenditures and to increase private consumer expenditures as the economy expanded. The objective was to offset the inherent

---

[22] National Planning Association, *Long-Range Projections for Economic Growth: The American Economy in 1970*, Planning Pamphlet No. 107, Washington, D.C., October 1959, p. 5.

TABLE III

The U.S. National Economic Accounts for 1957
and Colm's National Economic Budgets for 1965 and 1970
(in billions of 1958 dollars)

Expenditures for gross national product	1957 National economic accounts (actual)	1965 National economic budget (projected)	1970 National economic budget (projected)
Personal consumption expenditures	290.3(64%)	408.8(64.6%)	514.5(65.2%)
Business investment expenditures	73.0(16%)	97.3(15.4%)	120.8(15.3%)
Government expenditures	88.7(20%)	126.8(20.0%)	154.8(19.5%)
Gross national product	452.0(100%)	632.9(100%)	790.1(100%)

Source: National Planning Association, *Long-Range Projections for Economic Growth*, 1959.

tendency in the capitalist system of private business investment to be excessive and to create surplus productive capacity which would lead to a recession when the nation's capacity to consume fell behind its capacity to produce.

The policy implications of Colm's 1965 and 1970 national economic budgets point to the following policy positions. His budgets imply that gross national product should grow at an average rate of 4.2 per cent a year with unemployment reduced to 3.5 per cent. This is taken to be a desirable and feasible annual economic growth rate. A higher growth rate would require more governmental controls than we now have because it would create new inflationary pressures and production bottlenecks. Business, labor and political leaders and public opinion in general are currently not prepared to accept new governmental controls. It is therefore "prudent," in Colm's opinion, to accept as a goal an annual growth rate somewhere between 4 and 4.5 per cent a year.

Colm's judgment models or national economic budgets for 1965 and 1970 also point to the need for an expansion of government services. Economic growth does not automatically expand all sectors of the economic system in a balanced manner. The tendency is for the public parts of the economy to lag behind the private parts. Industrial growth needs many services "such as resource development including water supplies and soil conservation, aids to transportation and urban development, public education, research and

training, as well as public health programs."[23] Market forces alone
will not provide these services in adequate amounts for securing
sustained and high economic growth. It is therefore up to the government to make certain that there is a "balanced advance" in the
provision of public services and capital facilities. Colm's national
economic budgets for 1965 and 1970 maintain the proportion of
gross national product going into the public sector at 20 per cent,
as this product annually expands at the rate of 4.2 per cent. The
expansion of public services would be financed primarily from increased tax revenues.

Three special problems for the 1960's are recessions, the imbalance in taxing power between the federal government and the state
and local governments and inflation. All three issues raise important
policy problems. Since most of the public services needed by private
business are provided by the state and local governments, but the
tax revenues arising from economic growth go mainly to the federal government, the federal government must provide more public
services or share more of its revenues with the state and local governments. Colm does not recommend any particular solution to this
problem, but does argue that "a workable economy in 1970" requires a solution to this problem. His national economic budgets
for 1965 and 1970 are based on the assumption that a workable
solution to the problem of the imbalance in taxing power between
the federal government and the state and local governments is found.

Colm's national economic budgets also look forward to the elimination of recessions and the inflation that leads to them. New policies
with regard to price and wage adjustments are necessary. Credit
and fiscal policies can be effective in curbing the demand inflation
resulting from excess aggregate demand, but not against administered price and wage or cost push inflation. Business in general
would have to be severely depressed by restrictive credit and fiscal
policies before the power of large corporations and large unions to
raise prices and wages in an inflationary way could be effectively
curbed. Administered or sellers' inflation can be satisfactorily
curbed, in Colm's opinion, only by adopting some new institutional
arrangements. His proposals along this line include creating in the
Executive Office of the President a price-wage productivity agency
under the general policy guidance of the Council of Economic

---

[23] *Ibid.*, p. 18.

Advisers.[24] In addition there would be established in each major industry a price-wage-productivity board which would be staffed by business and labor representatives selected from the membership of the President's Labor-Management Policy Committee by the President's price-wage-productivity agency. The individual industry boards would submit reports concerning the facts relating to productivity improvements in the industry and related matters in any situation where actual or imminent price or wage behavior might appear to run contrary to the price and wage guideposts. These industry fact finding reports would be reviewed by the Council of Economic Advisers, and the President would be authorized to transmit them to the Congress with his recommendations concerning proposed wage or price increases.

This would be a method of trying to make wage and price guideposts workable. It is Colm's position that the American economic system cannot operate satisfactorily without price and wage guideposts.[25] The desired goal is not the abandonment of these guideposts but a remodelling of them. He is in agreement with the general philosophy of wage-price guideposts which is based on the proposition that incomes of all types should increase in accordance with the increase in average national productivity. The two deficiencies of the Kennedy-Johnson wage-price guideposts were that they tied wage increases to increases in worker productivity, but made no allowance for increases in the cost of living; and that they had a precise standard or limit for wage increases but no precise standards or limits for profits and other non-wage incomes. To remedy these defects Colm would make some allowance in wage adjustments for increases in the cost of living as well as for productivity improvements. In addition, while he does not propose precise standards or limits for non-wage incomes, he would look at incomes policy in the context of tax, social and other policies. His proposals for a federal price-wage-productivity agency and for industry price-wage-productivity boards would make it possible for business, labor and the government to tackle the price-wage or infla-

---

[24] House of Representatives, Subcommittee of the Committee on Government Operations, *Hearings on H.R. 11916, Congressional Review of Price-Wage Guideposts, Statement of Dr. Gerhard Colm*, Washington, D.C., Sept. 12, 1966, p. 6.

[25] Hearings before the Joint Economic Committee, *The 1967 Economic Report of the President, Testimony of Gerhard Colm, Chief Economist, National Planning Association*, 90th Congress, 1st Session, Part 4, Feb. 20-23, 1967, Washington, D.C., pp. 883-893.

tion problem jointly. Colm asserts that there can be no solution to this problem without the cooperation of all the interested parties.

National Economic Programming and Balanced Growth

Colm's general position with regard to the American economic system is that it cannot, if unregulated, expand without creating imbalances or discrepancies among different types of expenditures. There are two main imbalances: first, an imbalance between the public and private sectors, and, secondly, an imbalance within the private sector between private consumption and business investment. The imbalance between the public and private sectors arises because there is no mechanism that automatically keeps the two sectors in balance. The private market system cannot function as a balancing agent in this situation because public services are not usually provided at a price. Decisions to direct economic resources into the public sector are non-market decisions. They are political or governmental decisions which are made collectively with public support at the federal, state and local levels. The problem here is to improve the way in which economic resources are made available to the public sector. First, there is a need to secure more collaboration among the governments at various levels, since many public needs go beyond the jurisdiction of any one government. Problems of water supply, transportation, air pollution, flood control and health frequently require collective efforts by a number of governmental jurisdictions. Priorities among public services need to be established with the cooperation of federal, state and local governments. In some cases this will involve federal financing of state and local public services. Furthermore, more collaboration is needed to see to it that the total amount of government spending is in conformity with overall national economic policy. The total purchases of goods and services by the federal, state and local governments should add up to what is required by the American economic system when it is growing at an annual rate of between 4 and 4.5 per cent.

Colm believes that the process by means of which decisions are made as to what kinds and how many economic resources shall be diverted to the public sector stands in need of much improvement. Some progress has been made along these lines in recent years but much remains to be done. The main improvement that he recommends is to tie the public sector in with national economic programming. This means that government purchasing of goods and services at all government levels should be programmed on a long-term basis. Federal, state and local fiscal budgets, besides being made annually, should be projected on a five or ten year basis to fit in with five and ten year national economic budgets. Government appropriations at all levels could then be viewed as a part of the overall priorities set forth in the national economic budgets.

The second major imbalance relates to the tendency for private business investment to become excessive in relation to the economy's capacity to consume. In a competitive small-scale economy any such tendency would be soon corrected by market forces. All private business investment would have to stand the test of the competitive market system. Small competitive firms could not finance themselves from retained earnings as large corporations now do, and so they would have to borrow funds from the competitive capital market. When investing in plant and equipment proved to be unprofitable, self-correcting competitive market forces would very quickly reduce private investment. Prices would fall, investment would be reduced and consumption would rise soon enough to prevent any major discrepancy or gap between the capacity to produce and the capacity to consume from developing. This would occur in the competitive market economy where investing in the small-scale competitive firm does not require a large capital commitment, nor a long time between investment and sales of output produced by the new plant and equipment.

In the modern market economy with its large oligopolistic sector the self-correcting competitive forces are no longer strong enough to prevent the development of a serious imbalance between investment and consumption. Large-scale business enterprises finance a large part of their investment in new plant and equipment from retained earnings. These investments are not submitted to the test of the capital market, since this market is bypassed. Potentially excessive investment that might have been discouraged by adverse reactions to appeals for outside funds is not deterred. Nor does the riskiness of large capital commitments and of long periods of time between investment and securing income from this investment act so forcefully as to curb a rate of private investment that cannot be sustained. Booms feed upon themselves so that for a time self-reinforcing forces win out over self-correcting forces. Both business and government suffer from a "myopia induced by the pressure of current events," and the boom turns into overexpansion of the nation's capacity to produce in relation to its capacity to consume.[26] For example, the boom period 1955 to 1957 was accompanied by a capital buildup which became overextended in relation to consumption. The consequence of the unbalanced ratio of investment to consumption was the recession of 1958.

Colm does not believe that any economic program can eliminate all fluctuations from a private enterprise economy. He is confident, however, that more can be done to reduce economic fluctuations than has as yet been accomplished. He is convinced that national economic programming could be used to come closer to the goals of sustained economic growth and full employment. While recessions do correct the imbalances between investment and consumption, they do so at too high a cost—retarded economic growth, high unemployment and price instability. It is his position that national economic programming would be a step forward in curbing recessionary developments. The use of national economic budgets would make it possible to keep all the components of total national expenditures in a better balance than we have achieved up to now. This would be the case, Colm believes, because the national economic budget would quantify a sustainable investment-consumption balance, and would make it easier to secure agreement among the government, business and organized labor concerning the economic policies that should be adopted to achieve the desired investment-consumption balance.

Both the government and private business have their respective roles to fill in national economic programming. The government must have "the strength and skill to deal with any dangerous imbalances in the domestic economy that cannot be corrected without government action."[27] The government should take a long view which would consider the performance of the economy in relation to its potential. The long term national economic budget should be used as a quantitative guide to sustained growth and full employment with price stability. Private business should likewise take the long view and place less reliance on records of past business and current market conditions as guides to future expectations. Private business planning would be based on the confidence that the government could fill its role successfully in supplementing the private market economy with policies and programs that would lead to

---

[26] *Long-Range Projections for Economic Growth*, p. 11.
[27] *Ibid.*, p. 20.

the achievement of the national goals presented in the long term national economic budget.

Colm's General Indirect National Economic Planning

Colm's objective is the successful operation of a "free enterprise economy" in which public policies are needed to supplement market forces. What he envisions is a combination of public and private planning in which collaboration would be more prominent than economic controls. Also since the government's role would be only a residual and supporting role, decentralized private initiative would continue to be the dominant feature of the economy. What would provide coordination or integration of private and public enterprise would be the fact that both private and government decision makers would be using "as a common frame of reference the prospective growth of the economy as a whole."[28] It is this common frame of reference that would provide the needed consistency among private and public economic decisions.

Colm's national planning can be best described as overall or general indirect planning. It is overall for the reason that it provides a general framework for an analysis of the functioning of the total economy and for the national economic programming which supplements the private market economy. It is a form of indirect planning since it does not envisage setting up fixed production targets for specific industries or business enterprises. Nor does Colm's planning contemplate the use of any direct wage, price or investment controls. Whatever controls are to be used are to be indirect and along the lines of currently accepted fiscal and monetary policies which work indirectly on the levels of production, consumption, investment and employment. Colm's national planning is similar to the strategic national planning that was recommended by J. M. Clark in the 1930's.[29] Both Clark's and Colm's national planning would operate only at strategic points in the economy where fiscal, monetary, government spending, wage and price policies would have an impact.

Colm's national economic planning is in some ways similar to the kind of national planning carried on in France, Norway, Sweden, and the Netherlands today. Both his and West European planning do not duplicate the blue print, comprehensive direct planning found

---

[28] *The Economy of the American People*, p. 140.
[29] John M. Clark, *Social Control of Business* (Second edition; New York: McGraw-Hill Book Co., 1939) p. 465.

in the Soviet Union and other communist countries. Colm's national planning emphasizes the differences between democratic and totalitarian national planning such as is carried on in the communist countries. If Colm's proposals for national economic programming were to be adopted in the United States, it would be because the Congress and the public had come around to the position that they approved this type of planning.

Although Colm's national economic planning is in its fundamentals similar to the kind of planning being carried out in most democratic West European countries today, it should be pointed out that these countries make more use of direct economic controls than is recommended by Colm. For example, most West European countries have direct foreign exchange controls especially in relation to capital movements out of the country. In addition, the governments in these countries usually have the power to regulate prices, although this power is usually used only in the form of general price freezes and then only in national emergencies. Also the West European countries frequently make use of direct investment controls in the form of building or construction licenses which supplement credit controls. In some West European countries there is also the licensing of individual bond issues. It is clear that West European national planning makes much more use of direct economic controls than is envisioned by Colm's national planning proposals. Critics of Colm's planning proposals would argue that he underestimates the need for direct economic controls. They assert that his planning program would inevitably move in the direction of more direct controls than he has considered. If the experience of Western Europe is any guide in this connection, it would appear that more direct economic controls than we now have in the United States might be required for the successful execution of a national planning program. This would not mean, however, that the essentially democratic nature of Colm's planning program would be fundamentally jeopardized. This has not occurred in Western Europe, and there is no good reason to believe that it would happen in the United States. In both situations it is up to the people to decide whether or not they want national planning, and how far they want to go in carrying it out.

The Improvement of National Economic Guidance

As a first step towards improving our system of national economic guidance Colm would improve the execution of the Employment Act of 1946.[30] This Act makes provision for close cooperation among the federal government, industry, agriculture, labor and state and local governments in pursuing the objectives of the Act. Nothing, however, has been done to provide formally for joint consultation among these interest groups. Consultations with separate interest groups have usually been infrequent and always informal. Colm would have the joint consultative committees envisaged by the Employment Act meet regularly with the Council of Economic Advisers at least once each quarter. In addition he would have the *Economic Report of the President* present each year a national economic budget for the coming year, and also a budget for the following five years. The annual economic budget would indicate what increases in production, income and expenditures would be needed for the achievement of full employment in the coming year. The five year national economic budget would give a longer run perspective for an evaluation of foreseeable trends. This long term economic budget could be used to analyze the long term problems of economic growth and alternative resource uses. Alternative long term national economic budgets could be used in an exploratory way to analyze different paths of economic development.

Colm would also have the annual *Budget Message of the President* present a five year fiscal budget outlook so that the Congress and the public could see how the fiscal budget would be used to accomplish the national objectives set forth in the five year national economic budget. Five and ten year fiscal budget projections would show the expansion of federal government revenues over the five or ten year projection period, and for what purposes these growing revenues would be spent. As the economy grows, the existing tax rates under full employment will lead to an increase in government revenues. The long-term fiscal budget projection may then allow for tax reductions, for increased government spending, for sharing of federal tax revenues with state and local governments or for some combination of these arrangements. The purposes for which the increased government revenues may be spent would be indicated by the long term national economic budget. Federal fiscal budget projections should therefore be related to and integrated with the economic projections or long-term national economic

---

[30] Joint Committee on the Economic Report, *Hearings before the Joint Committee, January 1956 Economic Report of the President*, 84th Congress, 2d Session, Washington, D.C., Jan. 31-Feb. 28, 1956, pp. 694-697.

budgets. Colm points out that this would require cooperation between the Bureau of the Budget and the Council of Economic Advisers.[31]

The presentation of a long term federal fiscal budget outlook and a long term national economic budget would provide the Congress and the public with the information required for considering the need for changes in private and public economic policies. This information would also be of interest to the joint consultative committees provided for by the Employment Act, which Colm would have working closely with the Council of Economic Advisers. Not only could advice be secured from these joint consultative committees, but also their cooperation and support for the national economic guidance program could be enlisted. The representatives of business, labor and agriculture on the joint consultative committees could inform their respective organizations about the government's program for national economic guidance, and could seek to broaden the public support for this program.

In his 1968 study of the problem of the expansion of government programs in recent years, *Program Planning for National Goals*, Colm made further proposals for the improvement of the national economic decision making process. He suggested that the determination and evaluation of national goals could be done more effectively by establishing the post of a new Special Assistant to the President for Plans and Priorities, who would be concerned with these plans and priorities within the framework of the President's general view of the nation's future. In addition there would be set up in the Executive Office of the President an Office for the Appraisal of National Goals and Programs which would be staffed with professional analysts and would be concerned with the appraisal of long-term goals and programs. There would also be a need for a Citizens' Committee on National Goals and Priorities and a special congressional committee for the appraisal of plans and programs in the light of national needs. The Citizens' Committee would keep the President and the Congress informed about the public's views with regard to what should be the nation's goals and programs and what should be the priorities among these goals and programs. A special congressional committee supplied with an adequate pro-

---

[31] Gerhard Colm and Peter Wagner, *Federal Budget Projections, A Report of the National Planning Association and the Brookings Institution* (Washington: The Brookings Institution, 1966) p. 16. The Bureau of the Budget has now become the Office of Management and Budget.

fessional staff of analysts would enable the Congress to make its own independent appraisal of the President's proposals with regard to desirable national goals and their priorities. This tripartite citizen-presidential-congressional appraisal system would ensure a thoroughgoing appraisal of the directions that the nation's economic and social development would be taking.

Colm is well aware that public-private economic planning in the United States is not immediately around the corner. Nor can this type of democratic planning be successfully developed in a short time. It will take much experimentation and a willingness to try new ways of adjusting to the technological change that is rapidly and extensively transforming the American economy. Colm believes that it is feasible to educate the American public to the need for public-private economic planning. To this end he has been associated with the educational efforts of the National Planning Association which has established a Center for Economic Projections and a Center for Priority Analysis.[32] The Center for Economic Projections carries on research in how to improve the analytical foundations and methods of making long range projections. It publishes regular and continuing series of five to fifteen year economic and demographic projections for the nation, states and metropolitan areas. These projections are of interest to business, labor organizations and government officials who are concerned with investment, marketing, manpower, fiscal or program planning. Conferences and technical workshops provide a meeting ground for the exchange of ideas concerning long-range planning and projections. They also help planners in industry and public agencies with the development and use of long-range projections.

The Center for Priority Analysis engages in research relating to the problem of national priorities. The Center carries on a continuous audit of national goals and the resources available to secure these goals. Studies have been made to identify national goals, and to determine the dollar cost and the manpower and raw materials requirements for securing these goals. Research has also been directed to the manner in which decisions are made concerning national goals and how this process can be improved. The aim of the Center's research program is to identify the individuals and groups in the public and private sectors of the economy who make decisions affecting national goals, and to improve their participa-

---

[32] National Planning Association, *1964 and 1965 Report on Activities*, Washington, D.C., 1966, pp. 17-22.

tion in this decision making process by making them aware of the alternative goals available to society and the need to establish priorities among these alternatives.

The Economics of National Economic Programming

Colm's analysis of American capitalism and its prospects is supported by a version of economics that goes beyond the standard economics of today. He refers to a "new economics" towards which we are working, and which he believes is more useful than standard economics for explaining the economic world in which we live. Colm points out that what economists are concerned with is interpreting economic reality. But they are always interpreting an ever changing scene since "The reality of economics is dynamic."[33] In order to interpret the emergent economic reality the economist has to make some assumptions that will aid him in his work of economic explanation. These assumptions, if they are to be "live" and in accordance with the observable facts, should emphasize the emerging nature of the economic world and not its current nature. What is important about economic reality is not its features that have already been shaped or established but its features that are currently coming into being. Colm explains that Adam Smith based his economic theorizing on the assumption that the economic system was a free competitive system when in fact the actual system of his day was the non-competitive mercantilist system. Likewise, Karl Marx assumed that technological progress and large scale monopolistic industry were prominent features of the West European economy when he made his analysis of the capitalist system. In reality the economic system of his day in the United Kingdom and on the continent was predominantly small scale and competitive in nature. Both Smith and Marx made the emergent features of the economic world and not the predominantly existing features the basis for their economic theorizing. This is precisely what Colm has done. He has taken the emerging main feature or aspect of the economic world to be its tendency to move towards intervention or planning. His economic theorizing is about an economic system that has crossed the threshold into an age of interventionism and planning. Just as Smith and Marx were futuristic in their approach to economic reality so also is Colm's economics oriented towards the future.

Economic reality for Colm is an evolving process undergoing historical development. This evolving process has passed through a

---

[33] "Economics Today," *Essays in Public Finance and Fiscal Policy*, p. 338.

number of stages, and is currently moving from a regulated "market economy" to a planned "organizational economy." Interpretation of the development of the economic system is not a mere extrapolation of past trends. These trends are not "necessary" developments over which mankind has no control. On the contrary these trends can be influenced or shaped by human action. As he puts it, "In social development the trend is not a 'natural' or necessary development. It may be shaped by human action, and one of the elements in its formation is the theoretical conception of the economic system. The theorist influences, mostly to a minor degree but sometimes as an important factor, the historical development that he is interpreting. Hence the social responsibility of economic theory."[34]

Colm explains that the approach of an economist to economic reality is determined by the historical situation in which he lives. As this situation changes and crises arise because society has failed to make the appropriate adjustments, traditional economic assumptions are revised and a new approach to economic reality is established. This occurred in the 1930's when the classical approach with its emphasis on equilibrium and order proved no longer to be a satisfactory approach for an interpretation of the economic world of that time. Both the classical and the Marxian approaches were based on the assumption of "economic automatism." The classical economists believed that the economic system would automatically gravitate towards a just and efficient competitive order, while the Marxians held the view that capitalism would automatically move to its ultimate self-destruction. In 1937 Colm based his economic analysis on the assumption that interventionism had replaced automatism. He explained that "The economic order has today reached a point where action will brook no delay." The only question was the type of action to be pursued. He assumed that it would be possible to steer a "middle course" between communism and fascism.

Colm's framework of assumptions included the assumption that the traditional patterns of life, while shaken by modern industrial developments, were not being dissolved or destroyed. Consequently there was still a chance to "pursue a 'middle course' of reconstruction within the traditional social pattern." In other words, he felt that the remodelling of capitalism was still a feasible goal which could be achieved by a program of government intervention in the market economy. In this situation economic science must become "constructive," since we cannot rely on natural forces for the crea-

[34] *Ibid.*, p. 339.

tion of a perfect market economy. We must take as our starting point a "man made economy" and not one that is supposed to reflect the automatic functioning of market forces. If it is accepted that the economy is man made, it can be altered and adapted to technological change.

Colm's new approach to economic reality calls for "a realistic analysis of the actual functioning of economic life." This means a broadening of the scope of economics to include the management problems of large scale enterprise and of powerful labor organizations and the problems of public and private planning. In 1937 Colm described the new emerging feature of the economic system as "interventionism" which seemed to place him in the same camp as Keynes who, in 1936 in his *General Theory of Employment Interest and Money*, laid the theoretical foundations for a program of government intervention. By 1954 Colm had moved far beyond Keynesian interventionism to the "new economics" of national planning or programming. In 1954 he referred to this fundamental change in his economic approach by observing that "There is no good term for characterizing the present state of the economy and the present task of economics in the Western World. I would not choose today the term 'interventionism,' which I used in this essay in 1937. Interventionism stresses the fact that the modern government had to accept additional responsibilities in a predominantly free market economy. This was a one sided view, which was influenced by the experience of the depression period."[35] Interventionism implies too narrow a role for the government in the modern economy. Since 1937 Colm has come to see that the newly emerging feature of the economic world is not interventionism but national planning, which assigns the government a much larger role in economic affairs than does interventionism.

Colm is well aware of the significance of the Keynesian revolution in economic thinking. He would agree that what Keynes had to say about employment, interest and money marked a big advance beyond Alfred Marshall and Arthur C. Pigou. He would also agree that many of Keynes's policy recommendations have been found useful in combating depression or recession. But Colm would point to serious limitations in the work of Keynes. Keynes did not read the future accurately enough with the consequence that he failed to grasp that the major industrial nations were going beyond

---

[35] *Ibid.*, p. 334 fn.

intervention towards planning. Keynes did not have an adequate long-range view because he failed to take account of technological change and its impact on the structure and functioning of the economy. Keynes's economics remained compensatory or manipulative. With his exclusive "treasury" outlook or approach he proceeded to try to manipulate the economy into the desired position of full employment. He called for no joint consultation on a formal basis of representatives of business, labor, agriculture, local and central government. Instead he kept the nation's major economic interest groups at arm's length. He had no interest in published national economic budgets which could have been a basis for joint consultation and collaboration among the representatives of the nation's organized economic interests and the government.

From Colm's point of view Keynes's economics is too compensatory or remedial and not preventive enough. Instead of analyzing the economic situation and taking early steps to prevent the development of unworkable wage-price-profit relationships or an unbalanced investment-consumption relationship, Keynes thought primarily in terms of adopting policies and measures that would compensate for or remedy non-sustainable economic relationships that were allowed to develop with inflationary or deflationary consequences. Colm explains that "It is true that fiscal policy in its original and simplest conception is designed to combat inflation or deflation. This means that compensatory fiscal policy is more suited to combating the results than it is the causes of economic maladjustments. It would be preferable, at least under peacetime conditions, if these maladjustments themselves could be prevented before they cause large swings of inflation or deflation."[36] This means that fiscal policy should be associated with long-range wage and price policy to improve collective bargaining; with a price policy that prevents excessive profit margins and retained earnings above those justified by investment needs; and with efforts to get private business to "regularize" its program for investment planning. These are matters that did not particularly interest Keynes. Had he been more concerned with these issues his economics would have been less compensatory and more preventive than it turned out to be.

Colm observes that the present day followers of Keynes in the United States adhere rather closely to Keynes's original position. Under the pressure of changing events the Keynesians, especially

---

[36] Gerhard Colm, "Fiscal Policy and the Federal Budget," *Essays in Public Finance and Fiscal Policy*, p. 214.

in government circles where reality is distorted with much more difficulty than in academic circles, have made some small advance beyond the Keynes of 1936. Some Keynesians will now quantify the national economic growth rate goal, and will even make long term projections of the size of the gross national product. The recent interest in wage and price guidelines marks an advance beyond the Keynes of the 1930's. But, in spite of these advances in Keynesian policies and programs, the Keynesians of today hold substantially to the position Keynes had in the 1930's. The current Keynesians still cling to the predominantly "treasury approach," still mainly substitute manipulation of economic affairs for collaboration in these affairs, and still refuse to publish national economic budgets and to encourage joint consultation. They also still fail to adopt a long range view of economic evolution which gives due weight to technological progress and the need for an exploratory and innovatory approach in the handling of our major economic problems. It is obvious that whatever he is Colm is not a Keynesian.

The Logic of Economic Evolution

Colm's "new economics" is concerned with both an initial or current state of the economy and a future or terminal state towards which he believes the current American economic system is moving. Colm's initial state is the condition of the economy as he now sees it. This current state or condition of the economy is the product of a long evolutionary process which is converting the formerly free market economy into an "organizational economy" in which large government, business and labor organizations are reducing the area of competitive enterprise, and are interfering with the free functioning of the market system. The failure of government intervention of the Keynesian type to secure a balanced growth of the economy demonstrates the need for national planning. It is at this point in his economic analysis that Colm becomes concerned with his future or terminal state of the economy. This terminal state is based on the economic relationships in Colm's initial state, but it is not a mere extrapolation of these current relationships. Over time these economic relationships of the initial state are altered by technological change and by the purposeful actions of individuals and groups. The future is linked to the past but it is never a mere reproduction of the past.

The nation's economic system is changing under "the impact of technical progress." Colm points out that the development which the economy is undergoing contains irrational and unpredictable elements. Nevertheless, the course of economic development is subject to man's influence and may be shaped by him to some extent. The economist has the responsibility of moving beyond his interpretation of economic development to show how the economy may be steered towards a situation in which sustained economic growth, full employment and price stability may be secured. This situation is Colm's future or terminal state or situation in which the economy would be planned along lines similar to those being followed today by a number of the democratic West European countries. The link between Colm's initial state of the economy and its future or terminal state is national economic programming. This programming shows how we may move from the current initial state to the future terminal state by constructing long-term national economic budgets, and by developing economic policies that will aid us in accomplishing the goals projected in the national economic budgets.

In his analysis of the course of economic evolution in Western Europe and the United States, Colm has turned up no laws of economic development which inevitably point to the next stage in the evolution of the capitalist system. Nor is it possible to squeeze what Colm describes as "the peculiarities of economic development" into a mathematical or statistical formula. There is, however, a logic of economic evolution which reflects technological progress and indicates the technological limits or conditions to which an evolving economic system must adapt itself. There is a "vital task of adaptation" to technological change to which economists can and should contribute, but there is no assurance that this adaptation will inevitably lead to any particular type of economic system. Economists and others must put forth an effort to create the kind of economic system that they want.

Welfare Economics in Action

Does Colm's analysis of a possible planned economy of the future go beyond the proper scope of economics? He agrees that this kind of economic analysis transcends economics as a purely descriptive or a purely analytical science. His economics is "an example of 'constructive economics' or 'welfare economics' in action."[37] Colm's constructive economics has a much broader scope than conventional or standard economics. He places the economic system in a

---

[37] "Setting the Sights," *Essays in Public Finance and Fiscal Policy*, p. 358.

political and social framework which both influences and is influenced by the economic system. As he explains it, "present day economics must be constructive, and therefore both realistic and imaginative, integrating political, sociological and psychological elements into the theoretical framework."[38] Colm is impatient with a narrow analytical economics which pays excessive attention to the refinement of traditional or inherited economic theory, and whose concern is largely with "the abstract creations of scholars floating on air above the struggle waged in the field of actual social life." In developing his "constructive economics" Colm does not dispense with standard economic theory. He finds the contributions of micro and macro economists very useful as far as they go. The point is that the work of these standard economists does not go far enough in its explanation of the dynamic real economic world. Keynes's economics was a great advance beyond Alfred Marshall's economics. But even so Keynes had no theory of the evolving capitalist system, and he paid no particular attention to the impact of technological change on the structure and functioning of the developing economic system. Standard economics, in Colm's opinion, is particularly deficient in its capacity to explain the nature and problems of the evolving capitalist system. Only by broadening the scope of economics as traditionally viewed can the economist approach the task of explaining the developing economic system in a realistic manner. In broadening the scope of standard or conventional economics the economist develops what Colm describes as a "social or political economics."[39] The economist has a responsibility to pursue theorizing that exhibits a certain "social responsibility." Excessive refinement of theoretical concepts has no relevance for the reason that it contributes nothing towards the solving of the problem of an historical situation. Colm explains that "The most important duty of science is that it should understand the task it has to fulfill in a specific historical situation." Economists should understand what is on the social and economic agenda, that is to say, what the main economic problem of their time is, and should then direct their purely academic work towards solving this problem. It is Colm's position that the main economic problem of our particular "historical situation" is how to guide our economy towards sustained growth, full employ-

---

[38] "Economics Today," p. 343.
[39] Conference on Research in Income and Wealth, *Long-Range Economic Projection*, Volume Sixteen (New York: National Bureau of Economic Research, 1954) p. 39.

ment and price stability. His solution to this problem is national economic programming with the aid of national economic budgets. In working out this solution Colm's "welfare economics in action" not only analyzes statistics and interrelations among economic variables, but also "becomes a tool for private and public action by projecting the results [of economic analysis] into the future."

Economists are currently very much interested in economic decision making on two levels; namely, the level of the individual firm and the level of the governmental department. As Colm sees the problem, what is required is decision making at the national level that will coordinate decision making at these two levels. This overall decision making would be achieved through what he has described as "concerted national planning."[40] Colm defines concerted planning as "a system of decision making." Decision making at the national level would consist of setting policy goals, developing programs and projects for moving towards these goals within a specific time, designing policies for mobilizing resources required by these programs and projects and providing a mechanism for making adjustments to unexpected developments. Like business decision making, governmental decision making is carried on under conditions of uncertainty because there are always factors such as foreign markets, foreign capital movements and the responses of people to government measures which are outside government control.

The essence of national decision making is priority analysis which seeks to achieve a nationally approved relative balance among such programs as defense, space, oceanics, urban renewal, rapid transportation, education, health, law enforcement and the like. National decisions as to the "best" uses of resources are a task that involves political, social and economic considerations. They are the joint products of the deliberations of both governmental and private groups. Colm explains that "National goals and priority analysis can never be defined and determined solely by the use of statistical and other techniques."[41] These techniques such as national economic budget projections and computerized economic models can help the decision makers arrive at more "knowledgeable and better informed decisions," but they cannot themselves determine what should be the national goals. Decisions about national goals and priorities are in the final analysis a matter of judgment which reflects the value

---

[40] Gerhard Colm and Luther H. Gulick, *Program Planning for National Goals*, p. 16.
[41] *Ibid.*, p. 18.

premises of the individuals and groups participating in the decision making process. Hence decision making at bottom is a matter of value or preference and not of technique. The decision making process at the national level gives rise to compromises among individuals and groups with conflicting value preferences. For this reason Colm finds that it is very important to have all major interest groups participate in the national decision making process.

In developing his concept of national decision making Colm utilizes the holistic approach which blends the roles of economic, social and political factors.[42] National decision making goes beyond conventional economic analysis since it is concerned with the social and political environment in which planning is carried on. Just as business enterprises today have increasingly come to recognize "some degree of responsibility for creating a social environment for efficient production and mutually advantageous management-labor relationships," so also the government in its decision making should take into account the total economic, social and political situation in which it makes decisions with regard to the use of economic resources. If economists are to grapple effectively with the problems associated with national decision making, they must in Colm's opinion adopt an holistic approach that goes far beyond the scope of economics as it is conventionally viewed.

According to Colm's interpretation it is very important to push economic analysis into the realm of national decision making because in the future public decision making will be more important than private decision making in the work of achieving high levels of economic and social development. What is especially crucial in the future is not what private business does but what government does. As Colm puts it, "Now the greatest contribution to economic growth and welfare could be made by the expansion of high priority government programs."[43] More resources will in the future have to be poured into large-scale government programs in research and development concerned with the war on poverty, urban renewal, the farming and mining of the oceans, enlarging the supply of fresh water, curbing air pollution and providing new methods of rapid

[42] Gerhard Colm, *Integration of National Planning and Budgeting*, Center for Development Planning, National Planning Association, Methods Series No. 5, Washington, D.C., March 1968, p. 6.

[43] Gerhard Colm, "Man's Work and Who Will Do It in 1980," *America 1980, The William A. Jump–I. Thomas McKillop Memorial Lectures in Public Administration 1965*, edited by Robert L. Hill, The Graduate School, U.S. Department of Agriculture, Washington, D.C., August 1965, p. 21.

transportation. Economics in the future will be more of an "economics of national priorities" and less of an "economics of private priorities." This does not mean that the private enterprise system will disappear or that private priorities are unimportant. On the contrary the new economics of national priorities will be solidly based on "new methods of government-business cooperation." Colm explains that economic growth inevitably results in some degree of structural and institutional change. "Change in governmental and social institutions is much slower than change in technology and management. Institutions change usually when the need is long overdue, when their defects have made the need abundantly clear and when it is recognized that knowledge and ability exist to make the revised or new institutions work." A part of this institutional change will give rise to new methods of bringing the private sector into the national decision making process. It will also call for the modernization of government procedures as they relate to the national decision making process.

Colm has greatly strengthened the work of institutional economists by filling in a serious gap in their analysis. The pre-World War II institutionalists had come to the conclusion that the United States and the major West European countries had entered a plan age, and that there was then a need to work out some kind of democratic national economic planning program. Prior to 1939 the institutionalists were stymied in their handling of the national planning problem because they could not quantify their planning proposals. In 1939 Clark discussed a social or national economic budget as the point of departure for his "social-liberal" planning, but he was unable to make much progress with his planning proposals because he could not quantify his social budget. Similarly, Wesley C. Mitchell, Rexford G. Tugwell and Gardiner C. Means were unable to do much with their planning proposals because they had no quantitative basis for their proposals. Colm has removed this obstacle in the path of the pre-1939 institutionalists as the result of his pioneering work in the area of national economic budgeting. He has successfully demonstrated to the institutionalists how they can quantify their national planning program, and how they can make concrete proposals with respect to national.economic programming.

Colm's science of national economic programming neatly complements the work of economists such as Clarence E. Ayres and John K. Gailbraith. Our analysis of the work of the latter two economists has revealed that the least satisfactory part of their work relates to their proposals for translating economic theory into economic practice. The planning proposals of Ayres and Galbraith remain vague and somewhat elusive. The goals of Ayres's "reasonable society" and Galbraith's "society of excellence" have both qualitative and quantitative aspects. Their qualitative goals have quantitative impacts which reveal themselves in the form of demands upon the nation's supply of scarce economic resources. No matter how highly qualitative a national goal is it necessarily gives rise to a demand for a share of the nation's gross national product. In other words, all national goals should be budgeted for in competition with one another. It would strengthen the work of Ayres and Galbraith if they could show the overall economic impact of their planning proposals. This can be done by turning to Colm's national economic budgeting with its quantification of national goals on a high priority basis.

CHAPTER VII

NEO-INSTITUTIONAL ECONOMICS:
ITS NATURE AND SIGNIFICANCE

Having surveyed the work of Ayres, Galbraith, Myrdal and Colm we are now in a position to summarize their views with respect to the nature and scope of economics. These heterodox economists emphasize the point that the social sciences are together concerned with an analysis and interpretation of the functioning of the total social system. Social scientists take the social system to be an evolving pattern or complex of human relations which is concerned with the ways in which mankind meets its wide variety of needs. The total social system breaks down into a number of subsystems each one of which deals with a special area of human need. Thus we have the subsystem dealing with the need for goods and services, the subsystem concerned with the government or administration of human activities, and the subsystem that is interested in justice or the adjustment of conflicting claims and the assignment of rewards or punishments. Although each social science is interested in a special part of the total social system, it does not ignore the interrelations between social subsystems or the impact of the total social system on each social subsystem.

What is important about all the social sciences is that they deal with different aspects of the social world or with what Myrdal refers to as "social reality." Myrdal's view of social reality, which he defines as a "dynamic process" and not a "static balance," is a view of an evolving social system of which the economic system is a subsidiary part or subsystem. This economic system which provides a supply of scarce goods and services to meet a variety of human needs is analyzed by Myrdal within the framework of the total social system. To explain the economic system fully Myrdal and other neo-institutionalists assert that economists must relate the economic system to the total framework or social system of which it is a subsidiary part. It is this emphasis upon the economic system as a part of the larger social system that makes Myrdal's economics of integration a type of "social economics."

Economics as a Social Science

The views of Myrdal and other neo-institutionalists with respect to the definition and scope of economics reflect their views concerning the nature of social and economic reality. These views in turn reflect the neo-institutionalists' views concerning the differences between the physical and the social sciences, and therefore the differences between physical and social science data. As we shall see, the conventional economists do not make the same distinction between physical and social science data that the neo-institutionalists make, and consequently the conventional economists arrive at views on the definition and scope of economics that are very different from the views of the neo-institutionalists. Whereas the conventional economists, following their classical and neo-classical predecessors, pattern their economics after the physical sciences, the neo-institutionalists do not fashion their economics after the physical sciences. Instead they keep their economics a "social" science that is to be distinguished at all times from what passes as physical science.

The basic difference between the physical and the social sciences is not in their methods of carrying on scientific investigations, but rather it is in the nature of the data that they analyze. The data or matter investigated by the physical scientists have two qualities that distinguish them from social science data. First physical science data do not change their nature over time, and secondly since they do not have any purposive aspect they do not in any way raise the question of wants or ends. Although over aeons of time the universe may evolve and the nature of physical matter may change, for all practical purposes the physical scientist can consider his data to be of an unchanging nature, and he can take the physical world to be a stable, non-evolving system of relationships among physical data. In addition physical science data have nothing to do with values, ends or purposes. Particles of matter are not value creating or value carrying data. They do not move about the universe with the aim of achieving their values or satisfying their wants. They are set in motion as the result of the action of blind natural forces that have nothing to do with purpose or value.

The situation is quite different with regard to the social world and the data found in it. The data of the social world which concern the social scientist are not only evolving data but also purposeful data. Since the structure and functioning of the social system are usually in a state of flux, the relations between men and the social world in which they live are subject to dynamic change. Although some societies may appear for a time to be stable or stagnant, in general social systems move cumulatively in either an upward or downward direction. Whereas unchanging duration is the essence of the physical world, dynamic change is the essence of the social world. Galbraith has emphasized this point with the observation that "In the physical sciences—chemistry, physics, biology—change is associated only with discovery, with the improving state of knowledge. The matter being studied does not change. In economics as in other social sciences, there is change both in the state of knowledge and in what is being studied. There is improvement in the knowledge of the way prices are established. There is also change in the *way* prices are established. This will happen as the small proprietorship with no control of its market gives way to the giant corporation which has such control, or as both make way for government price fixing."[1] In the opinion of Galbraith and the other neo-institutionalists a full understanding of economic data can be achieved only by taking account of the fact that this data is by its very nature developmental or evolutionary. Economic and all other social science data are cultural data which reflect the advance of science and technology, and which therefore necessarily proliferate, change or evolve. While for some analytical purposes the economist may ignore the changing and unstable nature of his data, a full understanding of this data requires the economist to subordinate this assumption of the fixity and stability of economic data to the more realistic assumption of the essentially evolutionary nature of this data.

As has already been explained, the physical sciences deal with data that involve no question of purposes, ends or values. The situation with respect to the social science data is quite different. All social science data relate to man and his relations with other men in some form of society. Man as a social phenomenon and as the central concern of the social sciences is a datum that cannot be divorced from the concept of ends or purposes if the study of this datum is to be classified as a "social science." Human behavior becomes "social" when it involves two or more individuals whose behavior is guided by ends or purposes. The behavior of an iso-

---

[1] John Kenneth Galbraith, *The New Industrial State*, p. 410.

lated individual which absorbs the attention of so many conventional economists is not "social" behavior. There are no social relations or social problems in Robinson Crusoe's world. One can inquire how an isolated individual might behave in a situation in which means or resources are scarce, and thus learn something about the nature of this type of individual behavior. No one can properly deny that something can be learned about economic behavior by observing how the isolated individual might function in an environment of scarcity. The isolated individual, however, is a deviation from the real individual who is a social and not an isolated man. The basic or ultimate concern of social science is man in a society and not man in a cultural vacuum. Those conventional economists who make the behavior of the isolated man the fountainhead of economics strip man of his cultural bearings, and end with a view of economics that finds the essence of this science in a mental state—the making of a choice among alternative uses of scarce means. One cannot get very far in understanding the problems of mature industrialism or of organized capitalism by inquiring into the behavior pattern of the isolated individual. Social science deals with the individual as a social product, as the product of a social system in which many individuals have wants or values that are culturally conditioned, and that are sometimes in harmony and sometimes in conflict with the wants or values of other individuals. These actual or existing wants or values can be studied objectively by the social scientist. He can inquire into how men acquire wants or ends, what factors influence the nature of these wants, how they affect the course of economic behavior, what obstacles there are to the achievement of these wants, and what factors are favorable to their achievement.

Neo-Institutional Economics as a Social Science

Nothing distinguishes neo-institutionalists from conventional economists more than the concern of the former with human wants or ends and the lack of concern of the latter with these aspects of human activity. Just as the physical scientist excludes all concern with values or goals from his analysis of the data of the physical world, so also the conventional economist declares that economics has no concern with ends or goals. In the analyses of the conventional economists the ends of the individual making choices among alternative uses of scarce means are taken as given data which do not fall within the proper scope of economics. According to the conventional interpretation economics deals with how choices are made among alternative uses of scarce means but not with the ends for which these means are used. As one specialist in decision theory has explained, "rationality, as decision theory thinks of it, has nothing to do with what you want, but only with how you go about implementing your wants."[2] In likening human data to physical science data the conventional economist eliminates from human data the purposive aspect of this data. After eliminating this purposeful aspect the conventional economist then proceeds to develop the mechanics of choice which become the basis for the prediction of how a rational decision maker would behave if he were to act according to the dictates of the principle of the best alternative.

The neo-institutionalists do not agree with the assertion of the conventional economists that economics should have no concern with ends or wants. When Galbraith explains how the large industrial corporation induces consumers through various selling practices to want the goods that it produces, he is objectively analyzing how important individual wants are created. When he points out that the market is to some extent a want creating as well as a want fulfilling system, he is calling attention to a prominent feature of economic activities as they are carried on in the mature industrial economy. When Colm focusses his attention on the "possible corruption of taste" and the "cultural recession" that flow from the ingenious mass advertising and sales promotion activities of the large business enterprises, he is referring to the ways in which demand in the market place is manipulated by these large corporations. When Myrdal inquires into the "materialistic 'Babbittism'" that is so characteristic of economic life in the western industrialized nations, he is concerned with a cultural climate that nourishes a highly commercialized life style, and that greatly influences what people declare their economic wants to be. To say that human wants are culturally conditioned is not to say that culture is some overwhelming force to which individuals blindly or helplessly react. On the contrary the individual is a self-active and creative person who can to some extent select the ways in which he is influenced by the cultural milieu. The cultural milieu can influence how human wants are created but does not "determine" them. In their analysis of the want determining process the neo-institutionalists do not accept the doctrine of a simple blind cultural determinism.

---

[2] Ward Edwards, "Decision Making," *International Encyclopedia of the Social Sciences*, Vol. 4, p. 35.

When the neo-institutionalist examines the economic decision maker as a purposeful individual functioning in a social system, he is not converting economics into a "normative" science. The neo-institutionalist as a scientist has no concern with "what ought to be." As a scientist he analyzes the existing wants or goals held by individuals, groups and nations and inquires into how these values or goals were created and how they influence the course of economic activity. When Myrdal states that the ultimate purpose of economics is "to find out where we are heading," he is interested in analyzing the current wants or goals that are dominant in the nation's economy, and in explaining how they give direction to the development of this economy. As a scientist it is not the neo-institutionalist's intention to impose his goals or values on any one or to suggest what should be the direction in which the economy should move. When Ayres states that economics is a "science of value," he means to say that neo-institutional economics studies the actual values or wants that lie behind the prices of the market place. His discussion of "ceremonial" and "technological" values is a discussion of goods that according to scientific understanding do not or do contribute to the maintenance of the life process. Like other neo-institutionalists Ayres asserts that wants or goals can be scientifically analyzed without invading the normative area of "what ought to be." If the neo-institutionalist wishes to advocate the acceptance of certain wants or goals, and many of them do not hesitate to do so, they understand that they are then no longer acting in the capacity of scientific investigators but instead are advocates of reform.

Since the neo-institutionalists do not pattern their economics after the physical sciences, they view the economic system as an evolving process which changes its structure and functioning over time. The economic system of the western world has passed through many stages of development since the period of antiquity. What are of special interest to the neo-institutionalists are the changes that have occurred in the industrial system of the advanced western nations since the fourth quarter of the nineteenth century. These changes have given rise to a "mature industrialism" or an "organized capitalism" which exhibits very significant differences from the prior stage of small-scale competitive capitalism. Since they are concerned with an evolving economic system, the neo-institutionalists give a strong futuristic bent to their economic analyses. They are very much interested in current economic trends and what these trends seem to imply for the future. Unlike the conventional economists whose primary concern is with the current economic situation and short-run market developments, the neo-institutionalists look at the present and near future economic situations but only against the backdrop of long-range developments.

The Economic System as a Process

In their long-range view of the economic system the neo-institutionalists substitute the concept of "process" for the concept of "equilibrium." These heterodox economists do not deny that for some analytical purposes the concept of equilibrium is a useful concept. This is the case where analysis is focussed on the short run activities of the individual firm or industry. Economists are also interested in the short run equilibrium of the economic system as it moves through periods of expansion and contraction. But in the long run the economic system is an evolving process and not a static equilibrium. This process undergoes a cumulative development in which various factors act and react upon one another in a cumulative process of circular causation. Where the cumulative movement has been upward towards higher levels of output and improved living conditions, the growth of large-scale industry, the urbanization and democratization of society, the growth of the labor movement and the spread of mass education have cumulatively reinforced one another in such a way as to further the industrialization process and to expedite the movement towards the establishment of the welfare state. The process of cumulative circular causation is accompanied by tension and conflict among the nation's major economic interest groups. Conflicts of interest with regard to the sharing of the national income, the participation of labor in management, the quality control of production, the assigning of responsibility for unpaid social costs and the prevention of environmental deterioration give rise to tensions and conflicts among economic interest groups. According to the neo-institutionalist interpretation tension and conflict are normal features of the adjustment process through which the economic system passes. Where the conflict is not so serious as to undermine the economic system, it leads eventually to cooperation and adjustment among the contending groups. Unlike the equilibrium situation envisioned by conventional economists where an automatic harmony of interests is assumed to exist, the economic process as viewed by the neo-institutionalists has inherent in it the conflict and tension that may lead to a created or managed harmony of interests. Where the cumulative movement of the economic process is downward, tension and conflict may lead to a magnification of disequilibrium and social and political dislocation, a decline in total output and a further deterioration of the nation's economy. The dynamics of the economic process is the circular cumulative causation which results in adjustment to technological change through conflict and cooperation. This dynamics removes institutional and attitudinal lags by giving rise to new institutions and attitudes which permit the movement of the economic process to higher levels of output and improved levels of living.

While both the neo-institutionalists and the conventional economists use the concept of the economic system, the concept used by the neo-institutionalists is basically different from that of the conventional economists. The economic system as viewed by the neo-institutionalists is a part of the total social system. What holds this "socio-economic" system together is not a set of equilibrating market forces but instead a set of cohesive or coherent social, political and economic forces. These forces are grounded in the institutions and attitudes associated with individual, group and class actions which contribute to the coherence of the socio-economic system. The essence of the neo-institutionalist concept of the economic system is found in social coherence rather than in the mechanical equilibrium which is the essence of the conventional concept of the economic system.

The economic system of the neo-institutionalists is an open system whereas the economic system of the conventional economists is a closed system.[3] When the neo-institutionalists developed their concept of the economic system as a process they constructed it in such a way as to leave this process open to change and development and a lack of harmony between private firm efficiency and overall social efficiency. Their concept of the economic system as a dynamic evolving process is not built on the assumption that self-correcting market forces will always maintain the equilibrium of the economic system, or on the assumption that optimal efficiency of the microeconomic unit will necessarily lead automatically to the optimal efficiency of the total economic system. In this manner the neo-institutionalists have kept the economic system, when viewed as a process, an open system into which disequilibrating forces can be

---

[3] For a similar view see K. William Kapp, "In Defense of Institutional Economics," *The Swedish Journal of Economics*, Vol. LXX, No. 1, 1968, p. 7.

introduced as an integral feature of economic activity. The situation is quite different with the conventional economists' view of the economic system as an equilibrium system. These orthodox economists take the economic system to be a closed system in which it is assumed that self-correcting forces will always preserve equilibrium. Whatever deviations from equilibrium occur will sooner or later be eliminated by the self-correcting forces of the competitive markets. Furthermore conventional economists, by assuming that the micro economic unit or business firm is internally efficient in an optimal way, necessarily conclude that the total economic system is optimally efficient. This is so because the economic system as regarded by conventional economists is no more than the sum of a large number of optimally efficient micro economic units. For the conventional economist what is true of the part is also true of the whole. Consequently in the conventional view of the economic system micro economic unit efficiency and overall systemic efficiency go hand in hand. There can be no conflict between private and social efficiency because no account is taken in pure theory of the importance of diseconomies in the form of unpaid social costs and unrealized social values. Furthermore disequilibrating forces such as technological, social and political change cannot alter the structure and functioning of the economic system in equilibrium since these forces are relegated by conventional economists to Lionel Robbins's "sociological penumbra" or to the *ceteris paribus* pound.

In the opinion of the neo-institutionalists the equilibrium concept of the economic system held by the conventional economists is quite unrealistic. They assert that the conventional economists' concept of the economic system is an oversimplification and a pale reflection of the real economic world. When used to explain the real world the conventional concept of the economic system causes economists to fail to come to grips with many of the pressing problems in that world which give rise to considerations of social costs and social values as well as private costs and market values. These pressing problems also call attention to the impact of disequilibrating factors on the structure and functioning of the economic system and the direction in which it is moving.

When the neo-institutionalists view the industrial system as an evolving process they raise two very important questions not included by conventional or orthodox economists within the scope of economics. These questions are: What causes the industrial system to change, and where is it going? When the neo-institutionalists turn to the question of what it is that causes the economic system to change, they observe that the development of the industrialized nations over past decades has not been a haphazard and merely accidental development. On the contrary this development has responded to the stimulus of certain factors and has taken on shape or form as a result of this response. The trends in the development or evolution of the modern industrial system have in a special way reflected the impact of technological change as a cultural imperative. Science and technology act as cultural imperatives in the sense that they set broad limits within which economic development necessarily occurs. When industrial technology fosters the growth of small-scale industry, economic trends cannot give rise to a large-scale economic system in which collective action dominates individual action, and in which large economic interest groups play major roles in economic affairs. When the reverse is true and science and technology favor the growth of large-scale industry, then economic trends necessarily lead to the appearance of an economy of collective action and large economic power groups. In other words, given a situation in which there are a large skilled population, many economic resources, private property, freedom of enterprise, political stability and a large-scale industrial technology, the logic of development necessarily points in the direction of modern industrialism with its large private business enterprises, trade unions, farm organizations, active governments, administered markets and conflicts of interest.

Although social and political factors cannot be ignored, the major active factor that gives momentum to the economic process is its changing, proliferating industrial technology and the science on which this technology is based. Science is by its own nature proliferative. It expands through a cumulative process in which scientific ideas or concepts are unceasingly brought together in new combinations. Science is by nature dynamic and the sponsor of new ideas and continuous change. The state of the industrial arts or technology, being the offspring of science, has the same dynamic proliferative nature as does science. The dynamics of science is reproduced in the dynamics of technology. In a similar way the dynamics of technology is reproduced in the dynamics of cultural or institutional development. Since the institutional structure of society rests on a technological foundation, technological change necessarily gives rise to institutional change but within the limits set by the nature of the technological change. The latter change is primary and determinative whereas institutional change is secondary and resultant for the most part. This does not mean that man is a mere pawn at the beck and call of blind technological forces. Man is himself responsible for further progress in science and the resultant changes in technology. But the accumulated science and technology—the accumulated intellectual contributions of past generations of scientists and technicians—have come to have an existence of their own which sets limits to what mankind can do at any one point in time. For example, the accumulated science and technology of today call for a world of large-scale collective action and institutions which mankind can modify but not eliminate. Unless he is willing to run counter to all major technological trends, man must accept the fact that he will be living in a world of large-scale collective action in control of individual action. To think of returning to a small-scale atomistic and competitive world where collective action is conspicuous by its absence and individual action would be the order of the day is to engage in wishful and unrealistic thinking.

Technological change as the prime mover in the logic of economic development does not act alone. It combines with political and social changes of many kinds to increase the momentum of economic development. Since 1900 two world wars, the severest depression of all times, the cold war, the emergence of the newly developing nations and recurring international crises have combined with technological change to alter greatly the institutional bases of national economies and of the world economy. Under the combined influence of these dynamic factors the institutional structure of the capitalist system has reflected the transition from *laissez-faire* capitalism to welfare capitalism, and more recently to guided or directed capitalism.

The logic of economic development constructed by the neo-institutionalists calls attention to the lags in the evolution of society's institutional structure as this structure responds slowly to changes in society's technological foundation. Institutions involve customary ways of doing things and inherited attitudes of individuals. Individuals and groups possessing power and privilege are unwilling to accept changes in the institutional arrangements that support this power and privilege. Owners and managers of large corporate enterprises oppose the efforts of organized labor to broaden the collective bargaining process. High income groups resent the setting up of new government programs that protect or enlarge the incomes of disadvantaged marginal groups. In the world economy technological developments call for new international arrangements if the international economy is to be prosperous and to meet the needs of all nations, both those that are industrialized and those that are newly developing. New institutions in the form of international planning programs and agencies, international foreign aid programs, regional common markets and international production and price stabilization boards are needed to eliminate the lag or discrepancy that has arisen between the technological forces creating an international economy and the inherited national institutional arrangements and nationalistic attitudes found throughout the world.

When the neo-institutionalists analyze the evolving economy in terms of the logic of development, they are interested in the emerging shape of the economy. There is nothing teleological, however, about the neo-institutionalists' logic of economic development. This logic does not point to any specific future economic arrangements or future type of economic system. While this logic indicates that economic systems will probably become more collective in the future and therefore probably more planned in the future, as technological progress increasingly brings individuals, groups and nations into closer communion, the precise shape of any nationally programmed economy is not foretold. The logic of economic development does not predict whether or not a people will turn to capitalism, socialism, communism, fascism or some combination of these systems. All that the logic of economic development states is that when economic development occurs in the western world it will probably be of a collective or programmed nature.

The Definition of Neo-Institutional Economics

Definitions are important not only for the light that they may throw on the essential nature of a subject, but also because of what they reveal about the individuals who make these definitions. The definition of standard economics provided by Lionel Robbins, and other orthodox economists reveals not only their interest in a static view of the world, but also their preference for a psychological or mental approach to economic analysis. What interests these conventional economists is primarily the individual chooser or decision maker who is confronted with a situation in which a decision about the use of scarce means is to be made. What is lacking in the conventional definitions of economics as the "science of choice" or the "science of efficiency" is reference to the changing, developing world within which the individual decision maker operates, and to the web of sometimes conflicting, sometimes harmonious social relationships that surrounds the individual decision maker. When conventional economists find the roots of economics in a mental state (choosing) and in the physical world (diminishing returns), they have an excessively restricted interest in what is historical or cultural, and in what is collective or social. These scientific blind spots associated with conventional definitions of economics are revealed as a lack of concern about the economic system as an evolving system, about technology as a factor leading to basic changes in the structure and functioning of this system, about the importance of economic interest groups and how they use their economic power, and about the ways in which private and public economic wants are determined and how they guide the economy.

The neo-institutionalists do not deny that the definitions of economics supplied by conventional economists over the past century throw considerable light on the nature of economics. What they object to is the narrowness that is placed upon the nature and scope of economics by standard definitions. Views on the definition and scope of a science cannot be completely separated because a definition, in purporting to catch the essential nature of the science, also necessarily indicates how far the scientist proposes to extend his inquiries in order to comprehend or fully grasp the nature of his science. The neo-institutionalists find that conventional definitions of economics, being too narrow, also lead to excessively narrow views regarding the scope of economics. What the neo-institutionalists do when they define economics is to place the conventional economist's individual chooser or decision maker in an institutional framework or concrete economic system such as "mature capitalism." Even the conventional economists do not leave their isolated "Crusoean" decision maker on his remote island unconnected with the real world. They are willing to go so far as to place him in an exchange economy that turns out to be not the "mature capitalism" of today but a hypothetical competitive economic system that is reminiscent of the competitive capitalism of a century ago. Conventional economists are aware that the capitalist system has been modified in important ways since the third and fourth quarters of the nineteenth century. Since they regard these modifications, however, as merely deviations from the competitive norm of business enterprise, they do not take them to be evidence of the appearance of a new phase in the evolution of capitalism—evidence of the appearance of a mature industrial system in which decision makers, whether they are businessmen, trade union leaders, consumers or government officials, behave quite differently from the decision makers who operated in the competitive capitalism of the mid-nineteenth century.

Ayres speaks for the neo-institutionalists when he defines economics to be the "study of the economy" or of that part of the social process that provides mankind with the material goods and services that it wants. The economic system is the means by which men organize themselves in the effort to secure a supply of scarce goods and services. Economic systems vary in their capacity to overcome the scarcity of goods and services. Primitive tribal economies do not do very well at this job of providing goods and services with the result that most people in them remain at or near the minimum or subsistence level. Advanced industrial systems do a better job of providing goods and services. With a large section of their population assured a much more than basic minimum supply of goods and services, the simple problem of scarcity recedes into the background. In the modern affluent industrial societies the main issue is not how to secure a subsistence level of living for the majority of the population but instead what kinds of goods should be produced and at whose demand, at what point should leisure take preference over more production, and what are the social costs of an ever increasing gross national product. To say that economics is the science of scarcity, and that without scarcity there would be no science of economics, does not tell us very much about the problems of an affluent society. The scarcities faced by an isolated individual on a remote island are not very relevant to the problems of scarcity or the lack of it in the advanced affluent industrialized societies. If economics is to be a social science, it must deal with scarcity in a social or cultural setting where some groups may be affluent while others are impoverished, where some groups have much influence in the determination of what kinds of goods shall be produced and others have no or very little influence, and where reducing the scarcity of privately produced goods may increase the scarcity of such public goods as clean air, pure water, scenic beauty, uncongested urban areas, communal quiet, ecological balance and a well-preserved historical heritage. Scarcity has both individual and social aspects which can be satisfactorily investigated only when economics becomes a study of the evolving economic system within which the economic decision making process is embedded.

When Ayres defines economics as the study of the economy he does not ignore the operations of the market system. On the contrary his economics pays special attention to the price system and how it functions in a mature phase of the development of the private enterprise system. He does what all neo-institutionalists do, and that is to place the price system in an institutional framework which reflects not the competitive system of pure or analytical economics but the mature industrial system that has developed in the western world. Unlike the definitions of the conventional economists Ayres's definition of economics does not emphasize what is mental, non-cultural and static. Instead his definition looks at individual economic behavior as a social or cultural product. In addition his definition of economics emphasizes the economic system as a cumulative cultural process that is moving along the path of industrialization.

Galbraith duplicates Ayres's approach to economics when he places the economic decision making process in the "larger matrix of change" from which has issued the mature industrial system. For Galbraith economics becomes the study of the "economy of opulence." Likewise Myrdal is concerned with what he calls the organizational state and organized capitalism. In Myrdal's view the economic system is a "dynamic economic process of cumulative causation" in which the forces of the market place support the momentum towards self-reinforcement, imbalance and disequilibrium. This interest in the dynamic cumulative economic process makes the economic analyses of the neo-institutionalists futuristic in the sense that they focus their attention on the emerging shape of the economic system. As Colm has put it, what are important are not the current features of the economic system but its emerging features.

Unlike conventional economists the neo-institutionalists examine the act of choosing among alternative uses of scarce resources within the framework of a real world of historical time and geographical place. What primarily concerns the neo-institutionalists is the act of choosing or decision making in the modern industrial world that stretches from Sweden and West Germany to the United States and Canada. Other neo-institutionalists could as well be primarily interested in the communist or newly developing areas of the world. In the opinion of the neo-institutionalists the act of economic choosing or decision making must be embedded in one

or another cultural situation, if the economist is to have a full understanding of the nature of economic activities. It is for this reason
that the neo-institutionalists make the subject matter of economics
"the study of the changing patterns of cultural relations which
deal with the creation and disposal of scarce material goods and
services by individuals and groups in the light of their private and
public aims."[4]

Neo-Institutionalism and the Reconstruction of Economic Science

The work of the neo-institutionalists since 1945 points in the
direction of a reconstruction of the science of economics. This reconstruction, as Lowe explains, involves a shift from economics as a
science of prediction to a science of control.[5] When the economic
system was small-scale and competitive in the nineteenth century,
the orthodox economics of the time included generalizations which
were the basis of predictions as to how producers, investors and
consumers would act. Capital was mobile, investing and producing
time spans were short, consumers had little income beyond what
was needed for necessities and the international economy was relatively stable. In these circumstances where producers' and investors'
expectations were positive and certain, the economist could make
predictions based on the principle of profit maximization and the
law of supply and demand. Since the economy was assumed to be
in or moving towards an equilibrium, the main concern of the
orthodox economist was with the prediction of the course of economic activities. The competitive economy was an automatic
orderly economic system in which the economist, viewing the economy from the outside, generalized in a predictive manner about the
behavior of producers, investors, workers and consumers.

With the shift from *laissez-faire* capitalism to "organized" or
"mature" capitalism with its high degree of capital immobility, long
time span from original investment to final production, unpredictable
consumer behavior and great international instability, economic
expectations became a destabilizing rather than a stabilizing force.
As a consequence of this transition from a stable predictable economic system to a highly uncertain economy "the role of theory

---

[4] Allan G. Gruchy, *Modern Economic Thought, the American Contribution*, p. 552.

[5] Adolph Lowe, *On Economic Knowledge: Toward a Science of Political
Economics* (New York: Harper and Row, 1965) pp. 128-161.

is in the process of a drastic change. Economics as a medium of passive contemplation, observing and systematizing autonomous processes, is gradually being converted into *Political Economics*, namely, into an instrument of active interference with the course of these processes."[6] Keynes made a step in the direction of changing economics from a science of prediction to a science of control when he pointed out in *The General Theory* that investors' and producers' expectations were no longer the stabilizing force that they had once been, and that therefore control in the form of intervention by the government was necessary to restore the orderliness of the mature industrial economy. But in the opinion of the neo-institutionalists Keynes did not go far enough in developing a new economics of public control. The indirect controls of Keynesian economists have not proven capable of reducing to an acceptable degree the volatility and uncertainty of private economic decision making. Keynesian intervention is not adequate to cope with the shocks to the mature industrial economy coming from the automation of the "cybernetic revolution," the expanding power of economic interest groups and the continuing international instability.

The neo-institutionalists' economics of public control does not dispense with the basic Marshallian and Keynesian economic concepts. Instead it finds these concepts quite useful for the analysis of various types of static and short-run economic problems where the equilibrium concept has some relevance. What the neo-institutionalists do is to go beyond conventional economics to broaden the scope of economics so that room will be made for an economics of public control. Since this involves placing the core economic process within the framework of political and social institutions, there are no precise limits to the scope of economics. As Myrdal has explained, whatever is relevant to the explanation of an economic problem should be included within the scope of economics. Data should be selected according to their relevance to whatever problems are being investigated. In other words, the neo-institutionalists' economics of public control is of an interdisciplinary nature since it draws heavily upon social psychology, sociology and political science. To the neo-institutionalist any thought of keeping economics segregated from other social sciences by allotting it a particular narrow field of inquiry whose limits are somehow logically or definitionally determined is totally unacceptable.

---

[6] *Ibid.*, p. 91.

We may conclude our analysis of the nature and scope of neo-institutional economics by pointing out that this type of economics is compatible with the new mathematical and econometrical methods of economic inquiry. Econometric model building, input-output analysis and operations research are all very closely related to the national economic budgeting which has such an important role in the construction of the future or terminal state of the economy with which the neo-institutionalists are concerned. Input-output analysis is a necessary first step in making annual and longer term national economic budgets. Econometric models of the total economy also throw light on the structural relationships of this economy and may be used to reveal the impact of economic policy changes on these structural relationships. In those western countries that practice national economic budgeting such as the Netherlands, France and the Scandinavian countries considerable use is made of econometric techniques and input-output economics in constructing national economic budgets and in using these budgets as the basis for economic policy formulation and execution. These countries use econometric models of their economies to reveal the consequences for investment and consumption of choosing alternative economic growth rates and to reveal the probable impact of tax, wage, profit and other economic policies on the price level or the levels of imports and exports.

While the neo-institutionalists welcome progress made in the development of mathematical and econometrical procedures of inquiry, they also emphasize the limitations of these procedures. Mathematical and econometrical techniques of scientific inquiry are useful for the purpose of revealing the structural and functional relationships of the existing economic system in so far as this system responds to equilibrating tendencies in its market system. They are also useful for the analysis of short-run developments within the economic system as it fluctuates between inflationary expansion and deflationary contraction. But when it comes to analyzing long-term or secular developments these techniques have very limited application. As Myrdal has explained, economists can not yet construct an econometric model of the evolving, changing economic process. This is so because, while there is a mathematics that can be used in an analysis that is applicable to an economic equilibrium, there is no mathematics that is applicable to the kind of disequilibrium observed by the neo-institutionalists in the dynamic evolving economic process.[7] There is no mathematics of the evolving process. Mathematical and econometric techniques are useful when the data can be quantified. When the neo-institutionalist turns to qualitative as well as quantitative data relating to the evolution of organized or mature capitalism, he finds that he must go beyond mathematical and econometric techniques of inquiry because the analyses of technological change and value structures do not lend themselves to conventional mathematical and econometrical treatment. In the opinion of the neo-institutionalists it is not possible to reduce the logic of industrialization to mathematical or econometrical formulation.

It is the view of the neo-institutionalists that contemporary conventional economists permit the mathematical and econometrical techniques of investigation and analysis to dominate them, to limit their areas of study and to restrict their view of the proper scope of the science of economics. In other words they adjust their areas of economic study and their views of the nature of economics to the requirements of their mathematical and econometrical methods of inquiry instead of regarding these methods as only one of a number of ways of comprehending economic reality. Conventional economists have a tendency to "technicalize" the science of economics. By the technicalization of economics is meant an excessive concern with highly specialized areas of investigation and with the development of mathematical techniques of investigation that aid these highly specialized studies. This technicalization leads to a neglect of the larger issues and to an emphasis upon what Myrdal has referred to as "petty, short term problems." Galbraith has also emphasized the tendency of the technical specialist to see small problems in isolation from the large problems besetting the economy. As he puts the matter, "Bigness and market power, in other words, are but one part of a much larger current of change. To see them in isolation from other changes is artificial. In part it is what results when a social discipline passes however partially from the custody of scholars to that of specialists and mechanics."[8] Both

[7] Kapp has pointed out that "Certainly the mathematics of the calculus and of differential equations which are adequate for the description of tendencies towards stable equilibria offer no solution to the analytical description of the process of circular inextricable interdependencies 'where cause and effect interweave'. . . ." K. William Kapp, "In Defense of Institutional Economics," p. 13 fn.

[8] *Hearings before the Subcommittee of the Select Committee on Small Business, United States Senate, Planning, Regulation, and Competition,* Washington, D.C., June 29, 1967, pp. 6-7.

Myrdal and Galbraith do not deny the value of specialization and the search for more refined methods of investigation, but they do object to the tendency of economists to drop their economic analyses at the point where technical matters are no longer of importance, and to refrain from relating their highly specialized technical work to larger economic problems. Especially in the United States economic specialists and technicians construct elaborate econometric models of the economy, and then fail to draw any inferences from their work as to how it might be used to program the activities of the whole economy. Myrdal explains that he is not complaining "that more and more labor is devoted to less and less interesting things," because everything is interesting. His complaint is that economists do not devote more of their energies to "what really matters and, not least, to what is controversial."[9] The excessive concern with specialization, refinement of investigational techniques and quantification of economic data becomes a screen with which the conventional economist shields himself from the larger significant issues. Well equipped with statistical and econometric tools the conventional economists rarely think of long term developments and trends, but instead focus their attention on the economic ups and downs from quarter to quarter and half year to half year. In government service they concern themselves too frequently with the smaller day-to-day "brush fire" problems to the neglect of the larger national and international issues.

Neo-institutional economics is much more than an extension of conventional economics. It accepts much from the latter type of economics, but it does not merely build on or extend this type of economics. Neo-institutional economics introduces a way of understanding the real economic world that is different from the approach used by conventional economists. Neo-institutional economics is distinguished from orthodox economics by what Myrdal has described as its "large view," a view in which the economy is taken to be an evolving cumulative process rather than an unchanging equilibrium. Neo-institutional economics is a cultural or social science which borrows extensively from related social sciences. It avoids the twin intellectual pitfalls of scientism and technicalization by not attempting to fit economics into the natural science mold and by eschewing overspecialization and excessive concern with technicalities. Above all neo-institutional economics is a relevant and realistic type of economics for the reason that its main concern is

---

[9] Gunnar Myrdal, *An International Economy*, p. 307.

with the major economic problem of national economic guidance which is the overriding problem of the second half of the twentieth century. As a science neo-institutionalism does not tell mankind what its economic goals should be, but it does indicate how mankind may proceed in attaining whatever goals it may wish to achieve.

The Conventional View of the Nature and Scope of Economics

Conventional definitions of economics currently closely follow along the lines laid down a third of a century ago by Lionel Robbins in his well-known *An Essay on the Nature and Significance of Economic Science* (1932). It is Robbins's position that economics is "the science which studies human behaviour as a relationship between ends and scarce means which have alternative uses."[10] According to Robbins's interpretation the essence of economics is to be found in the act of choosing so that at bottom economics is the science of choice. Although choosing among alternative uses of scarce means usually goes on in an exchange economy, it is not necessary to have such an economy in operation in order to observe the fundamentals of economic behavior. Robbins explains that the operation of the laws of choice "are best seen when contemplating the behaviour of the isolated individual" in a Crusoe economy where the isolated individual must make choices among alternative uses of both scarce means and scarce time. He goes on to explain that economics is not concerned with the ends or uses to which scarce means are put. Furthermore the economist has no concern with the technical and social environment in which the act of choosing by individuals is carried on. As he puts this matter, "The subject-matter of Economics is essentially a series of relationships. . . . Ends as such do not form part of this subject matter. Nor does the technical and social environment. It is the relationships between these things and not the things in themselves which are important for the economist."[11] As a study of a series of relationships concerned with the act of choosing economics becomes essentially a body of logical principles that govern the behavior of rational individuals.

The subjectivistic and abstract approach of Robbins and other conventional economists to the problem of defining economics has the following consequences with respect to their view of the eco-

---

[10] Lionel Robbins, *An Essay on the Nature and Significance of Economic Science*, p. 16.
[11] *Ibid.*, p. 38.

nomic system. The economic system is made up of a number of decision makers who seek to maximize gain or utility through the market or exchange system. Since no attention is paid by Robbins and other conventional economists to technological advance as a factor altering the structure and functioning of the economic system, this system is regarded by the conventional economists as being both static and non-historical in nature. The view of the economic system that dominates conventional economics is not that of a system undergoing irreversible changes that make it increasingly less competitive. Conventional economists do not deny the fact of technological change, but they never open the door in their analyses to the kind of technological change that leads to the evolution of the economic system and the transformation from competitive capitalism to "organized" or "mature" capitalism. Furthermore, since in the conventional view of economics human ends are taken as given data, this view makes no room for an analysis of the private and national goals that provide guidance for the nation's economy. The economic system of concern to conventional economists is not a goal directed system in which there is a wide array of private and national goals arising from the search for a large variety of private and social values. The only goal or objective to which attention is given by orthodox economists is the maximization of gain or utility by decision makers. Since the individual decision maker is assumed to know how and when gain or utility is maximized, no questions are raised by conventional economists about the nature of specific economic wants, how demands for these wants are created and how they contribute to the maximization of private and social utility.

What Robbins and other orthodox economists do is to peel back the outer layers of economic reality until they come to what they describe as the ultimate subject matter of economics. This inner truth or essence turns out to be the laws of choice which are held to be independent of all concrete historical economic systems. The laws of choice that explain how rational individuals follow the principle of the best alternative use are said to be universal in the sense that they are independent of all historical time and geographical place. Robbins explains that "it is clear that the phenomena of the exchange economy can be explained by *going behind* such relationships and invoking those laws of choice which are best seen when contemplating the behaviour of the isolated individual."[12] Having tracked down what he takes to be the ultimate subject matter of the science

---

[12] *Ibid.*, p. 20.

of economics, Robbins then retraces his steps from Crusoe's isolated world and returns to the exchange economy. After all the world has little interest in the economy of the isolated individual. In the exchange economy men choose among alternative uses of scarce means in the market place where all items for sale are tagged with prices. Although Boulding like Robbins defines economics as a "generalized theory of choice," he hurries on to say that "In my view the basic abstraction of economics is the phenomenon of exchange, wherever this occurs, and the central problem of economics consists in the understanding of how exchange organizes society."[13] And since the most important single consideration in any exchange is the ratio of exchange or terms of trade as revealed by prices, Boulding finds that "price theory is therefore central to economics." In short economics in the hands of Robbins, Boulding and other standard economists becomes "market" or "price" economics.

These orthodox economists do not go beyond the exchange economy or market system to develop a theory of capitalism or a theory of the maturing industrial economy as do the neo-institutionalists. Their views on the nature and scope of economics prevent them from doing so. Instead they are content with a very limited version of economics. Since they find the fountainhead of economics to be the pure act of choosing, they find it very difficult to clothe this abstraction, never venturing as economists much further than the "phenomenon of exchange." If they should happen to go beyond the phenomenon of exchange, as some of them have, to discuss such matters as the theory of organization, social dynamics or the technological revolution, these conventional economists regard such matters as being outside the proper scope of economics and therefore as having nothing to do with economics.

The neo-institutionalists admit of a great debt to the long line of economists from Smith to Keynes. As has already been explained, they do not dispense with the basic concepts of what passes today as conventional or standard economics. The neo-institutionalists do not deny that economic activity has its rational aspect, and that a study of the axioms of rational conduct is helpful in analyzing economic activity. They acknowledge the usefulness of such concepts as marginal rates of substitution and opportunity costs. The neo-institutionalists do not ignore the importance of the theory of maximizing behavior

---

[13] Kenneth E. Boulding, "Is Economics Obsolescent?" a review of Adolph Lowe's *On Economic Knowledge: Toward a Science of Political Economics*, in *Scientific American*, Vol. 212, No. 5, May 1965, p. 140.

or the principle of the best alternative. Nor do they deny the value
of such Keynesian concepts as the propensities to consume and to
save, liquidity preference, the multiplier and the accelerator. What
the neo-institutionalists do is to go beyond supply and demand and
beyond saving and investment to inquire into such factors as market
power and market domination that affect supply and demand and
the institutional arrangements and the value structures that influence income distribution, saving and investment. The neo-institutionalists are not satisfied with an economics that is largely limited
to a study of the mechanics of price and income determination.
They want to break through the equilibrium mold that encases
micro and macro economic analyses both of which are reducible to
the mechanics of equilibrium analysis.

From Economic Automaticity to Economic Control

The automatically functioning free competitive economic system
theorized about by conventional economists had considerable relevance to the real economic world in the period 1775-1875 when
the economies of the United Kingdom and the United States were
small scale in nature, the masses of the population were poor and
individuals were strongly induced to improve their economic lot
by a cultural climate that placed a high premium on economic
success. Government played a minor role in economic life and the
unregulated competitive markets were left free to determine production and exchange relations. To a great extent the competitive
economic system in the years 1775 to 1875 did function automatically although some of the conditions required in theory for
perfect competition, such as equal knowledge on the part of buyers
and sellers, an equitable distribution of income and the production
of uniform products were not present. In spite of these deviations
from the criterion of perfect competition the body of pure economic
theory developed by economists in the nineteenth century had considerable predictive value. It could be predicted that in the real world
buyers would reduce the quantity demanded and sellers would increase the amount supplied when prices rose. Also when profits
declined below their normal level in an industry, mobile capital
could be expected to be transferred to more profitable industries.

The neo-institutionalists point out that, since the emergence of
big business and the decline of competition in the fourth quarter
of the nineteenth century, the competitive model of standard
economics has become less and less relevant to the real economic

world. In important areas of the modern industrial economy large-scale oligopolistic industry has replaced small-scale competitive industry, capital has become increasingly immobile, the planning horizons of businessmen have been considerably lengthened and market expectations have become increasingly uncertain. For a large part of the population poverty has been replaced by affluence, much consumer spending has become discretionary spending, the public sector has grown much more rapidly than the private sector and governments have intervened extensively in economic affairs. As a consequence of these developments automaticity has become a much less important feature of economic life than it was prior to 1875. The former automatic functioning of the market system has been greatly reduced by the appearance of major economic interest groups with considerable power to influence the price determining process. In spite of the industrial progress made prior to 1929 the economies of Western Europe and the United States were plunged into the worst depression of the capitalist era. By 1929 the body of pure economic theory had lost much of its relevance to the actual economic world and hence much of its predictive value. In the depression years people bought less and producers supplied less when prices fell. Heavy capital investment remained sunk and immobile in unprofitable industries. The economy's self-correcting forces by 1929 were no longer strong enough to offset the deviations from competitive behavior which threatened to undermine the competitive system. After 1929 these self-correcting forces of the market place were replaced in large part by self-reinforcing forces which magnified rather than corrected the consequences of deviations from the norms of competitive behavior.

Since 1929 automaticity as a feature of economic life has receded before the advance of control as a new feature of economic activities. The decline in the automatic functioning of the competitive economic system has been accompanied by the rise in the economic control exercised by large industrial enterprises, large labor unions and large governments. When competition declined after 1875 business, labor and agriculture organized to offset the adverse consequences of this decline. These organized economic interest groups acquired the power to control sources of supply, markets and consumers. After 1929 governments in the advanced industrial societies came to realize the need to offset private economic control by enlarging public economic control in the national interest. Since 1945 governments in Western Europe and the United States have energetically enlarged their areas of control at the expense of the groups that formerly had considerable private economic power. The same pattern of public control did not develop in the West European countries and the United States. There is a wide variation between the pattern of economic control in the Scandinavian countries, the Netherlands and France at one end of the scale and the pattern of economic control in West Germany, the United Kingdom under the British Conservative Party and the United States at the other end of the scale. National patterns of economic control cover the wide range from limited intervention along Keynesian lines to overall national economic planning along Scandinavian lines. In all these advanced industrialized countries, however, economic control has taken precedence over economic automaticity as the dominant feature of economic activities. This means that the key issue in the modern industrial society revolves around economic control, what form it should take and how it should be applied to the nation's economy. This does not mean that the free market system has been completely eliminated or that its automatic functioning has entirely disappeared. On the contrary the control programs of Western democratic governments, even those carrying economic control as far as national planning, seek to preserve the essentials of the private enterprise system and much of its remaining automatic functioning. But this is done by providing a framework of public economic control within which the private enterprise system freely operates as long as it meets the standards of performance required by established national economic goals. Economic controls are used by governments in the modern industrial society to ensure that private economic performance is satisfactorily coordinated with public economic performance.

Control, Automaticity and Economic Theory

An important question is: What has been the impact of the further industrialization of Western Europe and the United States, with its accompanying increase in economic control and decline in economic automaticity, on economists and their economic theorizing? The reactions to these developments on the part of the conventional economists and the neo-institutionalists have been markedly different. Conventional economists continue to cling to their narrow view of economics as "the science of choice" or "the science of efficiency" in which the competitive model remains the ultimate criterion and the point of departure for economic analysis. These conventional economists do not deny that the "mature capitalism" of today is very different from the *laissez-faire* competitive capitalism that existed when neo-classical economists defined economics as "the science of wealth." They still adhere, however, to their basic model of a competitive economy and regard non-competitive developments as deviations that are undesirable and should be eliminated whenever possible. The Chicago school would go so far as to legislate the non-competitive elements of the modern industrial economy out of existence. By law they would eliminate bigness from economic activities, and by law they would plan to establish an unplanned competitive economy. These pulverizationists, if they had their way, would turn back the stream of technological progress by pulverizing the modern large-scale economy and replacing it with a resurrected small-scale competitive economy.

The Keynesian school, unlike the Chicago school, endeavours to freeze the modern industrial economy in its present position with the aid of vigorous antitrust action accompanied by fiscal and monetary policies that do not alter the basic structure of the economy. Economic control for the Keynesian means regulation or intervention but never planning. It means trying to alter the behavior of businessmen, workers and consumers with the aid of fiscal, monetary and other economic policies but without changing the basic framework or institutional structure of the nation's economy. While various policies to alter economic behavior are proposed by the Keynesians, no new institutional arrangements such as a national planning board or permanent wage-price board are recommended by the Keynesians. Instead of considering the desirability of new institutional arrangements when their economic policies turn out to be ineffective, the Keynesians turn to an "exhortatory" or "jaw bone" type of economic policy which relies unsuccessfully upon persuasion and exhortation to achieve economic goals.

The reaction of the neo-institutionalists to the decline in competition, the rise of large-scale business enterprise and the growing inadequacy of the competitive model of the conventional economist as a device for explaining and predicting economic activities has been to develop a new model of a mature industrial economy. In this model the core of the economy is made up of large-scale industries such as the steel, oil, chemical, automobile, transportation and communication industries. It is the large industrial corporation that dominates the core of the private enterprise system with its leadership in research and development, contacts with large labor unions, major role in production serving the needs of governments at all levels and large influence on consumer behavior. Surrounding the core of oligopoly and monopoly industries are the middle-size imperfectly competitive industries and the surviving small-scale manufacturing industries, farming and retailing. Dominating the private sector of the economy is the public sector which accounts for the consumption of a large part of the nation's total output, and for a sizeable part of the nation's investment and employment. This public sector also involves the government in the role of a directing agent which provides guidance for the nation's economic affairs. In the industrial society of today the government supplements and directs the private enterprise system through the use of various economic controls.

It is this shift in interest from "automaticity" to "control" that separates the neo-institutionalists from orthodox economists. It is also the source of the basic difference between the model of the economy that is found at the core of conventional economics and the model that is central to the theorizing of the neo-institutionalists. This shift in interest from the automatic working of the competitive economy to the controlled functioning of the large-scale industrial economy results in a shift in interest from predicting the outcome of spontaneous economic behavior to controlling spontaneous behavior. The neo-institutionalists do not predict the course of economic behavior on the basis of what individuals are expected to do automatically in a competitive situation where the objective is to maximize gain or utility, and self-correcting forces in the market place are expected to lead to the establishment of an equilibrium. Instead the neo-institutionalists with the aid of national economic budgets set forth a planned future economic state or situation in which various macro national goals are to be achieved along with the micro goals of the individuals and groups operating in the private enterprise sector. This planned terminal or future state or situation is an objective which is to be secured by making various institutional changes and by applying various controls at strategic spots in the economic system.[14] The micro goals of the private sector are coordinated with the macro goals of the public sector so that the two types of goals may be secured together. If it is necessary for the achievement of national goals, private planning for micro goals may be altered by the government with the aid of appropriate national economic policies. In this manner private and public economic deci-

[14] Adolph Lowe, *op. cit.*, pp. 133-139.

sion making may be harmoniously integrated. From the government's point of view this outcome is not predicated on the basis of some automatic functioning of the nation's economy. Instead it is to be achieved through planning and the use of appropriate economic controls.

The Policy Implications of Neo-Institutional Economics

The kinds of economic policies that are recommended by economists and the relative importance that they attach to short-run and long-run policies reflect their views with respect to the nature and scope of economics and the kinds of economic analyses that they make. Behind each economist's policy proposals lies his theory of economic regulation or control. These theories range all the way from theories that call for a minimum of regulation or intervention to those that lead to considerable national economic planning. With respect to problems of economic policy and regulation or control economists fall into three general categories. The first category thinks in terms of the competitive ideal and proposes to keep the economic system competitive or to make it more competitive where it has deviated from the competitive ideal. These economists propose to break up or curb bigness wherever it occurs in the economy, including bigness in the government area. They rely upon a few policy measures to guide the economy and especially upon monetary policy which would keep the money supply growing at the same rate as the nation's gross national product. It is the position of this "monetarist" school that changes in the money supply are the primary cause of changes in overall economic activity, and it should therefore be possible to secure economic stability by regulating the money supply. The Chicago school led by Milton Friedman falls in this first category which may be described as "monetarist" to distinguish it from the second category of economists who are described as "fiscalists." This second category includes the Keynesians who do not pursue the competitive ideal with the same avidness as does the Chicago school. Since they emphasize the role of tax policy and other fiscal measures in the guidance of the economy, these "fiscalists" while not ignoring monetary policy nevertheless place much less emphasis on it than do the monetarists. It is the position of the fiscalist school of economists that fiscal policy, including changes in tax rates and government spending, should be given special consideration in any program for stabilizing the economy because changes in incomes are the primary cause of changes in overall economic activity. Economists who were in the service of the Kennedy and Johnson Administrations such as Walter Heller, Gardner Ackley and Arthur Okun are representative of the Keynesian or fiscalist school.

The members of the monetarist and fiscalist schools can lay claim to being standard or orthodox economists in terms of economic policy recommendations. They are the economists who have dominated government policy making in the United States since 1945. They are both simplistic in their policy approaches since they oversimplify economic problems by excluding from their analyses of these problems such complicating matters as the impact of the technological and organizational revolutions of recent decades on the structure and functioning of the industrial system, and the consequences of the increase in the power of the nation's major economic interest groups to interfere with the operations of the private market system. Both the fiscalists and the monetarists are guilty of the sin of simplism which is the reduction of a problem to a false simplicity by ignoring complicating factors. This simplism leads conventional economists to emphasize the view that economics is largely a matter of "market economics." Their policy proposals are likewise simplistic in nature and lead to a heavy reliance upon only a few policy measures such as fiscal and monetary measures for the guidance of the nation's economy. Standard economists adopt the untenable position that somehow antitrust action can be relied upon to handle successfully the problem of the market power of large industrial enterprises and large labor unions. Consequently they really ignore the problem of economic power and do not deal effectively with the ability of large corporations and labor unions to raise prices and wage rates. The policy recommendations of conventional economists are designed to interfere as little as possible with the operations of the private enterprise system. Although they do not always agree upon the extent to which intervention in the nation's economic affairs should be carried, standard economists assert that intervention should never lead to national economic planning even of the democratic indicative type.

The third category of economists from the viewpoint of economic policy and control is that of the neo-institutionalists. The two major features of neo-institutionalist economic policy proposals that distinguish them from the proposals of standard economists are the use of national economic budgets and the provision for joint consultation and cooperation between the government and the nation's major economic interest groups in the formulation of policy. Neo-institutionalists find that national economic budgets are very important in the construction of both short-run and long-range economic policies, because these budgets enable the government to supplement the private market system in its work of allocating the nation's economic resources. This is so because the private market system has a limited capacity to guide the economy towards the achievement of national economic goals. For example, the private market system cannot decide how total national output is to be divided between the economy's private and public sectors, since public goods usually have no price tags on them and people do not express their preferences for these goods through the private market mechanism. Decisions regarding the division of the nation's economic resources between the private and public sectors or decisions with regard to the relative importance of private and public production can not be expected to arise automatically from the operations of the private market system. They must be made outside this system by the government working in cooperation with the public and its representative interest groups. It is at this point that the national economic budget has an important role to play. The consequences of any public decisions with regard to the division of economic resources between the private and public sectors show up in the national economic budget as national economic goals which are quantified as components of aggregate demand and aggregate supply. In this manner national economic budgets become the basis for considering alternative national economic goals, for securing consistency among these goals as shares of the total national output and for providing a basis for agreement among federal, state and local governments and the nation's many economic interest groups with regard to national goals.

The national economic budget also provides a framework within which fiscal, monetary, wage, price and other economic policies can be coordinated. Each of these policies has an impact on the supply and demand items in the national economic budget. Discussions between the government and major economic interest groups about various economic policies and their probable impacts on the economy can be related to the national economic budget and given a quantitative basis. These impacts can be analyzed with the aid of the national economic budget and a basis may then be laid for agreement by the government and major economic groups about the final selection of both short-term and long-term economic policies.

In neo-institutionalist policy formulation national economic budgeting is associated with joint consultation between the government and major economic power groups and also with the direct participation of these groups to some extent in the policy construction process. Standard economists have failed to realize that economic policy making in advanced industrial countries with high pressure economies and strong economic pressure groups cannot be successfully carried on when these groups have no effective role in the policy making process. It is the position of the neo-institutionalists that national economic policies cannot be successfully executed without the close cooperation of organized interest groups and the government. A good example of the failure of national economic policy that was formulated without adequate prior joint consultation and that was carried out without the cooperation of the government, business and labor was the failure of the wage and price guidelines during the Kennedy and Johnson Administrations in the years 1962-1968. Experience with these guidelines in Western Europe since 1945 very clearly indicates that they have no chance of success without the cooperation of all interested parties.

The neo-institutionalists criticize standard short-run economic policies for curbing inflation and reducing economic instability on the ground that these policies place too much reliance on fiscal and monetary measures and can only secure price stability at the price of heavy unemployment. The neo-institutionalists' proposals for securing short-run economic stability seek to curb inflation without increasing unemployment and without retarding economic growth. This would be done by enlarging the anti-inflationary policy mix to include the use of wage, price and profit guidelines. In 1969 Galbraith strongly criticized the Nixon Administration's anti-inflationary program because it took no action against inflationary wage and price settlements in the organized sector of the nation's economy.[15] It was his position that a heavy reliance on monetary restraint with no mechanism for controlling the wage-price spiral created by organized business and organized labor could eventually curb inflation but only at the cost of high unemployment and retarded economic growth.

The differences between the long range economic policy pro-

---

[15] "Letters to the Editor," *The Wall Street Journal*, Sept. 2, 1969.

posals of the neo-institutionalists and conventional economists are striking. Not making use of published long term national economic budgets, conventional economists have no way of showing the Congress and the public what demands would be made upon the nation's gross national product if its combined economic and social goals were to be achieved. National goal setting and achieving since 1945 under the guidance of conventional economists in the United States has been a very unstructured procedure. There has been very limited cooperation among the federal, state and local governments with regard to the establishing of national economic and social goals. Furthermore there has been very little joint consultation between governments and major economic interest groups with regard to these goals. Also the Congress has had little opportunity to view the national goals in their entirety since no national economic budgets are presented to it by the Council of Economic Advisers, the Director of the Office of Management and Budget or any other government agency. In the absence of a well structured and well publicized way of analyzing and agreeing upon national goals strong lobbying interests have been able to exert an undue influence on the national goal setting process. The neo-institutionalists call for a modernization of government structures and procedures at all levels so that a more orderly way of considering and establishing public economic and social goals may be instituted. The main concern of this modernization of government goal establishing procedures would be to make national economic budgeting the foundation of all long-term national economic policy formulation.

Short-term and long-term economic policy making on the basis of joint consultation and national economic budgeting has become standard practice in many West European countries since the end of World War II. The Scandinavian countries, the Netherlands and France have been in the vanguard of nations that have sought in recent decades to modernize governmental procedures and the process of economic policy formulation so that economic policies would be more effective in achieving national economic and social goals. In recent years the United Kingdom, Belgium and Italy have moved in the same direction. In these countries national economic budgeting and joint consultation have been widely employed in dealing with both short-term and long-range economic problems. Experiments have also been carried on with wage, price and profit policies in the search for more sophisticated ways of dealing with the problem of economic instability in the post war high pressure industrial economies. While it is agreed that much remains to be done to improve wage, price and profit policies in the West European countries, it is also agreed that it is not politically feasible in these countries to curb economic instability and inflation by placing major reliance on restrictive fiscal and monetary policies which result in high unemployment and retarded economic growth. The United Kingdom in the years 1951-1962 tried the Keynesian "stop-go" policy based on fiscal and monetary adjustments and came to the conclusion in 1962 when the National Economic Development Council was established that the retarded economic growth caused by the "stop-go" policy was neither economically justifiable nor politically acceptable.[16]

In the early post World War II years in the United States there was a considerable interest in national economic budgeting and joint consultation as devices for improving the formulation and execution of economic policies. This interest was derived from the experience with the national economic budgeting and joint consultation that were carried on during the war years. With the cessation of hostilities in 1945 it was felt by many economists who had been in government service during the war that some of the experience with national economic budgeting could be applied to a peacetime economy. The Employment Act of 1946 opened the door to both national economic budgeting and cooperation between the federal government and the nation's major economic interest groups. The Council of Economic Advisers in 1949 recommended the use within government circles of the national economic budget concept to provide a quantitative basis for economic policy formulation. The Council also recommended experimentation with joint meetings of representatives of industry, agriculture, labor and consumers and the Council for the consideration of policy problems.[17] The Economic Report of the President for 1950 included a five year (1950-1954) national economic budget which set forth the goal of a higher consumption economy than had existed in the early post war years. From 1951 until 1958 the staff of the Joint Committee on the Economic Report incorporated annual full employment national economic budgets in the Committee's annual reports to the

---

[16] National Economic Development Council, *Growth of the United Kingdom Economy, 1961-1966* and *Conditions Favourable to Faster Growth*, London, Her Majesty's Stationery Office, 1963.

[17] Council of Economic Advisers, *Business and Government*, Fourth Annual Report to the President, Washington, D.C., U.S. Government Printing Office, December 1949, pp. 29-37.

Congress. These annual budgets were designed first to cope with the problem of inflation that had arisen from the Korean War and later with the problem of securing sustained economic growth with price stability. Looking forward to the problems of the post Korean War period the United States Department of Commerce in 1952 analyzed the post war period in terms of a four year (1952-1955) national economic budget which projected income and product developments during the years 1952-1955 on the assumption of continued high level prosperity.[18] With the change in political administration in 1953 interest in government circles in national economic budgeting and joint consultation declined. National economic policy making then reverted to the simplistic format of the conventional economists with its heavy emphasis on manipulatory fiscal and monetary measures without the use of national economic budgets.

The neo-institutionalists are well aware of the advances in economic policy making that have been made since the onset of the depression of the 1930's. The Keynesian anti-depression program left a permanent deposit in the form of an understanding of the roles of fiscal and monetary policies in securing economic stability which had not existed prior to 1929. The "new economics" of the Kennedy and Johnson Administrations was the culmination of a long process of education on the part of the American public with respect to the use of fiscal and monetary policies as stabilizing measures. The neo-institutionalists do not repudiate the valuable lessons that Keynes taught with respect to the importance of fiscal and monetary policies. It is their position, however, that time has moved on and that the advanced industrialized economies of Western Europe and the United States are now much too complicated to be guided effectively by the simplistic policies of the fiscalist and monetarist schools. It is the neo-institutionalists' position that it will take much more than limited intervention to domesticate the technological explosion of recent decades so that it will serve mankind rather than make mankind the victim of an age in which technological advances override human values.[19] As the report of the National Academy of Sciences on *Technology: Processes of Assessment and Choice* points out, the development of technology in our society

---

[18] United States Department of Commerce, *Markets after the Defense Expansion*, Washington, D.C., U.S. Government Printing Office, 1952, p. 83.

[19] Committee on Science and Astronautics, U.S. House of Representatives, *Technology: Processes of Assessment and Choice*, Report of the National Academy of Sciences, Washington, D.C., July 1969, p. 115.

will not be adequately controlled until there are sufficient "opportunities for meaningful public participation in choices [with regard to technology and its use] having major public consequences." The neo-institutionalists assert that it is only through some form of national planning that technological advance and its applications to industry can be monitored in such a way as to minimize "technological surprise," and to make certain that the program of technological assessment "takes into account the changing values, sensitivities and priorities of society."[20]

Criticisms of Neo-Institutional Economics

Ever since Veblen published *The Theory of the Leisure Class* in 1899 the kind of economics that is associated with the terms "institutionalism" and "neo-institutionalism" has been subject to a constant stream of criticism. This criticism can be divided into two general categories, one category being on the theoretical level and the other on the policy level. On the theoretical level the main criticism is that the neo-institutionalists have what are to conventional economists unacceptable views with respect to the nature and scope of economics. The conventional economists who reduce economics to market or price economics assert that the neo-institutionalists would dispense with price theory, or do not understand fully the implications of price theory or are generally unfavorably disposed towards price theory. Abba P. Lerner, Paul T. Homan and A. B. Wolfe criticize Ayres on the ground that he rejects price theory or that he does not grasp the fundamental contributions of price analysis.[21] These criticisms of Ayres miss the point that he is well aware of the allocative and rationing roles of the price system, and that he does not dispense with price theory as it has been developed by standard economists. What Ayres does is to carry his analysis beyond the market price system to inquire into the value structure that finds expression through this system. Ayres points out that the market price system tells us nothing about the value structure of society that lies behind the exchange ratios in the market place. His critics can disagree with his analysis of the

---

[20] *Ibid.*, p. 116.

[21] Abba P. Lerner, review of Ayres's *The Theory of Economic Progress* in *The American Economic Review*, Vol. XXXV, No. 1, March 1945, p. 162; Paul T. Homan, review of Ayres's *Toward a Reasonable Society* in *The American Economic Review*, Vol. LIII, No. 1, March 1963, p. 148; and A. B. Wolfe, review of Ayres's *The Theory of Economic Progress* in *Political Science Quarterly*, Vol. LIX, December 1944, p. 622.

relations between the value structure of society and the market price system, but they are in error when they say that he rejects standard price theory or is not aware of the functions of the price system as far as they have been developed by conventional economics.

Similarly distorted criticisms are levelled against Galbraith and Myrdal. Walter Adams states that it is Galbraith's position that "the industrial giant performs society's planning function.... The market is dead ... and there is no good reason to regret its passing." James E. Meade argues that Galbraith implies that "planning and the use of the market-price mechanism are incompatible," while P. T. Bauer criticizes Myrdal on the ground that his analysis of international economic development proceeds on the basis of a "rejection of market prices and costs."[22] It is quite clear that Galbraith does not assert that the market is dead. On the contrary it is Galbraith's position that the market is very much alive, but that it is significantly different from the competitive market that absorbs so much of the attention of conventional economists, and which is the unrealizable goal of those who place their faith in antitrust action to restore the competitive market system. The criticism by Meade that economists like Galbraith envision a planned economy without a price system is groundless. It is Galbraith's view that the planning imposed on the economy by large industrial corporations distorts the price system by injecting a high degree of inflexibility into it. In a more rationally planned economy the free price system would be in a better position to perform its rationing and allocative functions. In their eagerness to condemn all national planning as a "blue print for technocracy," Galbraith's critics seem to suggest that he is only a simple minded technocrat who does not realize that a production system cannot function effectively without a price system. Technocracy and the technocrats who drew some attention in the 1920's and 1930's have long since been forgotten except by those who are very short of critical ammunition. There is nothing in common between the neo-institutionalists of today and the technocrats of the 1920's and 1930's except the belief that conventional economics falls far short of being an adequate tool for explaining

---

[22] Walter Adams, "The Military-Industrial Complex and the New Industrial State," *The American Economic Review*, Vol. LVIII, No. 2, May 1969, p. 652; J. E. Meade, "Is 'The New Industrial State' Inevitable," *The Economic Journal*, Vol. LXXVIII, No. 310, June 1968, p. 375; and P. T. Bauer, "International Economic Development," *The Economic Journal*, Vol. LXIX, No. 273, March 1959, p. 121.

the real economic world.

The argument of P. T. Bauer that Myrdal's discussion of the problems of underdeveloped countries is carried on in terms of a "price-less economics" is based upon a faulty interpretation of Myrdal's objective. It is not his purpose to make a conventional analysis of balance of payments and foreign exchange problems. Instead it is Myrdal's purpose to explain that the gap between rich and poor nations can be reduced only by avoiding what the free market dictates, and by acting as "non-economic" men who are prepared to go beyond what private international markets would dictate and to give special aid to the poor underdeveloped countries. Myrdal's economics is not "price-less" in any theoretical sense. It is only "price-less" in the sense that in his opinion free market price and cost considerations should not alone dictate the relations between rich and poor nations.

Kenneth E. Boulding's criticism of Adolph Lowe, which presumably would be applicable to all heterodox economists like Lowe and hence to the neo-institutionalists, is to the effect that Lowe and similar economists suffer from a disease which Boulding invents and describes as *Preisschmerz*. Boulding explains that "Preisschmerz is a sort of woe about the price system that seems to be an inescapable accompaniment of progressive thought, and that turns into a serious handicap when progressive thinkers [like Lowe and other heterodox economists] put their ideas into practice."[23] This imaginary disease or alleged antipathy towards prices is said by Boulding to seem to cause Lowe and other heterodox economists to regard "price theory" as a "relic of a by-gone free-market economy," and to consider price economics as something that "can be thrown in the ash can as a relic of an earlier day." This is a complete misinterpretation of Lowe and the neo-institutionalists who have nothing against price theory *per se*, but who do have much against the way in which conventional economists use price theory as an adjunct of a narrow "price economics." To assert that Lowe and the neo-institutionalists are suffering from the disease of *Preisschmerz* would be on a par with asserting that Boulding and other conventional economists are suffering from the disease of *Preisliebe*, an infatuation with prices. Neither accusation could be said to be on a scientific level, or to merit serious critical consideration. Boulding goes on to say that those heterodox economists who think

[23] Kenneth E. Boulding, review of Lowe's *On Economic Knowledge: Toward a Science of Political Economics*, p. 140.

that price theory is "merely a matter of technology" are like "the economic planner who thinks that economics is just technology" and who "is in for some rude shocks."[24] We can all agree with Boulding that any planner who ignores the role of the price system in the operation of a planning program is indeed a poor economist, and would be in for some rude shocks if he hoped to plan an economy successfully without using a price system. But where are such benighted anti-price economists to be found except in some backward communist countries? Certainly not among the neo-institutionalists. Lowe states explicitly in *On Economic Knowledge* that the kind of economic planning that he would be favorably disposed towards is French indicative planning which is constructed around the preservation of the private enterprise system and its price system.[25] Likewise Myrdal's view of national planning is along the lines of Swedish national planning in which the price system plays a key role. Colm's national planning is of the same general type as Lowe's and Myrdal's planning but adjusted to American circumstances. No neo-institutionalist says or even suggests that price theory is merely a matter of technology, and no neo-institutionalist would equate economic planning with technocracy.

A second major criticism of neo-institutionalism made by conventional economists is that the neo-institutionalists have indefensible views with respect to the scope of economics. This criticism asserts that the neo-institutionalists have enlarged the boundaries of economics so far as to include what would be better classified as sociology, cultural anthropology or economic philosophy. J. E. Meade agrees that Galbraith's studies of the affluent society and the new industrial state contain a "very important core of truth." He admits that Galbraith's writings may require a "fundamental rethinking of the basis of much economic philosophy," but this rethinking according to Meade would not go on within the boundaries of economics. As he puts it, "It is not, perhaps, the professional duty of the economist as such to give the answers to these basic psychological and ethical questions" raised by Galbraith.[26] John Hicks describes Myrdal's work in recent decades as a turning "away from economics towards sociology." Both Meade and Hicks object to the broadening of the scope of economics by Galbraith and Myrdal because they agree with other conventional economists that the

---

[24] *Ibid.*, p. 142.
[25] Adolph Lowe, *op. cit.*, p. 156 fn.
[26] J. E. Meade, *op. cit.*, p. 383.

proper scope of economics is limited to what throws light on how the market organizes society. This view of the scope of economics limits economics in so far as it is a matter of economic theory to "pure" or "analytical" economics. Descriptive material about the economic system is used only to illustrate what Robbins calls "the historical manifestations of 'scarcity'."

The conventional approach to economics deprives the economic historian of the possibility of making any economic generalizations that go beyond the generalizations of pure economic theory. With economic history reduced to the menial task of providing illustrative material for use by pure theorists who wish to demonstrate the applicability of their economic laws to the real world, the science of economics cannot wander far from the "phenomenon of exchange." Economics from Meade's and Hicks's point of view cannot be concerned with any theory of the evolving economic process, with the impact of technological change on the structure and functioning of the economic system, with the logic of industrialization or with the theory of "mature" or "organized" capitalism. For Meade and Hicks as for other conventional economists there is no possibility of moving from a theory of the market system to a theory of the industrial system in which the market system is embedded. This outcome does not disturb the conventional economist because he is satisfied to limit economics to a study of market phenomena. What separates the neo-institutional economist from the conventional economist with respect to the scope of economics is not only a difference in philosophical outlook but also a fundamental disagreement concerning the nature of social science. These basic differences lead the neo-institutionalists to broaden the scope of economics to include the evolving economic framework within which the market system functions. They seek to explain not only a market system but also an economic system. In pursuing this goal they find the orthodox view of the proper scope of economics to be quite unacceptable.

A third criticism made of neo-institutional economics by orthodox economists is that the neo-institutionalists in broadening the scope of economics convert economics into a normative science. Meade finds that Galbraith discusses ethical questions and so goes beyond the work of the professional economist. P. T. Bauer criticizes Myrdal for suggesting that "the validity of economic propositions depends on value judgments." Lerner argues that Ayres confuses "value as price and value as morally significant ideals of individual or social behaviour."[27] Boulding objects to "political economics" for the reason that it includes the goals of the economy within the scope of economics. The assertion that the neo-institutionalists make economics a normative science derives from a failure of conventional economists to distinguish between a *study* of human goals and an *evaluation* of these goals. The neo-institutionalists both study and evaluate economic goals but they keep their study and evaluation of goals quite separate. When they study how individual and collective goals influence the functioning of the economic system, the neo-institutionalists make scientific studies of ascertainable, existing economic goals or wants, and they analyze what "is" and not what "ought to be." At this point in their work they do not make economics a normative science. At a later point when they have left the realm of scientific analysis and have put on the hats of reformers the neo-institutionalists as reformers and as individual voters but not as scientists express their private preferences for various economic goals. To say that the neo-institutionalists convert economics into a normative science is not supported by the facts. Such an accusation can only come from those conventional economists whose eagerness to exclude all studies of goals or wants from economics prevents them from correctly assessing the position of the neo-institutionalists with regard to the study and the evaluation of human goals.

A fourth criticism of neo-institutional economics takes the form of the assertion that the neo-institutionalists are economic or technological determinists. This means that their work is supposed to be vitiated by an overemphasis on the importance of technological change in economic life. For example Adams presents the view that Galbraith's thesis in *The New Industrial State* "rests on the unproved premise that corporate giantism is the inevitable product of technological determinism."[28] Galbraith is interpreted by Adams as building his case for the new industrial state on the assumption of "technological inexorability." In contrast to Galbraith Adams finds the fountainhead of business giantism to be "unwise, man-made, discriminatory, privilege-creating governmental action." According to this interpretation the *bête noire* to be feared is not technology but bad big government. Meade moves along the same line as Adams when he states that "Professor Galbraith is, I think, essentially an

---

[27] P. T. Bauer, *op. cit.*, p. 106 and Abba P. Lerner, *cit.*, p. 162.
[28] W. Adams, *op. cit.*, p. 652.

economic determinist."[29] Meade explains that in the spectrum between extreme materialism and extreme idealism Galbraith is "too
near the former and too remote from the latter." No explanation
is offered by Meade as to how he places Galbraith in such a nebulous
spectrum. Doubtlessly Meade's strong preference for an analytical,
non-evolutionary approach to economics would have something to
do with how he categorizes economists who broaden economics to
include a study of the impact of technological change on economic
activities. When the neo-institutionalists are labelled "economic
determinists" or "technocrats" they are also accused of belittling
man's role in society, and of adopting a teleological view which
states that technological change will inevitably lead to human progress. Wolfe argues that Ayres is in error when he makes the
individual exist for the technological process rather than the reverse.
Homan criticizes Ayres for implying that science and technology
create democracy, while Lerner cannot accept what he believes to be
Ayres's interpretation that a principle of progress is at work in the
technological continuum.

The neo-institutionalists do not deny that other factors than
technological change such as domestic and international social and
political developments have had much to do with the shaping of
economic activities. What they assert is that among a number of
factors technological change is a cultural imperative in the hard
and fast world surrounding the individual that cannot be ignored
if we are to understand the real economic world. Furthermore the
neo-institutionalists do not accept the view that scientific advance
and technological change inevitably lead to human progress. It is
their position that scientific advance and technological change in
our complicated world make human progress possible but do not
guarantee it. Nor do the neo-institutionalists take man to be the
mere plaything of blind technological forces. On the contrary they
observe that man is a self-active creative individual who cannot
make over the entire social world, but who can provide some direction for the evolution of this world. Those conventional economists
who find the work of the neo-institutionalists contaminated by a
technological taint do so because they are overly zealous in their
efforts to narrow down the scope of economics, and to close the
door on the suggestion that economists should take account of
technological change in their analyses of economic developments.

A fifth criticism levelled against the neo-institutional economists

---

[29] J. E. Meade, *op. cit.*, p. 375.

is to the effect that their economic policy proposals would lead to a diminution of the freedoms of the individual. F. A. Hayek sees Galbraith's policy proposals leading to an ever bigger government that would exercise a coercive influence over individuals. By taxing people and forcing them to take public goods and services instead of privately produced goods and services the government, in Hayek's opinion, would coerce any dissenting minority that did not want the public goods preferred by the majority.[30] Henry C. Wallich observes "a new puritanism" running through Galbraith's writings that "would make no great contribution to an economy that requires incentive goods to activate competition and free markets. Neither would it be compatible with the freedom that we value."[31] The arguments that Hayek and Wallich present against Galbraith and other neo-institutionalists are the arguments of those economists who are on principle opposed to the expansion of government activities. This is in line with the anti-state predilection dominating conventional economists to which Myrdal has called attention. The neo-institutionalists would concede that when government concern for the direction of economic activities is increased, as in the case of the indicative planning in France, the Netherlands and the Scandinavian countries, some of the freedoms of minorities may be curbed. But at the same time the freedoms of the majority are increased, for otherwise they would not vote for governments that favor indicative national planning. It would be cynical for any social or economic critic to say that in a democracy the majority of people vote for an economic system that reduces their freedoms. It is the position of the neo-institutionalists that in the western democracies people will over the years choose the type of economic system that will best provide for their wants and freedoms. This does not mean that a majority of the citizens should ignore the legitimate interests of any dissenting minority. The economic system to which the neo-institutionalists' policy proposals would lead would be based upon a participatory democracy in which all interests would be heard, and in which the principle of compromise would see to it that the freedom of the majority would not mean the slavery of minorities. This is the meaning of the "politics of compromise" in a participatory democracy.

---

[30] F. A. Hayek, "The *Non Sequitur* of the 'Dependence Effect'," *The Southern Economic Journal*, Vol. XXVIII, No. 4, April 1961, pp. 346-348.
[31] Henry C. Wallich, "Public versus Private: Could Galbraith Be Wrong?" *Harper's Magazine*, Oct. 1961, Vol. 223, No. 1337, p. 14.

quite different from the framework provided by conventional equilibrium economics. It has been the primary concern of the post war
neo-institutionalists to provide a new framework of interpretation
and to make broad-brush studies of the evolving industrial system
within this framework. Others who are to follow can make more
specialized studies and fill in some of the details not supplied by
Ayres, Galbraith, Myrdal, Lowe and other heterodox economists.

Neo-Institutionalism and the New Political Economy

It is now widely recognized that a very considerable broadening
of the interests of economists has occurred in recent decades. This
development has led to a tendency to refer to economics as "political
economy."[36] With government so important a factor in economic
life it is not surprising that the term "political economy," once
widely used by the classical economists, should again become
fashionable among economists. When the science of economics was
first given shape in the eighteenth century by the French Physiocrats
and Adam Smith, government played a very prominent role in
economic affairs. A number of West European nations were then
emerging from the mercantilist era which had flourished for over
two centuries. Adam Smith and other early classical economists
had an overall or totalistic approach which led them to analyze the
exchange economy in a much larger framework of reference than
that of the later neo-classicists. The early classical economists never
reduced economics to "economic analysis." For Adam Smith and
other classical economists the science of economics was more an
inquiry into the wealth of nations than the wealth of individuals,
and hence a study of political economy. When the neo-classical
economists appeared on the scene after 1850 they narrowed the
definition and scope of economics which then became mainly the
study of the wealth getting and wealth using activities of individuals operating in the private market place. By the fourth quarter
of the nineteenth century economics was well established in academic circles as "market economics" or "price economics." This
trend towards a narrow view of economics was brought to the attention of the general public in 1890 when Alfred Marshall, Professor
of Political Economy at Cambridge University, published his *Prin-*

---

[36] As John S. Gambs has put it, "the great economic problem of the
Twentieth century is political." See his *Man Money and Goods* (New York:
Columbia University Press, 1952) p. 320.

ciples of Economics and laid the term "political economy" to rest for half a century.

The renewed interest in economics as "political economy" after 1929 coincided with the interest in macro economics that was stimulated by the publication of Keynes's *The General Theory of Employment Interest and Money* in 1936. The new macro approach not only looked at the economic system in a totalistic or aggregative way, but also opened the door to a large role for government in economic affairs. Private and public enterprise now became closely interwoven and economists began to write about "directed" or "guided" capitalism. This was a return to some extent to the view of the early classical economists who had investigated the economics of individual behavior but within the framework of the total national economy. With the government not only being an important factor in economic life but also becoming increasingly more important as it took on the role of a guiding agent, it is not surprising that economists came to regard Keynesian economics as a new form of "political economy."

It has been the usual practice of the older institutionalists and the neo-institutionalists to consider their type of economics to be "political economy." As has already been explained, John R. Commons spoke for the pre-1939 institutionalists when he explained in his *Institutional Economics* (1932) that it was his purpose to develop "the whole of a rounded-out Political Economy." He went on to explain that he was not dispensing with the analytical economics of the neo-classicists, but was incorporating it in a larger analytical framework which related the market system to the nation's legal and political structure. This framework was the evolving capitalist system which in his time had reached the stage of "banker capitalism." It was Commons's position that his study of economic transactions in the framework of banker capitalism was better described as "political economy" than as "economics." A third of a century later Adolph Lowe was to follow Commons by referring to his broad version of economics as "Political Economics." This Political Economics which deals with the theory of controlled economic systems assigns a large role to the government in the mature industrial system.

The political economy of the neo-institutionalists differs from the Keynesian version of political economy in two important ways. These two differences relate to the fundamental approaches to economic studies adopted by the neo-institutionalists and the Keynesians. The approach of the neo-institutionalists is evolutionary and interdisciplinary, while that of the Keynesians is essentially static and non-interdisciplinary. The early institutionalists and the later neo-institutionalists have an holistic approach to the study of the economic system. This holistic approach leads these heterodox economists not only to concern themselves with the economic system as a whole, but equally important is the fact that it causes them to regard the economy as an evolving whole.[37] Keynes and the Keynesians do not have the holistic approach because their macro approach while it is aggregative or totalistic is not evolutionary. They consider the whole economy to be a non-evolving aggregate sum or total of economic relationships. Unlike the neo-institutionalists Keynes and the Keynesians do not have a theory of capitalist development or a theory of industrialization.[38] On this point they do not differ from their orthodox Marshallian predecessors. The difference between the micro approach of Marshall and the macro approach of Keynes is not that Marshall's approach is static, while Keynes's approach is evolutionary. On the contrary both the micro and the macro approaches are static or non-evolutionary. The basic difference between Marshall's approach and that of Keynes is that Marshall's approach is particularistic and concerned with the parts of the economy, while Keynes's approach is aggregative and concerned with the whole economy.

The political economy of the neo-institutionalists differs from that of the Keynesians in more than being evolutionary in its approach. The neo-institutionalists have an interdisciplinary approach that is quite lacking among the Keynesians. When the neo-institutionalists turn to a study of the economic system as a process, they find that an explanation of the course of economic development must take "non-economic" as well as "economic" factors into account if a satisfactory explanation is to be worked out. While a study of narrow market problems may not require much concern with non-economic factors, this is not the case when the economist turns to a study of the maturing industrial system or the development of underdeveloped countries. A full grasping of the nature of economic problems frequently requires an understanding of the sociological, psychological and political factors involved as well as the economic factors. It is the position of the neo-institutionalists that if an econo-

[37] Allan G. Gruchy, *Modern Economic Thought*, p. 4.
[38] Allan G. Gruchy, "J. M. Keynes's Concept of Economic Science," *The Southern Economic Journal*, Vol. XV, No. 3, January 1949, p. 259.

mist is to be prepared to understand economic problems fully, he must have some acquaintance with the contributions of the related social sciences. And if he is to be in a position to make significant policy proposals, he must be able to take account of the importance of non-economic factors in solving economic problems. The Keynesian who clings to a narrow view of the nature and scope of economics, and who therefore refuses to open his economic analysis to a consideration of such matters as the impact of technological change on the structure and functioning of the economic system, the importance of major economic power groups and the role of the nation's value structure in guiding the economic system, is in a poor position in the opinion of the neo-institutionalists to analyze economic problems and to make proposals for their solution.

Neo-Institutionalism and the Economics of Dissent

A review of economic literature reveals that there are many kinds of economic dissenters.[39] Some of these dissenters, who criticize the way the current economic system operates, are outside the academic world and do not concern themselves to any great extent with the inadequacies of standard or conventional economics. We have in this area such dissenters as Michael Harrington, Vance Packard, Ralph Nader, David Bazelon and William H. Whyte Jr., who have called attention to the deficiencies of the modern industrial system by focusing public concern on such issues as the poverty problem, the weak voice of the consumer, the dominant role of the large industrial corporation in the guidance of the economic system and the values imposed upon the community by those who place private gain above public welfare. Other economic dissenters, who are members of the academic community, direct their criticism at the science of economics as it is handled by conventional economists. These academic dissenters range all the way from those at one end of the scale who simply want somehow to make conventional economics more realistic to those at the other end of the scale who seek to reconstruct economics and make it over more in the image of a social than a natural science. The dissenters who merely want to make standard economics more realistic call for more empirical feedback in the work of the conventional economists so that conventional economic theory and actual economic practice may be more closely related. This can be done, these mild dissenters say, by going

---

[39] Allan G. Gruchy, "Neo-Institutionalism and the Economics of Dissent," *Journal of Economic Issues*, Vol. III, No. 1, March 1969, pp. 4-5.

beyond highly mathematical economic analysis to take account of much of the data left out of their economic analyses by the model builders. This is to be done by disaggregating the macro economic analysis of the model builders and paying more attention to micro economic analysis. At no time, however, does this type of economic dissenter ever consider converting the search for economic realism into a desire to reconstruct conventional economics by altering its fundamental nature.

Other economic dissenters in the academic world find that the scope of standard economics is too narrow. Since economic problems are frequently also social or political in nature, these dissenters assert that the economist should analyze economic problems in a broader framework than is used by conventional economists, especially those with a strong quantitative bent. These economic dissenters who are unwilling to limit themselves to the scope of economics as it is conceived by standard economists are not, however, interested in any fundamental reconstruction of conventional economics. They would eliminate the narrowness of standard economics not by reconstructing it but by pursuing an interdisciplinary approach in which conventional economics would be combined with other social sciences in the analysis of human problems and in the effort to find solutions to these problems. The economic dissenters who merely want conventional economics to have more empirical feedback, or those who recommend integrating conventional economics with the other social sciences in some kind of interdisciplinary arrangement, present no real challenge to conventional economics. This is the case because economic dissent of these types leaves intact the narrow view of the nature and significance of economics held by conventional economists.

Neo-institutionalists as economic dissenters go beyond merely trying to make conventional economics more empirical and hence more realistic, and also beyond applying an interdisciplinary approach to economic problems. Their economic dissent leads to a fundamental reconstruction of conventional economics. The dissent of the neo-institutionalists is positive and constructive in the sense that it challenges the fundamental view of economics cultivated by conventional economists, and offers a different view of economics to replace that of the conventional economists. The neo-institutionalists offer a social science in place of a technical science, and they substitute a "systems economics" for the conventional "market economics." As has already been explained, this systems economics includes taking the economic system to be an evolving process, analyzing the impact of technological change on this process and inquiring into the role of individual and group goals or values in providing direction for the nation's economy. All these important matters are ignored by conventional economists and by those economic dissenters who never get as far as considering the need for a fundamental reconstruction of economics along the lines indicated by the neo-institutional economists.

The question may be asked: What is it that makes a neo-institutionalist a neo-institutionalist? In answering this question one should not expect to create an image to which all economists who are categorized as neo-institutionalists must neatly conform. The special interests of individual neo-institutionalists will necessarily lead them to emphasize different areas of economic analysis in which they are especially interested, and therefore to draw attention only to special aspects of neo-institutionalism. It is possible, however, to indicate in a general way what it is that constitutes the essence of neo-institutionalism, and what it is that distinguishes neo-institutionalists from other types of economists. The fundamentals of neo-institutionalism can be discussed in terms of the neo-institutionalists' philosophical outlook, their definition of economics, their view of its scope and their proposals for the more effective working of the modern industrial system.

The neo-institutionalists have a common pragmatic philosophical outlook which leads them to view economic reality—the real economic world—as an evolving process or pattern of human relations. They avoid the logical positivism that underlies standard economics and that leads standard economists to find the essence of economic reality in a static pattern of logical relationships—in what Lionel Robbins has described so well as the "shadowy abacus of forms and inevitable relationships." Instead of reducing economic reality to a pattern or model of static logical relationships the neo-institutionalists find the essence of economic reality in an evolving economic system. For the neo-institutionalist economic reality is a concrete cultural phenomenon to which logical analysis is applied in uncovering its real nature, but at all times the neo-institutionalist subordinates "logical analysis" to "concrete interpretation."

The philosophical outlook of the neo-institutionalists leads them to view economics as the study of the part of the evolving social system that is concerned with the provision of scarce material goods and services. For all neo-institutionalists economics is the study of the developing economic system of which the private market system is a subsidiary part. They do not dispense with the market economics of the conventional economists. Instead they go beyond this market economics to develop, as has been pointed out, a "systems economics" which while not dispensing with equilibrium economic analysis nevertheless moves far beyond it. The neo-institutionalists' broad definition of economics leads to a similarly broad view of the scope of economics. This broad view makes it possible to study technological change, its impact on the industrial economy and the pattern or logic of industrial development that canalizes the flow of technological change. This concept of the logic of industrial evolution is the colligating concept that unifies the neo-institutionalists' analyses of the course of industrial development. It should be noted, furthermore, that the neo-institutionalists' interpretation of industrial development is not limited to equilibrium analysis. On the contrary the working out of the process of industrialization is marked by a high degree of disequilibrium which can in the opinion of the neo-institutionalists be eliminated only through some program for national economic guidance.

Since the neo-institutionalists take the economic system to be an evolving pattern of human relationships, they necessarily raise the question of the direction in which this pattern is moving. They are very much concerned about the future state of the economy that may be emerging. They observe that this future state of the economy is influenced by many different factors such as the desires of consumers as expressed through the private market system, the power exercised by major economic interest groups and the kind of guidance provided by governments. The neo-institutionalists see a need for more and not less government supervision of the process of industrial development, and they assert that some form of democratic indicative national planning is the kind of national guidance that will enable the general public to have its wants more fully met. The specific economic policy recommendations of the neo-institutionalists are made within the framework of this indicative national planning.

It is quite clear that there is a well-defined overall image to which the economist must conform if he is to be described as a neo-institutionalist. This does not mean that all economists who may be described in this manner will neatly fit the image of the typical neo-institutionalist constructed above. Not all neo-institutionalists have well developed views with respect to the nature and scope of economics. When we turn, however, to an overall survey of the work of Ayres, Galbraith, Myrdal, Colm and other neo-institutionalists there emerges a common way of comprehending economic reality that can properly be described as "neo-institutionalist." It is this common way discussed above that makes a neo-institutionalist a neo-institutionalist, and that distinguishes him from the representatives of conventional or orthodox economics.

BIOGRAPHICAL NOTES

Clarence E. Ayres

Clarence E. Ayres was born in Lowell, Massachusetts, in 1891. After receiving his bachelor's and master's degrees in philosophy at Brown University, Ayres went on to the University of Chicago where he completed his graduate work in philosophy. The untimely death in 1915 of Robert F. Hoxie, an early institutionalist, prevented Ayres from carrying on his graduate work on the relations between ethics and economics under Hoxie's direction. He received his doctoral degree from the University of Chicago with a thesis on "The Nature of the Relationship between Ethics and Economics."

Ayres began his academic career as an instructor in philosophy at Amherst College. From 1917 to 1924 he taught at Amherst College and Reed College where he offered courses on ethics and economics. In 1924-1925 Ayres was an associate editor of *The New Republic*. In 1928 he returned to academic work as a lecturer in the Experimental College of the University of Wisconsin. In 1930 Ayres joined the Department of Economics at the University of Texas where he remained until he retired in 1969. Although he served for some time as a director of the San Antonio Branch of the Federal Reserve System (1954-1959) and was a member of the Commission on the Southwest Economy (1950-1953), Ayres devoted most of his time to academic pursuits.

Ayres's earliest writings were in the fields of science and philosophy. While at the University of Texas he specialized in the field of institutional economics, and sent many of his graduate students to positions in universities in the Southwest and West where they continued to work in the institutionalist tradition. His basic views on the nature of institutional economics were presented in *The Theory of Economic Progress* (1944). Ayres's research on the meaning of human welfare and the means of attaining it culminated in the publication of *Toward a Reasonable Society, the Values of Industrial Civilization* in 1961. In 1966 Ayres was elected the first president of the Association for Evolutionary Economics which had been formally organized in 1965 to advance the cause of neo-institutionalism and other forms of economic dissent.

341

John Kenneth Galbraith

John Kenneth Galbraith was born near Iona Station, Ontario, Canada in 1908. He graduated from the University of Toronto in 1931 and continued his interest in agricultural economics at the University of California, where he obtained his doctoral degree in 1934 with a thesis on "California Counties and Their Expenditures." Galbraith began his academic career as an instructor in economics at Harvard University in 1934. He continued in the academic field until he entered government service during the Second World War in 1940.

During his government service Galbraith served first as an economic adviser and assistant to Chester Davis who was the agricultural representative on the National Defense Advisory Committee. In 1941 he transferred to the Office of Price Administration where he became involved in the wartime price control program. In 1943 Galbraith became a director of the United States Strategic Bombing Survey and was concerned with the effect of bombing on the economies of Germany and Japan. In the same year he was appointed director of the United States State Department's Office of Economic Security Policy which prepared to take charge of economic affairs in post war Germany and Japan.

From 1943 to 1948 Galbraith was a member of the Board of Editors of *Fortune* magazine, and in 1949 he returned to Harvard University. Since the end of the Second World War Galbraith has displayed a deep interest in the interrelations between economics and politics in American life. During the 1950's he was a key figure in the presidential campaigns of Adlai E. Stevenson. This close association with politics continued into the Kennedy Administration during which he was Ambassador to India for the years 1961-1963. After 1963 Galbraith withdrew from the mainstream of American politics and became a critic of the Johnson Administration on the ground that it was responsible for a socially undesirable ordering of the nation's social and economic priorities. He continued to be an active participant in the liberal wing of the Democratic Party as represented by the Americans for Democratic Action. In 1968 Galbraith was elected national president of the Americans for Democratic Action, and in 1971 he was elected president of the American Economic Association.

Much of Galbraith's time since 1951 has been devoted to writing for the general public on such issues as the changing nature of

American capitalism, the affluent society, the new industrial state, and the problems of the underdeveloped countries. Among his many writings his *American Capitalism, the Concept of Countervailing Power* (1952), *The Affluent Society* (1958), and *The New Industrial State* (1967) have aroused a great deal of public interest. Galbraith's well established reputation abroad was attested to by the invitation in 1966 to deliver the Reith Lectures over the British Broadcasting System. Over the years Galbraith has served as a consultant to many private and government organizations, and he has frequently appeared before congressional committees concerned with major economic and political problems.

Karl Gunnar Myrdal

Karl Gunnar Myrdal was born in Gustafs, Sweden, in 1898. He graduated in law and economics from the University of Stockholm and obtained his doctorate of law and economics in 1927 by which time he was a lecturer in political economy at the University of Stockholm. During the years 1925-1929 he travelled extensively in Germany, France, the United Kingdom and the United States. For the period 1930-1931 he was an assistant professor in the Postgraduate Institute of International Studies in Geneva.

During the 1930's Myrdal combined an academic career with an active political life. In 1933 he was appointed to the Lars Hierta Chair of Political Economy and Public Finance at the University of Stockholm which had previously been occupied by Gustav Cassel. During the 1930's Myrdal was active in the field of social security, and he frequently served as an adviser to the government on financial, economic and social questions. He turned to social engineering as a device for constructing the Swedish welfare state. His interests were focussed on the population, family and housing problems. In collaboration with his wife, Alva Myrdal, who is also a social scientist, Myrdal published extensively with regard to population and related problems. He served as a Social Democratic member of the Swedish Senate, a member of the Swedish Housing and Population Commission and a deputy member of the Board of Governors of the National Bank of Sweden.

In the late 1930's Myrdal turned to a study of the negro problem in the United States. During the years 1938-1943 he conducted investigations of the negro problem in the United States for the Carnegie Foundation and in 1944 published his well-known *An American Dilemma*. In 1944 Myrdal was chairman of the Swedish

Postwar Economic Planning Commission which laid down the broad guidelines for national planning in Sweden during the postwar years. From 1945 to 1947 Myrdal was Minister of Trade and Commerce in the Social Democratic Government. In 1947 he became the Executive Secretary of the United Nations Commission for Europe, a position that he occupied until 1957. In 1960 he returned to the University of Stockholm as a professor of international economics. In recent years Myrdal has travelled extensively in the developing countries, especially in Southeast Asia. It was on the basis of his observations made in this area that he wrote his monumental *Asian Drama, An Inquiry into the Poverty of Nations* in 1968. As a frequent visitor to the United States since 1929 Myrdal has been a leading interpreter of American affairs for the Swedish public.

Gerhard Colm

Gerhard Colm was born in Hanover, Germany, in 1897 and died in Washington, D.C., in 1968. At the University of Freiburg he worked in the field of sociology under Max Weber who died before Colm completed his doctoral thesis on "The History and Sociology of the Uprising in the Ruhr, 1920-1921." After leaving Freiburg Colm turned from sociology to statistics and did postgraduate work in the latter field at the University of Berlin. From 1922 to 1926 Colm was a statistician in the German Federal Service. He returned to academic life in 1927 when he joined the economics faculty of the University of Kiel where he became the deputy director of research in the Institute of World Economics until 1932.

In 1933 Colm left Germany for the United States where he joined the economics faculty of the New School for Social Research in New York and remained there until 1939. In that year Colm began his career in government service in Washington, D.C., which continued until 1952. He served as a fiscal adviser in the United States Department of Commerce and the Bureau of the Budget during the years 1939-1946. In 1946 he became a member of the economics staff of the Council of Economic Advisers soon after the Council was established by the Employment Act of 1946. In 1952 Colm left the Council to become the chief economist of the National Planning Association, a position that he held until December 25, 1968.

When Colm entered government service in the United States he specialized in the field of public finance. His work at the Council of Economic Advisers gave him an opportunity to broaden his interest in the public sector. By 1946 his major concern had shifted from the fiscal budget to the national economic budget which became his primary interest while working at the National Planning Association. Colm enlarged the activities of this Association by arranging for the establishment of the Center for Economic Projections (1962), the Center for Priority Analysis (1962), and the Center for Development Planning (1963). These centers developed Colm's basic thesis that in our large scale complex industrial economy national priorities should be clearly identified, and should be balanced with available national resources with the aid of national economic budget projections. He made information with regard to these projections available to both private industry and the government for the guidance of private and public policy formulation.

Over the years after Colm entered government service in 1939 he appeared before many congressional committees where his views on a wide variety of economic problems received widespread attention. In 1966 Colm who was active in the Association for Comparative Economics was elected president of this Association. He was very much interested in developing this Association on an international basis with the hope of bringing together economists from many parts of the world who are concerned with the field of comparative economic systems.

BIBLIOGRAPHY

CHAPTER I

Aron, Raymond, *Progress and Disillusion, the Dialectics of Modern Society* (New York: Frederick A. Praeger, Inc., 1968).

Ayres, Clarence E., *The Industrial Economy* (Boston: Houghton Mifflin Co., 1952).

Clark, John M., "Statement of Dr. John Maurice Clark, Professor of Economics, Columbia University," *Hearings before a Subcommittee on Manufactures*, U.S. Senate, Washington, D.C., U.S. Government Printing Office, 1931.

Colm, Gerhard and Gulick, Luther H., *Program Planning for National Goals*, Planning Pamphlet No. 125, Washington, D.C., National Planning Association, 1968.

Galbraith, John K., *The New Industrial State* (Boston: Houghton Mifflin Co., 1967).

Kahn, Herman and Weiner, Anthony J., *The Year 2000, A Framework for Speculation on the Next Thirty-Three Years* (New York: The Macmillan Co., 1967).

Keynes, John M., *The General Theory of Employment Interest and Money* (New York: Harcourt Brace and Co., 1936).

Mishan, Ezra J., *The Cost of Growth* (New York: Frederick A. Praeger, Inc., 1967).

Myrdal, Gunnar, *Challenge to Affluence* (New York: Pantheon Books, 1962).

National Economic Development Council, *Growth of the United Kingdom Economy, 1961-1966*, London, Her Majesty's Stationery Office, 1963.

Perroux, François, "The Domination Effect and Modern Economic Theory," *Social Research*, Vol. 17, June 1950.

Robbins, Lionel, *An Essay on the Nature and Significance of Economic Science*, Second Edition (London: The Macmillan Co., Ltd., 1935).

Samuelson, Paul A., *Economics, an Introductory Analysis*, Sixth Edition, (New York: McGraw-Hill Book Co., 1964).

Senate Committee on Government Operations, Subcommittee on National Security and International Operations, *Planning—Programming—Budgeting, Initial Memorandum, Official Documents, and Selected Comments*, Washington, D.C., U. S. Government Printing Office, 1967.

U. S. Department of Health, Education, and Welfare, *Toward a Social Report*, Washington, D.C., U. S. Government Printing Office, 1969.

CHAPTER II

Burns, Arthur F., *Wesley C. Mitchell: the Economic Scientist* (New York: National Bureau of Economic Research, 1952).

Clark, John M., "Economics and the National Recovery Administration," *American Economic Review*, Vol. XXIV, March 1939.

Clark, John M., *Studies in the Economics of Overhead Costs* (Chicago: University of Chicago Press, 1923).

Clark, John M., "The Socializing of Theoretical Economics," *The Trend of Economics*, R. G. Tugwell (ed.) (New York: Alfred A. Knopf, 1924).

Clark, John M., "Toward a Concept of Social Value," *Preface to Social Economics* (New York: Farrar and Rinehart, 1936).

Clark, John M., "Toward a Concept of Workable Competition," *American Economic Review*, Vol. XXX, June 1940.

Commons, John R., *Industrial Goodwill* (New York: McGraw-Hill Book Co., 1919).

Commons, John R., *Institutional Economics* (New York: The Macmillan Co., 1934).

Dorfman, Joseph, *The Economic Mind in American Civilization*, Volumes Four and Five, 1918-1933 (New York: The Viking Press, 1959).

Dorfman, Joseph, "The Source and Impact of Veblen's Thought," *Thorstein Veblen: A Critical Reappraisal*, Douglas F. Dowd (ed.) (Ithaca: Cornell University Press, 1958).

Dowd, Douglas F., *Thorstein Veblen* (New York: Washington Square Press, 1966).

Friday, Charles B., "Veblen on the Future of American Capitalism," *Thorstein Veblen, The Carleton College Veblen Seminar Essays*, Carlton C. Qualey (ed.) (New York: Columbia University Press, 1968).

Friedman, Milton, "Wesley C. Mitchell as an Economic Theorist," *Journal of Political Economy*, Vol. LVIII, December 1950.

Gruchy, Allan G., *Modern Economic Thought, The American Contribution* (New York: Prentice-Hall, Inc., 1947).

Gruchy, Allan G., "The Influence of Veblen on Mid-Century Institutionalism," *American Economic Review*, Vol. XLVIII, May 1958.

Gruchy, Allan G., "Veblen's Theory of Economic Growth," *Thorstein Veblen: A Critical Reappraisal*, Douglas F. Dowd (ed.) (Ithaca: Cornell University Press, 1958).

Koopmans, Tjalling C., "Measurement without Theory," *Review of Economic Studies*, Vol. XXIX, August, 1947.

Kuznets, Simon, "The Contribution of Wesley C. Mitchell," *Institutional Economics: Veblen, Commons, and Mitchell Reconsidered* (Berkeley: University of California Press, 1963).

Mitchell, Wesley C., *Business Cycles* (Berkley: University of California Press, 1913).

Mitchell, Wesley C., "Human Behavior and Economics," *Quarterly Journal of Economics*, Vol. XXIX, November 1914.

Mitchell, Wesley C., "The Prospects of Economics," *The Trend of Economics*, R. G. Tugwell (ed.) (New York: Alfred A. Knopf, 1924).

National Resources Planning Board, "Toward Full Use of Resources," *The Structure of the American Economy*, Part II, Washington, D.C., U. S. Government Printing Office, June, 1940.

Patten, Simon N., *The New Basis of Civilization* (New York: The Macmillan Co., 1912).

Reisman, David, *Thorstein Veblen: A Critical Interpretation* (New York: Charles Scribner's Sons, 1953).

Report of the President's Research Committee on Social Trends, *Recent Social Trends in the United States* (New York: McGraw-Hill Book Co., 1933).

Schumpeter, Joseph A., "Mitchell's Business Cycles," *Quarterly Journal of Economics*, Vol. XLV, November 1930.

Seligman, Ben B., *Main Currents in Modern Economics, Economic Thought since 1870* (New York: The Free Press of Glencoe, 1963).

Tugwell, Rexford G., "Experimental Economics," *The Trend of Economics*, R. G. Tugwell (ed.) (New York: Alfred A. Knopf, 1924).

Tugwell, Rexford G., "The Fourth Power," *Planning and Civic Comment*, Part II, April-June 1939.

Veblen, Thorstein, *Absentee Ownership and Business Enterprise in Recent Times* (New York: The Viking Press, 1938).

Veblen, Thorstein, "A Policy of Reconstruction," *Essays in Our Changing Order*, Leon Ardzrooni (ed.) (New York: The Viking Press, 1934).

Veblen, Thorstein, *The Theory of the Leisure Class* (New York: The Macmillan Co., 1912).

Veblen, Thorstein, "The Opportunity of Japan," *Essays in Our Changing Order*, Leon Ardzrooni (ed.) (New York: The Viking Press, 1934).

Watkins, Myron W., "Veblen's View of Cultural Evolution," *Thorstein Veblen: A Critical Reappraisal*, Douglas F. Dowd (ed.) (Ithaca: Cornell University Press, 1958).

CHAPTER III

Ayres, Clarence E., "Institutionalism and Economic Development," *Southwestern Social Science Quarterly*, Vol. XLI, June 1960.

Ayres, Clarence E., "Ideological Responsibility," *Journal of Economic Issues*, Vol. 1, June 1967.

Ayres, Clarence E., "Piecemeal Revolution," *Southwestern Social Science Quarterly*, Vol. XXX, June 1949.

Ayres, Clarence E., *The Divine Right of Capital* (Boston: Houghton Mifflin Co., 1946).

Ayres, Clarence E., *The Problem of Economic Order* (New York: Farrar and Rinehart, 1938).

Ayres, Clarence E., *The Theory of Economic Progress* (Chapel Hill: University of North Carolina Press, 1944).

Ayres, Clarence E., *Toward a Reasonable Society* (Austin: University of Texas Press, 1961).

Cooley, Charles H., *Human Nature and the Social Order* (New York: Charles Scribner's Sons, 1902).

Dewey, John, *Reconstruction in Philosophy* (New York: Henry Holt and Co., 1920).

Dorfman, Joseph, *Thorstein Veblen and His America* (New York: The Viking Press, 1934).

Gottlieb, Manuel, "Clarence E. Ayres and a Larger Economic Theory," *Southwestern Social Science Quarterly*, Vol. 41, June 1960.

Higgins, Benjamin, "Some Introductory Remarks on Institutionalism and Economic Development," *Southwestern Social Science Quarterly*, Vol. 41, June 1960.

Mitchell, Wesley C., "The Role of Money in Economic Theory," *The Backward Art of Spending Money* (New York: McGraw-Hill Book Co., 1937).

Robertson, Jack E., "Folklore of Institutional Economics," *Southwestern Social Science Quarterly*, Vol. 41, June 1960.

CHAPTER IV

Adams, Walter, Mueller, Willard F., and Turner, Donald F., Hearings before the Senate Subcommittee of the Select Committee on Small Business, *Planning, Regulation, and Competition*, Washington, D.C., U. S. Government Printing Office, June 29, 1967.

Dennison, H. S. and Galbraith, J. K., *Modern Competition and Business Policy* (New York: Oxford University Press, 1938).

Galbraith, John K., *American Capitalism, The Concept of Countervailing Power* (second edition; Boston: Houghton Mifflin Co., 1956).

Galbraith, John K., "A Review of a Review," *The Public Interest*, Number 9, Fall 1967.

Galbraith, John K., "Market Structure and Stabilization Policy," *Review of Economics and Statistics*, Vol. XXXIX, May 1957.

Galbraith, John K., "Statement of John Kenneth Galbraith," *January 1965 Economic Report of the President*, Hearings before the Joint Economic Committee, Washington, D.C., U. S. Government Printing Office, February 24, 1965.

Galbraith, John K., *The Affluent Society* (Boston: Houghton Mifflin Co., 1958).

Galbraith, John K., *The Liberal Hour* (Boston: Houghton Mifflin Co., 1960).

Gruchy, Allan G., *Comparative Economic Systems, Competing Ways to Stability and Growth* (Boston: Houghton Mifflin Co., 1966).

Heilbroner, Robert L., review of Galbraith's *The New Industrial State*, *The New Republic*, Vol. 157, July 8, 1967.

Kristol, Irving, "Professor Galbraith's 'New Industrial State'," *Fortune*, July 1967.

Saulnier, R. J., review of Galbraith's *The New Industrial State*, *New York Review of Books*, Vol. 8, June 29, 1967.

Solow, Robert M., "The New Industrial State," *The Public Interest*, Number 9, Fall 1967.

CHAPTER V

Krishnaswamy, K. S., "Some Thoughts on a Drama," *Finance and Development* Vol. 6, March 1969.

Myrdal, Gunnar, "Adjustment of Economic Institutions in Contemporary America," *Institutional Adjustment, A Challenge to a Changing Economy*, Carey C. Thompson (ed.) (Austin: University of Texas Press, 1967).

Myrdal, Gunnar, *An American Dilemma, The Negro Problem and Modern Democracy* (New York: Harper and Brothers, 1944).

Myrdal, Gunnar, *An International Economy, Problems and Prospects* (New York: Harper and Brothers, 1956).

Myrdal, Gunnar, *Asian Drama, An Inquiry into the Poverty of Nations* (New York: Pantheon Books, 1968).

Myrdal, Gunnar, *Beyond the Welfare State, Economic Planning and Its Implications* (New Haven: Yale University Press, 1960).

Myrdal, Gunnar, *Development and Under-Development*, Fiftieth Anniversary Commemoration Lectures, National Bank of Egypt, Cairo, 1956.

Myrdal, Gunnar, *Monetary Equilibrium* (New York: Augustus M. Kelley, 1962).

Myrdal, Gunnar, *Population, A Problem for Democracy* (Cambridge: Harvard University Press, 1940).

Myrdal, Gunnar, *Realities and Illusions in regard to Inter-Governmental Organizations*, L. T. Hobhouse Memorial Trust Lecture, No. 24, London, Oxford University Press, 1954.

Myrdal, Gunnar, *Rich Lands and Poor, The Road to World Prosperity* (New York: Harper and Brothers, 1957).

Myrdal, Gunnar, "The Trends towards Economic Planning," *The Manchester School of Economic and Social Studies*, Vol. XIX, January 1951.

Myrdal, Gunnar, *Value in Social Theory* (London: Routledge and Kegan Paul, Ltd., 1958).

Prebisch, Raul, *The Economic Development of Latin America and Its Principal Problems*, United Nations Economic Commission for Latin America, New York, 1950.

Rosen, George, a review of Myrdal's *Asian Drama, American Economic Review*, Vol. LVIII, December 1968.

Wicksell, Knut, *Interest and Prices (Geldzins und Guterpreise)* (London: Macmillan and Co., Ltd., 1936).

CHAPTER VI

Clark, John M., *Social Control of Business* (Second edition; New York: McGraw-Hill Book Co., 1939).

Colm, Gerhard, *Long-Range Projection*, Comments by Gerhard Colm, Conference on Research in Income and Wealth, National Bureau of Economic Research, New York, 1954.

Colm, Gerhard, "Economics Today," *Essays in Public Finance and Fiscal Policy* (New York: Oxford Press, 1955).

Colm, Gerhard, "Economic Planning in the United States," *Zeitschrift des Instituts für Weltwirtschaft*, Weltwirtschafliches Archiv, Hamburg, 1964.

Colm, Gerhard and Wagner, Peter, *Federal Budget Projections*, a Report of the National Planning Association and the Brookings Institution, The Brookings Institution, Washington, D.C., 1966.

Colm, Gerhard, "Fiscal Policy and the Federal Budget," *Essays in Public Finance and Fiscal Policy* (New York: Oxford Press, 1955).

Colm, Gerhard, *Integration of National Planning and Budgeting*, Center for Development Planning, Methods Series No. 5, National Planning Association, Washington, D.C., 1968.

Colm, Gerhard, "Is Economic Planning Compatible with Democracy?" *Essays in Public Finance and Fiscal Policy* (New York: Oxford Press, 1955).

Colm, Gerhard, "Man's Work and Who Will Do It in 1980," *America 1980*, the William A. Jump—I. Thomas McKillop Memorial Lectures in Public Administration, Robert L. Hill (ed.), The Graduate School, U. S. Department of Agriculture, Washington, D.C., 1965.

Colm, Gerhard, "National Economic Budgets," *Essays in Public Finance and Fiscal Policy* (New York: Oxford Press, 1955).

Colm, Gerhard, "Setting the Sights," *Essays in Public Finance and Fiscal Policy* (New York: Oxford Press, 1955).

Colm, Gerhard, *The American Economy in 1960*, Planning Pamphlet No. 81, National Planning Association, Washington, D.C., 1952.

Colm, Gerhard, *The Economy of the American People*, Planning Pamphlet No. 102, National Planning Association, Washington, D.C., 1958.

Colm, Gerhard, "The Nation's Economic Budget, a Tool of Full Employment Policy," *Studies in Income and Wealth*, Conference on Research in Income and Wealth, National Bureau of Economic Research, New York, 1947.

Hearings before the Joint Economic Committee, *January 1956 Economic Report of the President*, Testimony of Gerhard Colm, Washington, D.C., U. S. Government Printing Office, January 31-February 28, 1956.

Hearings before the Joint Economic Committee, *The 1967 Economic Report of the President*, Testimony of Gerhard Colm, February 20-23, 1967, Washington, D.C., U. S. Government Printing Office.

House of Representatives Subcommittee on Government Operations, *Congressional Review of Price-Wage Guideposts, Statement of Dr. Gerhard Colm*, Washington, D.C., U. S. Government Printing Office, September 12, 1966.

National Planning Association, *Long-Range Projections for Economic Growth: The American Economy in 1970*, Planning Pamphlet No. 107, Washington, D.C., 1959.

National Planning Association, *National Budgets for Full Employment*, Planning Pamphlets Nos. 43 and 44, Washington, D.C., 1945.

National Planning Association, *1964 and 1965 Report on Activities*, Washington, D.C., 1966.

CHAPTER VII

Adams, Walter, "The Military-Industrial Complex and the New Industrial State," *American Economic Review*, Vol. LVIII, May 1969.

Bauer, P. T., "International Economic Development," *Economic Journal*, Vol. LXIX, March 1959.

Boulding, Kenneth E., "Is Economics Obsolescent?" a review of Lowe's *On Economic Knowledge*, *Scientific American*, Vol. 212, May 1965.

Council of Economic Advisers, *Business and Government*, Fourth Annual Report to the President, Washington, D.C., U. S. Government Printing Office, 1949.

Edwards, Ward, "Decision Making," *International Encyclopedia of the Social Sciences*, Vol. 4.

Galbraith, John K., "Letters to the Editor," *The Wall Street Journal*, September 2, 1969.

Gambs, John S., *Man Money and Goods* (New York: Columbia University Press, 1952).

Gruchy, Allan G., "J. M. Keynes' Concept of Economic Science," *Southern Economic Journal*, Vol. XV, January 1949.

Gruchy, Allan G., "Neo-Institutionalism and the Economics of Dissent," *Journal of Economic Issues*, Vol. 1, March 1969.

Hayek, F. A., "The Non Sequitor of the 'Dependence Effect'," *Southern Economic Journal*, Vol. XXVIII, April 1961.

Homan, Paul T., review of Ayres's *Toward a Reasonable Society*, *American Economic Review*, Vol. LIII, March 1963.

House of Representatives Committee on Science and Astronautics, Report of the National Academy of Sciences, *Technology: Processes of Assessment and Choice*, Washington, D.C., U. S. Government Printing Office, July 1969.

Kapp, K. William, "In Defense of Institutional Economics," *Swedish Journal of Economics*, Vol. LXX, 1968.

Knox, A. D., review of Myrdal's *Economic Theory and Under-Developed Regions*, *Economica*, Vol. XXVII, August 1960.

Lerner, Abba P., review of Ayres's *The Theory of Economic Progress*, *American Economic Review*, Vol. XXXV, March 1945.

Lowe, Adolph, *On Economic Knowledge: Toward a Science of Political Economics* (New York: Harper and Row, 1965).

Meade, James E., "Is 'The New Industrial State' Inevitable?" *Economic Journal*, Vol. LXXVIII, June 1968.

National Economic Development Council, *Conditions Favourable to Faster Growth*, London, Her Majesty's Stationery Office, 1963.

The Economist, "Galbraith's Republic," review of Galbraith's *The New Industrial State*, Vol. CCXXIV, September 9, 1967.

The Economist, review of Galbraith's *The Affluent Society*, Vol. CLXXXVIII, September 20, 1958.

U. S. Department of Commerce, *Markets after the Defense Expansion*, Washington, D.C., U. S. Government Printing Office, 1952.

Wallich, Henry C., "Public versus Private: Could Galbraith Be Wrong?" *Harper's Magazine*, Vol. 223, October 1961.

Wallich, Henry C., *The Cost of Freedom, A New Look at Capitalism* (New York: Harper and Brothers, 1960).

Wolfe, A. B., review of Ayres's *The Theory of Economic Progress*, *Political Science Quarterly*, Vol. LIX, December 1944.

INDEX